CONFLICTING WORLDS

New Dimensions of the American Civil War

T. Michael Parrish, Editor

Emory M. Thomas

INSIDE THE CONFEDERATE NATION

ESSAYS IN HONOR OF

EMORY M. THOMAS

EDITED BY

LESLEY J. GORDON AND JOHN C. INSCOE

LOUISIANA STATE UNIVERSITY PRESS

BATON ROUGE

Published by Louisiana State University Press

Manufactured in the United States of America
Louisiana Paperback Edition, 2007
FIRST PRINTING

DESIGNER: *Andrew Shurtz*
TYPEFACE: *Adobe Caslon*
PRINTER AND BINDER: *Edwards Brothers, Inc.*

LIBRARY OF CONGRESS CATALOGING-IN-PUBLICATION DATA

Inside the Confederate nation : essays in honor of Emory M. Thomas / edited by Lesley J. Gordon and John C. Inscoe.

p. cm. — (Conflicting worlds)

Includes bibliographical references and index.

ISBN 0-8071-3099-0 (cloth : alk. paper)

1. Confederate States of America—Politics and government. 2. Nationalism—Confederate States of America—History. 3. Group identity—Southern States—History—19th century. 4. Confederate States of America—Social conditions. 5. United States—History—Civil War, 1861–1865—Social aspects. I. Thomas, Emory M., 1939– II. Gordon, Lesley J. (Lesley Jill) III. Inscoe, John C., 1951– IV. Series.

E487.157 2005
973.7'13—dc22

2005002805

ISBN-13: 978-0-8071-3231-9 (paper : alk. paper)

The paper in this book meets the guidelines for permanence and durability of the Committee on Production Guidelines for Book Longevity of the Council on Library Resources. ♾

Contents

MEMORY AND LEGACIES

Preface

IN A TALK AT A CITADEL CONFERENCE IN CHARLESTON IN 2000, Emory Thomas mused over when the last book would be written about the Civil War. "How long, O Lord," he asked, "will this plethoric outpouring of books about the Civil War continue?" Rather than speculate as to whether and when that landmark publication might be, Thomas suggested that it might be more important to try to understand "why so many people seem so hell-bent to buy every last scrap of history about the war—good, bad, and indifferent."[1]

Thomas himself has generated a sizeable portion of the "good" history produced on the war, not only through his own books, articles, and essays but also as the mentor, advisor, and director of over a dozen doctoral dissertations, nearly all of which have been published as books and in many cases have set their authors off on prolific scholarly careers that continue to produce even more "good" history on the war.

Thomas himself hit the ground running on his own scholarly career. Only four years after completing his dissertation at Rice University in 1966, he published not only his dissertation, *The Confederate State of Richmond,* but also his seminal work *The Confederacy as a Revolutionary Experience,* a remarkable feat for a young assistant professor then in the third year of his long and fruitful career at the University of Georgia. The following pages will deal much more with the scholarly output of that career, one that lasted over thirty-five years until—by all accounts but his own—his much too early retirement in 2002. But it did not end there, for Thomas spent the next two springs in Charleston, where he held the Mark W. Clark Distinguished Visiting Professorship at the Citadel.

It was only in the latter part of his career in Athens that Thomas took on the equally significant role as scholarly mentor. He directed the work of thirty-two graduate students, fourteen of them at the Ph.D. level, the other eighteen as master's students, in what was long a heavily weighted M.A. program at Georgia. The vast majority of those students earned their degrees in the 1990s as Thomas emerged as the most sought after of faculty advisors, and many students came to UGA specifically to work with him. Thomas, together with Bill McFeely, who attracted a number of good students himself during those years, made the Civil War and Reconstruction fertile ground for graduate students at Georgia and inspired a wide range of solid, often groundbreaking scholarship from a sizeable cohort of very able students, most of whom continue to be productive historians in their own right today.

In answering the question he himself raised at the Citadel Conference as to why the publication of books on the Civil War shows no signs of waning, Thomas declared that this is so because the war era "continues to speak to contemporary questions—questions about race, community, and identity."[2] That along with the human drama that continues to fascinate Americans will, he thinks, continue to fuel the ongoing outpouring of inquiry about the war and those caught up in it. It is no coincidence that these are the issues and qualities reflected in the essays presented here, most of which wrestle in one way or another with identity, community, or race and explore the dilemmas and strains posed by the burdens of all facets of life in the Confederacy, from home front to battlefield.

As with any essay collection, this project has been a widely collaborative effort from its inception. The editors are very grateful to Brian Wills, who, along with Lesley Gordon, originally conceived the idea of a *festschrift* for Thomas as his retirement loomed. All of the authors enthusiastically agreed to contribute original essays to this volume. About two-thirds of them were once graduate students who worked under Thomas at UGA, some earning doctorates and some master's degrees. The rest of the essayists are either departmental colleagues and/or distinguished scholars who count Thomas as a close friend, all of whom eagerly accepted the invitation to join in this celebration of his career and its influence on so many others. The editors appreciate the timely manner in which the contributors produced and revised their works and the patience they have maintained through a process that has taken somewhat longer than any of us originally anticipated.

The UGA History Department, under the leadership of Chair Edward J. Larson, a close friend of Thomas, has been behind this project from the beginning and sees this effort as one of several ongoing ways in which the department and the university can and has paid homage to Emory Thomas and his legacy.

We appreciate the early interest in the project by LSU Press and by Michael J. Parrish, who edits their Conflicting World Series and who also provided the manuscript with an unusually meticulous and helpful reading, as did another anonymous reader. To varying degrees their insights have much improved almost every essay in the volume. We are especially grateful for all the time, thought, and support Sylvia Frank Rodrigue at the press gave to this project from its inception. Others on the staff—Rand Dotson and George Roupe—as well as freelance editor Kevin Brock, also have been a pleasure to work with and have contributed much to the improvement of the book as it has moved through their very capable editorial hands.

Sheree Dendy—copyeditor extraordinaire—has lent her skills to this project with the same skill and dedication that she has with so many projects at UGA, from her many years with the *Georgia Historical Quarterly* and more recently with the *New Georgia Encyclopedia.* Her efforts have greatly lightened the burdens of this volume's nominal editors, and they—along with nearly all of the contributors, many of whom count Sheree as a friend and have worked with her before—are very grateful for the close attention and care she has given to our work and the many ways in which she has improved our prose.

And finally, all of us in Athens are enormously in the debt of the man we honor here for the variety of ways he has enriched and enlivened not only the academic environment in which history is taught and in which young historians are trained at the University of Georgia, but also for the many ways in which he and his wife, Fran, have long enhanced the social life of the department. His presence is much missed there but his legacy is firmly entrenched. We hope that this volume represents in some small way our collective gratitude for all that he has meant as scholar, mentor, colleague, teacher, and friend.

NOTES

1. Emory M. Thomas, "Clio at Climax: Apocalypse and the American Civil War," in *Warm Ashes: Issues in Southern History at the Dawn of the Twenty-First Century,* ed. Winfred B. Moore Jr., Kyle S. Sinisi, and David H. White Jr. (Columbia: University of South Carolina Press, 2003), 5.

2. Ibid., 6.

INSIDE THE CONFEDERATE NATION

Introduction

JOHN C. INSCOE AND LESLEY J. GORDON

IN JANUARY 1861, AS THE UNION CRUMBLED AROUND HIM, PRES. James Buchanan turned in exasperation to Sen. Robert Toombs of Georgia. "Good God, Mr. Toombs," the president exclaimed, "do you mean that I am in the midst of a revolution?" "Yes, sir," the senator replied. "More than that, you have been there for a year and have not yet found it out."[1]

If indeed this "revolution" had been a long time in coming, it was only in early 1861 that it took tangible—and for many others, like the hapless Buchanan, recognizable—form. In February representatives from seven southern states created the Confederate States of America. They elected their own president, drafted a constitution, and formed a provisional government. Although the United States of America refused to recognize the legitimacy of this new government, for all intents and purposes, the South had created a nation. Of course, the CSA's existence soon proved to be an embattled and short-lived one.

Since its demise, many have tried to understand why the Confederacy failed and why the South lost the war; others have wondered how the CSA lasted as long as it did. Historians have pondered whether an identifiable "nationalism" or unique sense of corporeal identity existed among white southerners. Still others have argued that there was no real nationalism; instead localism, states' rights, and political dissent displaced, indeed subverted, any enduring loyalty to the South's central government. By the same token scholars have debated whether and in what ways the transformations brought on by secession and the formation of a nation were indeed "revolutionary" either in intent or in practice.[2]

Emory M. Thomas was one of the first to enter this important debate in 1971 with his book *The Confederacy as a Revolutionary Experience,* followed by a more complete study in 1979, *The Confederate Nation, 1861–1865.*[3] While both works recognize Confederate nationalism as a shared worldview held by a majority of white southerners, Thomas argues that southern secession, nation building, and armed conflict entirely transformed "the very way of life they had seceded to defend."[4] Formed to preserve the "status quo," the warring Confederacy found itself revolutionizing many basic aspects of southern culture. The result was a more centralized, more industrialized, more socialized, and even less patriarchal society than had ever existed before 1861. War proved revolutionary, though when faced with the most radical change of all, abolishing slavery, Confederates balked. In the end, though, much of the dramatic change wrought by the war proved temporary.

More than a quarter century after the publication of Thomas's seminal books, the debate about Confederate nationalism has not subsided. There continues to be a great fascination with the southern experiment of nation building. Scholars continue to contest the very definition of southern nationalism.[5] Over the past twenty years, we have learned far more about ordinary people's wartime experience—soldiers and civilians, blacks and whites, men and women, loyal and disloyal—and about how those experiences, individually and collectively, shaped both the perceptions of and allegiances toward the new nation under whose jurisdiction southerners found themselves living and for whose survival they were forced to sacrifice.[6]

Yet there is still a good deal to discover about what the southern nation meant—or failed to mean—to familial relationships, political affiliations, and individual identities. This collection of essays by Emory Thomas's students, friends, and colleagues is an attempt to further explore the place of southerners within the Confederacy and how they came to see themselves and others differently because of the new nation within which they suddenly found themselves. With much of the focus here on individuals, on households, on communities, and on particular regions of the South, we can begin to appreciate the sheer variety of circumstances southerners faced over the course of the sectional crisis and the war and how they chose to respond to—or merely to cope with—the difficult realities of life in the Confederacy. These variables influenced public as well as private matters, so diplomats, policymakers, journalists, and soldiers—high and low—also figure prominently in these essays. From secession through defeat, self- and local interests often collided with the larger objectives of that nation, and many of the essays that follow reveal the myriad tensions resulting from the disparities between the expectations and the realities imposed by a nascent nationalism and its citizens' commitment to it.

William C. Davis sets the stage with a reexamination of the Fort Sumter crisis. He reminds us of the ambivalence that still marked sentiments on both sides of the Mason-Dixon Line up to that point in the crisis. The test of wills that played out in Charleston's harbor demonstrated not only how far certain southerners were willing to go with their "experiment in revolution" but also the dilemma Union officials, from President Lincoln to Sumter's commander, Robert Anderson, faced in responding to the first real challenge posed by the new nation.

A number of the essays probe specific areas of the Confederacy in terms of how they contended with the dramatic upheavals the war imposed. David McGee draws from a larger community study of North Carolina's capital during and after the war to analyze here the initial transformation Raleigh underwent after secession. He builds on Thomas's distinctions between internal and external revolutions to probe the long- and short-term effects caused by the tremendous demographic, economic, governmental, and racial changes the city's residents experienced during the war's opening months.

Brian Wills investigates the ways in which residents of Suffolk and the surrounding area of southeastern Virginia exhibited nationalistic sentiments toward the Confederacy—the governmental seat of which lay less than a hundred miles away. When occupied by Federal forces in May 1862, local residents' patriotism and sense of national purpose were again tested, and Wills's description of the interplay between occupiers and occupied reveals much about the sometimes shifting, sometimes steadfast nature of loyalties and disloyalties under pressure.

Like Wills, John Inscoe examines the response of southern civilians to Federal incursion on their homes and communities. More specifically he chronicles the behavior of elite white women during one of the final affronts by Union forces—Stoneman's raid through western North Carolina in April 1865. Inscoe suggests that the comforts of their class allowed these women to withstand that invasion relatively unscathed. Their own accounts of what they witnessed and endured reflect their great satisfaction in their defiance and steadfastness when faced by the enemy. They portrayed themselves in postwar narratives as true Confederates even as they knew that their cause was lost.

Two authors look to specific states in assessing the duration of Confederate identity and nationalistic support at the state level. Rod Andrew takes on all of Georgia but narrows his focus to a single moment in time—the congressional elections of 1863. He uses the campaign rhetoric of candidates seeking a seat in the Confederate Congress in Richmond to measure the extent of popular support for the Richmond government and its policies at the war's midpoint and challenges the conventional wisdom that these elections served as a widespread repudiation of Jefferson Davis's administration. That election served not only as a referendum on states' rights sentiment versus that of the southern nation and its authority; Andrew also demonstrates that the issues raised and debated by candidates in Georgia's ten congressional districts illustrate just how the electorate conceived of the concept of nationalism at this crucial point in the Confederacy's existence.

Christopher Phillips focuses on two states that never became part of the Confederacy, Kentucky and Missouri, but illustrates how their residents' southern identity sometimes overlapped with Confederate identity, both during and after the war. Slavery's existence in both states, and the traumas its destruction inflicted on their white populations, Phillips argues, was crucial to their ultimate sense of themselves as southerners and the extent to which they embraced the Lost Cause through commemorations to a nation and a cause they had chosen not to become part of in 1861.

In several essays certain groups of southerners not necessarily defined by geographic bounds serve to illuminate other aspects of the Confederacy's effect on its citizens. Like Rod Andrew, Keith Bohannon chooses a particular moment in time to measure southern commitment to the national cause. In this case it is the reenlistment option open to soldiers in the Army of Tennessee in early 1864. Wintering in northwest Georgia in the aftermath of costly defeats in and around Chattanooga, Confederate leaders could hardly have chosen a more inauspicious time to put the continued devotion of their troops to such a test. And yet Bohannon demonstrates not only how many of those who had already devoted three years to Confederate service chose to extend their commitment to the cause but also the variety of motivations and inspirations behind their decisions.

Many of these veterans soon found themselves engaged in the Atlanta campaign, where among those civilians affected most dramatically were African Americans. Clarence Mohr provides a vivid sense of how Sherman's troops disrupted the peculiar institution in and around Atlanta and in so doing provided the first tastes of freedom to thousands of bondsmen and women. He also chronicles the many pursuits—military, medical, and industrial—through which both northern and southern armies utilized Georgia blacks and how those experiences ultimately shaped their emancipated status.

If Mohr explores the breadth of the African American experience brought on by contact with Union troops, Joseph Glatthaar takes a far more focused look at one of the more tragic consequences of those encounters. Thousands of former slaves from various parts of the Confederacy enlisted in the Federal army, where many discovered that wearing the Union blue did not mean an end to discrimination. Glatthaar examines a relatively unexplored aspect of that experience, the medical care accorded to those who served as U.S. Colored Troops. Not only did racial prejudice by Union medical personnel and military leaders result in often deplorable neglect and abuse for wounded or ailing black soldiers once under their care, but the conditions and locales in which they were forced to serve also proved detrimental to their health and led to far higher death rates than was true for their white counterparts.

Individual attitudes and actions can be as valuable as collective experience in contributing to our understanding of the relationship between the Confederate nation and its citizenry. Several essays in this collection highlight one or more such individuals whose writings allow us to understand the personal dilemmas often inherent in those forced to declare allegiance to the new polity under which they and their families found themselves. Frank Byrne looks specifically at the linkages between southern distinctiveness prior to the war and its transformation into nationalism—what Emory Thomas has called "secular transubstantiation," or how common elements of antebellum life generated a southern ideology after secession.[7] Byrne focuses on two southerners, journalist and political propagandist Daniel Hundley and novelist and diarist John Beauchamp Jones, whose written works reveal much about regional identity before the war. That regionalism intensified after secession and evolved into a strong sense of Confederate nationalism, which both men enthusiastically embraced through service—for one military, the other administrative—to the cause.

Jean Friedman's interest lies in the dynamics of family relationships and how they shaped allegiances before and during the war. It was through families that the war was most often cast as a moral crusade. She uses the contrasting paths taken by two unique individuals when the fighting broke out—Alfred Mordecai, an Orthodox Jew from North Carolina who commanded a U.S. arsenal near Albany, New York, and George William Bagby, a doctor-turned-journalist in Virginia—to examine the extent to which their parents provided the moral perspectives that shaped their beliefs and actions, specifically in terms of their commitment and contributions to the Confederacy. In both cases the men believed the choices they made to be honorable ones, though those choices proved ambivalent enough to conflict with the higher standards imposed by their parents.

Lesley J. Gordon explores another kind of personal relationship and how it helped shape and sustain personal feelings toward the Confederate cause. She draws on over a hundred letters exchanged between adolescent lovers—and after January 1864, newlyweds—from Thomas County in south Georgia. The steadfast affection of Bobbie Mitchell and Nellie Fondren for each other also served to maintain a strong devotion to the nation and cause for which he was fighting, even as they wavered between optimism and despair at its ultimate fate and their own future together. Like many soldiers in service to the Confederacy, the sentiments of a woman at home could fuel a man's resolve as much as anything happening in camp or on the battlefield. As Gordon demonstrates, in the case of these two young people, such influences flowed both ways.

Stories of individual black lives within the Confederacy are remarkably scarce, which makes Tom Dyer's reconstruction of Robert Webster's experiences in and around Atlanta during the war years so exceptional. A minor supporting player in Dyer's study of Atlanta's Unionist community, Webster moves center stage here in a complex portrait of a man who straddled black and white worlds as much as he straddled slavery and freedom. As a slave, a businessman, and a Unionist living in the exceedingly hostile environment of a major Confederate city, Webster reminds us that some southerners, often obscure and living on the margins, not only survived but also prospered in volatile environments.

Three authors view the Confederate nation in terms of its policymakers and on how crucial efforts by the Richmond government—both legislative and diplomatic—served not only to define the nation but to affect its endurance as well. Certainly Confederate nationalism in its fullest sense required recognition by other nations as to its legitimacy. James McPherson details a crucial turning point in the South's attempt to win that recognition from France and Great Britain. He traces the efforts by both northern and southern diplomats in London and Paris and demonstrates just how close to success the latter came in the summer of 1862, fueled by Confederate military success, only to be thwarted with the sudden reversal of battlefield fortune at Antietam.

The extent to which a government provides for its citizens is one mark of national strength. Jennifer Gross traces the shift in sentiment and legislative action in the Confederacy's acknowledgement of an obligation toward the widows and children of those soldiers who had died in its service. What began as private financial support for their families gradually became the responsibilities of local and then state governments, a process Gross delineates for three states—Virginia, North Carolina, and Georgia. As the number of indigents increased and the problem of alleviating poverty became more pervasive, Richmond officials finally took matters into their own hands, a development Gross attributes to a shift in the attitudes of the city's citizenry toward the authority and responsibility of their national government.

That most desperate and revolutionary of Confederate policy proposals—the arming of slaves—is the focus of David Dillard's essay. Given the military setbacks by the end of 1864, southerners had to confront the dilemma of whether a nation built with slavery as its foundation would have to sacrifice that institution in the name of self-preservation. It is a topic that has received considerable attention from historians, but Dillard provides fresh insights by localizing the debate and comparing the ways two very different Confederate communities—Lynchburg, Virginia, and Galveston, Texas—responded to the crucial question of whether slaves should become an added means of maintaining the army's dwindling manpower and the reasons for their varied sentiments.

Two essays focus on the Confederacy in hindsight and how its leaders took on new and different meanings through long-term reflection and memory. Glenna Schroeder-Lein, much of whose work has focused on medical aspects of the war, chronicles the postwar efforts of Confederate surgeons to organize in order to recreate and preserve their contributions to the cause. After several sporadic and tentative attempts, they ultimately came together only in 1898, when they formed the Association of Medical Officers of the Army and Navy of the Confederacy. Schroeder-Lein traces the organization's relatively brief existence from that point and its mixed record as a useful resource in recapturing and commemorating the role played by doctors and other medical personnel over the course of the war.

Nina Silber pays tribute to Emory Thomas as Robert E. Lee's biographer with her own take on the general's legacy in which she traces how and why his image evolved among both northerners and southerners after his death. She argues that by the turn of the century, Lee had emerged as the ultimate icon of national reconciliation in large part because he embodied so fully the late Victorian concepts of manhood and manly virtue. In perhaps the ultimate gesture in the ongoing "romance of reunion" between North and South that Silber has chronicled so effectively elsewhere, New Englander Charles Francis Adams brought that image to full fruition in 1907 in a glowing tribute to Lee not as Confederate commander, but as Anglo-Saxon gentleman.

As Russell Duncan and Jennifer Lund Smith point out in their thorough assessment of Thomas's career and his work, much of the significance of that work lies in the interpretive disputes that it has inspired. Certainly not all of his fellow scholars—or even all of his students—fully agree with his conception of the Confederate nation, the revolutionary nature of its existence, or even his characterization of Robert E. Lee. And yet the issues Thomas raised and the groundwork he laid in even thinking of the Confederacy in these terms have fueled much of the scholarship since.

The following essays, written and compiled to honor Emory Thomas, demonstrate how his students and colleagues have taken these questions to heart and have sought to test them through examination of particular individuals, communities, regions, or policies. In a 1983 essay entitled "Reckoning with Rebels," Thomas notes that "too often the Confederate past in Southern history has been the subject of myth and madness." He suggests that we take "a fresh look at the old facts of Confederate history [and] ask new questions of the old story." Only then "may the Confederacy emerge as more than the source of reaction and irrelevance."[8]

The essays here reflect the latest of now long-ongoing efforts to do just that. Taken together they should contribute to a greater appreciation of the vast and varied populace encompassed by the Confederate nation. Over the course of its four-year lifespan, personal feelings, consciences, and relationships; local and regional values and agendas; racial attitudes; and military fortunes all contributed to perceptions of nationhood and identity, which in turn determined how and to what degree its citizens chose to support the southern nation.

NOTES

1. Samuel Wylie Crawford, *Genesis of the Civil War: The Story of Sumter, 1860–1861* (New York: C. L. Webster, 1887), 148–49 (borrowed from unpublished manuscript by William C. Davis).

2. Examples of this vast literature include Richard E. Beringer, Herman Hattaway, Archer Jones, and William N. Still Jr., *Why the South Lost the Civil War* (Athens: University of Georgia Press, 1986); Paul D. Escott, *After Secession: Jefferson Davis and the Failure of Confederate Nationalism* (Baton Rouge: Louisiana State University Press, 1978); Harry P. Owens and James J. Cooke, eds.,

The Old South in the Crucible of War (Jackson: University Press of Mississippi, 1983); Drew Gilpin Faust, *The Creation of Confederate Nationalism: Ideology and Identity in the Civil War South* (Baton Rouge: Louisiana State University Press, 1988); Frank L. Owsley, *State Rights in the Confederacy* (Chicago: University of Chicago Press, 1925); Gary W. Gallagher, *The Confederate War: How Popular Will, Nationalism, and Military Strategy Could Not Stave Off Defeat* (Cambridge, Mass.: Harvard University Press, 1997); George C. Rable, *The Confederate Republic: A Revolution against Politics* (Chapel Hill: University of North Carolina Press, 1994); William C. Davis, *"A Government of Our Own": The Making of the Confederacy* (Baton Rouge: Louisiana State University Press, 1997); William C. Davis, *Look Away: A History of the Confederate States of America* (New York: Free Press, 2002); and William W. Freehling, *The South vs. the South: How Anti-Confederate Southerners Shaped the Course of the Civil War* (New York: Oxford University Press, 2001).

3. Emory M. Thomas, *The Confederacy as a Revolutionary Experience* (Englewood Cliffs, N.J.: Prentice-Hall, 1971); Thomas, *The Confederate Nation: 1861–1865* (New York: Harper & Row, 1979).

4. Emory M. Thomas, "Rebellion and Conventional Warfare: Confederate Strategy and Military Policy," in James M. McPherson and William J. Cooper, eds., *Writing the Civil War: The Quest to Understand* (Columbia: University of South Carolina Press, 1998), 42.

5. For example, see William Blair's careful definition of nationalism in *Virginia's Private War: Feeding Body and South in the Confederacy, 1861–1865* (New York: Oxford University Press, 1998), 152 n. 2; and Michael Fellman, Daniel Sutherland, and Lesley J. Gordon, *This Terrible War: The Civil War and Its Aftermath* (New York: Longman, 2003), 211–12.

6. A few examples include works on women and family: Drew Gilpin Faust, *Mothers of Invention: Women of the Slaveholding South in the American Civil War* (Chapel Hill: University of North Carolina Press, 1996); George C. Rable, *Civil Wars: Women and the Crisis of Southern Nationalism* (Urbana: University of Illinois Press, 1989); Catherine Clinton and Nina Silber, eds., *Divided Houses: Gender and the Civil War* (New York: Oxford University Press, 1992); and Catherine Clinton, ed., *Southern Families at War: Loyalty and Conflict in the Civil War South* (New York: Oxford University Press, 2000); on home-front communities: Daniel Sutherland, *Seasons of War: The Ordeal of a Confederate Community, 1861–1865* (New York: Simon & Schuster, 1995); Steven Elliott Tripp, *Yankee Town, Southern City: Race and Class Relations in Civil War Lynchburg* (New York: New York University Press, 1997); William Warren Rogers Jr., *Confederate Home Front: Montgomery during the Civil War* (Tuscaloosa: University of Alabama Press, 1999); Brian Steel Wills, *The War Hits Home: The Civil War in Southeastern Virginia* (Charlottesville: University Press of Virginia, 2001); David Williams, *Rich Man's War: Class, Caste, and Confederate Defeat in the Lower Chattahoochee Valley* (Athens: University of Georgia Press, 1998); Martin Crawford, *Ashe County's Civil War: Community and Society in the Appalachian South* (Charlottesville: University Press of Virginia, 2001); G. Ward Hubbs, *Guarding Greensboro [Ala.]: A Confederate Company in the Making of a Southern Community* (Athens: University of Georgia Press, 2003); and Edward J. Ayers, *In the Presence of Mine Enemies: War in the Heart of America, 1859–1863* (New York: W. W. Norton, 2003); on slavery and emancipation: Clarence Mohr, *On the Threshold of Freedom: Masters and Slaves in Civil War Georgia* (Athens: University of Georgia Press, 1986); Joseph Glatthaar, *Forged in Battle: The Civil War Alliance of Black Soldiers and White Officers* (New York: Free Press, 1990); and Ervin L. Jordan

Jr., *Black Confederates and Afro-Yankees in Civil War Virginia* (Charlottesville: University Press of Virginia, 1995); on Unionism and disaffection: Thomas G. Dyer, *Secret Yankees: The Union Circle in Confederate Atlanta* (Baltimore: Johns Hopkins University Press, 1999); Daniel Sutherland, ed., *Guerrillas, Unionists, and Violence on the Confederate Home Front* (Fayetteville: University of Arkansas Press, 1999); David Williams, Teresa Crisp Williams, and David Carlson, *Plain Folk in a Rich Man's War: Class and Dissent in Confederate Georgia* (Gainesville: University Press of Florida, 2002); John C. Inscoe and Robert C. Kenzer, eds., *Enemies of the Country: New Perspectives on Unionists in the Civil War South* (Athens: University of Georgia Press, 2001); Freehling, *South vs. the South;* and Margaret M. Storey, *Loyalty and Loss: Alabama's Unionists in the Civil War and Reconstruction* (Baton Rouge: Louisiana State University Press, 2004).

7. Emory M. Thomas, "Reckoning with Rebels," in Owens and Cooke, *Old South in the Crucible of War*, 7–8.

8. Ibid., 6.

Emory M. Thomas and the Confederate Imagination

RUSSELL DUNCAN AND JENNIFER LUND SMITH

> I first saw the photograph during a visit to the Library of Congress. . . . Because the army to which the young man belonged surrendered only one week after his death, no one can convince me that his death was anything but meaningless. . . . [T]his particular picture affected me immediately and has haunted me since. Recently I visited the place where the young Confederate soldier died. Maybe it was morbid curiosity; I hope it was more than that. I would like to think it was respect for the young man's life and life itself that made me want to see where he died. Whatever the reason I went to the Petersburg National Battlefield Park.
>
> EMORY M. THOMAS, *Travels to Hallowed Ground*

EMORY THOMAS HARBORS A CONFEDERATE IMAGINATION. Locating the past in the present, his sensibility is rooted in his birthplace—an a priori understanding that combines with his lifelong academic inquiry into the southern way of life. This is not to invoke any such miasma of geographical determinism as advanced by U. B. Phillips and others; instead we offer it as a complement to Thomas's credentials, as understood by William Faulkner. In *Absalom, Absalom!* Quentin Compson answers his northern roommate's question about living "among defeated grandfathers and freed slaves."[1] Compson's explanation that to understand the South "you would have to be born there" reflects the interplay of nature and nurture that informs human knowledge.[2]

Emory Morton Thomas was born "there" in Richmond, Virginia, on November 3, 1939, at a time when the numbers of defeated grandfathers and freed slaves had been notably reduced, though they still existed. Too young to remember the World War II years but certainly aware that the United States dominated the global order in the 1950s, Thomas tried to understand the significance of the memorials to the Confederate dead along the avenues and around the White House of the Confederacy in downtown Richmond. His patriotic allegiance to the United States confronted the fact of his being a white Virginian. Trying to define himself, Thomas got hooked on the newspaper editorials and radio broadcasts of Douglas Southall Freeman, who had been awarded the Pulitzer Prize in 1935 for his four-volume biography of Robert E. Lee. Thomas clearly recalled Freeman's "15-minute radio program at 8:00

in the morning, sort of a commentary on the day's events, and as far as I knew, everybody in Richmond . . . listened to Dr. Freeman at 8:00 in the morning. And only when Dr. Freeman was through . . . did I pack up my little books and trundle on off to Ginter Park Elementary School or Chandler Junior High School."[3] In a way Freeman symbolized an *un*defeated grandfather who wrote about Marse Robert, Superstar. Thomas readily admitted that, though he could not know it at the time, Freeman became "a constant in my life."[4]

In 1958 Thomas enrolled at the University of Virginia and pragmatically, if unimaginatively, decided on his major for the completely understandable reason of having made "an A in history."[5] He confessed to going to UVA not only "to get an undergraduate education, but also to play football. . . . I really wanted to be a football coach for a good portion of my adolescent and post-adolescent years."[6] Playing both offensive guard and linebacker for the Cavaliers, who lost twenty-eight straight games during Thomas's four-year tenure on the team—a school record—invited comparisons to military marches, flank attacks, defeat, the good fight, manhood, loss despite home-field advantages, and of being overrun by superior strength and numbers. Even the team mascot, the Cavalier, brought the myth of southern gallants to the gridiron. Reflecting later on the battle of First Manassas, Thomas wrote of the folly of such comparisons: "But this was no game and all analogies that link war to athletic contests are dangerous. Men died here. And those who survived did not shuffle off to locker rooms, take showers, and then meet wives or girl friends."[7]

One month before the October 1962 Cuban Missile Crisis, Thomas moved with his new bride, Fran, to Houston, where he entered the Ph.D. program in history at Rice University. Finally outgrowing his desire to coach football, he was convinced by Civil War historian Frank E. Vandiver of the "intellectual viability in [studying] the Confederate States of America."[8] Vandiver was already well respected for his work on southern industry and for a stunning biography of Thomas Jonathon Jackson.[9] Thomas was most impressed by one of Vandiver's newer pieces, "The Confederate Myth" (1961). This article not only confronted the Lost Cause histories and misconceptions of "a static, racist, states' rights, Confederacy" but also implored historians to repudiate all moonlight-and-magnolia "pseudo-past" mythologies.[10] Thomas became fast friends with another Vandiver student, Thomas L. Connelly, whose work at chipping away mythology to reveal history paralleled his own efforts.

While still at work on his dissertation, Thomas married and moved to Dayton, Ohio, to fulfill his active-duty obligation in the U.S. Army. Assigned not to Vietnam, he served instead in a missile battery that successfully "defended Cincinnati and Dayton against the evil empire during 1965 and '66 and '67."[11] Thomas completed his dissertation, "The Confederate State of Richmond," and received his Ph.D. in 1966. With one more year in uniform, he taught army extension courses for Wright State University. The next year he took his one—and only—full-time academic job at the University of Georgia.

The 1960s witnessed an outpouring of books about the Civil War at precisely the same time that the civil rights movement demanded a reinterpretation of the African American past. Feminists, immigrant laborers, American Indians, and students all aired grievances against the conformist society, and increasingly, young men were sent to fight and die in Vietnam for reasons still deemed meaningless to many critics. Meanwhile unreconstructed white southerners held fast to the old cultural interpretations, recited the "never" first spoken against the Supreme Court's decision in *Brown v. Board of Education* (1954) to integrate the schools, resisted the pleas by Martin Luther King Jr. for a colorblind society, and formed a "flag cult" around the "Confederate battle flag."

During these years of social disruption and civil conflict, Thomas searched for a history that made sense to modern southerners, who had been shaped too often by myth and memory—or a lack of both thereof. He explained: "To be a Southerner in the 1950s and 1960s was to share in such acts as church bombings in Birmingham; the murders of three civil rights workers in Philadelphia, Mississippi; the terrorizing of little children; and [the] assassination of Martin Luther King Jr. But however sick appeared the South's present in the 1950s and '60s, the past offered no cures. The Southern past seemed to offer only the heritage of guilt, reaction, disunion, racism, poverty, and oppression."[12] Thomas bravely admitted falling so far into despair over the events of the 1960s that in 1968 he told a New York magazine editor: "I am a liberal; I am not one of them. I am an unsouthern Southerner."[13] He soon regretted his apology and realized that it had been "a terrible and momentous thing to reject the past, even the recent past. I should have known better."[14]

C. Vann Woodward's *The Burden of Southern History* (1960) furthered the argument that southern history was marked more by change than continuity. The corpus of Woodward's writing influenced Thomas to challenge the static interpretations of the South.[15] In 1971 Thomas wrote: "Benumbed by the recent Civil War Centennial and revulsed by the perverse causes which come wrapped in the rebel flag, most Americans would just as soon erase the Confederate experience from the national memory. To a generation seeking a 'usable past' historians of the Confederacy have offered cavalry charges and lost causes. Thus the Confederate image in the American mind is a peculiar blend of reaction, myth and irrelevance."[16]

Having several articles to his credit, Thomas published two books in 1971 that challenged previous interpretations of the Confederacy and established his position in the vanguard of two revisionist movements: urban history and the new military history. He emphasized the roles of behavior and folk culture in shaping political ideology during rapidly modernizing times. *The Confederate State of Richmond: A Biography of the Capital,* his revised and expanded dissertation, led the way in connecting city stories with army campaigns. He argues that because of its geographical position and war role, "Richmond was the most governed city in the land."[17] Thomas inscribes this coming-of-age urban biography with traditional supports and changing life ways. In reviewing the book for the *Journal of Southern History,* Mary Elizabeth Massey called it "one of the first scholarly, comprehensive accounts of a Confederate city, despite the importance [of Richmond] to the war and to urban history."[18] She praised Thomas for his unique efforts revealing "that life in the Confederate capital was as significant, dramatic, and worthy of analysis as events on the battlefield."[19] Another Richmond scholar quietly stated, "This little book gives a useful, readable account of Richmond's military, political, social, and economic experiences as capital of the Confederacy."[20] And yet overall, scholarly reviewers were not especially taken with the native son's biography of the Confederate capital. One historian took particular offense at Thomas's appointment of a female gender to the city and of his ribald description of Union general Ulysses Grant "moving relentlessly against her defenses."[21] Apparent from this first book onward, two characteristics of Thomas's prose—not equally appreciated by all critics—are the readability of his writing and his capacity for humor. Simply put, Thomas fills his writings with grace and wit, something he shares with a long line of southern storytellers from Flannery O'Connor to Charles Frazier.

His other 1971 production, *The Confederacy as a Revolutionary Experience,* an installment in the New Insights in History series, continues to cause ripples in Civil War historiography, even if the book was both widely ignored and unenthusiastically reviewed at first publication. Thomas advances a novel interpretation of how four years of war changed the nature of Confederate dreams. Southerners, who had made a revolution to preserve a way of life, made another revolution by making sacrifices and pushing changes—in essence giving up what they had been fighting to preserve in the first place. Thomas writes:

"In the name of independence the Southerners reversed or severely undermined virtually every tenet of the way of life they were supposedly defending. The substantive revolution came only after the Confederacy was engaged in a fight for its life."[22] The South had gone to war to protect states' rights, the agrarian ideal, aristocracy, separate gender spheres, and most importantly a "peculiar institution." By war's end it had sacrificed these ideals in exchange for centralized government power, urbanization and industrialization, an increased democracy, former belles working in hospitals and factories, and even the turning of slaves into "men" who could fight in the Confederate army. Certainly this was a revolution.

Many historians have disagreed with Thomas and hold to the idea of a Confederate South true to, and continuous with, its roots. Summing up the opposition, Richard Current was skeptical, even unimpressed, as he rejected the idea of the Confederacy as a revolutionary change from the antebellum era.[23] Others have charged that Thomas overlooks the common southerner to focus on class conflict. Despite the early criticisms or silences, the book has aged well. In 1979 Michael Perman referred to *The Confederacy as a Revolutionary Experience* as being "provocative" and full of "brilliant insights."[24] In 1988, seventeen years after its initial publication, Richard E. Beringer, Herman Hattaway, Archer Jones, and William N. Still Jr. similarly described it as "path-breaking, marvelously provocative, and insightful."[25] Attesting further to its power, editors have included two different chapters from the book in historiographical anthologies.[26]

Acknowledging the debates among historians, James M. McPherson notes, "The field of Civil War history has produced more interpretive disputes than have most historical events."[27] Thomas has been influential in shaping these disputes. He describes his philosophy of historical inquiry in a seminal essay, "Honest to Clio: The New History of the Old South" (1972), arguing that simply telling what happened is not enough. Thomas explains that the "challenge of Southern history is to penetrate myths" and to explore the nuances "of myth and amnesia in the Southern historical mind."[28] He acknowledges that a few historians before the 1960s—including W. E. B. Du Bois, Charles Beard, Kenneth Stampp, and C. Vann Woodward—had broken the edifice shielding southern history. But it was only the scholarly "intensity of the past decade" wherein the "assault on Southern mythistory" had reached a critical mass by providing enough scholars disputing matters of consensus or conflict to encourage a vibrant intellectual discussion.[29]

In 1973 Thomas synthesized recent scholarship—including especially the findings of Allan Nevins, Raimondo Luraghi, Eugene Genovese, and Eric Foner—refining his own views of the Civil War and Reconstruction to publish a short textbook, *The American War and Peace: 1860–1877.*[30] Thomas explains the era as marked first and foremost by "a clash of ideologies or world views which made war a possibility, then defined the combatants' response to the conflict, and finally conditioned the peace."[31] In a comparative essay Steven Channing notes Thomas's clear narrative style, even while he charges Thomas with "sweeping and unsubstantiated generalizations."[32] Perhaps remembering that as a genre brief textbooks abound in generalizations, Channing recants: "The important questions are all asked aggressively—the distinctive nature of the sections, the forces behind secession and the northern decision for war, the revolutionary impact of warmaking, considerations of military strategy, and the main issues of Reconstruction."[33] In fact Thomas had done so well that Channing concludes, "One has to admire the author's ingenuity in packaging so much material in so brief a volume, and in so accessible a form."[34] In his review of the textbook, Grady McWhiney characterizes Thomas as a "liberal nationalist" who often writes "dramatic and informative" prose. McWhiney then focuses on several minor but "cumulative" errors, including, for example, Thomas's claim that Albert Sidney Johnston was "hit in a fleshy part of his thigh" or that Joseph Hooker was "knocked silly by a spent artillery shell."[35] This was only the opening salvo by military historians who have followed McWhiney in encouraging Thomas to focus on battlefield specifics or to expand his book chapters to include even more analysis of military actions.

Appearing in 1979, *The Confederate Nation: 1861–1865* remains Thomas's signature work and maintains a prominent place in university classrooms and among both the literate public and Civil War enthusiasts. Thomas here develops and further enhances the thesis he had established eight years earlier. But unlike the tepid reception given *The Confederacy as a Revolutionary Experience,* reviewers paid close attention to the release of the newest volume in Henry Steele Commager and Richard B. Morris's highly regarded New American Nation series. It also did not hurt that in a timely review in the highbrow magazine *The New Republic,* C. Vann Woodward praised Thomas's contributions as "serious, scholarly, readable, . . . a fresh and detached view of the whole subject."[36] Woodward anticipated others' criticisms—and in a comment that has always been the standard complaint by reviewers of Thomas's work, stated that if Thomas "encounters complaints from his readers about his brevity on most subjects he can take comfort in the reflection that they want more. It is one mark of a good book that it whets appetites."[37]

Thomas and Woodward have been fellow travelers among the neoprogressives in highlighting conflict and change over continuity in southern history. *The Confederate Nation* continues to have such an important place in our understanding of what the war wrought as well as in interpretative disputes that it is worthy quoting Thomas at length:

> In the beginning the Confederate South was a cause, the sanctification of the Old South status quo. Because the South began as a section instead of a nation, the cause of Southern nationalism most often found negative expression within the United States. In 1861, however, the cause was incarnate. The Confederacy was the political expression of Southern nationalism and the logical extension of ante-bellum Southern ideology. At that point the process of positive identification began. . . .
>
> . . . [T]he war experience began to test and temper the new nation. By the spring of 1862 the Confederacy had been tried and found wanting. The Southern nation had suffered a series of shocks and setbacks which threatened its continued existence. Then, when their national experiment seemed almost a failure, Confederate Southerners began to respond to their circumstance by redefining themselves—or, more precisely, by defining themselves as a national people. . . .
>
> . . . Southern belles came off their pedestals and labored in hospitals and factories for the cause. . . .
>
> . . . In the end Southerners themselves decided for emancipation in the vain hope of national survival. . . .
>
> In April 1865, the Confederate struggle had but one goal: independence, the ability to exist as a people. . . .
>
> . . . Having sacrificed or been willing to sacrifice most of the ideological tenets they went to war to defend, ultimately Confederate Southerners were willing to lose their national life in order to save life itself.[38]

Woodward agreed with Thomas's explanation and added: "Historians have been too much inclined to see the South's war for independence as an extension of the old order and essentially a part of it. They have looked to post-war history, to Reconstruction and the New South to find the sources to social change and the beginnings of the region's break out of its preindustrial past. Thomas has demonstrated that we should have begun the search for the origins of change further back in the Confederacy itself."[39]

Others have disagreed with Thomas's central contention that the Confederate South differed strikingly from the Old South. They also confirmed Woodward's prediction that Thomas had whet their appetites for more. Some scholars have argued that *The Confederate Nation* had insufficiently attempted to explain the role nationalism played, or did not play, in the military defeat of southern armies.[40] J. Mills Thornton III disagreed that any fundamental alterations in society and ideology could be placed in the Confederate South, and his belief that a strong southern yeomanry could resist planter power and ideology—call it hegemony—put him in direct opposition to Thomas's leftist thesis. Thornton went as far as to declare Thomas's depiction of the Old South as "poppycock."[41] We must take that response as high praise for Thomas and others of his ilk, who see planter dominance and change among the history of the southern states.

Whether one supports a thesis of continuity or change, every serious book on the subject of the Confederate States of America in the past twenty years has been informed by, spawned from, or written as rebuttal to *The Confederate Nation*. The authors of *The Elements of Confederate Defeat* differentiate between the "administrative nationalism" they find in Thomas's work and the "mystical or spiritual sense" of nationalism they see lacking in the Confederacy.[42] Clearly spawned from Thomas's conclusions and questions concerning a "crisis of identity," Drew Gilpin Faust locates a spiritual nationalism in evangelical religion and the defense and reform of slavery but shows how, ultimately, unity fell apart in the face of internal contradictions. She concludes that southern nationality and American nationality proved to be very much alike in the end.[43]

By 1981 Thomas was widely recognized as "the foremost historian of Confederate experience."[44] That year the University of Mississippi honored his importance to historiography by sponsoring a symposium, "which was generated from [his] provocative scholarship." Two years later a half-dozen symposium participants contributed to *The Old South in the Crucible of War*, a book of essays confronting or supporting Thomas's ideas.[45] It has now been more than two decades since the release of *The Confederate Nation*, and Michael Perman's assessment that "Thomas has produced the best one-volume history of the Southern Confederacy" remains as valid today as when he wrote it in 1979.[46]

Thomas has made a conscious effort to bridge what he calls "the history gap," defined as "that space of mind which separates professional historians from the general public . . . the vacuum that too often exists between scholarly monography and conventional historical wisdom."[47] Thomas's "readable, literary style" and particularly his ability to explain "military strategy lucidly" makes his work accessible to the public at large.[48] *The Confederate Nation* led the way, and two of his next three books were also main selections of the market-driven History Book Club. From the early 1980s to the mid-1990s, Thomas turned to biography to explode the "mythistory" suffocating two of the most significant warrior-saints in Confederate iconography and hagiography. It was a daunting task. In delving into the lives of J. E. B. Stuart and Robert E. Lee, Thomas determined to go beyond a military analysis to reveal the humanity lurking behind or inside the two legends. As he would have done while he lived, Stuart rode around Lee to go first.

The *New York Times* and *Chicago Tribune Books* featured favorable commentaries on *Bold Dragoon: The Life of J. E. B. Stuart* when it was published in 1986. The *Tribune* reviewer praised Thomas for going "a long way toward making [Stuart] intelligible to a post-centennial generation," and the *Times* reviewer noted Thomas's ability to make "scattered and complex cavalry actions admirably clear."[49] The historical journals gave generally favorable reviews. Joseph Glatthaar and Gary Gallagher echoed one another in calling *Bold Dragoon* "the best biography of Stuart" and "the standard life of Stuart" respectively.[50] Glatthaar believed the strength of Thomas's Stuart is in "the character analysis of the Confederate cavalryman," and Gallagher applauded Thomas's "compelling portrait of a combative, robust, talented man determined to make the most of life."[51] As usual these military-minded historians wanted more from Thomas than he was willing to give and chastened him, gently, for a "failure to give adequate attention to several aspects of Stuart's military operations and relationships."[52]

As he had done in his monographs and would do with his biography of Lee, Thomas explores the crisis of identity and the search for self-actualization in Stuart; in so doing he proves himself to be a psycho-historian. The questions of "Who am I?" and "How do I present myself?" are multifaceted, postmodern, and far-reaching queries that depend on moral judgments, decisions about self versus family and community, and the ways in which individuals and societies are forced to compromise between change and tradition, life and death. Thomas has consistently explored how life happens and how people respond with limited amounts of power over circumstances, even over themselves. There is a collision of ambition, hard work, chance, desires, and fulfillment as opportunity holds out its hand or defers to do so. Some people seek fame and others crouch from glory. Thomas's Stuart wanted the former and became a master manipulator of his image:

> There is a very good reason why Stuart the man became so quickly and completely Stuart the metaphor. That reason is Stuart himself. He began the metaphor-making process while he lived, and he succeeded.
>
> He was warrior, knight, and cavalier; his life was mission, quest, and lark.... It was an ambitious role and a bold facade, and somewhere beneath an actor's mask was Stuart the finite human being.[53]

Thomas took away the mask, something Stuart or previous biographers were never able to do—and it was more of a tragedy for the general because he "confused fame with greatness."[54]

Thomas changed horses—or genres—almost immediately, trailing the Stuart book with *Travels to Hallowed Ground: A Historian's Journey to the American Civil War* (1987). Allan Millet mused mightily on this unique piece in Thomas's repertoire: "Those who sup at the table of Civil War history have been of late consuming full course meals, heavy fare on how the North won and the South lost, how misplaced Celtic ardor killed a generation of Southern youth, how such giants as A. P. Hill and J. E. B. Stuart fought their battles and leaders. Emory Thomas, one of the most accomplished chefs of the 'full course meal' . . . , has given us . . . a light snack, a watercress sandwich of Civil War history. . . . Thomas's descriptive narrative and his reflections show the same high literary quality, keen insight, and patience with the human condition that grace his other books."[55] But the volume was also meant for academics, as James Lee McDonough stressed in his review: "This is a book that will be most meaningful to those who know the war, who know the land where it was fought, and who themselves have reflected on the significance, then and now, of that great struggle."[56]

In *Travels* Thomas tells vivid stories derived from intersections of past and present. He closes the "history gap" and helps soothe public fears over academic abstractions by going to the physical places anyone can visit. Thomas helps make history accessible. For him "history is a creative, interpretive response to experience. It is, or ought to be, art which springs from life and at the same time attempts to expand and deepen an understanding of the human experience."[57] The purpose of history is to inspire people to think, and, as has been demonstrated repeatedly in this essay by reviewers using the word "provocative," Thomas has been faithful to Clio. History compels people to confront life in the present tense and teaches "about the persistence of change in human affairs . . . [even though] paradoxically change and continuity seem both to be historical constants."[58]

One of Thomas's favorite short stories is Bobbie Ann Mason's "Shiloh," precisely because of its look at the historical imagination or lack of it. Leroy and Norma Jean—their names indicate a crisis of identity and role-playing: "le Roi," the King (Elvis), and Marilyn Monroe—are adjusting to each other during the latter part of a long marriage. Their lives changed when Leroy was disabled, forced to quit his coast-to-coast truck-driving job, and started staying at home. Thomas is interested in Mason's use of the pair as metaphor for past and present, history and myth: "They have known each other so long they have forgotten a lot about each other. They could become reacquainted."[59]

Pulling memory and history into the present, Mason writes: "At Christmas, Leroy bought an electric organ for Norma Jean. She used to play the piano when she was in high school. 'It don't leave you,' she told him once. 'It's like riding a bicycle.'"[60] Norma Jean buys "The Sixties Songbook" and says, "I didn't like these old songs back then. . . . But I have a crazy feeling I missed something."[61] She is not alone: "Leroy has grown to appreciate how things are put together. He has begun to realize that in all the years he was on the road he never took time to examine anything. He was always flying past scenery. . . . Now that Leroy has come home to stay, he notices how much the town has changed. . . . Nobody knows anything, Leroy thinks. The answers are always changing."[62]

Thomas links Mason's "Shiloh" to the geographical Civil War Shiloh and to the historical imagination in a chapter in *Travels* entitled "Art, Life, and Shiloh," a title reflecting his definition of history. Thomas understands Leroy and Norma Jean: "These people are troubled and frustrated for a number of reasons. One of the reasons they are troubled and frustrated is history, or the lack of it rather, the rootless, aimless detachment from time and place that afflicts many middle American moderns."[63] As Mason writes of Leroy: "He is leaving out the insides of history. History was always just names and dates to him."[64] To connect with the past, Leroy and Norma Jean go on a picnic to Shiloh National Battlefield Park. Thomas follows them there and concludes: "The place 'so full of history' compels them to confront life. Under very different circumstances, the same thing happened to me."[65]

Thomas is well known for his attention to primary-source research, secondary-source synthesis, and interpretive schools. In 1993, with Richard Current and others, he was an editor of the four-volume *Encyclopedia of the Confederacy*. Among the thousands of entries and contributors to the project, no one was surprised that Thomas took on the massive task of writing "Bibliography and Historiography" for a Civil War literature that has, maybe, 100,000 titles. He decided to divide books about the Confederacy into three dominant themes: "Apology," "Continuity or Discontinuity," and "Southern Distinctiveness." Thomas called the apologists "neo-Confederates" who aim at vindicating the loss; history as apology finds "the uses and perversions of Confederate history" to its liking.[66] Those in the continuity-or-discontinuity category differ on the question "To what extent did the Confederacy provoke or provide fundamental change in the American South?"[67] Those who argue for southern distinctiveness encompass scholars who "see Southerners as 110% Americans" and those who see them as a distinct people—before, during, or/and after the Confederate period. Thomas indicates that whichever the category and whatever the interpretation, the issues dealing with humans are "pregnant with subtle complexities."[68]

In 1995 he returned to biography and focused on the most myth-laden figure in the Confederate pantheon. *Robert E. Lee: A Biography* also confronts the constants in Thomas's own life: Douglass Southall Freeman, the Confederate memorials in Richmond, and Thomas's particular Confederate imagination. Also influential and important to this book were Thomas's long association with Thomas L. Connelly and his myth-debunking works on Lee: *The Marble Man: Robert E. Lee and His Image in American Society* (1977) and, with Barbara Bellows, *God and General Longstreet: The Lost Cause and the Southern Mind* (1982).

In his self-described "post-revisionist" examination of Lee, Thomas offers a less perfect man than Freeman's Lee or the myth-embracing cinematic Lee of Ken Burns, though a better man than described by Connelly and his interpretive descendant, Alan Nolan.[69] For Thomas, Lee "was a greater man than he was a general," and he "was a great person, not so much because of what he did (although his accomplishments were extraordinary); he was great because of the way he lived, because of what he was."[70] Thomas provides a psychological life of a tragic hero who made the most of the paradoxes in the human condition. Lee learned strict self-control in order to have freedom. He was nonconfrontational, yet he ordered horrific battles. He endured an unsatisfying marriage and family life because of his overpowering religious belief that "evil was selfishness" and that the "great duty of life is . . . the promotion of the happiness & welfare of our fellow men."[71] Lee "appreciated absurdity in the human condition and refused to take himself or anyone else too seriously." He was most unlike J. E. B. Stuart.[72]

Historians have recognized Thomas's Lee as a valuable contribution to the body of work focusing on the general as well as on the Civil War. Carol Reardon and Steven Woodworth praised the interpretation, and Michael Parrish called it "a perceptive biography that achieves balance between Lee's personal and professional lives."[73] George Rable wrote that the book was "both intelligent and quirky" but conceded that "Thomas usually strikes the right note. He is empathetic without being uncritical."[74] "Quirky" for Rable means that Thomas infers too much, connects history with contemporary imagery, and in Rable's mind, the "dichotomy between words and actions may offer less insight about Lee in particular than about human beings in general."[75] Thomas must appreciate the ironies in the critique, for he has always stressed interpretation, viewed the past as interwoven with the present, and argued for a common humanity for Lee.

For his insights into Lee and as a way to mark his position as the leading scholar on the Confederate South, the Southern Historical Association honored Thomas with a roundtable session on Robert E. Lee at the New Orleans meeting in 1995. Panel members included Bertram Wyatt-Brown, Nina Silber, William J. Cooper, Grady McWhiney, Gabor Boritt, and James I. Robertson—a group representing disparate interests from the personal to the political, from the home front to the battlefield. The packed house of three hundred people included many of the leading scholars of the Civil War. As Thomas flashed pictures for his scrapbook, his colleagues affirmed the importance of his work to their understandings of the Confederate States of America.[76]

Even with his substantial continuing contribution in writing history, Emory M. Thomas is preeminently a teacher. His classroom manner, with its respect for various opinions, and his continuing thirty-year habit of opening his home—and Fran's—to graduate students have had enormous ramifications on literally hundreds of thousands of other students, that is, his students' students' students. He has promoted the happiness and welfare of his charges through the sheer fun of exploding firecrackers in a four-by-eight-foot sandbox to recreate the Battle of the Crater, charging up Kennesaw Mountain battlefield to demonstrate something or the other, dancing often with us to Joan Baez's "The Night They Drove Old Dixie Down," hitting softballs for the

"Last Chance Saloon Gang," writing hundreds of recommendations highlighting our strengths, or lending an ear to our various wanderings. The Confederate South of our understanding is "his." And his Confederate imagination has had an influence on the academy of professional historians, remaking history in readable, playful, and provocative ways to replace the "Mint Julep mythology" with a usable story.[77]

NOTES

1. William Faulkner, *Absalom, Absalom!* (New York: Vintage Books, 1936), 361.

2. Ibid.

3. Emory M. Thomas, interview by Brian Lamb, C-SPAN, Sept. 10, 1995, "Booknotes," www.booknotes.org/Transcript/?ProgramID=1268, 5.

4. Ibid., 4.

5. Ibid., 5.

6. Ibid.

7. Emory M. Thomas, *Travels to Hallowed Ground: A Historian's Journey to the American Civil War* (Columbia: University of South Carolina Press, 1987), 30.

8. Ibid.

9. Frank E. Vandiver, *Ploughshares into Swords: Josiah Gorgas and Confederate Ordinance* (Austin: University of Texas Press, 1952); Vandiver, *The Mighty Stonewall* (New York: McGraw-Hill, 1957).

10. Frank E. Vandiver, "The Confederate Myth," *Southwest Review* (Summer 1961): 199–204, cited in Emory M. Thomas, "Honest to Clio: The New History of the Old South," Lamar Lecture Series (Macon, Ga.: Wesleyan College, 1972), 8.

11. Thomas, interview by Lamb, 6.

12. Thomas, "Honest to Clio," 20.

13. Ibid.

14. Ibid.

15. For C. Vann Woodward's themes of change versus continuity, see his *Origins of the New South, 1877–1913* (Baton Rouge: Louisiana State University Press, 1951); *Reunion and Reaction: The Compromise of 1877 and the End of Reconstruction* (Boston: Little, Brown, 1951); *The Strange Career of Jim Crow* (New York: Oxford University Press, 1955); and *The Burden of Southern History* (Baton Rouge: Louisiana State University Press, 1960).

16. Emory M. Thomas, *The Confederacy as a Revolutionary Experience* (Englewood Cliffs, N.J.: Prentice-Hall, 1971), ix.

17. Emory M. Thomas, *The Confederate State of Richmond: A Biography of the Capital* (Austin: University of Texas Press, 1971), 63.

18. Mary E. Massey, review of *The Confederate State of Richmond,* by Thomas, *Journal of Southern History* 4 (1971): 647–48.

19. Ibid., 648.

20. Thomas Senior Berry, review of *The Confederate State of Richmond,* by Thomas, *American Historical Review* (Feb. 1974): 231.

21. William Hanchett, review of *The Confederate State of Richmond,* by Thomas, *Journal of American History* 59 (Mar. 1972): 1018–19.

22. Thomas, *Revolutionary Experience,* 134.

23. Richard N. Current, review of *The Confederacy as a Revolutionary Experience,* by Thomas, *Journal of American History* 58 (Sept. 1971): 466–67.

24. Michael Perman, review of *The Confederate Nation,* by Thomas, *American Historical Review* 84 (Dec. 1979): 1481.

25. Richard E. Beringer, Herman Hattaway, Archer Jones, and William N. Still Jr., *The Elements of Confederate Defeat: Nationalism, War Aims, and Religion* (Athens: University of Georgia Press, 1988), 20.

26. Chapters have been incorporated into Allen Weinstein and Frank Otto Gatell, eds., *American Negro Slavery: A Modern Reader,* 2nd ed. (New York: Oxford University Press, 1973); Paul D. Escott and David R. Goldfield, eds., *Major Problems in the History of the American South,* vol. 1 (Lexington, Mass.: D. C. Heath, 1990); and Michael Perman, ed., *Major Problems in the Civil War and Reconstruction* (Lexington, Mass.: D. C. Heath, 1990).

27. James M. McPherson, "Could the South Have Won?" *New York Review of Books,* June 13, 2002.

28. Thomas, "Honest to Clio," 7. As furthering his understanding of "mythistory," Thomas cites George B. Tindall, "Mythology: A New Frontier in Southern History," in *The Idea of the South: In Pursuit of a Central Theme,* ed. Frank E. Vandiver (Chicago: University of Chicago Press, 1964), 1–15.

29. Thomas, "Honest to Clio," 8.

30. Emory M. Thomas, *The American War and Peace: 1860–1877* (Englewood Cliffs, N.J.: Prentice-Hall, 1973).

31. Ibid., xiv.

32. Steven Channing, "The Civil War Centennial: A Revival?" *Reviews in American History* 3 (June 1975): 270.

33. Ibid.

34. Ibid.

35. Grady McWhiney, review of *The American War and Peace,* by Thomas, *Journal of Southern History* 40 (Feb. 1974): 146.

36. C. Vann Woodward, review of *The Confederate Nation,* by Thomas, *The New Republic,* Mar. 17, 1979, 25, 27.

37. Ibid., 27.

38. Emory M. Thomas, *The Confederate Nation: 1861–1865* (New York: Harper & Row, 1979), 297–99, 305.

39. Woodward, review of *Confederate Nation,* 27.

40. Charles Roland, review of *The Confederate Nation,* by Thomas, *Journal of American History* 66 (Dec. 1979): 654–55; Perman, review of *Confederate Nation,* 1481.

41. J. Mills Thornton III, "The Confederacy as a Novelty Item," *Reviews in American History* 8 (Mar. 1980): 57–62.

42. Beringer et al., *Elements of Confederate Defeat,* 24, 25, 217.

43. Drew Gilpin Faust, *The Creation of Confederate Nationalism: Ideology and Identity in the Civil War South* (Baton Rouge: Louisiana State University Press, 1988), 84.

44. Harry P. Owens and James J. Cooke, eds., *The Old South in the Crucible of War* (Jackson: University Press of Mississippi, 1983), viii.

45. Ibid. Paul D. Escott, Lawrence N. Powell, Michael S. Wayne, Leon F. Litwack, Michael Barton, and Thomas B. Alexander contributed essays to the volume.

46. Perman, review of *Confederate Nation,* 1481.

47. Thomas, "Honest to Clio," 26.

48. Thornton, "Novelty Item," 61.

49. John S. Peterson, review of *Bold Dragoon: The Life of J. E. B. Stuart,* by Thomas, *Chicago Tribune Books,* Dec. 28, 1986, 5; Richard Snow, review of *Bold Dragoon,* by Thomas, *New York Times Book Review,* Dec. 21, 1986, 46.

50. Joseph T. Glatthaar, review of *Bold Dragoon,* by Thomas, *Journal of American History* (Mar. 1987): 1042; Gary W. Gallagher, review of *Bold Dragoon,* by Thomas, *American Historical Review* (Apr. 1988): 505.

51. Gallagher, review of *Bold Dragoon,* 505.

52. Ibid. Also see Michael C. C. Adams, review of *Bold Dragoon,* by Thomas, *Civil War History* (June 1986): 269–70.

53. Thomas, *Bold Dragoon,* 299.

54. Ibid., 300.

55. Allan R. Millett, review of *Travels to Hallowed Ground,* by Thomas, *Civil War History* (June 1988): 172.

56. James Lee McDonough, review of *Travels to Hallowed Ground,* by Thomas, *Journal of Southern History* 54 (Nov. 1988): 668.

57. Thomas, *Travels to Hallowed Ground,* 60.

58. Ibid., 61.

59. Bobbie Ann Mason, "Shiloh," in *Shiloh and Other Stories* (New York: Harper & Row, 1982), 9.

60. Ibid., 3.

61. Ibid.

62. Ibid., 2, 3, 5.

63. Thomas, *Travels to Hallowed Ground,* 46.

64. Mason, "Shiloh," 16.

65. Thomas, *Travels to Hallowed Ground,* 60.

66. Emory M. Thomas, "Bibliography and Historiography," in *Encyclopedia of the Confederacy,* ed. Richard Current et al., 4 vols. (New York: Simon & Schuster, 1993), 1:165–66.

67. Ibid.

68. Ibid., 167.

69. Ken Burns, *The Civil War* (Florentine Films, 1991); Alan T. Nolan, *Lee Considered: General Robert E. Lee and Civil War History* (Chapel Hill: University of North Carolina Press, 1991). See

also Emory M. Thomas, review of *Lee Considered,* by Alan T. Nolan, *American Historical Review* 97 (Apr. 1992): 618–19.

70. Thomas, interview by Lamb, 1; Emory M. Thomas, *Robert E. Lee: A Biography* (New York: W. W. Norton, 1995), 14.

71. Ibid., 414.

72. Ibid.

73. Carol Reardon, review of *Robert E. Lee,* by Thomas, *Journal of American History* 83 (June 1996): 218–19; Steven Woodworth, review of *Robert E. Lee,* by Thomas, *American Historical Review* 102 (Feb. 1997): 192; T. Michael Parrish, "The R. E. Lee 200: An Annotated Bibliography of Essential Books on Lee's Military Career," in *Lee: The Soldier,* ed. Gary W. Gallagher (Lincoln: University of Nebraska Press, 1996), 590.

74. George Rable, review of *Robert E. Lee,* by Thomas, *Journal of Southern History* 62 (Nov. 1996): 811.

75. Ibid.

76. Five years after the SHA meeting, Thomas published *Robert E. Lee: An Album* (New York: W. W. Norton, 2000), a visual account of how historians and mythmakers have portrayed Lee over the years.

77. Thomas used the term "Mint Julep Mythology" in "Honest to Clio," 15.

NATIONALISM AND IDENTITY

Striking a Revolution's First Blow

WILLIAM C. DAVIS

IN HIS INAUGURAL ADDRESS GIVEN MARCH 4, 1861, TUCKED BEtween the leaves of the olive branch of peaceful reconciliation with the South, Abraham Lincoln inserted his determination to use "all the power at my disposal" to hold U.S. property and enforce its laws—everywhere. The right of secession did not exist, he said; the Union was perpetual and indissoluble.[1]

Those he referred to as "my dissatisfied fellow countrymen" thought otherwise. When Lincoln assumed his office, the Confederate States of America had been an accomplished fact for fully a month, at least on paper. Its leaders had framed a constitution, established the executive and congressional branches of government, chosen Jefferson Davis of Mississippi for its president, and commenced the task of raising an army for its own defense. Their motivations may have been mixed. A few had wanted to separate from the North and the old Union for more than a generation. Others found a fatal threat to slavery in the swelling population of the free states and their inevitable expansion westward. Some feared that government in Washington was growing too strong and that, backed by a free-state majority in Congress, it could force unwelcome economic and social evils on the South.

There was no "solid" South, then or later. A host of often-conflicting interests made up the southern constellation. While one-fourth of southern whites who were eligible to own slaves actually did own them, the other three-fourths of the decision-making population, mostly poor white farmers, felt little common cause with the planter oligarchs who governed in most states. In every new Confederate state there were serious political, social, and economic divisions between the peoples of the hilly and more isolated interior and the rulers who lived on the coastal tidewater plains. But as is so often the case, the potential threat of outside interference could bind all sides on at least the one paramount common interest of self-defense. Lincoln's threat to use "all the power" at his disposal did more to bring the majority of southerners together as Confederates than all the speeches of the politicians and the fire-eating demagogues.

Lincoln's stated determination to hold U.S. property was the sticking point, for he would have to take back what southerners were now taking from the Union. A host of fortresses, arsenals, customhouses, treasury branches, and more sat spotted throughout the South, easy targets for the secessionists. Indeed hardly was secession accomplished before the southern firebrands began seizing federal buildings. On December 27, 1860, South Carolina militia occupied Fort Moultrie and Castle Pinckney at Charleston without incident. Three days later they took the city's federal arsenal. A week later, even before seceding, Alabama soldiers seized the arsenal at Mount Vernon, and Georgians grabbed Fort Pulaski near Savannah from its garrison—a sergeant and a civilian caretaker. In the weeks that followed, forts at Mobile, Alabama; St. Augustine and Pensacola, Florida; New Orleans; and elsewhere continued to fall into the hands of the secessionists.

Either ungarrisoned completely or else manned by a few caretakers, the forts were easy prey. So were the rest of the southern arsenals and public buildings. Arguing that these installations on southern soil were therefore southern property, the seceding states asserted their unquestioned right to them. President Lincoln, however, assumed the position that the forts and other facilities had been, and still were, the property of all the people of the original federal Union. Refusing to recognize the right or even the possibility of secession, he saw it clearly as his duty to hold what he could and reclaim what he lost. As early as December he had privately declared that if such federal property, and especially the forts at Charleston, should fall into the hands of the secessionists, then the Union "must retake them."[2]

From the very first it was those forts in the Charleston harbor—and one in particular—that drew the attention of the nation, of both nations. For while almost every other piece of Union property fell without even a show of resistance, it was not to be so here in the city already coming to be called the "Cradle of the Confederacy." How appropriate it is, with that irony so beloved of history, that the one city that symbolized and championed secession above all others should also be the place to test just how far southerners would go with their experiment in revolution—and how far Lincoln would go in attempting to prevent it.

In a way it was only accident that put U.S. troops in the Charleston forts for, unlike those others that were unmanned, Sumter and Moultrie were still under construction. Fort Moultrie, whose antecedents went back to the Revolution, housed the actual garrison, whose chief object was to oversee the construction of massive Fort Sumter out in the harbor. Built upon a manmade island of rubble—most of it from New England, incidentally—Sumter had been "in progress" for more than thirty years and was still unfinished. Although its fifty-foot-high outer wall was complete and most of the interior casemates stood ready to hold their seacoast defense cannon, few of those guns had yet been mounted, while many of the fort's interior appointments, including barracks, were mere temporary wooden structures.

Back in 1846, when Jefferson Davis was a congressman from Mississippi, he had introduced a proposal that the garrisoning of such coastal-defense forts be taken over from federal troops by local state militia. Nothing ever came of his suggestion, but if it had, there would have been no trouble in Charleston in 1861. Instead there was a garrison of regular-army soldiers, eighty-five of them. It was not much, certainly no match for the dozens of southern militia units that gathered in the city immediately after South Carolina seceded in December. But as so often happens at great moments, the affairs of nations rested not upon the numbers of either side, but upon a single man.

Maj. Robert Anderson possessed the stuff of heroes. He had demonstrated that during the Mexican War, when he fought until felled by three bullets. If he was to be a hero now, many assumed it would be on the side of the revolutionaries, for he was a Kentuckian, a man of decidedly southern sympathies, a slaveowner, and married into an old Georgia family. More than that, his personal friendship with Jefferson Davis went back over thirty-five years to their West Point days together. Davis regarded him as "a true soldier and man of the finest sense of honor," and in the 1850s, when Davis was secretary of war, he oversaw Anderson's promotion to his current rank.[3]

Yet Anderson was truly a man caught in the middle, between his ties of blood and friendship to the South and the bonds of a soldier's loyalty to the Union and the flag he had served all his professional life. Anderson had campaigned in the Black Hawk War with his old friend Davis. But in that same war, he swore into volunteer service Abraham Lincoln as well. In December 1860, with South Carolina seceding and both men about to become rival presidents, Anderson faced questions posed to few other American soldiers before or since.[4]

From the first he saw no other course than his duty as an officer, though he would try his mightiest to do that duty short of actual conflict, playing diplomat as well as soldier. Poor Anderson had only taken command of the Charleston forts in November 1860, with the situation deteriorating all around him ever since. Failing to get any guidance from the comatose Buchanan administration, he had to act on his own. On December 23, just days after South Carolina left the Union, the first real instructions came from Secretary of War John B. Floyd, and they consisted of a thinly veiled suggestion that he should surrender rather than risk injury in any attack that would mean certain loss of the forts anyhow.[5] Things were happening that Anderson knew nothing about, including a two-week-old promise made by President Buchanan to South Carolina governor Francis Pickens that federal authorities would do nothing in Charleston to alter the status quo. Status quo was the essence of Buchanan; Anderson was made of other stuff. He would act.

Shortly after arriving in Charleston, Anderson had determined that neither Moultrie nor the mainland installations, including Castle Pinckney set on an island close to the city, were defensible against attack. Only Fort Sumter, unfinished as it was, offered real protection to his garrison. Anderson reported this impression to Floyd soon after taking his command, and the secretary of war authorized him to remove his troops to Sumter if threatened, though he never actually expected it to happen. Thus Floyd, Buchanan, and South Carolinians all met a healthy surprise on the morning of December 27 when daybreak revealed Moultrie and the other forts abandoned, their cannon spiked, stores either removed or destroyed, and Anderson and his men and their flag safely ensconced in Fort Sumter. When Governor Pickens demanded that the garrison return to Moultrie, citing President Buchanan's status quo promise, Anderson calmly replied, "I cannot and will not go back."[6]

And now, forced to action by the major's decision, Buchanan even began to show some spine. When South Carolina emissaries demanded that Anderson return to Moultrie, the president told them no. "We are ruined if Anderson is recalled or if Sumter is given up," one of the president's men declared.[7] Then Buchanan went even the next step by trying to send supplies to the garrison at Fort Sumter, but when the *Star of the West* approached the harbor on January 9, South Carolina guns opened fire and drove her away.

For a time many expected this to start outright war, for each side charged the other with unwarranted aggression. But nothing came of it immediately. Buchanan tried once more to calm affairs and hold on to peace long enough for him to leave office, while to the south more states continued to secede, and South Carolina bided its time, awaiting the organization of the new Confederate government before pressing the issue once more at Charleston. Inside Sumter itself Anderson simply prayed to the Almighty "that He will be pleased to save us from the horrors of civil war."[8]

It was a prayer unanswered. The new Confederate States of America was barely three weeks old when on March 1 Pres. Jefferson Davis sent Brig. Gen. P. G. T. Beauregard to take command of the forces in and around Charleston and to prepare its batteries for an attack upon Sumter if it should be ordered. In Washington, Abraham Lincoln relieved a tired Buchanan of his responsibilities and perhaps learned then for the first time the real nature of Anderson's plight. His supplies would soon run out, and unless revictualed the garrison might face being starved into submission. In the fort itself the men became increasingly restive as they awaited events. "We are in daily expectation of a commencement" of hostilities, wrote a private. "That they intend to bombard us is evident."[9]

Lincoln's intent seemed less certain at first. Thanks to dissent within his own cabinet, his Secretary of State William H. Seward was giving Confederate representatives signals that Sumter would be abandoned, while Lincoln, unaware of Seward's doings, wavered back and forth on the issue before determining on March 30 to take steps to succor the garrison. He would send food only, but if the Confederates tried to prevent that, then troop ships would land reinforcements at Sumter as well.

Neither came to pass. In the face of mounting pressure in the South to drive Anderson away, and seeing that Lincoln, not Seward, was making the decisions in Washington, Jefferson Davis finally decided that it was time for an ultimatum. Through Beauregard the Confederate government on April 11 demanded that the garrison surrender. When Major Anderson met with Beauregard's emissaries, he flatly refused to do so. But then he asked if the batteries ringing the harbor would open fire upon him without warning. When told that they would not, Anderson thought he saw a glimmer of hope. He might yet avert the firing of a first shot that could lead the North and South into the abyss of civil war. "I shall await the first shot," he stated, "and if you do not batter us to pieces, we shall be starved out in a few days." His meaning was clear: there was no need to open fire at all. Once his garrison was out of supplies, he could honorably evacuate the fort, the Confederates would have it, and the crisis in Charleston would have been settled without bloodshed.[10]

Beauregard, an old friend of Anderson, was no less anxious to avert a conflict. Telegraphing Davis in Montgomery that Anderson would soon be out of supplies, he was told by the president that he could hold his fire if the major would give a definite time at which he would evacuate. Just after midnight on April 12, Beauregard's aides again rowed out to the fort. Anderson stalled for time when they relayed Davis's conditions, then finally told them that he would leave the fort by noon on April 15.

The major knew that a relief expedition was on its way to Charleston. The date he gave would allow sufficient time for the supply ships to arrive, if they were coming. But this was not good enough for Beauregard, for the major's promise to evacuate was conditioned upon his not receiving new instructions from Washington or supplies in the interim. The general's aides did the only thing they could do. They politely informed Anderson that Charleston's batteries would open fire upon Sumter in one hour. Shaking each of the emissaries by the hand, the major bade them farewell, saying, "If we never meet in this world again, God grant that we may meet in the next."[11]

In that, the last hour of American peace, American innocence, thousands of men in and around Fort Sumter pondered what was to come. Anderson and his officers wakened their men to prepare them. Soldiers in Charleston's batteries chafed with excitement, now that the thing was going to start at last. Local citizens stayed awake or tried to rest, according to their mood. Mary Chesnut, wife of one of Beauregard's emissaries, frankly confessed to her diary: "I do not pretend to go to sleep. How can I?"[12] And oddly enough, among some of the hotheads who helped foment this crisis, there were sudden cold feet.

Leaving Fort Sumter, the Confederate aides first landed at Fort Johnson, due west of the fort. They ordered Capt. George S. James to fire at the appointed time a signal shell from his battery, which would commence the bombardment. Present was a leading secessionist from Virginia, Roger A. Pryor, who had fought long without success to get his state to secede. Arriving in Charleston just two days before, he promised a crowd of Carolinians: "I assure you that just as certain as tomorrow's sun will rise upon us, just so certain will Virginia be a member of the Southern Confederacy; and I will tell your Governor what will put her in the Southern Confederacy in less than an hour by a Shrewsbury clock. *Strike a blow!*"[13] Remembering his speech, Captain James offered Pryor the honor of firing the signal gun, of striking the first blow. The Virginian suddenly lost all his bluster and boast. "I could not fire the first gun of the war," he said.[14] But Lt. Henry S. Farley could. At 4:30 on the morning of April 12, 1861, he pulled a lanyard that sent the signal shell rocketing into the air above Fort Sumter. Years later some would claim that it burst into a fiery palmetto, the symbol of South Carolina.

Thus, finally, after generations of talk and debate, bombast and posturing, threat and withdrawal, Americans North and South had at last come to blows. Most were still baffled at how it could have happened or why it was happening now rather than some other time. But the answer to their bewilderment lay all about them. Now at last the stakes were great enough for the South to risk a bid for independence. Another generation might see more and more free states admitted and the end of southern parity in Congress. The threat that scenario posed to southern life was too great for this crisis to pass away as had those before.

Equally important was the fact that only now was the nation ready for a civil war. Had the sections come to blows thirty or even twenty years earlier, there would have been no contest. In 1840, with almost all small arms in the country still smoothbores, with transportation by rail still in its infancy (even in the North), with telegraphic communication still a relative novelty, and with almost no heavy industry at all in the South, the sections simply could not have fought a real war anywhere approaching the magnitude or nature of the one now commenced.

In 1861, however, just as the ideological polarization and hysteria in the old Union reached the point where brother could fire upon brother, so had the technological development of the country ensured that each could fire with deadly force and with a steady supply of weapons to equip the millions of men of military age north and south of the Mason-Dixon Line. For especially in the past decade, there had come to fruition a technological revolution begun decades before, called, for want of a better name, the American system. It was in essence the forerunner of modern mass production. Weapons and machinery of war that formerly had to be made slowly and by hand were now made almost entirely by machine, by something approaching assembly-line techniques. Further, advances in ballistics now gave, through rifling, a major advance in range and accuracy. Add to this the thirty thousand miles of railroads that could now transport men and material almost anywhere east of the Mississippi, telegraph lines that brought instant communication wherever men chose to string the wires, a pool of manpower in both sections sufficient to field armies on a truly massive scale, a spirit of localism and independence that dated back to colonial times, and political and social issues that simply did not admit compromise, and Americans in 1861 had all the ingredients of that "irrepressible conflict" Seward spoke about.[15]

Thus, consciously or unconsciously, North and South had waited until they had the capability to wage a real war before they started one. Both the democratic nature of the country and its people, with its advantages and its flaws, and the growth of the country as an industrial nation were intimately linked in producing a distinctive war such as could not have been fought at any earlier time, nor anywhere else on the globe.

On that part of the continent called Charleston, South Carolina, the signal shell from James's battery commenced a bombardment that lasted thirty-three hours and that could have but one outcome. Anderson kept his men under cover at first, deciding not to return fire until after dawn. When he offered Capt. Abner Doubleday the honor of firing Sumter's first shot, the captain showed none of Pryor's hesitance. He was delighted. And so were the Confederates. They had feared at first that Sumter would not fire back, that their victory would be cheapened by being too easy. Shortage of powder and shot compelled Anderson to pace his fire, and in any case he offered only a show of resistance rather than a serious return fire. But whenever a gun from Sumter got off a shot, many of the Confederates manning the batteries actually set aside their business and mounted their own works to cheer on the garrison. Anyone looking on should have guessed then and there that it was going to be a peculiar war.[16]

The gunfire ceased that evening, only to resume the next day with renewed ferocity. Sumter's wooden buildings took flame. The fire from the Confederate—already they were called "Rebel"—batteries was so great that Anderson could only risk working six of his own guns. The relief expedition sent by Lincoln was even then arriving off the harbor mouth, but with the firing going on, there was no safe way for the ships to come in to Sumter.

Then just after noon on April 13, a shot cut down the U.S. flag. Thinking that Anderson had lowered it intentionally, an emissary rowed to the fort to propose surrender. After some confusion over who was authorized to receive the capitulation, Anderson agreed. He had done all he could do. The next day, with full honors to their flag, the valiant garrison of Fort Sumter paraded out of the fort after firing a fifty-gun salute. It should have been one hundred guns, but an accident halfway through killed one soldier and mortally wounded another. After that, Anderson was anxious simply to get himself and his men aboard the ships that would take them home. Ironically the first men to die in the Civil War were thus killed only after their engagement had ended. It was, said newspaperman Horace Greeley, an almost bloodless opening to the bloodiest war in American history.[17]

The fall of Fort Sumter electrified North and South alike. The question on every man's lips was, what will happen next? Some in the Confederacy thought that Sumter was an end of it. There would be no war. The Yankees, thus chastised, would let the southern states withdraw in peace. Armistead L. Burt of South Carolina foolishly boasted that he would personally drink every drop of blood shed as a result of secession, so confident was he that Lincoln would not fight. Others were less sanguine. Secretary of State Robert Toombs of Georgia, once hot for war, reputedly prophesied that the taking of Sumter "will wantonly strike a hornet's nest." "Legions now quiet will swarm out and sting us to death," he warned. "It is fatal."[18]

The outpouring of emotion in the Union was instant, and staggering. "The heater is on fire," wrote a Boston man on April 21. "I never knew what a popular excitement can be. . . . Nobody holds back. Civil war is freely accepted everywhere."[19] A Philadelphian declared that "the assault upon Fort Sumter started us all to our feet, as one man. . . . We are to a great degree at present, and will shortly be throughout, an armed nation."[20] And while young men of the North began to rush in martial euphoria to enlist and chastise the Rebels before the summer was out, a few thought they saw a long and hard road ahead. "May be it won't be such a picnic as some say it will," an Indiana farm boy wrote in his journal. Learning that his cousins in the South had already enlisted, he wondered "if I were [in] our army and they should meet me would they shoot me?" He could only conclude, "I suppose they would."[21]

Indeed they would, and they did. Thus, as Lincoln would say, "the war came."

NOTES

1. James M. McPherson, *Ordeal by Fire: The Civil War and Reconstruction* (New York: Alfred Knopf, 1982), 110.

2. E. B. Long, *The Civil War Day by Day: An Almanac, 1861–1865* (Garden City, N.Y.: Doubleday, 1971), 701–2.

3. W. A. Swanberg, *First Blood: The Story of Fort Sumter* (New York: Scribner's, 1957), 34–35.

4. Ibid., 34.

5. U.S. War Department, *The War of the Rebellion: A Compilation of the Official Records of the Union and Confederate Armies,* 128 vols. (Washington, D.C.: Government Printing Office, 1880–1901), ser. 1, 1:103 [hereinafter cited as *OR;* all references to ser. 1].

6. Samuel Wylie Crawford, *Genesis of the Civil War: The Story of Sumter, 1860–1861* (New York: C. L. Webster, 1887), 422–24.

7. McPherson, *Ordeal by Fire,* 141.

8. *OR,* 1:134–44.

9. John Thompson to his father, Feb. 1861, John Thompson Letters, Public Record Office, Belfast, Northern Ireland.

10. Crawford, *Genesis of the Civil War,* 422–24.

11. Ibid., 494–96.

12. Mary Boykin Chesnut, *A Diary from Dixie,* ed. Ben Ames Williams (Boston: Houghton Mifflin, 1949), 36.

13. Crawford, *Genesis of the Civil War,* 305.

14. R. U. Johnson and C. C. Buel, eds., *Battles and Leaders of the Civil War,* 4 vols. (New York: Century, 1884–87), 1:76.

15. David A. Hounshell, *From the American System to Mass Production, 1800–1932* (Baltimore: Johns Hopkins University Press, 1985), 15–16.

16. Swanberg, *First Blood,* 301.

17. Ibid., 322.

18. Pleasant A. Stovall, *Robert Toombs: Statesman, Speaker, Soldier, Sage* (New York: Cassell, 1892), 226.

19. Henry Steele Commager, ed., *The Blue and the Gray: The Story of the Civil War as Told by the Participants,* 2 vols. (Indianapolis: Bobbs-Merrill, 1950), 1:40, 41.

20. Ibid., 41.

21. Ibid., 40.

A Revolution in Raleigh: The Early Transformation of a Confederate State Capital, 1861

DAVID H. McGEE

SHORTLY AFTER 5:30 P.M. ON MAY 20, 1861, A MAN STEPPED ONTO the west balcony of North Carolina's state capitol building in Raleigh. Making his way through the throng of people gathered there, he walked to the railing and dropped a white handkerchief. "Deafening shouts" of approval rose from the hundreds of spectators gathered on the grounds below. The dropped handkerchief was the signal for red-shirted gunners of the Ellis Light Artillery to push people away from their six cannons arranged along the square. Amid the ringing of church bells, cheering, and waving handkerchiefs, the artillerymen commenced firing the one-hundred-gun salute that announced North Carolina's secession from the Union.[1]

The secession of North Carolina ushered in a period of vast change for the residents of Raleigh. Such transformation was not unique to the city. As Emory Thomas argued in *The Confederacy as a Revolutionary Experience,* the act of secession brought about revolutions in the states throughout the Confederacy. But what type of revolution had secession brought to those living in North Carolina's capital city? Thomas describes two types of revolution as taking place in the Confederacy. The first he labeled an external revolution that stemmed from the efforts of radical southerners who rebelled against the United States and created a new government in an effort to maintain and "preserve the Southern way of life" developed during the antebellum period. But this external revolution in turn spawned a second, internal revolution that "engulfed the status quo" it sought to defend by profoundly changing southern political, economic, and social relationships.[2]

Raleigh, North Carolina, serves as a case study showing how one southern city found that joining the Confederacy brought both types of significant change to the ways of living that Thomas describes. As residents became caught up in the rebellion against one government and the formation of another, they (like so many others in the South) found their lives transformed by the process. In a matter of months, they watched as their city grew rapidly in population, saw women openly (and with society's approval) participate in political activities, heard slaveholders question the continued existence of the "peculiar institution" in front of their slaves, witnessed the growth of new industrial businesses in and around the city, and saw state and local governments intervene in daily activities to an extent previously never seen. Taken individually many of these changes seemed small and unimportant; but taken as a whole they represented a revolutionary change in the way that people lived and related to their government.[3]

By the time North Carolina seceded from the Union in 1861, Raleigh had been the state capital for nearly seventy years. During that time the city grew from little more than a roadside tavern to a regional trading center for the Piedmont of North Carolina. When census takers conducted their count in 1860, they found approximately eight thousand people living in Raleigh and within two miles of its city limits. Much of the population growth here (as in so many inland cities during the mid-nineteenth century) came with the advent of the railroads.[4]

The coming of the railroads also brought an increase in trade and a consequent increase in the ties between Raleigh merchants and their counterparts in the North. During the latter part of the secession crisis, these commercial links help explain why many of the city's white population remained hostile to the idea of breaking away from the United States. The events surrounding John Brown's 1859 raid on Harpers Ferry and his subsequent trial temporarily excited the feelings of many against those they saw as radical northerners, whose actions and words would inevitably "sound the death-knell of the union." But the turmoil quickly passed, and the attention of Raleigh's residents returned to the more mundane aspects of their daily lives. Even after the election of Abraham Lincoln, most people in the city steadfastly refused to consider seceding until after they saw what actions the Republican president would take. In February 1861 North Carolina held a referendum on whether to hold a secession convention. The city's voters rejected the proposal by a margin of more than two to one.[5]

Much of the pro-Union sentiment evaporated immediately following the attack on Fort Sumter and Lincoln's call for troops. In early May 1861 Gov. John Ellis called a convention of North Carolina delegates for a special session to chart the state's course regarding secession. Wake County voters selected as their delegates Raleigh residents George Badger, Kemp P. Battle, and William W. Holden, three men who had strongly opposed secession in February but had since changed their stance. On the afternoon of May 20, these three men joined the other delegates as the convention took only a few hours to unanimously pass an ordinance of secession and ratify the Provisional Constitution of the Confederate States of America.[6]

In public Raleigh residents presented a united front supporting secession. President Lincoln's call for troops, according to William Holden, "as by a stroke of lightning, made the North wholly North and the South wholly South." All the Raleigh newspapers echoed this sentiment, calling on southerners to unite to protect their humanity and religion, their soil, their honor, and their slaves. During the latter half of April and early May, residents held mass meetings in the city to show their support for secession and help prepare for coming events. Reports from these meetings reveal that when it came to rallying support for secession, people spoke in terms of a South "united in a common destiny" versus a North united by what one commentator called "the madness of the [northern] people." Even the newspaper of the Wake County Workingmen's Association, which had railed against the secessionists the previous year, dropped its heated attacks to endorse disunion. The only hint that some might want to consider the welfare of North Carolina before that of the South as a whole came when Holden, who was editor of the state's most prominent newspaper, the *North Carolina Standard,* called upon the secession convention to deal only with breaking from the Union and let the people of the state "*determine hereafter what our future relations will be.*" This exception aside, it appears that the bulk of Raleigh's white population sought to tie their fortunes to that of the new Confederate nation.[7]

Despite public proclamations of joy, murmurs of unease could be heard in some quarters. They echoed an earlier generation of North Carolinians who had faced the prospect of rebelling against the British government. Now as then, the people of Raleigh differed on the wisdom of severing ties with one nation and bonding with another. While some openly embraced the idea of joining the Confederacy, others did so with reluctance. R. H. Whitaker remembered that as his family sat around the dinner table on the night North

Carolina seceded, his father remarked that they had eaten breakfast in the United States but were now dining in the Confederate States. The older Whitaker feared that "we will not be as well off when we get back into the United States as when we left." As George Badger listened to the cannonade, the ringing church bells, and the shouts for joy, he informed a friend that he believed the people of Raleigh were celebrating a tragedy and "the death knell of slavery." Still, Whitaker and Badger agreed with those who believed that their duty now was to support the state in its decision.[8]

Behind the public facade of unanimity, some people living in and near Raleigh continued to support the United States. Their voices remained muted because they feared reprisal given the prevalent secessionist atmosphere. Francis Hathcock, who lived just outside the city, told a neighbor that he was so opposed to secession that he would rather give up everything he owned than engage in rebellion against the United States. He remained loyal to the Federal government, refusing any support to his three brothers who enlisted in the Confederate army. Tyrell Gill faced a similar rift in his family when two of his sons volunteered to fight. One of the most outspoken Unionists before Fort Sumter, attorney Bartholomew F. Moore persisted in maintaining that secession was wrong and would hurt the South much more than it would help. But he shared his thoughts on the issue only with his family instead of airing them publicly. Kate Curtis, a student at St. Mary's, also noted that more than a few people disliked the idea of secession. A week after Lincoln's call for troops, she deduced that there were "still a great many unionists about" from the number of hisses drawn by the Confederate flags at the front gate of the school. Clearly not everyone in Raleigh accepted the legitimacy of this rebellion against the U.S. government.[9]

Slaves living in Raleigh also paid attention to the events swirling around them. Although the editor of the *North Carolina Christian Advocate* claimed that they were the most orderly, easily governed, and well-behaved African American population in the state, they listened carefully for information about the coming war. Hannah Crasson remembered her master, John William Walton, calling her father and two uncles to him on the day North Carolina seceded. Walton told the three male slaves that a war had begun between the North and the South. He stated that "if the North whups [the South] you will be as free a man as I," but if the South won, he continued, "you will be a slave all your days." Hannah also recalled hearing Walton's son boast that southerners would be able to "eat breakfast at home, go and whup the North, and be back fer dinner." She laughingly noted that the table was set for four long years before he came back for dinner. Other former Raleigh slaves also remembered hearing similar claims of an easy Confederate victory as they listened to the conversations of their masters' families. Behind a facade of indifference and obedience, the city's black population waited to see how this war would transform their lives.[10]

Much of the radical activity that Emory Thomas describes in *The Confederacy as a Revolutionary Experience* took place from 1862 until the end of the war. But in Raleigh, many of the revolutionary changes that affected that city occurred at the beginning of the war. As residents considered what secession meant to them, they became caught up in a whirlwind of change as the city became the center for the state's military preparations. In just a matter of a few weeks, thousands of soldiers arrived to be mustered in to state service and begin training at the camps of instruction located throughout the city. Legislators and other officials took over many of the hotels, boardinghouses, and spare rooms of friends as the state government worked to prepare North Carolina for war. Meeting the material needs of so many new people called for some sacrifice among Raleigh's permanent residents; but at the same time it also created opportunities for many.

When the first soldiers arrived in Raleigh in response to Governor Ellis's instructions, they found themselves camping wherever they could find room because no preparations had been made for them. William Boylan offered the grounds of his estate off Hillsborough Street (on the western edge of the city) to the men of the Ellis Light Artillery. Others camped briefly in the open lots of Burke and Caswell Squares, at the railroad depots, in various churches, at boardinghouses, on the grounds of the new hospital for the insane, at private homes that were rented or donated, and in the pine groves along the edge of the city. By the second week of May, Raleigh's population had risen by more than half as over five thousand men arrived from all over the state. Charles Manly aptly described the situation to a friend when he noted that the city had "become a military camp."[11]

The chaos subsided somewhat after Col. Daniel Harvey Hill quickly converted the state fairgrounds into a camp of instruction. While Camp Ellis (named after the governor) did not offer luxurious accommodations—one soldier described his company's quarters as "horse stall No. 55"—it provided shelter and a place for troops to begin their training. As soldiers continued to flow into Raleigh, Camp Ellis soon became overcrowded (the number of soldiers there jumped from 920 to 2,500 in one week) and unhealthy. Adj. Gen. J. F. Hoke ordered two other camps established just outside the city: Camp Mangum, on land adjacent to the North Carolina Railroad approximately four miles from the capitol square, and Camp Crabtree (also known as Camp Carolina), several miles north of the city on the plantation of Kimbrough Jones.[12]

Many of the men in the camps of instruction required medical assistance. To meet their needs the state created the position of surgeon general to oversee the medical treatment of soldiers. Raleigh physician Charles Johnson received appointment to the post. He selected local doctors E. Burke Haywood as chief surgeon for the general hospital to be established in the city and J. B. Hardy and Peter E. Hines to care for the troops at the camps of instruction. Haywood immediately set to work locating and preparing the military hospital, but because he also supervised the physicians at the camps of instruction, it took him nearly seven months to have a permanent facility ready to receive soldiers.[13]

The younger residents thoroughly enjoyed the presence of the many new soldiers. At St. Mary's School for Girls, the students rushed to make Confederate flags to fly at the front gate of the school and later made and presented a company flag to the Ellis Light Artillery. The young boys gathered at the Raleigh rail depot almost every day to watch trains full of men arrive and depart. Some of them carried Confederate flags, which they waved to the passing carloads of troops.[14]

While the young people of Raleigh celebrated the coming of thousands of soldiers, the large number of young men camping in and around the city (many of whom were away from the supervision of their families for the first time) meant the situation was ripe for rowdiness. When the Anson Guards unexpectedly arrived in the city, they met with a chilly reception. The troops spent their first night in Raleigh in makeshift shelters at Camp Ellis. Deciding those quarters did not suit them, the men took possession of the county courthouse. The soldiers created a stir when they placed guards in the street around the building and refused to allow local residents to pass without a permit. These actions angered Governor Ellis and a number of prominent citizens. Residents probably breathed a sigh of relief when the company moved on to Weldon a few days later.[15]

More serious problems arose when soldiers slipped into the local taverns for a drink. Although the commanders at the training camps tried to keep their men from obtaining alcohol, the troops managed to acquire it anyway. W. P. Baker, an intoxicated soldier from the 26th North Carolina, attempted to force his way into the home of two women late one night. One woman ran to a neighbor's house to get help. The neighbor returned armed with a pistol and ordered the soldier to stop. When Baker drew a bowie knife, the neighbor shot and critically wounded him. Another group of drunken soldiers, armed with swords and bowie knives, tried to force their way into the city jail to release two comrades who had been arrested for disorderly conduct. Mayor Root arrived and appealed to the gathering crowd of residents to help him arrest the soldiers. Since the local citizens carried no weapons, they gently "declined the polite invitation." A messenger soon returned with another group of soldiers, who promptly arrested their comrades and returned them to camp. Fortunately few such incidents were reported.[16]

For the most part the large number of troops in the city presented more opportunities than problems for local residents. Although David Schenck (a state legislator from western North Carolina) complained that "everything is in confusion here—the city is full of soldiers and officers, every grocery and saloon is full of them," Raleigh merchants enjoyed the increased business. They advertised all manner of wares for sale to the soldiers—from items that made camp life easier to a variety of weapons that included swords, bowie knives, and the new Colt revolving pistols. The city's tailors and seamstresses also touted their abilities to make fine new uniforms for the men, especially the officers. Other businesses benefited as well. The formation of the camps of instruction demanded the services of carpenters to erect or modify buildings; the hundreds of orders flowing out of governmental offices required clerical services and stationery; and bakers furnished fresh bread to feed the men. Seeking cartridge boxes and belts for the new troops, the adjutant general authorized leatherworker Thomas Breem to make five thousand sets as quickly as possible at a cost of no more than $5.50 apiece. The government sought the services of almost everyone who could provide products or labor. In early June, James D. Hollister found that his skills as a machinist were in more demand than his ability to shoulder a rifle when Adjutant General Hoke ordered that he be detailed to return home and make percussion caps. Military officials even called on slaveholders to send any men they could spare to help repair the defenses at Fort Macon on the North Carolina coast.[17]

Raleigh officials faced their greatest challenge in providing the basic necessities and equipment for the soldiers. North Carolina (like other southern states) entered the war almost totally unprepared to equip large numbers of troops. The Adjutant General's Office announced in newspapers what each soldier should bring with him, but few recruits arrived at the camps of instruction with everything Hoke recommended, even though people in the communities where the companies had been recruited made an effort to provide the needed clothing and accoutrements. In addition no one was prepared to feed the more than five thousand soldiers who descended on the capital during the first months of the war. To complicate matters even more, the state government soon found that it had more enlistees than it had weapons and ammunition.[18]

The burden of clothing, feeding, and arming the troops fell primarily on those serving in the Adjutant General's Office, many of whom came from Raleigh. Lawrence O'B. Branch, who had recently resigned from the U.S. Congress, found that he had his hands full as head of the North Carolina Quartermaster General's Department during the first few months of the war. His many responsibilities included finding transportation to move over twenty thousand new recruits, procuring adequate shelter at the camps of instruction in Raleigh and at other locations across the state, procuring and storing massive quantities of food (a single shipment to one camp contained fifty thousand pounds of bacon and thirty thousand pounds of flour), and putting what weapons that could be found in North Carolina into the hands of the soldiers. Raleigh residents Rufus Tucker, John Devereux, Daniel G. Fowle, James J. Iredell, A. M. Lewis, Thomas D. Hogg, and Moses Bledsoe served as procurement officers under Branch. The skills and contacts these men gained as merchants and attorneys before the war no doubt aided their efforts in locating the sources of supplies and negotiating the contracts involved in providing for the soldiers.[19]

The actions that Hoke, Branch, and the junior officers in the Adjutant General's Office took in fulfilling their duties occasionally surprised Raleigh residents accustomed to little government interference in their lives. In April Adjutant General Hoke informed state supreme court justice Thomas Ruffin that he had confiscated a cargo of flour being shipped to the judge for the troops concentrating in Raleigh. Hoke justified his actions by noting that the soldiers needed all the provisions they could get. Perhaps fearful of antagonizing the most powerful and respected legal authority in the state, Governor Ellis had his personal secretary send Ruffin a note thanking him for his "patriotic action" in "forwarding" the flour for the troops. The secretary echoed Hoke in explaining the necessity of the action.[20]

On other occasions state procurement officers Rufus Tucker and John Devereux used their authority to forcibly purchase or rent storage space from the city's residents. George W. Mordecai, the wealthiest person in the county, received notice that the Quartermaster Department was taking land belonging to a person for whom he served as guardian. The only choice he had in the matter was whether he wanted to receive cash or Confederate bonds in payment. In June state authorities also seized heavy metal rollers from William C. Lee's mill to manufacture percussion caps for rifles. Lee complained about the seizure to his friend William Holden. The editor warned officials that unless Lee promptly received fair compensation for his equipment, he would bring the matter before the state legislature. The government quickly appraised the rollers and gave Lee fifty dollars for them. Although Ruffin, Mordecai, and Lee enthusiastically supported the Confederate war effort, the manner in which authorities confiscated their property challenged the very notions about the sanctity of private-property ownership that lay at the heart of the rebellion against the U.S. government.[21]

State confiscation of property proved to be only one of the revolutionary changes brought about in the effort to provide clothing and equipment for the soldiers. This undertaking quickly involved the women of Raleigh in activities that went beyond their normal experiences as well. As soon as Governor Ellis issued his call for volunteers, women set to work preparing clothing and accoutrements for local soldiers. A week after the first shots were fired at Fort Sumter, John H. Bryan informed a friend that local women had already organized and begun to gather to make clothes and mattresses for the troops. Their organizations in Raleigh grew out of groups already in existence. Members of the female missionary association of the Baptist Church organized the first large-scale effort to produce goods for the troops. In the basement of the church, women cut material and distributed it to others to sew into uniforms. They pressed into service every sewing machine they could find in the city. When the number of volunteers involved grew too large to fit in the church basement, they commandeered other quarters—first the Governor's Office and then the Hall of the House of Commons in the state capitol. According to the *State Journal,* even a number of free black women offered their services and worked alongside the others. Within a month the city's newspapers were publishing long lists of contributions as women from every church (as well as those who were not members of a congregation) in the city united in activities to outfit the soldiers. The women of Raleigh joined others throughout the South in preparing their men for war.[22]

The state certainly needed such contributions. The massive recruiting taking place across North Carolina during the summer of 1861 left the state government unable to provide clothing and gear for most of the troops. Without the materials donated by the women of Raleigh and others throughout the state, North Carolina could not have fielded as many troops so quickly. By transferring an activity—making uniforms and other military equipment—long deemed acceptable by society from the private to the public sphere, the city's women exercised their political power in support of the Confederacy.[23]

The efforts that local political, civic, and religious leaders employed to enlist the support of Raleigh's white population for the war effort also exceeded anything the city's residents had experienced. At almost every turn the people found themselves bombarded with appeals to join together to defeat the Yankees and win freedom for the Confederacy. Newspapers, public speeches, and Sunday sermons all promoted the same message—it was the duty of all white residents of Raleigh to provide whatever aid they could to the South in this hour of crisis.

Dozens of articles, poems, and letters that appeared in the city's newspapers during the late spring and summer of 1861 framed their appeals to the people in two ways. To establish the duties to which each individual should respond, writers first called on the citizens' sense of honor and patriotism. They urged the men to show "true courage" and rise up against the oppression and tyranny that "Lincoln and his myrmidons" wanted to force upon the South. Writers also spoke of the need for every white man in Raleigh to prove himself worthy of his ancestors "who fought and fell at Alamance and King's Mountain" during America's struggle for independence. Other newspaper pieces emphasized the need for women to participate in the struggle if the South were to win, employing much the same type of language as used in the appeals to men. Mary E. Gorman wrote an article on female patriotism that hearkened back not only "to the days of '76, when the women of the Revolution" performed patriotic deeds to stop oppression, but also to the "high souled patriotism" of Grecian mothers, whose memory was treasured in the "hearts of all lovers of country." In a poem written to commemorate the presentation of a flag to the Oak City Guards, Jane Wilson echoed these sentiments as she described how women must have the strength to make sacrifices in answer to their "country's call."[24]

The newspapers also focused on more concrete concerns. Governor Ellis set the tone in his first proclamation after rejecting Lincoln's call for troops. He exhorted the people to defend their homes, hearths, and dearest interests against the Union army. Other writers urged the men of Raleigh to quickly meet the "invading foe" at the border rather than wait for the enemy to arrive at their doorstep. To emphasize the dire nature of the situation, some sought to demonize Federal forces by speaking of invading legions composed of hirelings, foreigners, and fanatics thirsting "for the life-blood of those you most cherish."[25]

Raleigh's religious leaders, like many of the city's political leaders, supported the Union before the firing on Fort Sumter. But following Lincoln's call for troops, they joined together in calling on the people to act and in giving their sanction to the Confederate cause. Ministers such as Frederick Fitzgerald, T. E. Skinner, William Pell, and Joseph M. Atkinson (representing the Baptist, Methodist, Presbyterian, and Episcopal denominations in the city) stressed in sermons and newspaper articles that the South was the aggrieved party in this conflict. They maintained that southerners were "perfectly satisfied, morally and economically," with their longstanding institutions and answered only to God for their actions. The ministers emphasized that the U.S. government was wicked and the morally mad northerners, filled with "wrath, malice, hatred, and revenge," had forced the war on the people of the South. Pell argued that in such a climate of hostility, defending the South was divinely sanctioned because "self-defense is no less a law of religion than of nature."[26]

This combination of appeals—based on obligations of honor, patriotism, and protecting one's home and loved ones, along with the moral sanction provided by ministers—touched at almost every angle that could be used to persuade a man to support the Confederate revolution. But questions persisted. Would the appeals be enough to convince Raleigh's workers, clerks, and shopkeepers to become soldiers? Could they persuade the city's women to allow their men to leave home and to provide goods for the southern army as well as support themselves during the war? Would the division between the city's nonslaveholders and slaveowners that flared up in a debate over ad valorem taxation the previous year keep people from joining the Confederate cause?

Raleigh's leaders attempted to address these problems in their efforts to recruit support from a broad base. Seeking to soothe fears of lower-class families who faced possible financial hardships if adult males (especially those who were the only ones providing an income for the household) joined the army, former governor Charles Manly, along with prominent Raleigh businessmen John Bryan and Moses Bledsoe, publicly called on the various public authorities to see that no soldier's family suffered from lack of necessities. The Wake County Court responded the following month by levying a 10 percent surcharge to each person's taxes for the year. The court authorized county officials to spend up to fifty thousand dollars to support the families of "indigent volunteers."[27]

The city's elite also worked to alleviate possible class tensions over slavery. Newspaper articles, public speeches, and sermons conspicuously omitted direct mention of the institution from discussions about supporting the Confederacy. They instead spoke about defending the rights and institutions of the South. The closest anyone came to publicly making slavery a fundamental war issue occurred when religious leaders placed much of the blame for the conflict on abolitionists in the North.[28]

In many ways the activities of Raleigh's white female population mirrored those of their male counterparts. Although societal norms precluded women from being in combat, the war provided opportunities for them to participate in public and political affairs in ways normally forbidden. Using existing women's organizations and staying primarily within established gender roles, many Raleigh women aided the Confederate war effort by working energetically to recruit men for the army; furnish food, clothing, and accoutrements for the troops; and instill in the soldiers moral and patriotic virtues. Given the limitations placed on their gender by society, the city's women played as active a role in supporting the Confederacy as the men.[29]

As soon as Governor Ellis rejected Lincoln's call for troops, some women in Raleigh began urging the men to fight. One identified only as "Lady" wrote the *Raleigh Register* claiming that the women of the city needed no home guard to defend them, telling the men to join the army, "where they are needed." Every week one or more of the city's newspapers carried letters or poems written by local women that called upon men to enlist. These women also participated at public events designed to recruit troops, often providing food and drink for the men at musters and on several occasions making and presenting flags for the local companies to carry into battle. By engaging in such activities, women employed skills normally associated with the domestic sphere to show their political support for the Confederacy.[30]

But some did not restrict their recruiting activities to only the men. They aimed many of the pieces they published at other local women, trying to convince them that sacrificing their menfolk to service in the army was the honorable and patriotic thing to do. Just as men had spoken of the heroic actions that their Revolutionary War ancestors had engaged in during battle, the women harkened back to the activities of their female forebears. A woman who assumed the patriotic nom de plume "Daughter of the Old North State" penned a poem addressed to the "North Carolina Volunteers." In it she states:

There is not a lass in all the land,
Who could bestow her tiny hand
Upon a coward base . . .
Frail, gentle mothers bid you fight,
Sweet sisters say, defend the right,
Ne'er shrink, cries Lady love.

Ostensibly speaking to men in this passage, the writer also sent a message to Raleigh's mothers, sisters, and sweethearts that they had a duty to bid their men to enlist in order to defend their region's honor. Other female writers spoke of how women, even though "every eye with tear may fill," should bravely relinquish their men for the Confederate cause.[31]

The language used to convince Raleigh's women to sacrifice for the war effort differed significantly from that aimed at men. Efforts to recruit male support emphasized the concrete goals of defending one's home from invaders as much as notions of patriotism and honor. But appeals to women focused narrowly on the abstract ideals. In her poem for the flag presentation to the Oak City Guards, Jane Wilson writes of men who fought with honor to defend their homes against the "northern hirelings" and of women who proudly sacrificed their men so their state would not be shamed. A woman writing under the name "L. L." told (as did almost all such writers) of mothers and wives raising their voices in prayer for the safety of their men and God's blessing on their cause. Limiting such appeals to abstract ideals produced mixed results in terms of enlisting soldiers. Only 10 percent of the city's male heads of households joined the army during the first year of the war. No doubt the wives of some men influenced them to stay at home by pointing out that the more immediate concerns of providing for their families took precedence over high-toned ideals.[32]

As the summer of 1861 came to a close, it became clear that Raleigh residents sought to shape the revolutionary aspects of this war in their own terms as much as possible. The city's African Americans appeared mostly content to adopt a watch-and-wait attitude, observing what went on around them to determine their best course of action. The majority of white citizens willingly gave public voice to their support and provided material aid for the Confederacy. Most men and women responded to the call for clothing and supplies by providing items (both voluntarily and for profit) desperately needed by the southern army. The attack on Fort Sumter and Lincoln's call for troops had acted as "a stroke of lightning," which severed the bonds that tied most Raleigh residents to the Union. This led to a series of rapid changes in the city—a rebellion against the existing national government, a doubling of the population, a massive shift in the economy, government interference with private property, slaveowners discussing the possibility of slavery ending, public participation of women in political affairs, and increased involvement of the state and local governments in everyday life. Many questions remained about the breadth and depth of these changes, but in the summer of 1861, the people of Raleigh, North Carolina, would certainly have seen these changes as revolutionary.

NOTES

1. Charlotte E. Grimes, "Sketches of My Life," Grimes Family Papers, Southern Historical Collection, University of North Carolina, Chapel Hill (hereinafter cited as SHC), 12–13; Elizabeth Reid Murray, *Wake: Capital County of North Carolina,* vol. 1, *Prehistory through Centennial* (Raleigh: Capital County, 1983), 459; John G. Barrett, *The Civil War in North Carolina* (Chapel Hill: University of North Carolina Press, 1963), 15–16; Moses N. Amis, *Historical Raleigh: With Sketches of Wake County and Its Important Towns* (Raleigh: Commercial Printing, 1913), 131–32. According to the reminiscences of eyewitnesses, the firing of the cannon brought about Raleigh's first casualties of the war. A young boy recalled that the concussion from the first cannon broke windows in the Haywood residence and the stores all along the upper end of Fayetteville Street. Things went better with the second gun, however, as a perfect ring of smoke accompanied its firing, which people took as a sign the South would be crowned with victory. David Brainard Whiting, "Reminiscence," North Carolina Department of Archives and History, Raleigh (hereinafter cited as NCDAH).

Joseph L. Seawell noted that the first blood shed by a Raleigh resident in the war also occurred here. After cleaning the barrel of one cannon after it had fired, one of the artillerymen accidentally hit a bulldog with the end of the rammer. Already upset by the noise of the guns, the angry dog promptly attached his teeth to the behind of the offending cannoneer. Seawell claimed that it took three men to get the dog off the poor gunner. Joseph Lacy Seawell, *Law Tales for Laymen* (Raleigh: Alfred Williams, 1925), 16–18.

2. Emory M. Thomas, *The Confederacy as a Revolutionary Experience* (1971; repr., Columbia: University of South Carolina Press, 1991), 43–57.

3. The changes that transformed Raleigh at the beginning of the Civil War also took place in differing degrees in other southern cities. Ernest B. Furgurson has discussed how Richmond was affected by the influx of soldiers on the civilian population, the shift in the city's economy, and the new roles of women. *Ashes of Glory: Richmond at War* (New York: Alfred A. Knopf, 1996), 54–67. LeeAnn Whites has described the political role that Augusta, Georgia, women played at the beginning of the war. *The Civil War as a Crisis in Gender: Augusta, Georgia, 1860–1890* (Athens: University of Georgia Press, 1995), 41–63. Stephen Elliott Tripp has provided a view into the transformation of class relations among the white population of Lynchburg, Virginia. *Yankee Town, Southern City: Race and Class Relations in Civil War Lynchburg* (New York: New York University Press, 1997), 86–90.

4. Eighth U.S. Manuscript Census, 1860, Wake County, N.C., Population Schedule and Slave Schedule, NCDAH; David H. McGee, "'On the Edge of the Crater': The Transformation of Raleigh, North Carolina, Households and Communities during the Civil War Era" (Ph.D. diss., University of Georgia, 2000), 1–12. Many of the people who considered themselves residents of Raleigh technically lived outside the narrowly drawn boundaries of the city. Those people living within two miles of the city limits are counted as residents for this study because many of them worked in the city, attended church in the city, frequently socialized with others in the city, or in their correspondence indicated that they were residents of Raleigh.

5. *North Carolina Standard,* Nov. 2, 16, 1859, Mar. 6, 1861; McGee, "Edge of the Crater," 75–80, 91–92; Daniel W. Crofts, *Reluctant Confederates: Upper South Unionists in the Secession Crisis* (Chapel Hill: University of North Carolina Press, 1989), 207–13, 330.

6. Barrett, *Civil War in North Carolina,* 15–16; *North Carolina Standard,* May 22, 1861. According to Marc W. Kruman, the only debate that occurred during the first day of the convention was whether to pass an ordinance of secession or a declaration of revolution. When the former passed, the convention moved quickly to conclude the day's business. *Parties and Politics in North Carolina, 1836–1865* (Baton Rouge: Louisiana State University Press, 1983), 210–20.

7. *Spirit of the Age,* Apr. 24, 1861; *Church Intelligencer,* May 9, 1861; *Biblical Recorder,* Apr. 24, 1861; *Raleigh Register,* Apr. 24, May 1, 1861; *North Carolina Christian Advocate,* Apr. 29, 1861; *Weekly Ad Valorem Banner,* Apr. 25, 1861; *North Carolina Standard,* Apr. 24, May 1, 8, 1861.

8. Murray, *Wake,* 458–59; Grimes, "Sketches," 12–13; R. H. Whitaker, *Whitaker's Reminiscences: Incidents, and Anecdotes* (Raleigh: Edwards and Broughton, 1905), 47; George E. Badger quoted in Hugh Talmadge Lefler and Albert Ray Newsome, *North Carolina: The History of a Southern State* (Chapel Hill: University of North Carolina Press, 1954), 425.

9. Cases of Francis W. Hathcock (no. 3,583) and Tyrell Gill (no. 4,637), Southern Claims Commission Case Files (1877–83), Records of General Auditor's Office, Records of Third Auditor's Office, RG 217, National Archives; Murray, *Wake,* 457; Kate Curtis to John H. Curtis, Apr. 22, 1861, quoted in Martha Stoops, *The Heritage: The Education of Women at St. Mary's College, Raleigh, North Carolina, 1842–1982* (Raleigh: St. Mary's College, 1984), 57.

10. *North Carolina Christian Advocate,* Apr. 29, 1861; George P. Rawick, ed., *The American Slave: A Composite Autobiography,* vol. 15, *North Carolina Narratives,* pt. 2 (Westport, Conn.: Greenwood, 1941), 192, 223. Peter Kolchin notes that in much of the South, slave reactions to the beginning of the war mirrored those of Raleigh slaves. *American Slavery, 1619–1877* (New York: Hill and Wang, 1993), 203–5.

11. *North Carolina Standard,* May 1, 15, 1861; *Raleigh Register,* May 1, 8, 1861; Barrett, *Civil War in North Carolina,* 14; Murray, *Wake,* 460; David H. McGee, "The Twenty-Sixth Regiment North Carolina Troops, CSA" (M.A. thesis, Virginia Tech, 1992), 9. Among the individuals who donated their land as campsites for the troops were William Boylan, Thomas Lemay, and Kenneth Rayner. The Adjutant General's Office also rented houses or rooms from Fabius J. Haywood and Sarah Reid. J. F. Hoke to various correspondents, May 2, 3, 21, 30, 1861, A.G. Book 13, N.C. Adjutant General's Office, NCDAH. The best description of the early military activities in Raleigh can be found in Richard W. Iobst, "North Carolina Mobilizes: Nine Critical Months, December, 1860–August, 1861" (Ph.D. diss., University of North Carolina, Chapel Hill, 1968), 236–45.

12. General Orders No. 4, Apr. 24, 1861, and Hoke to John Ellis, May 25, 1861, A.G. Book 13; *Raleigh State Journal,* May 1, 8, 1861; *Charlotte (N.C.) Western Democrat,* May 7, 1861; Murray, *Wake,* 460–61; McGee, "Twenty-Sixth Regiment," 16.

13. Charles E. Johnson to E. Burke Haywood, Apr. 29, May 11, Nov. 11, 30, 1861, and Peter Hines to E. Burke Haywood, Dec. 8, 1861, Haywood Family Papers, SHC; Hoke to Dr. J. B. Hardy, May 13, 1861, A.G. Book 13; Iobst, "North Carolina Mobilizes," 133–36. In late April, Burke Haywood found himself in an awkward situation when he agreed to support Charles Johnson for the surgeon general's post. He learned soon after his endorsement that his brother, Fabius J. Haywood, also sought the position. There seemed to be no hard feelings in the family even though Johnson received the position.

14. Louise [?] to "Dear Carrie," Apr. 30, 1861, quoted in Stoops, *The Heritage,* 57, 60; *Raleigh Register,* June 15, 1861; Whiting, "Reminiscence"; George R. Bryan to Mary Shepard Bryan, June 8, 1861, John H. Bryan Papers, NCDAH. One student, Kate Curtis, watched most of these events but took no part, "not considering it the most delicate work that a lady could do." Stoops, *The Heritage,* 57. Other young women seemed to enjoy watching the soldiers as much as the students at St. Mary's. While writing to his wife, William Battle informed her that their daughter Catharine had gone with her friend Patty to watch the regimental drill at one of the camps of instruction. William Battle to Lucy Battle, June 27, 1861, Battle Family Papers, SHC.

15. W. A. Smith, *The Anson Guards* (Charlotte, N.C.: Stone, 1914), 10–11; Iobst, "North Carolina Mobilizes," 281.

16. *Charlotte (N.C.) Western Democrat,* Aug. 13, 1861; *Raleigh Register,* Aug. 7, 28, 1861. Although Baker was not expected to live, he later recovered and served in another regiment.

17. David Schenck Diary, May 30, 1861, quoted in Iobst, "North Carolina Mobilizes," 240. *North Carolina Standard,* May–July 1861; *Raleigh Register,* May-July 1861; *Raleigh State Journal,* May 8, 22, 1861; Hoke to various correspondents, May 14, 17, June 3, 1861, A.G. Books 13, 15, N.C. Adjutant General's Office, NCDAH; *Spirit of the Age,* Apr. 24, 1861.

18. Adjutant General Hoke recommended that each soldier have "two pairs of pants (very loose), two sack coats, two shirts, two pairs of shoes, a felt hat (if caps were not provided), a knapsack, a haversack, a canteen, a blanket, a rubber overcoat, and as few drawers, socks, and undershirts as possible." While a number of men came to camp with such surplus items as musical instruments, large camp chests, and the occasional bedstead, few possessed all the items contained in Hoke's list. *Greensbourough (N.C.) Patriot* (semiweekly), May 10, 1861; Barrett, *Civil War in North Carolina,* 23–24; Walter Clark, *Histories of the Several Regiments and Battalions from North Carolina in the Great War, 1861–'65,* vol. 1 (Raleigh: E. M. Uzzell, 1901), 1, 23–24, 37, 39–42 (hereinafter cited as *N.C. Regiments*).

19. Various correspondence, orders, and circulars, Apr. 25, May 1, 7, 9, 21, 23, A.G. Book 13; Circular, May 18, 1861, A.G. Book 15; W. W. Morrison to L. O'B. Branch, May 21, 1861, and Wm. Johnston to Daniel G. Fowle, May 21, 1861, A.G. Book 21, N.C. Adjutant General's Office, NCDAH; *North Carolina Standard,* May 15, 1861; Murray, *Wake,* 465, Clark, *N.C. Regiments,* 23–24, 37. A good description of the activities and challenges faced by the men in the various branches of the Adjutant General's Office can be found in Iobst, "North Carolina Mobilizes," 120, 550–66.

20. Hoke to Thomas Ruffin, Apr. 25, 1861, Hoke to R. S. Tucker, May 14, 1861, A.G. Book 13; Graham Dawes to Ruffin, Apr. 25, 1861, in J. G. de Roulhac Hamilton, ed., *Papers of Thomas Ruffin, 1787–1870,* vol. 3 (New York: AMS, 1973), 146.

21. John Devereux to George W. Mordecai, Nov. 1, 1861, George W. Mordecai Papers, SHC; Iobst, "North Carolina Mobilizes," 494. Seizing Justice Ruffin's flour was not enough for the Commissary Department. Only a few days later, Rufus Tucker wrote the judge asking for a donation of several carloads of straw to help the soldiers who were forced to sleep on "naked Boards" because of a lack of cover. Tucker to Ruffin, Apr. 27, 1861, in Hamilton, *Papers of Thomas Ruffin,* 148.

22. John H. Bryan to Kelly H. Lewis, Apr. 22, 1861, Bryan Papers; Mary Badger Hale to sister, Aug. 16, 1861, Badger Family Papers, SHC; Grimes, "Sketches," 13–14; *Raleigh State Journal,* May 1, 1861; Iobst, "North Carolina Mobilizes," 521; David H. McGee, "'Home and Friends': Kinship, Community, and Elite Women in Caldwell County, North Carolina, during the Civil War," *North Carolina Historical Review* 74 (Oct. 1997): 363–88; Drew Gilpin Faust, *Mothers of Invention: Women of the Slaveholding South in the American Civil War* (Chapel Hill: University of North Carolina Press, 1996), 20–29.

23. Iobst, "North Carolina Mobilizes," chap. 8; Whites, *Crisis in Gender,* 47–54.

24. *Raleigh Register,* Apr. 24, May 15, June 5, 1861; *North Carolina Standard,* Apr. 24, May 1, 8, 1861; *Spirit of the Age,* May 8, 1861; *Biblical Recorder,* May 1, June 19, 1861.

25. *North Carolina Standard,* Apr. 24, 1861; *Raleigh State Journal,* May 1, 22, 1861; *Raleigh Register,* May 15, July, 17, 1861; *Spirit of the Age,* May 15, 1861; *Biblical Recorder,* Apr. 24, 1861; *North Carolina Christian Advocate,* Apr. 29, 1861; *Church Intelligencer,* Aug. 2, 1861.

26. *Biblical Recorder,* Apr. 24, May 1, 15, June 26, July 10, 21, 1861; *North Carolina Christian Advocate,* Apr. 29, 1861; *Church Intelligencer,* May 9, 30, 1861. Some of the sermons received such acclaim from those who heard them that they were repeated before different congregations and published in broadside form for distribution throughout the state. The sermons of Episcopal bishop Thomas Atkinson of the North Carolina Diocese were particularly popular. Thomas Atkinson, *Christian Duty in the Present Time of Trouble: A Sermon Preached at St. James Church, Wilmington, N.C.* (Wilmington: Fulton and Price, 1861); Atkinson, *Extract from the Annual Address of the Rt. Rev. Thomas Atkinson, D.D. to the Convention of the Diocese* (Raleigh: Office of the *Church Intelligencer,* 1861).

27. *North Carolina Standard,* May 1, 1861; *Spirit of the Age,* June 5, 1861; Minutes for May Term, 1861, Wake County Court of Pleas and Quarter Sessions, NCDAH.

28. The only articles directly mentioning slavery simply commented on how well slaves had behaved so far in Raleigh and in Virginia. Neither of these made any tie between slavery and the war. *North Carolina Christian Advocate,* Apr. 29, 1861; *North Carolina Standard,* May 1, 1861. The only other specific reference to slavery in newspapers was the publication of North Carolina's new law defining treason, which made anyone who advised or conspired with a slave to "rebel or to make insurrection in this State" liable for the crime. *North Carolina Standard,* May 15, 1861.

29. For discussions of how women were designated as noncombatants by society, see Jean Bethke Elshtain, *Women and War* (New York: Basic Books, 1987), xi, 166, 181; and Drew Gilpin Faust, "Altars of Sacrifice: Confederate Women and the Narratives of War," in *Divided Houses: Gender and the Civil War,* ed. Catherine Clinton and Nina Silber (New York: Oxford University Press, 1992),

172. Anne Firor Scott provides a good description of how women's long apprenticeship in voluntary associations prepared them to step in the roles assigned them during the Civil War. "On Seeing and Not Seeing: A Case of Historical Invisibility," *Journal of American History* 71 (June 1984): 9, 12. George C. Rable describes how the activities of southern women fell within the boundaries established for female behavior. *Civil Wars: Women and the Crisis of Southern Nationalism* (Urbana: University of Illinois Press, 1989), 47.

30. *Raleigh Register,* Apr.–Aug. 1861; *North Carolina Standard,* Apr.–Aug. 1861; *Spirit of the Age,* Apr.–May 1861.

31. *Raleigh Register,* May 22, 1861; *North Carolina Standard,* June 12, 1861. Elshtain provides a thorough discussion of the narratives designed to inform women of the "proper" roles to assume during wartime. *Women and War,* 142–68.

32. *Raleigh Register,* June 5, 1861; *North Carolina Standard,* June 12, 26, 1861; *Spirit of the Age,* May 15, 1861; *Church Intelligencer,* Aug. 2, 1861. Drew Gilpin Faust describes how many southern women felt torn by the conflict between honor (convincing men to enlist) and wanting a secure home life. See *Mothers of Invention,* 12–18.

Shades of Nation: Confederate Loyalties in Southeastern Virginia

BRIAN S. WILLS

IN *The Confederate Nation,* HISTORIAN EMORY M. THOMAS CREATES A powerful image of Confederate officials in their nation's capital awaiting news of the outcome of combat on the plains of Manassas in the summer of 1861:

> Back in Richmond it had been an anxious day for a lot of people. The capital was empty of soldiers, and the fact that July 21 was a Sunday accentuated the ominous quiet. All day in the sultry heat little knots of people gathered and dispersed; every horseman entering the city from the north attracted requests for war news.
>
> Across the street from the capitol in Mechanics Hall were the makeshift offices of the War Department. There Confederate officialdom assembled to wait out the suspense. The telegraph yielded nothing reliable. Secretary of War [Leroy] Walker damned his job and longed for action. The entire cabinet came and went, pacing and nervous. Howell Cobb, after sifting the fragmentary dispatches, announced that the battle at Manassas was a draw. Hot words followed, as men debated in complete ignorance. Night closed, and still the watch went on.
>
> Then Judah Benjamin burst into the hall with real news. . . . A telegram from the President had arrived [announcing a victory].

Thomas concludes, as did those Confederates in the wake of that significant first major battlefield success, "The Confederacy had committed its fate to battle and won. The Southern nation was at last a reality; the cause was triumphant."[1]

Of course, the battle of First Manassas, or Bull Run, was yet to be a "first," either in the sense of a combat action taking place in the same relative geographical location or as evidence of the consummation of a national birth. Nevertheless the outcome of the fight seemed to confirm the revolutionary heritage of a people that proudly claimed ancestral rights to the Revolution of 1776. Again Thomas captures the mood. "On the night of July 21, 1861, the Confederate States of America was just about everything its founders had envisioned the Southern nation to be. In the minds of its citizens at least the Confederacy was the confirmed expression of Southern nationalism."[2]

Advocates of the Confederacy may have been assured of its national existence, but over time some historians have been less so. Paul Escott has argued that even southern slaveholding planters, the very ones who had the most at stake in their new government, failed to sustain it. "This failure of Confederate nationalism," he writes, "was inseparably linked to the class system of the Old South."[3] Others have argued that self-interest outweighed national interest among many Confederate southerners.[4]

But historians William Blair and Gary Gallagher have underscored Thomas's views on the emergence and importance of nationalism for supporters of the Confederacy. Blair explains the influence of Vietnam and independence movements upon historical thinking by noting, "A generation that treated nationalism more skeptically, if not cynically, found Confederate patriotism wanting."[5] More recently Gallagher devoted a chapter of *The Confederate War* to the topic.[6] A growing body of work has dealt with the subject in one fashion or another, usually in an attempt to determine why women and men supported their "Cause" or, in the case of soldiers, risked their lives in combat for it. Clearly the existence and endurance of any meaningful sense of Confederate nationalism remains an open question.

Were the matter left to the Confederate fathers, they could assert that they had performed every task that a people could require in order to claim nationhood legitimately. They established a constitution and a governmental structure, provisionally elected its leaders, created forces for its defense to which thousands of their countrymen responded by enrolling in them, opened diplomatic contacts with at least a portion of the outside world, and now risked their fates and that of their new nation on the battlefield. There is no way to prove or disprove whether white southerners as a general rule would have discarded their efforts at nation building and voluntarily rejoined the Union had there been no war. Certainly their historical willingness to sustain that effort in battle suggests that many of them took the idea of Confederate nationalism seriously enough to stake their lives upon it.

In light of the ultimate failure of that experience on the battlefield, it is perhaps not nearly so ironic that many students of the period and of the region, not the least of them W. J. Cash, have continued to characterize the South as "a nation within a nation" long after any tangible expression had ceased to exist.[7] In his study of Georgia Unionists, Thomas G. Dyer argues that most nineteenth-century Americans would not have recognized a modern definition of the term "nationalism," if indeed they had used that term in the first place.[8]

Eric Hobsbawm's working definition of nationalism as existing when "any sufficiently large body of people whose members regard themselves as members of a 'nation'" is broad enough to include most mid-nineteenth-century white southerners.[9] Just as surely they fit Isaiah Berlin's description of "the conviction, in the first place, that men belong to a particular human group, and that the way of life of the group differs from that of others."[10]

Patriotism may not equate to nationalism, but it is an expression of it just as appearances of self-interest or even displays of disloyalty toward the larger state do not negate the existence of the national feeling generally. Again as Hobsbawm maintains: "We cannot assume that for most people national identification when it exists . . . excludes or is always or even superior to the remainder of the set of identifications which constitute the social being. In fact, it is always combined with identifications of another kind, even when it is felt to be superior to them."[11]

Once war began in 1861, dramatically complicating Confederate attempts to sustain their nation-building efforts, it also confirmed the sense of nationalism that made nation building possible in the first place. "The Confederacy posed to the North, to Europe, and to itself as a legitimate national state, in anticipation of the doctrine of 'self-determination of peoples,'" Emory Thomas has explained, with reference to the Wilsonian doctrine of the following century.[12] Nor was such thinking lost upon the government officials of other countries. Although British prime minister William E. Gladstone proved to be premature in his apparent case of oratorical exuberance, the British chancellor of the Exchequer was nonetheless correct when he asserted on October 7, 1862: "Jefferson Davis and other leaders of the South have made an army; they are making, it appears, a navy; and they have made what is more than either, they have made a nation."[13]

Whatever other nations' representatives might have thought of the South's national prospects, Confederate leaders had a vested interest in promoting and preserving the existence of the nation they had helped bring into being. It was expected that President Davis and his cabinet officials would tout that nation to its people and the world. Likewise it was assumed that at least some world leaders would take cognizance of that fact as well. But what did the people of the South think of the grand experiment to which they had been either witting or unwitting participants?

Perhaps some clues lie in a closer examination of a particular portion of the South. Indeed many people of southeastern Virginia experienced every facet of war, from the presence of Confederate forces to occupation by Union troops and finally a period of time in which much of the region remained between the opposing lines.[14]

Yet it should be noted that the region's citizens were not united in embracing even the idea of secession. Among those who supported the concept, there was widespread disagreement between those who wished to see Virginia secede immediately and those who preferred to wait for concerted action by the South as a whole. Others remained staunch Unionists, despite differences in degrees of willingness to exhibit such sentiments openly. Historian Daniel Crofts has noted this ambivalence among Southampton County voters for secession convention delegates, who elected Democrat John J. Kindred over Whig Charles F. Urquhart by 486 votes to 458, and the decision to support the referral of any action by a state convention to a popular referendum. Thus the voters "delivered a mixed verdict" by electing a secessionist delegate but expressing a preference for more deliberative action on the matter of secession itself.[15]

The public outpouring of support for the Confederate cause and nation in the opening phases of the conflict was unmistakable. Men rallied to local centers to join units as they were being formed. The town of Suffolk and the surrounding county of Nansemond produced nine companies of troops. Many of these units took names that reflected the current sentiment, but others harkened back to another time and another revolution with such nostalgic names as the Suffolk Continentals, the Marion Rangers, and the Nansemond Rangers.[16] Indeed one early arrival to the area from North Carolina, frustrated with his inability to obtain leave, judged his conditions against those of the soldiers of that earlier rebellion in a letter to his wife: "But, soldiers should not grumble. We are seeing a good time, when we take into consideration the soldiers of [17]76."[17]

Enthusiasm was easy to find in southeastern Virginia in the early days of the war. Southampton County farmer Daniel William Cobb sent a son into the service and expressed the war fever in his diary. When troops arrived from "Georgia and other states from a distant," he was pleased to find them "blood thursty for Lincon and Northern Yankies." He could only express the hope that God would "grant their success."[18] Later, as he pondered the reports he had heard of northern outrages, Cobb concluded resolutely, "No day passes but my prayer is to konker."[19]

When two local young men sought to obtain permission to raise a cavalry company, they did so with expressions of their devotion to the cause. "Tell Jeff Davis that we are in *for the war,* that we are not twelve month's volunteers," Thomas Upshaw wrote to Charles Riddick from Suffolk.[20] Riddick then dutifully forwarded the request to his brother, Nathaniel, a member of the Virginia House of Delegates, in a letter that reflected the same language and sentiments.[21] Their unit became Company C of the 13th Virginia Cavalry, the same regiment in which Daniel Cobb's son had enrolled in neighboring Southampton County.[22]

Of course local residents found the southern soldiers in their midst more than a reminder of peace and security; they were also a source of an often lucrative income. People of all types seem to have found ways to benefit from these Confederate connections. African American entrepreneur James T. Ayer sold so much material to southern forces that when he later claimed a Union pension, the government rebuffed it. The claim investigator insisted that the Suffolk resident "might as well have been in the employ of the [Confederate] Commissary Department."[23]

Military reverses in late 1861 and early 1862, as the Confederate States of America endured its first great crisis in confidence, dampened the mood of some but did not extinguish the flames of nationalism.[24] Word of the fall of Tennessee's Forts Henry and Donelson and Nashville, the first state capital in the Confederacy to fall, as well as defeats at Port Royal in South Carolina, at Mill Springs in Kentucky, and at Roanoke Island in North Carolina, filtered through the South with daunting regularity. Yet the setbacks did not mean the end of the Confederate experiment or generate widespread calls for an accommodation with the old government.

One Virginia Confederate posted in distant South Carolina decried the loss of Roanoke Island on the one hand as "shameful & cowardly" but demonstrated his dedication to the cause on the other with a stirring call to arms,

"Our motto must be victory or death." He could not entirely shake the feeling of despair at the battlefield defeats, but neither would he discard his belief in ultimate victory or his personal willingness to endure whatever might come in the pursuit of it. "The times are gloomy," Samuel McGuire admitted to his brother, "but we must not dispond, only work the more and strike the harder. May the good God preserve us and our cause!"[25]

Even as the monotony of camp life and drill replaced the initial excitement of enlistment, compounded by the frequently dreary news from the front, a profound sense of patriotism remained for many. Artillerist Channing Price reflected some disgruntlement when the Confederate Congress in Richmond implemented conscription as a device to keep southern armies filled with soldiers, but he attributed its passage to "a class of men who seem determined to grumble at everything done by the Authorities for the purpose of keeping our present Army in the field." He expressed his own satisfaction with the legislation, pronouncing it "a very proper Bill" that promised significant results.[26] What is more, the Suffolk correspondent for the *Petersburg Daily Express* seemed to confirm such positive expressions when he reported that "recruiting for old companies and joining new volunteer companies is going on rapidly."[27]

Union occupation of Suffolk in May 1862 further tested the devotion to the Confederacy of many local residents. For one young lad the confusion of uniforms led to a terribly unsettling moment, at least for his mother, when he shouted to passing Federal troops, "Hurrah for Jeff Davis!" The horrified look on his mother's face might have warned him that these words were no longer appropriate to the current state of affairs, but such rebuke as came his way was mild indeed. An officer guided his horse over to where the boy stood, still saluting, his words a faint echo on his lips. "You little traitor," he growled good naturedly as mother grabbed son by the arm and dashed inside the house to safety.[28]

For another resident there was geographic confusion. When told that the new arrivals hailed from Rhode Island, this Suffolk matron inquired simply, "Is that in North Carolina?" For the brief moments they remained on her doorstep, the New England soldiers attempted to assist her in the proper placement of their home state but finally gave up the fight as they reassembled to move on into camp. One of the men later recalled, "I left the old lady soliloquizing upon the causes which led to the war, and its probable result to both North and South."[29]

Even with the occupying Federals on reasonably good behavior and committed generally to the protection of private property, the general sense of patriotism and loyalty to the Confederacy among local residents failed to subside as the occupation continued. A Suffolk native boasted, "The Yanks say the people are the most obstinate they have ever seen." She praised the efforts of Suffolk's Methodist minister, William B. Wellons, who "preaches every Sunday and prays for the success of the confederate Arms, and for all in authority while the house [of worship] is filled with Yankees."[30] Another explained her feelings for the Union soldiers in no uncertain terms. "The more I see the Yankees," Mattie Prentiss vented to a friend in late June, " the worse I *hate* them."[31] The Federals noted the same obstinacy in residents, who often made little effort to hide their disdain. One wrote home to say that community children referred to the local men as all being "of[f] shooting Yankeys."[32]

It was precisely this type of open recalcitrance that contributed to a change in northern attitudes that would eventually lead to an alteration in Union policy.[33] "I reckon they will begin to draw the reins a little tighter now," an exiled Suffolk resident wrote her daughter.[34] Indeed, as it became clear that the "rosewater" policy was failing to produce much in the way of results regarding local pacification, the Federal soldiers themselves began to take action. A member of the 6th Massachusetts described to his wife the effect of camping on the property of "a capt. in the rebell army": "We are an expensive set to keep out the rebells will find out soon," he noted, illustrating the change from the general mode of protecting property, even of admittedly disloyal landowners, to a form of open season on their property and possessions as a means of punishing such disloyalty.[35]

Reverend Wellons found himself run out of Suffolk, replaced by Unionist ministers who professed to "preach the Gospel on its purity."[36] The provost marshal threatened to arrest civilians who persisted in displaying their secessionist beliefs in whatever form such demonstrations might take. For one resident this meant that life in occupied Suffolk was "almost as bad as being in prison."[37] Others engaged in passing information and goods on what some of them termed their "underground railroad," prompting occupation forces to react with increased stridency to interdict such activities.

Guerrilla activity, or bushwhacking, perhaps most distressed the Union troops and most likely provoked a strong response from them. "We haven't enough men in the field to whip the Rebs," one New Yorker lamented, "and if the North wants peace they must send men enough to clean [out] this part of the country entirely." Even were these Confederate sympathizers to surrender their weapons, "I wouldn't trust them," he explained. "In the daytime they are good union men, and at night the devils are out with their guns shooting our pickets or running provisions into Rebel camps."[38]

As this soldier indicates, the locals learned to proclaim themselves "good Union men" regardless of their true devotion to that cause whenever Federal soldiers appeared. The New Yorker concluded by writing, "Every man around here has taken the oath of allegiance, and [still] almost every one of them is known to be doing all he can for the Rebs, and they acknowledge it."[39] The deceptions were so commonplace that the safest and surest policy for Federal forces was to ignore such pronouncements and plunder anyway.

Certainly, as Union actions became increasingly heavy handed, the reactions they provoked often reinforced a sense of Confederate nationalism among the civilians they encountered. Following a raid into the little hamlet of Chuckatuck, one woman could barely contain her sense of outrage in a letter to her sister, despite the fact that the marauding Federals "did not steal as much as we expected they would." But even this relative moderation failed to spare the Union troops from her rancor: "I never had such indignant feelings toward them as I had yesterday when they came in flaunting *their flags* and looking as if the very earth belonged to them." Indeed it was the sight of the U.S. flag "that we once loved and reverenced" that seems to have offended her the most. Now the once-beloved standard was "so poluted and despised by the foul use to which it has been applied by the vile invaders of our lov'd, our native land," that she could scarcely bring herself to look upon it with anything but contempt.[40]

It must have seemed, to such individuals at least, as if there was to be no relief from Union occupation. Then, in mid-April 1863, Confederate lieutenant general James Longstreet approached the region with some twenty thousand veterans to challenge the Federal grip on Suffolk. Robert E. Lee's Army of Northern Virginia had struggled through a difficult winter desperately short of supplies, which the Confederate commander wanted to alleviate with this operation into occupied Virginia. Southern commissary and quartermaster agents expected a boon in untapped resources, provided they could move swiftly enough to secure them and transport the bounty back to the army.

The Federals had Brig. Gen. John James Peck's elaborate defensive network to assist them in holding Suffolk, whatever Longstreet's intentions might be. Peck's command remained on the alert, but as the Confederates settled into positions before Suffolk, the initiative lay with the southerners. They established masked batteries on the Nansemond River that endangered lightly armed Union river vessels and tested Union defenses for weaknesses.

In the meantime Confederate troops and wagon trains fanned out into southeastern Virginia and northeastern North Carolina to secure the supplies for which Longstreet primarily had come to the region. The agents encountered little resistance to their collection efforts outside of the handful of Unionists who attempted to hide their goods or run them into Federal lines. Even so, the haul was impressive.

Militarily, events turned for the worse for Longstreet and his men when a detachment of Union troops captured a Confederate battery holding an earthwork known as Fort Huger or Hill's Point. The blow struck at southern confidence, spurred recriminations among Confederate leaders on various levels, and led Longstreet to concentrate on defensive measures and his food-gathering mission. For the remainder of the campaign, Union gunboats continued to lob shells into Confederate lines, while sharpshooters from both sides took their toll on the unfortunates or the foolish who presented themselves as targets. Finally Union movements in central Virginia prompted General Lee to recall Longstreet. Despite two heavy reconnaissance operations on May 1 and 3, "Lee's War Horse" managed to undertake a phased withdrawal on May 4.[41]

In the aftermath of Longstreet's campaign, John A. Dix complained to General in Chief Henry Halleck: "Suffolk is no longer of any use to us as a position for making friends of the secessionists. The population there and in the surrounding country are bitter and implacable." Halleck agreed, though he might have pointed out that the existence of such sentiments meant that the occupation of southeastern Virginia had never been an object lesson in, as the later Vietnam-era phrase expressed it, "winning the hearts and minds" of the local people.[42]

John White, a South Carolina Confederate who remained stationed with other southern troops along the Blackwater River, expressed no diminution in his devotion to his cause, even if no outside help ever came to ensure ultimate victory for his side. In June 1863 he informed his sister: "Although we have fought well yet if we are conquored we need not look to Europe for help or sympathy, we do not desire the sympathys of the world." He remained determined to resist, particularly as he saw evidence of the shift of the Federals to a "hard war" policy. "We left . . . [the] Yankees on the oppo[site] side of the Blackwater burning houses and pillaging generally," he wrote. "They seem determined to be avenged on Rebeldom by acting the part of incendiaries and demons." Unhappily he had to admit that the Federals were enjoying success. "They have burned nearly all the dwellings between [the] Blackwater and Suffolk."[43]

The war turned on events happening elsewhere in July 1863, but white southeastern Virginians had their attentions largely occupied with what they were experiencing locally. To be sure, many sought what news came to hand to learn the fate of loved ones on distant battlefields such as Gettysburg, but Union forces in the region remained active and intrusive, demanding that a portion of the focus of the local populace remain closer to home.

Union brigadier general Edward A. Wild conducted an operation out of Norfolk that ranged deep into eastern North Carolina. Throughout the raid he hoped to conduct the military equivalent of a seminar on national identity. At its conclusion he reported, "Finding ordinary measures of little avail, I adopted a more rigorous style of warfare; burned their houses and barns, ate up their livestock, and took hostages from their families." The general was further convinced that if given a free hand to deal with guerrilla activity in the region, he "could rectify [the situation] in two weeks of stern warfare."

Unwittingly predicting the historical debate to come concerning matters of motivation, Wild noted his belief that "the property question touches the raw." He remained "convinced [that] it has always been, and will be, the controlling motive." Thus, by threatening property, Wild thought he could dictate a return to loyalty among the Confederates he encountered. "I should depend upon it not merely to recall the doubtful and the timid to their allegiance, but also to quench the ardor of the guerrillas themselves."[44]

Theoretically having taught these Confederate civilians the price of disloyalty to the Union, General Wild apparently failed to appreciate that his tactics might have produced only mixed results at best. He expressed great pleasure in the "rapid development of loyal sentiments as we progressed with our raid" without seemingly understanding that such loyalty as he observed often disappeared when he did. Wild's employment of former slaves as soldiers might have been an object lesson in his eyes, but it also strengthened the resolve of some to embrace the Confederate cause who might not otherwise have done so.

Indeed the general's definition of loyalty was certainly vague enough to accommodate those willing to appear to be loyal. "We found the majority of people along our track to be reasonably neutral," he explained, noting that they had verbalized to him any number of doubts and complaints about the war while also openly "sympathizing with the South." Wild felt that his actions produced the desired effect among those persons "disgusted with such unexpected treatment, it bred disaffection, some wishing to quit the business, [while] others [went] over the lines to join the Confederate Army."[45]

No act appears to have indicated the depth of loyalty to the Confederacy as much as the reluctance, if not outright refusal, of many local whites to take the oath of allegiance to the Union. At least two women from Suffolk made their way into North Carolina in late 1863 to seek assistance from Confederates stationed there. Brig. Gen. Matthew Ransom dutifully forwarded their concerns to his commanding officer, Maj. Gen. George Pickett. The women informed him, "[Union] General Butler has notified the citizens of Suffolk that they must take the oath of allegiance to the Federal Government or leave immediately." Naturally they did not wish to leave their homes, but neither did they wish to submit to an oath they could not make honestly. "They are loyal to the South, and wish your advice on the subject," Ransom observed. Clearly these women were unwilling even to appear disloyal if such an appearance could be avoided. Yet they were just as unwilling to "lose their all" by refusing the Union demands.[46]

When Pickett heard of their plight, he became thoroughly incensed at such treatment toward southern females. To Adjutant and Inspector General Samuel Cooper he wrote of the Federals, "You will see likewise that they are going to play the same game in Suffolk that they did in Norfolk, make all take the oath of allegiance to the Federal Government or confiscate their property." He bemoaned the fact that he lacked troops enough to prevent such wrongs from taking place or to succor the victims of them. "Still it makes my blood boil to think of these enormities being practiced, and we have no way of arresting them."[47]

Cooper shared Pickett's frustration. In an endorsement of the material that he sent on to President Davis for his perusal, Cooper offered his analysis: "It is impossible for the Department to answer the question propounded by General Pickett in respect to the deputation of ladies from Suffolk further than to state that taking the compulsory oath exacted of them by an infuriated [foe], for their safety, etc., should not, under the pressing necessities of the case represented by them, be considered as an indication of their want of fidelity to the Southern cause."[48] Under the circumstances of war, apparently it would be acceptable for such citizens to engage in a practical deception of the enemy concerning their loyalty to the Confederacy if attempting to safeguard their persons or property.

Yet any efforts to placate Union occupation forces often proved unsuccessful in warding off destruction. A Georgia newspaper sought to bring home the price of occupation to its readers by detailing the effects of Federal rule in distant Virginia: "The town of Suffolk, in Virginia, [was] once one of the beauties of the 'Union,'" the editor of the *Augusta Chronicle & Sentinel* explained. He offered a description from a correspondent with the *Petersburg Express* that estimated the town of 1,500 residents at the start of the conflict had declined to a population of "about 350 persons, of all sizes and color," by late 1863. The streets of Suffolk were now largely deserted, with two of its five churches "rendered unfit for use, and the others greatly injured."[49]

The toll of war spread beyond the population and public buildings to private dwellings as well. Homes the Federals commandeered while in the region suffered abuse. "The yards and gardens have all been destroyed, and many of the most beautiful family residences are ruined," the same newspaper writer observed. "For miles around Suffolk scarcely a tree has been left standing," he said, "and not a house or fence or anything, save old fortifications, rifle pits and small brush wood can be seen." The legacy of the previous spring's campaigning was the destruction of "half a million of property" by his estimation. Even so, the reporter concluded, "in spite of all their losses and their present condition, the citizens of Suffolk and Nansemond are true to the Southern cause, and suffering has only increased their love for Southern institutions."[50]

Of course not all area residents embraced the Confederate cause, or had ever done so. The Petersburg correspondent also admitted, "only a few having any claims to respectability have sympathized with the North."[51] Still, Unionists constituted a small minority compared to those southeastern Virginians who remained loyal to the Confederacy. But no doubt large numbers of area residents were not dissembling when they claimed loyalty to the Union. On several occasions Federal officers wrote on behalf of some of these individuals for privileges based upon past demonstrations of loyalty as well as a general belief in their devotion. For instance, an endorsement on behalf of a local farmer seeking permission to trade in cotton read, "Mr. Darden is a loyal citizen living on the road from Suffolk to Edenton."[52] While another, from Union general Charles K. Graham, included assurances of loyalty for a farmer near Chuckatuck who "gave me much valuable information." Graham concluded, "If the indulgence asked for is granted, I believe it will not be abused."[53]

Despite such illustrations of loyalty to the Union, other efforts, ranging from an attempt to hold elections for U.S. Congress in the region late in 1862 to raising a local company of Union soldiers, fell short of success. A correspondent for the *New York Daily Tribune* attributed the electoral disruption to enemy interference. "A few votes were cast in Suffolk, [but] no returns will be received from Isle of Wight, Windsor, or Smithfield," he noted in December, due to the fact that "the rebels from the other side of the Blackwater [River] came over to put a quietus upon Union men who might try to vote."[54]

While the Confederates might have been responsible for the paltry congressional election results in December 1862, they could hardly be blamed for the weak response when Union captain Hazard Stevens sought to raise a regiment of men to be designated the 1st Regiment Loyal East Virginians. In addition to patriotic fervor, recruiters counted upon the offer of a one-hundred-dollar bounty to encourage individuals to join the unit, promising twenty-five dollars immediately and the remainder at the end of presumably honorable service. Yet the reward was not sufficiently high to yield significant results. "I have used every effort to obtain recruits during your absence without any success whatever," a subordinate reported to Stevens. They had failed despite remaining "constantly employed . . . ; the Sergeant and myself have also exerted ourselves to the utmost but to no avail." Historian Richard Current certainly found such fruits inconsequential. "All together the efforts of Stevens and his subordinates netted only enough men to fill one company of the First Loyal East Virginia Infantry." Indeed the eighty-four men who stepped forward would not have constituted a full company in the early stages of the war.[55] Clearly this type of Unionism found poor soil in which to flourish in southeastern Virginia.

Yet for one group of people the choice of which side to support was unmistakable, even if it meant great risk to their lives. Many black southerners sought refuge early on within Union lines, particularly following the Federal occupation of Suffolk. Local planters complained of the loss of slaves and knew where most likely they would find them. Records suggest that slave men, women and children from as far as Gates County, North Carolina, moved into the area before any proclamation of emancipation and continued to do so afterward. In many instances Union soldiers themselves became liberators. The demands of war promised profound changes for southeastern Virginians of all stripes, dictating that difficult choices be made regardless of loyalties.

The loss of slaves was but one complaint for most white southerners as the war progressed. In the autumn of 1864, Southampton farmer Daniel Cobb registered a number of them in his diary. One of his strongest applied to the tax-in-kind policies of the Confederate government. "I sent my sheap to Murfrees Station that was called for, for the N. Army of Virginia," he noted in September. "They loud me 50 cts Per lbs per gross for No. 1 Lambs, etc."[56] Later he would send out "some 95 Gallons of Brandy to the Depot for Lee's Army."[57]

Afterward the complaints mounted, a sure sign that the relationship between this citizen and his government was under strain. Still, for all of his dissatisfaction, his compliance continued. Cobb was hardly pleased with the intrusion of the Richmond government upon his life and livelihood, but he was also unprepared to sacrifice his loyalty or the cause on which it was based.

Others felt similarly about the conditions war imposed on them. On the day after Christmas 1864, a lady in the area wrote that the holiday itself had been "the gloomiest that I have ever spent." Mary Riddick's family had suffered tremendously, and her feeling of having lost control over her own affairs sapped her energy and vitality. "The most distressing part of my poverty is seeing my children so much in need and not as heretofore have it in my power to aid them in any way." Yet, for all of the suffering they had endured, "there is still the same firm spirit of resistance as ever."[58]

In early 1865 Virginia politician and Suffolk native Nathaniel Riddick clung to the belief that independence might yet be won. "There is no doubt but we are at the crisis of this great Revolution, and that a few weeks or months will develop the issue," he wrote his daughter in mid-January.[59] If he had reason to think the situation would develop favorably for the Confederate cause, Riddick must surely have expected that the best path for such a resolution lay in diplomacy. "I would here say that we have sent peace commissioners to Washington at the invitation of Lincoln," he noted. "Vice-President [Alexander] Stephens, Senator [R. M. T.] Hunter and Judge [John A.] Campbell, late Asst. Secty of War are the men." He deemed the choices for the delicate, but important, mission "Capital selections" and concluded confidently, "The prospects for peace brighten."[60]

The Confederate delegation met with President Lincoln aboard the *River Queen* near Fort Monroe on February 3, 1865, but the results hardly cheered the hearts of their fellow countrymen. As historian E. B. Long observes, "Mr. Lincoln told a few stories, everyone was reasonably friendly, but nothing came of it or could come of it, considering the Federal demand for unconditional restoration of the Union and the Confederate demand for terms between the two independent nations."[61] Had Nathaniel Riddick known what was transpiring, he would doubtless have concurred, for while he still hoped to bring "a speedy close" to "this cruel war," he wanted only to do so "upon the basis of independence and other rights for which we contend."[62]

In February Riddick was busy at his duties in the Virginia House of Delegates. By this point the state government was reflecting the strain of a people struggling for their national survival. "Our Sessions now are mostly secret ones and much is transpiring of which it would not do for me to write," he told his daughter.[63] The same might have been said of the national Congress as well, which was undertaking the most profound debate in its existence.

One scholar of the Confederate Congress, Wilfred Buck Yearns, found that body unanimous in its "desire . . . to win the war." This did not mean that there was no opposition to various administration measures or even to the Davis government itself. Yet Yearns found that the opposition tended toward the "reform, not the wreckage, of the government."[64] No single issue perhaps reflects this tension as much as the debate over arming slaves for military service during the closing months of the war. Interestingly it was Virginia's legislature that acted to save the bill, which President Davis eventually signed, through its instructions to the state's two Confederate senators.[65]

In *The Confederacy as a Revolutionary Experience,* Emory Thomas suggests the extent to which the national government expressed a willingness, however reluctantly reached, to sacrifice the remaining principles of the Old South to secure Confederate independence. "The fact was that the Confederacy was prepared to let slavery perish and to fight on!"[66] In the eyes of enough southern leaders, the sense of nation predominated over all other matters, even maintaining the institution of slavery inviolate. "In the end Southerners themselves decided for emancipation in the vain hope of national survival," Thomas concludes. "In April 1865, the Confederate struggle had but one goal, independence, the ability to exist as a people."[67]

Of course this did not mean that individuals like Nathaniel Riddick were anxious to eliminate the institution of slavery, whatever expedient they might embrace in order to obtain southern independence. On February 25 he observed to his son John that if the Confederates should have to evacuate Petersburg and Richmond, "I have some things there I should certainly like to get away—negroes among other things—but I should not know what to do with them or where to carry them."[68] As late as March 20, the Virginia politician still clung to the notion that he might salvage all of his property, including his slaves. "Father['s] negroes are still in Petersburg," son Mills wrote to his sister, Anna. "He is at a loss to know what to do with them and his furniture."[69] Whatever the elder Riddick might have thought regarding the notion of arming slaves in the cause of the Confederacy, he never addressed the subject in his communications with the members of his family.

In any event it was too late. Such hope as remained in the hearts of white southerners would be shortly destroyed as Ulysses Grant broke through Robert E. Lee's lines at Petersburg, necessitating a general retreat and the evacuation of Richmond. The remnants of the Confederate government fled south, with Secretary of War John C. Breckinridge battling Jefferson Davis over the fate of their nation.[70]

At last even Nathaniel Riddick had to admit that the "military situation" was becoming "gloomier." "Poor Richmond is now in the hands of the Yankees," he told his daughter on April 5. Yet, desirous of placing even these worst of conditions in the most positive manner, the Virginia politician and family patriarch posited, "If it [the Army of Northern Virginia] moves off in the direction of Lynchburg and Danville as many suppose, Isle of Wight [and] Nansemond . . . may be among the most quiet parts of the State on the presumption that we are already under their rule."[71]

The struggle for national survival sputtered and finally died as the Confederate armies in the field surrendered east of the Mississippi, at places like Appomattox Court House and Bennett Place, and then finally across that great river too. Whatever the future might hold for the now lost cause of southern independence, or whatever they might feel about it, the verdict had been delivered on the battlefield.

"I feel very old now," a relative wrote to Anna Mary Riddick in June 1865. "I hope things will get more settled soon."[72] Things would be far from settled in the years ahead, but the Confederate States of America as a national entity was no more. Combat had consigned it to history (and literature and later cinema), where the gods have been content to let the generals rest, if not the matter of the existence and endurance of Confederate nationalism.

NOTES

1. Emory M. Thomas, *The Confederate Nation: 1861–1865* (New York: Harper & Row, 1979), 116–17. The author would like to thank Mark Clark for his assistance on questions relating to nationalism and the University Press of Virginia for use of material found in *The War Hits Home: The Civil War in Southeastern Virginia* (Charlottesville: University Press of Virginia, 2001).

2. Thomas, *Confederate Nation,* 117.

3. Paul D. Escott, "The Failure of Confederate Nationalism: The Old South's Class System in the Crucible of War," in *The Old South in the Crucible of War,* ed. Harry P. Owens and James J. Cooke (Jackson: University Press of Mississippi, 1983), 21.

4. See Lawrence N. Powell and Michael S. Wayne, "Self-Interest and the Decline of Confederate Nationalism," in ibid., 29–45.

5. William Blair, *Virginia's Private War: Feeding Body and Soul in the Confederacy, 1861–1865* (New York: Oxford University Press, 1998), 3.

6. Gary W. Gallagher, *The Confederate War: How Popular Will, Nationalism, and Military Strategy Could Not Stave Off Defeat* (Cambridge, Mass.: Harvard University Press, 1997), 61–111 passim.

7. Wilbur J. Cash, *The Mind of the South* (1941; New York: Vintage Books, 1969), viii.

8. Thomas G. Dyer, *Secret Yankees: The Union Circle in Confederate Atlanta* (Baltimore: Johns Hopkins University Press, 1999), 368.

9. E. J. Hobsbawm, *Nations and Nationalism since 1780: Programme, Myth, Reality* (New York: Cambridge University Press, 1990), 8.

10. Isaiah Berlin, *Against the Current: Essays in the History of Ideas* (New York: Penguin, 1982), 341.

11. Hobsbawm, *Nations and Nationalism,* 11.

12. Thomas, *Confederate Nation,* 105.

13. Quoted in D. P. Crook, *The North, the South, and the Powers, 1861–1865* (New York: John Wiley & Sons, 1974), 227–28. For assessments of the diplomatic efforts of the Confederate States of America in regard to the European nations, see in addition to Crook, Howard Jones, *The Union in Peril: The Crisis over British Intervention in the Civil War* (Chapel Hill: University of North Carolina Press, 1992); and Robert E. May, ed., *The Union, the Confederacy, and the Atlantic Rim* (West Lafayette, Ind.: Purdue University Press, 1995).

14. For an assessment of this region during the Civil War, see Wills, *War Hits Home.*

15. Daniel W. Crofts, *Old Southampton: Politics and Society in a Virginia County, 1834–1869* (Charlottesville: University Press of Virginia, 1992), 176–77.

16. Lee A. Wallace Jr., *A Guide to Virginia Military Organizations, 1861–1865* (Richmond, n.p., 1964), 53, 69, 109, 114, 126, 164, 286.

17. J. T. Hambrick to "Dear Wife," Camp Suffolk, Va., June 24, 1860, Hambrick and Paylor Papers, North Carolina Department of History and Archives, Raleigh.

18. Daniel William Cobb Diary, "1861, Tuesday, 14 [May]," Daniel William Cobb Papers, Virginia Historical Society, Richmond. See also an edited version of the Cobb diaries, *Cobb's Ordeal: The Diaries of a Virginia Farmer, 1842–1872,* ed. Daniel Crofts (Athens: University of Georgia Press, 1997).

19. Cobb Diary, "1861, Thursday, 13 [June]."

20. Thomas E. Upshaw to Charlie Riddick, Suffolk, Va., Friday night [Jan. 3, 1862], Riddick Family Papers (hereinafter cited as RFP), copies in possession of the author.

21. C. H. Riddick to Nathaniel Riddick, Portsmouth, Va., Jan. 6, 1862, ibid.

22. For information on this regiment, see Daniel T. Balfour, *13th Virginia Cavalry* (Lynchburg, Va.: H. E. Howard, 1985).

23. Ervin L. Jordan Jr., *Black Confederates and Afro-Yankees in Civil War Virginia* (Charlottesville: University Press of Virginia, 1995), 214.

24. See Bell I. Wiley, *The Road to Appomattox* (1956; New York: Atheneum, 1977).

25. Samuel McGuire to "My dear [brother]," near Pocotaligo, S.C., Feb. 22, 1862, Webb-Prentiss Papers, Alderman Library, University of Virginia, Charlottesville.

26. Channing Price to "Dear Mother," Camp Randolph near Suffolk, Va., Apr. 1862, R. Channing Price Papers, Southern Historical Collection, University of North Carolina, Chapel Hill.

27. *Petersburg Daily Express*, Feb. 20, 1862.

28. *History of the Eleventh Pennsylvania Volunteer Cavalry, Together with a Complete Roster of the Regiment and Regimental Officers* (Philadelphia: Franklin, 1902), 36.

29. Ansel D. Nickerson, *A Raw Recruit's War Experiences* (Providence, R.I.: Press Co., 1888), 40–41.

30. Missouri Riddick to Anna Mary Riddick, June 10, 1862, RFP.

31. Mattie J. Prentiss to Joseph Webb, June 1862, RFP.

32. William Henry Snow to "My very dear Wife," Camp Suffolk, Va., Sept. 17, 1862, William Henry Snow Papers, Southern Historical Collection, University of North Carolina, Chapel Hill.

33. For a study of this change in Union policy, see Mark Grimsley, *The Hard Hand of War: Union Military Policy toward Southern Civilians, 1861–1865* (Cambridge: Cambridge University Press, 1995).

34. Missouri Riddick to Anna Mary Riddick, June 10, 1862.

35. William Henry Snow to "My very dear Wife," Sept. 17, 1862.

36. Missouri Riddick to Anna Mary Riddick, June 10, 1862.

37. Mattie J. Prentiss to Joseph Webb, June 1862.

38. Hermon Clarke, *Back Home in Oneida: Hermon Clarke and His Letters,* ed. Larry F. Jackson and Thomas F. O'Donnell (Syracuse, N.Y.: Syracuse University Press, 1965), 85.

39. Ibid.

40. Eva to "My dear Sister," Chuckatuck, Va., Mar. 9, 1863, MacClenny Papers, Alderman Library, University of Virginia, Charlottesville.

41. Two works cover the Suffolk campaign, or the "Siege of Suffolk," as it is more popularly, but inaccurately, known. See Wills, *War Hits Home;* and Steven A. Cormier, *The Siege of Suffolk: The Forgotten Campaign, April 11–May 4, 1863* (Lynchburg, Va.: H. E. Howard, 1989).

42. John A. Dix to General in Chief Henry Halleck, May 10, 1863, in U.S. War Department, *The War of Rebellion: A Compilation of the Official Records of the Union and Confederate Armies,* 128 vols. (Washington, D.C.: Government Printing Office, 1880–1901), ser. 1, 18:711–12 (hereinafter cited as *OR;* all references to ser. 1); Wills, *War Hits Home,* 185.

43. John M. White to "Dear Sister Martha," June 16, 1863, John M. White Letters, Museum of the Confederacy, Richmond.

44. Edward A. Wild Report, Dec. 28, 1863, *OR,* 29(1):910–18.

45. Ibid.

46. Enclosure no. 4, DeBordenave to M. W. Ransom, [Dec.] 20, [1863], *OR,* 29(2):884.

47. Enclosure no. 3, M. W. Ransom to George Pickett, Dec. 20, 1863, ibid.; Pickett to Samuel Cooper, Dec. 20, 1863, ibid., 881–82.

48. Cooper endorsement, ibid., 882.

49. *Augusta (Ga.) Chronicle & Sentinel,* Jan. 3, 1864.

50. Ibid.

51. Ibid.

52. Robert M. Darden, Suffolk, Mar. 1, 1865, Hd. Qrs. Norfolk, Portsmouth & Defenses, Portsmouth, Va., Records of the U.S. Army Continental Commands, 1821–1920, RG 393, National Archives, Washington, D.C.

53. Jonas Walsavens, Norfolk, Apr. 4, 1865, ibid.

54. Quoted in the *Daily Richmond Examiner,* Dec. 31, 1862.

55. Richard Nelson Current, *Lincoln's Loyalists: Union Soldiers from the Confederacy* (Boston: Northeastern University Press, 1992), 24–26.

56. Cobb Diary, "1864, Friday, 23 [Sept.]."

57. Cobb Diary, "1864, Saturday, 15 [Oct.]."

58. Mary Taylor Riddick to Wilbur Disosway, Dec. 26, 1864, RFP.

59. Nathaniel Riddick to Anna Mary Riddick, Richmond, Jan. 16, 1865, ibid.

60. Nathaniel Riddick to Anna Mary Riddick, Richmond, Feb. 1, 1865, ibid.

61. E. B. Long, *The Civil War Day by Day: An Almanac, 1861–1865* (Garden City, N.Y.: Doubleday, 1971), 633.

62. Nathaniel Riddick to Anna Mary Riddick, Feb. 2, 1865, RFP.

63. Ibid.

64. Wilfred Buck Yearns, *The Confederate Congress* (Athens: University of Georgia Press, 1960), 225–26.

65. Ibid., 98. See chapter 7 for the debate in its entirety. For a fuller examination, see Robert F. Durden, *The Gray and the Black: The Confederate Debate on Emancipation* (Baton Rouge: Louisiana State University Press, 1972).

66. Emory M. Thomas, *The Confederacy as a Revolutionary Experience* (Englewood Cliffs, N.J.: Prentice-Hall, 1971), 131.

67. Thomas, *Confederate Nation,* 299.

68. Nathaniel Riddick to John, Richmond, Feb. 25, 1865, RFP.

69. Mills Riddick to sister, Mar. 20, 1865, RFP.

70. See William C. Davis, *An Honorable Defeat: The Last Days of the Confederate Government* (New York: Harcourt, 2001).

71. Nathaniel Riddick to Anna Mary Riddick, Louisa County, Apr. 5, 1865, RFP.

72. "Cousin" to Anna Mary Riddick, Woodlawn, June 1, 1865, RFP.

The Literary Shaping of Confederate Identity: Daniel R. Hundley and John Beauchamp Jones in Peace and War

FRANK J. BYRNE

THERE IS NO EVIDENCE TO SUGGEST THAT DANIEL R. HUNDLEY and John Beauchamp Jones ever met one another. Their private correspondence and numerous publications make no mention of the other. Nevertheless Hundley and Jones had much in common. Both men were born and raised in the slave South yet had been living in the North on the eve of the Civil War. Necessarily each man had only indirect ties to the agrarian South. Both supported the Confederate war effort, Hundley as a colonel of the 31st Alabama Infantry and Jones as a high-level clerk in the Confederate War Department. Most significantly each man wrote a number of publications that in varying degrees explored the meaning of sectionalism and regional identity in nineteenth-century America. Aiding the Confederate cause and surviving the war did not make Hundley and Jones particularly unusual individuals. Their lives and the books and articles they produced distinguished them from many of their fellow southerners. Very few of their neighbors could claim to have helped fashion a popular southern identity before the war, defended that ideal during the war, and lived long enough after the conflict to sustain their cherished southern virtues in print. Daniel R. Hundley and John Beauchamp Jones expended great energy reflecting upon and describing what it meant to be a white southerner.

Hundley and Jones are rather unusual historical figures because each wrote books that are well known to historians of the antebellum and Confederate South, while much about their lives beyond these two works remains obscure. Daniel R. Hundley's classic analysis of antebellum southern society, *Social Re-*

lations in Our Southern States (1860), has long been an important source for historians interested in understanding the complex relationship between race and class in the Old South. Early historical works by Ulrich B. Phillips and Kenneth M. Stampp and later studies by Eugene D. Genovese and Bertram Wyatt-Brown relied upon Hundley's insight into cultural features of the antebellum South. Likewise most studies of the Confederacy and the Civil War cite John B. Jones's *A Rebel War Clerk's Diary at the Confederate States Capital* (1866) as an important primary source.[1]

The list of major historians who have depended upon Jones's diary in order to understand the inner workings of the Confederate government and life in wartime Richmond includes Douglas Southall Freeman, Frank Vandiver, Bruce Catton, James M. McPherson, Gary W. Gallagher, and most recently Russell Weigley. Despite the interest in these two works, the dearth of personal papers Hundley and Jones left behind has relegated them to the footnotes of Civil War historiography. This neglect is unfortunate because the literature these men produced and the lives they led reveal much about the creation of southern identity during the era of the Civil War.[2]

The origins and meaning of Confederate identity for southern whites has long stirred debate and confounded simple explanation. Over thirty years ago historians began exploring this subject in earnest. Studies of Confederate nationalism, ideology, and identity began appearing on bookshelves and class syllabi. Many of these studies offered conflicting definitions of nationalism and its role in the Confederacy. The relative importance of nationalism, ideology, and identity within the Confederacy has been and continues to be a subject of great interest for historians even as they debate the very meaning of these terms.[3]

This chapter not only examines Hundley's and Jones's lives but also considers what southern identity meant to them. Apologists for the slave South and the Confederacy, both men suggest ways the apparent incongruities in the literature on southern and Confederate nationalism can be resolved. Their experience reveals how an intellectual defense of the antebellum social order and participation in Confederate institutions had a radical, even revolutionary effect upon white southerners. The efforts of these writers' "cultural creation," combined with their activities on behalf of a centralized and national state, reflected their southern identity and, perhaps, Confederate nationalism. It is also evident that this identity, even for thoughtful individuals like Hundley and Jones, often lacked coherence. They could articulate how slavery, breeding, and class relations distinguished the South from the North, but they did not or could not express an intellectual foundation for a separate national identity outside such Confederate institutions as the military and government.[4]

John Beauchamp Jones was far better known than Daniel R. Hundley. Born in 1810 in Baltimore, Maryland, Jones was a prolific novelist and journalist. Raised in Kentucky and on the Missouri frontier, little is known about his formative years. As a teenager he worked on his family's farm and mercantile establishment. As a young man he returned east, moving through several cities, including Philadelphia, where he wrote fiction and various newspaper articles. In 1840 Jones courted and married Frances Thomas Custis of Accomack County, Virginia. This advantageous match enabled Jones, still of only moderate means, to obtain a farm and timberlands in Virginia.

That same year he published in serial form his first novel, *Wild Western Scenes,* in the *Baltimore Saturday Visitor* after failing to find a publisher. The first and most popular of over a dozen novels, *Wild Western Scenes,* an adventure set on the Missouri frontier Jones experienced firsthand during his youth, went through many editions, with sales surpassing 100,000 copies. The following year Jones moved from the *Visitor* to the *Madisonian,* which at that time was the official Whig newspaper for Pres. John Tyler's administration. At this time it seems Jones did most of his writing, including *Wild Western Scenes,* while living on his newly acquired farm in Virginia and later while working in Washington, D.C., where the *Madisonian* was published. He played a significant role at the paper and enjoyed close ties with several members of the administration. When Tyler left office, Jones became the sole editor and proprietor of the *Madisonian* until it went bankrupt sometime during 1845.[5]

Over the next eighteen years, Jones wrote numerous novels, traveled with his family, and in 1857 established a weekly paper in Philadelphia called the *Southern Monitor.* Its mission was to alleviate sectional tensions by offering northern audiences an uncensored southern perspective by which they might better judge the untenable position of the slave states under Republican rule. In the first issue Jones declared that his paper's "defence of Southern rights and Southern institutions will be firm and uncompromising." His bold public statement on southern rights drew criticism from northern editors. A Pittstown, Pennsylvania, paper, for example, labeled the *Monitor* a "Slave Driving Journal." Nevertheless the opinions Jones espoused in its pages were consistent with those he had been expressing in his novels the preceding twenty years.[6]

The novels John B. Jones wrote between 1840 and 1860 are generally sentimental adventures that include stereotypical brave frontiersmen, parsimonious merchants, murderous Indians, and virtuous ladies in distress. While there is evidence to suggest that Edgar Allan Poe considered him one of America's best authors in 1841, Jones's body of work after *Wild Western Scenes* has not aged particularly well. His novels bear some resemblance to the historical novels of another southern author, William Gilmore Simms, but lack that South Carolinian's graceful prose and often interesting plot development. Still, Jones's work enjoyed a large audience throughout the United States and gave him an opportunity to put forward a version of southern identity rooted in race and class.[7]

Slaves are conspicuous by their absence in Jones's antebellum fiction. The few characterizations of slaves that make their way into his novels show them to be content and loyal to their owners. The institution itself is depicted as organic, even familial, with problems arising only when ignorant Yankees involve themselves one way or another in this most southern system. Northerners who move South and become slaveholders, Quakers, and every other variety of abolitionist are subject to criticism and ridicule in Jones's novels. In *The City Merchant* (1851) and *The Border War* (1859), subtitled *A Tale of Disunion,* he offers sympathetic portrayals of moderate Americans and condemns northern mobs, attacking fanatical abolitionists who had been guilty of sowing the seeds of hatred between the North and South. For Jones the latter two groups, the northern mob and abolitionists, were contradictory yet intertwined in an unstable northern society.

Jones presented an extended discussion on the dangers of sectionalism and abolitionism in the *Adventures of Col. Gracchus Vanderbomb* (1852). This convoluted tale recounts how Vanderbomb, born and raised "exactly" on the line dividing North and South, runs for political office both in New York and Virginia. A son of a Puritan father and southern mother, the protagonist is able to bridge the growing sectional divide. In a practical way he can transcend the physical division represented by the Mason-Dixon Line by living a portion of the year with his father in New York and part with his mother in Virginia. Shaped by both northern and southern ideals, Vanderbomb seems to offer the possibility of a spiritual rapprochement as well when he runs for the presidency. Along the way Jones offers what is intended to be a humorous characterization of Vanderbomb's father, a Yankee and reformed slave trader turned abolitionist. This son of Puritan New England is made intentionally ludicrous because he does not understand the contours of racial slavery in the South. For Jones, Vanderbomb's father embodies the negative extremes commonly found among Yankees, great racial antipathy (slave trader) and then dangerous sentimentality (abolitionism). Conversely white southerners, inherently conservative, accept the fact of racial hierarchy and the need for slavery. This is Jones's definition of southern identity, one he closely associates with Anglo-Saxon and northern European racial purity.[8]

There is a close association in Jones's fiction between race and character. That he made such connections, and that he clearly posited a racial hierarchy of European and non-European peoples, is hardly surprising considering that he wrote at a time when western intellectuals were demarcating what historian Ivan Hannford has described as "race as territory, race as environment and time, race as poetry, race as revolution, and race as class." Thus in his stories Jones defines the southerner and his "race" in part by what he is not. For example, in *Wild Western Scenes* Jones presents a character named Joe Beck, the loyal Irish servant of the protagonist. Beck functions as comic relief in this story of life on the Missouri frontier. He is loyal but simple and the first to run when confronted by bear or Indian. But his weaknesses highlight the virtues of the more noble male characters in the tale, most of whom, like Daniel Boone, hail from the South. Thus, despite the fact that there are few specific references to the extension of slavery, the Missouri Compromise, or other sectional issues in this novel, Jones uses his characters to exemplify his racial ideals.[9]

Ten years later, after publishing *Wild Western Scenes,* Jones detailed the psychological consequences of not maintaining racial or ethnic order in a northern community in *The Spanglers and Tingles.* Set in Philadelphia, the story's virtuous heroes, the poor but honest Spangler family, must live under the shadow of the crass nouveau riche Tingle sisters. As in most of Jones's novels, race and class order are restored in the final chapters when, through a series of improbable events, the protagonists come into great wealth and assume their rightful social position. In this example the crushing blow the Tingle sisters receive by losing their wealth through poor investments is compounded by the revelation that their grandfather's name was O'Tingle and that he spoke with a brogue. That he became a millionaire is of little account to the Tingle sisters in light of their tainted bloodlines. Naturally the Spanglers appear to descend from uncorrupted Anglo-Saxon stock.[10]

On the unlikely chance his loyal readers had not yet recognized the particular deficiencies of the Irish "race," in 1855 Jones wrote a "humorous tale" entitled *The Winkles,* in which the hero is a devout "Know-Nothing" and the villain "an instrument of the Jesuits." This novel sold over five thousand copies in only a few months. The most explicit case in which Jones employs a racial foil to underscore the particular attributes of southern identity can be found in his treatment of Jews.[11]

Historians who have read John B. Jones's famous wartime diary are familiar with his antipathy toward Jews. He describes them as moneylenders, speculators, and cowards whose activities were draining the lifeblood of the Confederacy. The same anti-Semitism so apparent in *A Rebel War Clerk's Diary* is also evident in Jones's prewar fiction. His novel *Life and Adventures of a Country Merchant* contains a scathing depiction of a Jewish merchant that is clearly designed not only to marginalize Jews and their perceived shortcomings but also to accentuate the wholesome virtues of "authentic" southerners. The story relates the experiences of two young Kentuckians named Jack Handy and Nap Wax as they attempt to make their fortunes on the Missouri frontier. Amid clearing land, occasional duels, and falling in love, Wax opens what becomes a successful dry-goods store. His only competition is a clever but malevolent Jewish merchant named Moses Rhino. A smuggler and land speculator, Rhino is depicted as a Shylock of the frontier. He steals from customers and creditors alike but lives a miserly existence himself. Wax, a wholesome but inexperienced southern boy, initially becomes a devotee of Rhino's sharp business practices. His agrarian friends warn Wax about the dangers of the commercial life, yet the apparent wealth that can be made by adopting Rhino's ways takes in the Kentuckian. It is only after witnessing the inevitable bankruptcy of the Jewish merchant and his own marriage to a righteous woman that Wax was "content to reap the gains of his legitimate business and became by degrees a man of wealth, and the happy head of a numerous family." The trope of the manipulative Jewish merchant as a threat to unsuspecting gentiles, predominately southerners, repeats itself in Jones's work.[12]

In the last book he published before the war, entitled *Secession, Coercion, and Civil War: The Story of 1861* (a reprinted version of *The Border War*), Jones offers yet another characterization of a Jewish merchant that foreshadows the tone of his wartime diary. The sectional plot in this novel depicts the North, dominated by the "Demon of Faction"—the Republicans—as the aggressor, calling for the destruction of the Constitution and ultimate secession. The Republican North is eventually defeated by a combined force of Federal and southern troops. Encompassed within this fantastic story, what one scholar has described as Jones's "wish-fulfillment," is an episode where a Jewish merchant in Philadelphia uses deception to trick a southern lady into offering her assistance to help him move his large trunk, ostensibly filled with "old scraps," while the streets abound with rioters. Straining with her burden, the young woman drops the trunk, whereupon a large number of gold coins spill across the pavement. As rioters fight over the treasure, the pathetic "old Jew begged, and struggled, and cursed in vain . . . and reproached her for not fulfilling her bargain." Jones assures the reader that good fortune protected this lady from falling into the clutches of the decrepit man. Like Nap Wax, this southerner learns to avoid the spiritually corrupted and racially unclean, be they Jewish, Irish, or even Yankee.[13]

The particular southern identity Jones presents in his antebellum fiction remained inchoate but nonetheless present. The noble white southerners in his novels defended slavery, promoted racial order, and accepted something akin to a republican hierarchy. Protagonists not only work hard and exhibit wholesome values but also benefit from their blood. A pattern emerges in Jones's work where the genteel, those descending from old Anglo-Saxon families, tend to rise a bit higher than the honorable democratic everyman. Considering Jones's own unremarkable background, such a conservative philosophy suggests his personal values as a southerner. When combined with the editorials he wrote for the *Southern Monitor* in the late 1850s, the whole reveals a man willing to abandon the Union he long supported to defend an idealized southern identity that he had helped disseminate.

Jones published the *Southern Monitor* in Philadelphia for well over three years (1857–61). Editing a newspaper that sought to end sectional strife by promoting a southern perspective allowed Jones to better formulate and spread his views on southern identity. The idea of southern nationality that is found in the pages of the *Monitor* reveals the influence of the sometimes conflicting arguments made by James D. B. DeBow and George Fitzhugh. Thus while encouraging the South to develop its own infrastructure and financial system, Jones could at the same time blame the Panic of 1857 on a free-labor, industrialized North that was too dependent upon the South. According to this argument, in 1857 the "great landed proprietors" of the South ended all purchases from most northern manufacturing and commercial firms in order to punish them for holding free-soil convictions "inimical to their [southern] rights and institutions." Jones defended such action, writing that "it is not in human nature to confer benefits on an enemy." Between predictable attacks on "Black Republicans" and calls for a cadre of teachers trained in the South, the *Monitor* presented sophisticated arguments that in various ways claimed that the "laboring classes are as much slaves of the 'lords of the loom' as are the negroes in South Carolina of their owners and more to be pitied. . . . They are weary, toil worn and depressed in spirit when their day's task is ended." Whether such editorials added anything new to an ideologically viable southern nationalism is unclear, yet Jones did much to popularize the idea of a unique southern identity before the war. Evidently his neighbors in Pennsylvania and New Jersey associated the writer and his paper with the secessionist cause. A mob sacked the office of the *Southern Monitor* after he and his family moved to Richmond, where he had obtained a position in the Confederate War Department.[14]

At the same time that John Jones relocated to Virginia, another son of the South was hastily tying up his affairs in Chicago, Illinois, so he too could return home. Daniel R. Hundley hailed from Limestone County, Alabama, where he was born in 1832. One of six children, Hundley's father, John H., and mother, Malinda, had migrated from Virginia to Alabama, where John, a successful medical doctor, operated a plantation and eventually became a preacher. As he grew older Daniel Hundley, having the necessary intellectual ability and financial support, studied at Bacon College in Kentucky, the University of Virginia, and Harvard University, where he earned his law degree in 1853. That same year the young man married his first cousin, Mary Ann Hundley of Virginia. Soon thereafter the couple moved to Chicago, where Mary's wealthy father had considerable real estate holdings. When not managing his father-in-law's interests in Illinois, Hundley enjoyed exploring his new community and submitting an occasional article for publication in national journals. Like Jones, he seems to have been both proud of his southern heritage and his adopted home. As a staunch supporter of Northern Democrat Stephen A. Douglas, Hundley positioned himself in the political middle ground during the 1850s, but his essential allegiance to his beloved South was never in doubt. The literature he produced between 1857 and 1860 represents an extended and sophisticated exposition on the subject of southern identity.[15]

Hundley's first known statement on politics and regional identity came with the publication of his article "The Evils of Commercial Supremacy" in an 1857 edition of *Hunt's Merchants' Magazine and Commercial Review.* Styled as a letter to the editor, the piece responded to an earlier article in the magazine that had predicted the continuing dominance of northern commerce despite the Panic of 1857. In a measured response Hundley disputed many of the specifics of the northerner's argument and contended that both North and South faced an "equal danger of decay, and that such decay proceeds from the corruptions, the riches, the luxuries, and the very growth of commerce itself." Reminiscent of the southern agrarian tradition, Hundley's article proceeded to build a historical case for the degrading influence "luxurious dissipation" had had upon the world's great civilizations. He called for a return to the virtues espoused by the country's "patriot sires" before the "insidious poison" of anarchy and despotism irreparably corrupted the body politic. "The Evils of Commercial Supremacy" offered a subtle defense of southern rights against the ascendancy of northern commerce by making the South's cause that of the American people as a whole. In short the South's resistance to the spiritual depravations inherent in rampant commercialism may well save the national soul. For Hundley the article must have seemed an auspicious beginning for an unknown writer.[16]

Hundley quickly published two more pieces that related directly to the growing sectional tensions within the United States. In 1857 he published a second article in *Hunt's Merchants' Magazine,* entitled "The Traffic in Coolies," and the next year he wrote a pamphlet, *Work and Bread; or the Coming Winter & the Poor.* In the former Hundley exposed what he believed to be the hypocrisy of abolitionists, particularly those in Great Britain, for their unrelenting attacks on southern slaveholders while they ignored white slavery and the trade in laborers in Asia and the islands of the Caribbean. Although the article represented his most pointed rebuttal to abolitionism to date, Hundley's defense of the South reveals its essential moderation by calling for an end to sectional strife. He posited slavery as a benign institution that recognized the slave's humanity, while "Old England's ships are triumphantly riding the seas, crammed with cargoes of human freight." According to Hundley, "In the one case the master's interest is on the side of humanity; in the other, it is just the contrary." He seems to suggest that by working together to end the "Coolie" trade, the North and South might bridge the sectional divide between them. The issue of wage labor versus slavery in America received a more extended treatment in Hundley's pamphlet.[17]

Like many of John Jones's articles in the *Southern Monitor, Work and Bread* bears the imprint of George Fitzhugh and other southern intellectuals. Hundley presents an implicit defense of slavery by depicting the plight of free workers in the North. Infused with his apparent sympathy for the workingman unable to support his family, Hundley attacks the commercial system and those individuals most responsible for oppressing the northern working classes. Denying fellowship with European "socialists," he subscribes to the "truth" of a social and racial hierarchy as outlined by Sen. James Henry Hammond in his famous "mud-sill" speech before Congress. In a free society, according to Hundley, "warfare is waged constantly between labor and capital, until the latter, being strongest, overrides the former, and drives the mechanic to the wall." When pushed to this extreme, workers will erupt in a "rebellion of the stomach" and anarchy will prevail. In order to avert social upheaval in the coming winter, the pamphlet recommends the creation of state charity funds that would alleviate the worst sufferings of the working classes. By detailing such problems *Work and Bread* provides a subtle defense of what is characterized as a more humane and stable slave South. Two years later Hundley offered a more original analysis of southern society in his now classic work, *Social Relations in Our Southern States*.[18]

Hundley's primary goal in *Social Relations* was to destroy the myth that seemed to exist in certain northern circles that only three classes existed in the South, "Negro slaves, Poor Whites, and Cavaliers." His study reveals the presence and interaction of several different classes in the South. Genteel planters, "Southern Yankees," and the important southern middle class are just a few of the specific groups defined by the Unionist Alabamian writing on the shores of Lake Michigan. Hundley's work, "a curious mixture of traditional values and contemporary modern ideas," according to one historian, professes to be a neutral investigation of southern life, but it should be more properly understood as a defense of and explanation for southern identity.

Ostensibly *Social Relations* concentrates on social classes, but Hundley reveals much when he writes, "We contend there is a great deal in *blood*." Reflecting the influence of the racial theories of Jules Michelet and southern thinkers closer to home, he argues that the South, like all societies, consists of a series of social classes based upon "types" that are inextricably rooted in climate, institutions, and race. Those factors that distinguish all white southerners from their northern countrymen include the region's warm weather, agrarianism, slavery, and breeding. He attests that those descendants of English cavaliers, true southerners, appreciate the foxhunt, warm friendship, and social stability, while in the free states "every species of pastime which hinders the making of money is regarded as sinful." He admits the presence of such an attitude in the South as well but describes it as an exception to the regional rule, embraced by what can only be described as a deviant strain of "Southern Yankees." The members of this class, often merchants, are portrayed as clever hypocrites who often survive by exploiting the region's sturdy yeoman farmers.

Concluding with a lengthy defense of slavery, once again based heavily upon the latest racial theories of the 1850s, Hundley ends *Social Relations* with a paean to "invincible King Cotton." What begins as an attempt to explain the South objectively to a northern audience becomes in actuality a strong argument for the existence and virtues of a unique southern identity. One year after the publication of *Social Relations,* Hundley's participation in the Confederate army would transform his own identification with the South into something closer to nationalism.[19]

The books and articles John Beauchamp Jones and Daniel R. Hundley wrote before the Civil War helped popularize the idea of an authentic, though somewhat ambiguous, southern identity built upon a foundation of slavery, race, and regional social institutions. Before the war these two men presented the ideological components of a viable Confederate identity. As Drew Faust, Paul Escott, and other historians have suggested, however, there were internal contradictions that plagued that identity. Such "races" as the Irish, Jews, and others were seemingly excluded from this regional identity, while the status of poor whites was often so marginalized as to place this class outside the mainstream of an idealized aristocratic, Anglo-Saxon South. Nevertheless, to quote Emory Thomas, both men's participation in the Confederate army and government proved the "revolutionary experience" that gave their regional identity a cogency it had lacked previously.[20]

Hundley and Jones supported the Confederate cause enthusiastically once their native states seceded from the Union. Their decisions did not necessarily entail severing the many ties they had established in their adopted northern communities. For example, Hundley claimed many "warm friends" in Chicago and "preferred living there to living in Alabama." Nevertheless, Hundley, like Jones, set aside whatever reservations he may have had and chose to remain true to his understanding of what it meant to be a loyal southerner. Once the two actively became involved in fighting and organizing the war, their devotion to the Confederacy, if not to all its leaders, was steadfast.[21]

Upon returning to his family home in northern Alabama, Hundley immediately set about raising a company from his old neighborhood in Limestone County. Elected captain, he and his troops left for war eager to fight. Hundley impressed those he met and rose quickly in the ranks; by April 1862 he became colonel of the Thirty-first Alabama. After serving in East Tennessee and the Department of Mississippi and Eastern Louisiana, in 1863 the Thirty-first Alabama was eventually reorganized and attached to Edmund W.

Pettus's brigade of John B. Hood's corps in Joseph E. Johnston's Army of the Tennessee. During this time Hundley handled the Thirty-first with great skill in several engagements. He and his regiment served in and around Vicksburg, Mississippi, where they fought with distinction at the battles of Chickasaw Bayou (December 27–29, 1862) and Port Gibson (May 1, 1863). At the latter encounter Hundley suffered a wound while leading his men in a rear-guard defense against several Federal assaults. Captured and subsequently exchanged after the fall of Vicksburg, Hundley led the Thirty-first in a virtual continual engagement with William T. Sherman's forces in north Georgia during the spring of 1864. It was during this campaign, at a battle near Big Shanty on June 15, 1864, that Federal forces captured Hundley and 152 of his men. The Alabama colonel was sent to a military prison on Johnson's Island in Lake Erie, where he spent the rest of the war.[22]

The months Hundley survived as a prisoner of war strengthened his commitment to the Confederacy and revealed his bold character. Obtaining paper wherever he could, he detailed his time in prison, as well as his complaints against the North, in a small diary that would later become the basis for *Prison Echoes of the Great Rebellion* (1874). The diary allowed him to explain his optimistic support for the Confederacy as well as his opposition to what he characterized as the brutal oppression instigated by the Federal government. The prison diary, unlike the tone of his antebellum writings, envelops its arguments in violent rhetoric. Hundley's invective against black troops, the treatment he received while imprisoned, and his ponderous reflections upon the coming Armageddon suggest an intellect that had been shaped, even scarred, by the experience of war. When not fulminating against his captors, Hundley planned an escape from Johnson's Island, which he accomplished on January 3, 1865. It seems he and at least one other Alabama officer made their audacious escape by impersonating Federal guards. Upon learning of the break out, the incensed commander of the prison notified local authorities and issued a one-hundred-dollar reward for their capture. A few days later a citizen in Fremont, Ohio, some twenty-five miles south of Johnson's Island, captured Hundley, whereupon the colonel was transported back to prison. At war's end Hundley took the oath of allegiance and days later was released from prison on July 25, 1865.[23]

As a clerk in the Confederate War Department, John Jones did not experience combat or risk imprisonment during the war. While Hundley led the Thirty-first Alabama and suffered as a prisoner of war, Jones confronted the difficult but far less perilous task of working in the Confederate government. Responsible for a number of clerical duties in the War Department, he had frequent contact with the secretary of war, numerous army officers, and even Pres. Jefferson Davis on occasion. A committed Confederate nationalist, Jones enjoyed many of the responsibilities his position demanded as he described them in his wartime diary. Those frustrations he did articulate—and they grew over the course of the war—focused upon what he considered to be the inferior quality of several Confederate leaders as well as the deprivations with which his family had to contend while living in Richmond. Through all his frustrations with incompetent politicians and generals, Jones's faith in the mass of his fellow citizens, a "military people" in his words, seemed to deepen. Even after the Confederacy's losses on the battlefield in the summer of 1863, Jones declared confidently that the U.S. government "would require a million bayonets to keep this people in subjection." Like many of his neighbors, he believed that the North would fail this "question of endurance." Hunger, inflation, and the carnage of the final two years of the conflict did not fundamentally alter Jones's faith in ultimate victory. Only after the surrender of the Army of Northern Virginia in the spring of 1865 did he acknowledge the South's inevitable defeat.[24]

It is evident from this brief overview of their wartime experiences that Daniel Hundley's service in the Confederate army and John Jones's work in the Confederate War Department powerfully affected these pro-southern Unionists. The journal Hundley kept while he commanded the Thirty-first Alabama and as a prisoner of war reveals a strong identification with the Confederacy. As a Douglas Democrat in 1860, he described himself as "ardently attached to the Union, and bitterly opposed to the abolitionists and the secessionists," whom he considered "*par nobile fratrum.*" Fighting with the Thirty-first Alabama, followed by a year spent as on Johnson's Island, radicalized Hundley's views. This "Revolution," as he once described it, reveals itself in his writing. Not only did he write patriotic letters to newspapers and encourage fellow soldiers to pray for salvation, but privately Hundley also conveyed a more extreme version of the southern identity he had articulated before the war.[25] His characterizations of northerners as a Yankee "race" acquired a more violent cast than they had in *Social Relations.* No longer are Yankees merely commercial men to Hundley by 1864: "A Yankee will be a Yankee and a leopard might change his spots or an Ethiopian his skin, sooner than any of the race ever learn that they are the most boastful & despicable of all races of the civilized earth. That they are the most boastful needs no proof, and their conduct in this war proves most unmistakably that they are the most despicable."[26] A deep, and apparently growing, fundamentalist religious sensibility became a critical feature of this southern worldview. When Hundley first witnessed a regiment of black troops dressed in blue, he could only make sense of the sight in apocalyptic terms. The "black shadow" reminded him of verses from Ezekiel that relate Israel's desperate war and eventual victory over the invader Gog. Hundley saw the Union, and its use of black troops in particular, as the modern equivalent of Gog's hordes. Such "despicable" conduct on the part of northerners, who did not know how to "honor God," served to strengthen Hundley's zeal for the Confederate cause.[27]

Jones's work in the Confederate War Department intensified his southern identity as well. Even after having lived in the North for many years, he compared the invasion of Yankee armies to the unthinking destruction produced by the armyworm, "which enters green fields in countless ways." Like Hundley, the war clerk labored for the cause both in his government post and by writing newspaper articles designed to "incite" the people to volunteer. When not performing either of these tasks, Jones wrote detailed entries in his diary on life in Richmond, the Confederate government, and the Yankee threat. When describing the latter he continued to view them as distinct from southern white men. For example, he describes Union general Joseph Hooker as a man gentlemen avoided because, "Yankee-like," he speculated in agricultural commodities. For Jones the war confirmed his belief that a cultural, even racial, divide existed between the North and South. His diary suggests that working in the War Department alongside many Confederate leaders heightened his awareness of regional differences and cultivated his southern nationalism. This same feeling induced him to denounce those southern leaders who prized the respective rights of their own states over the needs of the Confederate government. Such divisions, according to Jones, proved the ruin of the Confederacy.[28]

Following the war Hundley and Jones, like the vast majority of Confederate veterans, sought immediate work in order to support their families. Hundley returned to his family's home in Lawrence County, Alabama, where he engaged in the practice of law. Jones, who had suffered from consumption for a number of years, returned with his family to Accomack County along the eastern shore of Virginia, where he lived on the farm he acquired from his father-in-law. Predictably both men revived the literary careers the war had interrupted. Each revised his wartime diary for publication. Jones's effort assumed special urgency as it became clear that he would not live long after the war. He died on February 4, 1866, while *A Rebel War Clerk's Diary* was in press. Ironically the ailing southern partisan died near his old home in Burlington, New Jersey, where he was trying to interest J. B. Lippincott and Company in publishing his book. Hundley published his wartime diary in 1876. At the same time he edited a Huntsville, Alabama, newspaper called the *North Alabama Reporter*, which later became *The New South*. Hundley used these Redeemer Democratic papers to once again comment upon southern life while defending the region from the perceived criticism of outsiders.[29]

Emblazoned with a grim masthead that read "Learn to Suffer and be Strong," *The New South* carried many of the same messages as Hundley's antebellum work, albeit with a measure of circumspection that suggests the chastening effect of defeat. In its very first issue, Hundley's *New South* declared, "In this future, as in the past, we shall labor on unselfishly, fearlessly and hopefully, for the rebuilding of the waste places, for the restoration of our former prosperity, and for the education of the masses in everything which tends to develop a true manhood." Like the publication of Jones's diary in 1866, Hundley's postwar writing continued to articulate a clear understanding of southern identity. Rooted in blood and race during the antebellum period, southern "manhood" following the war became associated closely with the Lost Cause as well. Hundley's paper survived only a few short years, but he lived another two decades, dying in 1899.[30]

The tremendous scope of Daniel R. Hundley's and John Beauchamp Jones's writing demands the attention of those interested in exploring questions surrounding southern nationalism, identity, and politics. Over the course of their lives both men described, asserted, and even embodied variations of white southern identity. Reflecting their interest in regional characteristics, white supremacy, and blood, they did much to popularize the concept of unique northern and southern traits. Replete with passion, contradictions, and exceptions, their antebellum work pressed these arguments, while the Civil War seemed to give them real validity. Fortunate to survive the conflict, each continued to write about the South when possible. Although bitter on occasion, Hundley and Jones each recognized "the stern logic of facts" and accepted reunion with relative equanimity. By the end of their lives, both men could rightfully claim to have influenced the accepted thought on southern identity. Generations later historians are still coming to terms with their legacy.[31]

NOTES

1. See Ulrich B. Phillips, *American Negro Slavery* (New York: D. Appleton, 1918); Kenneth M. Stampp, *The Peculiar Institution: Slavery in the Ante-Bellum South* (New York: Alfred A. Knopf, 1956); Eugene D. Genovese, *The Political Economy of Slavery: Studies in the Economy and Society of the Slave South,* 2nd ed. (1961; Middletown, Conn.: Wesleyan University Press, 1989); Genovese, *The World the Slaveholders Made: Two Essays in Interpretation* (1969; Middletown, Conn.: Wesleyan University Press, 1988); Genovese, *Roll, Jordan, Roll: The World the Slaves Made* (New York: Pantheon Books, 1974); Bertram Wyatt-Brown, *Southern Honor: Ethics and Behavior in the Old South* (New York: Oxford University Press, 1982).

2. Douglas Southall Freeman, *Lee's Lieutenants: A Study in Command,* vols. 2–3 (New York: Charles Scribner's Sons, 1943, 1944); Frank E. Vandiver, *Their Tattered Flags: The Epic of the Confederacy* (New York: Harper's Magazine, 1970); Bruce Catton, *Terrible Swift Sword* (Garden City, N.Y.: Doubleday, 1963); James M. McPherson, *Battle Cry of Freedom: The Civil War Era* (1985; New York: Ballantine Books, 1988); Gary W. Gallagher, *The Confederate War: How Popular Will, Nationalism, and Military Strategy Could Not Stave Off Defeat* (Cambridge, Mass.: Harvard University Press, 1997); Russell F. Weigley, *A Great Civil War: A Military and Political History, 1861–1865* (Bloomington: Indiana University Press, 2000). The meager number of studies on Daniel R. Hundley and John B. Jones include Tommy W. Rogers, "Daniel R. Hundley's Contribution to Folklore," *Alabama Historical Quarterly* 30 (Fall and Winter, 1968): 203–18; Rogers, "D. R. Hundley: A Multi-Class Thesis of Social Stratification in the Antebellum South," *Mississippi Quarterly* 23 (Spring 1970): 135–54; Blanche Henry Clark Weaver, "D. R. Hundley: Subjective Sociologist," *Georgia Review* 10 (Summer 1958): 222–34; Clark Brockman, "John Beauchamp Jones" (Ph.D. diss., University of South Carolina, 1937); and Frederick R. Lapides, "John Beauchamp Jones: A Southern View of the Abolitionists," *Journal of the Rutgers University Libraries* 33, no. 2 (1970): 63–73. William J. Cooper Jr. provides a fine overview of Hundley's life and the significance of *Social Relations* in particular in an introduction to a reissued edition. See Daniel R. Hundley, *Social Relations in Our Southern States,* ed. William J. Cooper Jr. (1860; Baton Rouge: Louisiana State University Press, 1979), xiii–xlv.

3. Vandiver, *Their Tattered Flags;* Emory M. Thomas, *The Confederacy as a Revolutionary Experience* (1971; repr., Columbia: University of South Carolina Press, 1991); Thomas, *The Confederate Nation: 1861–1865* (New York: Harper & Row, 1979); Paul D. Escott, *After Secession: Jefferson Davis and the Failure of Confederate Nationalism* (Baton Rouge: Louisiana State University Press, 1978); Drew Gilpin Faust, *The Creation of Confederate Nationalism: Ideology and Identity in the Civil War South* (Baton Rouge: Louisiana State University Press, 1988). See also Lawrence N. Powell and Michael S. Wayne, "Self-Interest and the Decline of Confederate Nationalism," in *The Old South in the Crucible of War,* ed. Harry P. Owens and James J. Cooke (Jackson: University Press of Mississippi, 1983); George C. Rable, *Civil Wars: Women and the Crisis of Southern Nationalism* (Urbana: University of Illinois Press, 1989); Gallagher, *Confederate War.* For works that discount the presence or significance of Confederate nationalism, see Kenneth M. Stampp, *The Imperiled Union: Essays on the Background of the Civil War* (New York: Oxford University Press, 1980); and Reid Mitchell, "The

Perseverance of the Soldiers," in *Why the Confederacy Lost,* ed. Gabor S. Boritt (New York: Oxford University Press, 1992). For a provocative analysis of nationalism and the absence of popular will in support of the Confederate war effort, see Richard E. Beringer, Herman Hattaway, Archer Jones, and William N. Still Jr., *Why the South Lost the Civil War* (Athens: University of Georgia Press, 1986). For an earlier overview on the subject, see John McCardell, *The Idea of a Southern Nation: Southern Nationalists and Southern Nationalism, 1830–1860* (New York: W. W. Norton, 1979).

4. Faust, *Creation of Confederate Nationalism,* 8; Thomas, *Confederate Nation,* 298.

5. Brockman, "John Beauchamp Jones," 3–23, 75–77; "John Beauchamp Jones," in *Dictionary of American Biography* (Washington, D.C.: American Council of Learned Societies, 1932, 1933), 5(2):182–83.

6. *Southern Monitor* (Philadelphia), June 6, Aug. 8, 1857.

7. Brockman, "John Beauchamp Jones," ii. Poe did connect Jones with the "lighter literature" of Baltimore; see "John Beauchamp Jones," *Dictionary of American Biography,* 5(2):182. Jones republished several novels twice under different titles, so a measure of redundancy exists in any list of his works. The books he is known to have authored include *Wild Western Scenes* (1841); *Book of Visions* (1847); *Rural Sports: A Tale* (1849); *The Country Merchant* (1849?); *The Western Merchant* (1849); *The City Merchant* (1851); *Adventures of Col. Gracchus Vanderbomb* (1852); *The Spanglers and the Tingles* (1852); *The Monarchist* (1853); *Freaks of Fortune* (1854); *The Winkles* (1855); *The War Path* (1856); *The Border War: A Tale of Disunion* (1859); and *Secession, Coercion, and Civil War* (1861). For a useful discussion of William Gilmore Simms's fiction, see Charles S. Watson, *From Nationalism to Secessionism: The Changing Fiction of William Gilmore Simms* (Westport, Conn.: Greenwood, 1993).

8. Brockman, "John Beauchamp Jones," 21, 48; Lapides, "John Beauchamp Jones," 63–69.

9. J. B. Jones, *Adventures of Col. Gracchus Vanderbomb, of Sloughcreek, in Pursuit of the Presidency* (Philadelphia: A. Hart, 1852), 19–21, 43; Ivan Hannaford, *Race: The History of an Idea in the West* (Baltimore: Johns Hopkins University Press, 1996), 236; J. B. Jones, *Wild Western Scenes: A Narrative of Adventures in the Western Wilderness . . . ,* New Stereotype Edition (1841; Philadelphia: J. B. Lippincott, 1884), 10, 35–38. For ideological issues surrounding black-white relations in the South, see George Fredrickson, *The Black Image in the White Mind: The Debate on Afro-American Character and Destiny, 1817–1914* (1971; Middletown, Conn: Wesleyan University Press, 1987).

10. J. B. Jones, *The Spanglers and the Tingles; or, The Rival Belles* (Philadelphia: A. Hart, 1852), 41, 81, 85, 270.

11. Brockman, "John Beauchamp Jones," 24. It should be noted that Jones's characterization of Irish-Americans and Irish immigrants was hardly unique among nineteenth-century American writers. This said, his depictions of the Irish as a specific "type" or race is more pointed than that of others, particularly regional authors such as William Gilmore Simms or A. B. Longstreet. It should be noted that when late-antebellum writers referred to the Irish people, they almost always were describing more-recent Irish Catholic immigrants rather than the Scots-Irish or Anglo-Irish populations, most of whom immigrated to America in the eighteenth century. For one interpretation of these earlier Celts and their influence upon the South, see Grady McWhiney and Forrest McDonald, *Cracker Culture: Celtic Ways in the Old South* (Tuscaloosa: University of Alabama Press, 1989).

12. Jones made many passing references to the Jewish population in Richmond in his journal. His entry for December 20, 1864, is typical: "At an auction this morning, a Jew bid off an old set of

tablespoons, weighing twelve ounces and much worn, at $575. He will next *buy* his way out of the Confederacy." *A Rebel War Clerk's Diary at the Confederate States Capital,* 2 vols. (Philadelphia: J. B. Lippincott, 1866), 2:361. Quotes from and plot discussion based on J. B. Jones, *Life and Adventures of a Country Merchant: A Narrative of his Exploits at Home, during his Travels, and in the Cities,* 2nd ed. (1854; Philadelphia: J. B. Lippincott, 1857), 395, 338–43. This book was also published under the title *The Western Merchant* (1849). It is interesting to note that several of Jones's novels are set in Missouri Territory. This can be largely explained by the impression the region and its people left upon Jones when as a young man he lived there for a number of years. Indeed much of what he describes in his Missouri novels seems to have been autobiographical. Nevertheless it also seems likely that the sectional controversies within the future border state provided him with an excellent setting to explore broader issues of regionalism and personal identity.

13. J. B. Jones, *Secession, Coercion, and Civil War: The Story of 1861* (Philadelphia: T. B. Peterson and Brothers, 1861), 82–83; Jones, *The Border War: A Tale of Disunion* (New York: Rudd & Carleton, 1859), 44, 22–23, 499–501; Lapides, "John Beauchamp Jones," 63–64.

14. *Southern Monitor,* June 20, Aug. 29, Oct. 31, 1857; 1858–59 *Monitor* advertisements, John Beauchamp Jones Papers, Southern Historical Collection, University of North Carolina, Chapel Hill. For excellent examinations of DeBow, Fitzhugh, and other significant southern thinkers, see Genovese, *Political Economy of Slavery;* Genovese, *The Slaveholder's Dilemma: Freedom and Progress in Southern Conservative Thought, 1820–1860* (Columbia: University of South Carolina Press, 1992); Eric H. Walther, *The Fire-Eaters* (Baton Rouge: Louisiana State University, 1992), 1–8, 195–227; and Douglas Ambrose, *Henry Hughes and Proslavery Thought in the Old South* (Baton Rouge: Louisiana State University Press, 1997). Jones departed from Burlington, New Jersey, for Richmond, Virginia, on the morning of April 9, 1861, three days before the firing on Fort Sumter. His wife and children remained in Burlington for several weeks and finally rejoined him in late May. In his diary Jones expresses sadness about his family's hasty flight from New Jersey but concludes stoically, "The South is our only home—we have been only temporary sojourners elsewhere." *Rebel War Clerk's Diary,* 1:46.

15. Bio/timeline, Daniel Hundley Papers, Southern Historical Collection, University of North Carolina, Chapel Hill; Hundley, *Social Relations,* xiv–xxiv; Col. D. R. Hundley, *Prison Echoes of the Great Rebellion* (New York: S. W. Green, Printer, 1874), 6–9.

16. D. R. Hundley, "The Evils of Commercial Supremacy," *Hunt's Merchants' Magazine and Commercial Review* 36 (Mar. 1857): 316–17. Like Jones, Hundley conducted business in the North, in his case Chicago, Illinois, as late as April 1861. See Hundley Journal, Apr. 21, 1861, Hundley Papers.

17. D. R. Hundley, "The Traffic in Coolies," *Hunt's Merchants' Magazine and Commercial Review* 36 (May 1857): 570–73.

18. D. R. Hundley, *Work and Bread; or The Coming Winter & the Poor* (Chicago: James Barnet, Book and Job Printer, 1858), 15–16.

19. Hundley, *Social Relations,* xxviii–xxix, 36, 81, 136–38, 251 (italics in original); Hannaford, *Race,* 254–76; Walther, *Fire-Eaters,* 181–84.

20. Paul D. Escott, "The Failure of Confederate Nationalism: The Old South's Class System in the Crucible of War," in Owens and Cooke, *Old South in the Crucible of War,* 16–20. Both Faust and Escott emphasize how class conflict, religion, and concerns over slavery undercut Confeder-

ate nationalism. Faust concludes her analysis of the subject by noting: "Confederate nationalism prescribed change in the service of continuity, but then proved able neither to contain nor explain the ensuing transformations. . . . The notion of essentially conflicting interests within a single social or political order was incompatible with Confederate thought and belief, as it was with the republican evangelical, and nationalist doctrines on which that ideology was based." Faust, *Creation of Confederate Nationalism,* 84.

21. Hundley, *Prison Echoes,* 6.

22. U.S. War Department, *The War of Rebellion: A Compilation of the Official Records of the Union and Confederate Armies,* 128 vols. (Washington, D.C.: Government Printing Office, 1880–1901), ser. 1, 16:716, 24:703, 32:869 (hereinafter cited as *OR*); Hundley, *Social Relations,* xxi, xxiii; Chris Edwards and Faye Axford, *The Lure and Lore of Limestone County* (Tuscaloosa, Ala.: Portals, 1978), 196–97; Weigley, *Great Civil War,* 264–70; Albert Castel, *Decision in the West: The Atlanta Campaign of 1864* (Lawrence: University Press of Kansas, 1992), 280–81.

23. *OR,* ser. 2, 8:41–42; Hundley, *Prison Echoes,* 3–10, 18–22, 40–43; Hundley, *Social Relations,* xxii, xxiii.

24. Jones, *Rebel War Clerk's Diary,* 2:89, 91. Jones's wartime diary continued to reflect the anti-Semitism that appeared in his fiction before the war. He did not always trust the intentions of such leaders as Judah Benjamin and, like most southerners, did not appreciate the rather significant contributions Jewish southerners made on the battlefield. See Robert Rosen, *The Jewish Confederates* (Columbia: University of South Carolina Press, 2000).

25. Hundley, *Prison Echoes,* 6; Hundley Journal, Jan. 21, Apr. 29, Nov. 1, 1861, Hundley Papers. By all accounts an effective officer, Hundley also proved to be a spirited prisoner, being one of the few individuals to escape Johnson's Island successfully and evade Federal forces before being recaptured in Fremont, Ohio. See *OR,* ser. 2, 8:41–43.

26. Hundley Journal, Jan. 4, 1864.

27. Hundley, *Prison Echoes,* 40–43, 109.

28. Jones, *Rebel War Clerk's Diary,* 2:26, 55, 253, 447.

29. Brockman, "John Beauchamp Jones," 3–23, 75–77; "John Beauchamp Jones," *Dictionary of American Biography,* 5(2):182–83.

30. *The New South* (Huntsville, Ala.), May 25, 1876.

31. D. R. Hundley, "Prospectus," *The New South,* May 25, 1876.

The Saratoga That Wasn't: Confederate Recognition and the Effect of Antietam Abroad

JAMES M. McPHERSON

THE CAMPAIGN AND BATTLE OF ANTIETAM HAD CONSEQUENCES that reached far beyond the mountains, valleys, and fields of western Maryland where the fighting took place. Indeed the reverberations of this Confederate defeat were heard across the Atlantic in London and Paris. Like the secessionists of 1776 who founded the United States, the secessionists of 1861 who founded the Confederate States counted on foreign aid to help them win their independence. In the Revolution they got what they hoped for after the battle of Saratoga; French recognition of the fledgling United States and subsequent financial and military support were crucial to American success. In the Civil War southerners failed to achieve foreign recognition, which might have been crucial to Confederate success if it had happened. The outcome of the fighting near Sharpsburg, a Maryland village near Antietam Creek, was the main reason it did not happen; in that respect Antietam could be described as a failed Saratoga.

The principal goal of Confederate foreign policy in 1862 was to win diplomatic recognition of the new southern nation by foreign powers. Both North and South—one in fear and the other in hope—understood the importance of this matter. As early as May 21, 1861, Union secretary of state William H. Seward had instructed the U.S. minister to Britain, Charles Francis Adams, that if Britain extended diplomatic recognition to the Confederacy, "we from that hour, shall cease to be friends and become once more, as we have twice before been forced to be, enemies of Great Britain."[1]

Even if diplomatic recognition did not provoke a third Anglo-American war, southerners expected it to be decisive in their favor. "Foreign recognition of our independence will go very far towards hastening its recognition by the government of the United States," declared the *Richmond Enquirer* in June 1862. "Our independence once acknowledged, our adversaries must for very shame disgust themselves with the nonsense about 'Rebels,' 'Traitors,' &c" and "look upon our Independence . . . as *un fait accompli.*" Confederate secretary of state Judah F. Benjamin believed that "our recognition would be the signal for the immediate organization of a large and influential party in the Northern States favorable to putting an end to the war." Moreover "in our Confederate finances at home its effects would be magical, and its collateral advantages would be immeasurable."[2]

Benjamin was not just whistling "Dixie." Judging from the strenuous efforts by Union diplomats to prevent recognition and by the huge volume of Confederate news and editorial coverage of the issue in northern newspapers, foreign recognition of the Confederacy would have been perceived in the North as a grievous and perhaps fatal blow. It would have conferred international legitimacy on the southern nation and produced great pressure on the United States to do the same. It would have boosted southern morale and encouraged foreign investment in Confederate bonds. Recognition would also have enabled the Richmond government to negotiate military and commercial treaties with foreign powers.

This question, however, presented the South with something of a catch-22. Although Napoleon III of France wanted to recognize the Confederacy from almost the beginning, he was unwilling to take this step except in tandem with Britain. (All other European powers except perhaps Russia would have followed a British and French lead in that direction.) British policy on recognition of a revolutionary or insurrectionary government was coldly pragmatic. Not until it had proved its capacity to sustain and defend its independence, almost beyond peradventure of doubt, would Britain risk recognition of a new national state. The Confederate hope of course was for help in *gaining* that independence.

Most European observers and statesmen believed in 1861 that the Union cause was hopeless. In their view the Lincoln administration could never reestablish control over 750,000 square miles of territory defended by a determined and courageous people. And there was plenty of sentimental sympathy for the Confederacy in Britain, for which the powerful *Times* of London was the foremost advocate. Many Englishmen professed to disdain the braggadocio and vulgar materialism of money-grubbing Yankees. They projected a congenial image of the southern gentry that conveniently ignored slavery. Nevertheless the government of Prime Minister Viscount Palmerston was anything but sentimental. It required hard evidence of the Confederacy's ability to survive, in the form of military success, before offering diplomatic recognition. But it would also require Union military success to forestall that possibility. As Lord Robert Cecil told a northern acquaintance in 1861, "Well, there is one way to convert us all—win the battles, and we shall come round at once."[3]

In 1861, however, the Confederacy had won most of the battles—the highly visible ones at least, at Manassas, Wilson's Creek, and Ball's Bluff. And by 1862 the cutoff of cotton exports from the South to Britain and France due to both the southern embargo and the northern blockade was beginning to hurt the economies of those countries. Henry Adams, private secretary to his father in the American legation at London, wrote in January 1862 that only "one thing would save us and that is a decisive victory. Without that our fate here seems to me a mere matter of time." In February the *New York Tribune* acknowledged the critical foreign-policy stakes of the military campaigns then impending: "If our armies now advancing shall generally be stopped or beaten back, France, England, and Spain will make haste to recognize Jeff's Confederacy as an independent power." Only Union victories "prompt, signal, [and] decisive can alone prevent that foreign intervention on which all the hopes of the traitors are staked."[4]

Northern arms did win signal and decisive victories over the next several months that more than fulfilled the *Tribune*'s hopes, starting with Forts Henry and Donelson and Roanoke Island in February, followed by Pea Ridge and New Bern in March. In London the Confederate envoy, Virginian James Mason, conceded that news of the fall of Forts Henry and Donelson "had an unfortunate effect on the minds of our friends here." Charles Francis Adams informed Seward in March that as a consequence of northern success, "the pressure for interference here has disappeared." At the same time Henry Adams wrote to his brother in the army back home that "times have so decidedly changed since my last letter to you. . . . The talk of intervention, only two months ago so loud as to take a semiofficial tone, is now out of the minds of everyone."[5] The London *Times* ate crow, admitting it had underestimated "the unexpected and astonishing resolution of the North." Even Napoleon's pro-southern sentiments seemed to have cooled. From Paris the U.S. minister wrote in April that "the change in condition of affairs at home has produced a change, if possible more striking abroad. There is little more said just now as to . . . the propriety of an early recognition of the South."[6]

News from America took almost two weeks to reach Europe. In mid-May Henry Adams returned to the legation from a springtime walk in London to find his father dancing across the floor and shouting, "We've got New Orleans." Indeed, Henry added, "the effect of the news here has been greater than anything yet." It must have been, to prompt such behavior by the grandson of John Adams and son of John Quincy Adams. While Adams was dancing, James Mason was writing dispiritedly to Jefferson Davis that "the fall of New Orleans will certainly exercise a depressing influence here for intervention."[7]

Mason did not stop trying, however. He urged Lord John Russell, the British foreign secretary, to offer England's good offices to mediate an end to a war "ruinous alike to the parties engaged in it, and to the prosperity and welfare of Europe." Such an offer of course would be tantamount to recognizing Confederate independence. In a blunt reply Russell pointed out that "the capture of New Orleans, the advance of the Federals to Corinth, to Memphis, and the banks of the Mississippi as far as Vicksburg" meant "her Majesty's Government are still determined to wait." Nevertheless Mason worked his contacts among members of Parliament, who planned to introduce a motion in the House of Commons calling for recognition of the Confederacy. But Palmerston wrote in June, saying "this seems an odd moment to Chuse for acknowledging the Separate Independence of the South when all the Seaboard, and the principal internal Rivers are in the hands of the North. . . . We ought to know that their Separate Independence is a Truth and a fact before we declare it to be so."[8]

Therefore, as Charles Francis Adams informed Seward, even among skeptics in Britain, "the impression is growing stronger that all concerted resistance to us will before long be at an end." The danger of foreign recognition, Adams had earlier noted, "will arise again only in the event of some decided reverse."[9] Indeed it would, and those reverses were soon to occur as the pendulum of battle swung toward the Confederacy in the summer of 1862.

On May 30 and June 6, 1862, Union arms climaxed four months of victories with the occupation of Corinth, Mississippi, and the capture of Memphis. Maj. Gen. George B. McClellan's Army of the Potomac had advanced to within five miles of Richmond. But even as these events took place, the Confederate team of Stonewall Jackson and Robert E. Lee was beginning to strike back. Jackson's famous "foot cavalry" outmarched enemy forces in the Shenandoah Valley and won a series of victories that pumped up sagging southern morale. Lee took over the Army of Northern Virginia on June 1 and began planning a counteroffensive against McClellan, which he launched on June 26. By July 2 the Army of the Potomac had been driven back to Harrison's Landing on the James River in the Seven Days Battles, plunging northern morale to the lowest point in the war thus far. In the western theater too, the Union war machine stalled in the summer of 1862 and then went into reverse as Confederate forces raided through Tennessee and prepared to invade Kentucky.

These southern successes reopened the question of foreign recognition. They confirmed the widespread belief in Europe that the North could never subdue the South. The cotton "famine" was beginning to hurt workers as hundreds of textile mills in Britain and France shut down or went on short time. Unemployment soared. Seward's earlier assurance that the Union capture of New Orleans would lead to a resumption of cotton exports from that port was not fulfilled, as Confederates in the lower Mississippi Valley burned their cotton rather than see it fall into Yankee hands. Only a trickle of cotton made it across the Atlantic in 1862. The conviction grew in Britain and France that the only way to revive cotton imports and reopen the factories was to end the war. Pressure built in the summer for an offer by the British and French governments to mediate peace negotiations on the basis of Confederate independence.

As soon as news of Jackson's exploits in the Shenandoah Valley reached Europe (much magnified as it traveled), the government-controlled press in France and anti-American newspapers in Britain began beating the drums for intervention. The *Paris Constitutional* insisted in June that "mediation alone will succeed in putting an end to a war disastrous to the interests of humanity."[10] In similar language the London *Times* said it was time to end this war that had become "a scandal to humanity."[11] The "humanity" they seemed most concerned about were textile manufacturers and their employees. The U.S. minister to France, citing information coming to him from that country as well as from across the channel, reported "a strenuous effort . . . to induce England and France to intervene. . . . I should not attach much importance to these rumors, however well accredited they seem to be, were it not for the exceeding pressure which exists for want of cotton."[12] In mid-June the *Richmond Dispatch* headlined one story "Famine in England—Intervention Certain." Northern newspapers published many alarmist news stories and editorials about "British Intervention," "Foreign Intervention Again," and "The Intervention Panic"—all before news of the Confederates' upper hand in the Seven Days Battles reached Europe.[13]

Southerners hoped and northerners feared that the Seven Days would greatly increase the chances of intervention. "We may [now] certainly count upon the recognition of our independence," wrote the Virginia fire-eater Edmund Ruffin. The *Richmond Dispatch* was equally certain that this "series of brilliant victories" would "settle the question" of recognition.[14] Under such headlines as "The Federal Disasters in Virginia—European Intervention the Probable Consequence," northern newspapers regardless of party affiliation warned that "we stand at the grave and serious crisis of our history. The recent intimations from Europe look to speedy intervention in our affairs."[15]

Although perhaps not so critical as this rhetoric might suggest, the matter was indeed serious. "Let us hope that the North will listen at last to the voice of reason, and that it will accept mediation before Europe has recognized the Confederacy," declared the *Paris Constitutional.* On July 16 Napoleon III granted an interview to Confederate envoy John Slidell. The "accounts of the defeat of the Federal armies before Richmond," said the emperor, confirmed his opinion that the "reestablishment of the Union [is] impossible." Three days later Napoleon sent a telegram to his foreign minister, who was in London: "Ask the English government if it does not believe the time has come to recognize the South."[16]

The English seemed willing—many of them at least. The *Times* stated that if Britain could not "stop this effusion of blood by mediation, we ought to give our moral weight to our English kith and kin [i.e., southern whites], who have gallantly striven so long for their liberties against a mongrel race of plunderers and oppressors." The breakup of the United States, said the *Times* in August, would be good "riddance of a nightmare." The *London Morning Post,* semi-official voice of the Palmerston government, proclaimed bluntly in July that the Confederacy had "established its claim to be independent."[17]

Even pro-Union leaders in Britain sent dire warnings to their friends in the North. "The last news from your side has created regret among your friends and pleasure among your enemies," wrote John Bright to Sen. Charles Sumner of Massachusetts on July 12. "I do not lose faith in your cause, but I wish I had less reason to feel anxious about you." Richard Cobden likewise sounded an alarm with Sumner: "There is an all but unanimous belief that you cannot subject the South to the Union. . . . Even they who are your partisans & advocates *cannot* see their way to any such issue."[18]

From France Count Agénor-Etienne de Gasparin, who despite his title was a friend of the Union, wrote to Lincoln that only a resumption of northern military victories could stem the tide toward European recognition. Lincoln took this opportunity to reply with a letter expressing his determination to stay the course. Yet, he added in a tone of frustration, "it seems unreasonable that a series of successes, extending through half-a-year, and clearing more than a hundred thousand square miles of country, should help us to little, while a single half-defeat should hurt us so much."[19]

Unreasonable it may have been, but it was a fact. A pro-Confederate member of Parliament introduced a motion calling for the government to cooperate with France in offering mediation. Scheduled for debate on July 18, this motion seemed certain to pass. The mood at the American legation was one of despairing resignation. The current was "rising every hour and running harder against us than at any time since the *Trent* affair," reported Henry Adams.[20]

But in a dramatic moment, Prime Minister Palmerston temporarily stemmed the current. Seventy-seven years old and a veteran of more than half a century in British politics, Palmerston seemed to doze through parts of the interminable debate on the mediation motion. Sometime after midnight, however, he lumbered to his feet and in a crisp speech of a few minutes put an end to the debate and the motion (the sponsor withdrew it). Parliament should trust the cabinet's judgment to act at the right time, said Palmerston. That time would arrive when the Confederacy's independence was "firmly and permanently established." One or two more southern victories, he hinted, might do the job, but until then any premature action by Britain might risk rupture with the United States.[21]

This did not end the matter, though. James Mason wrote the following day that he still looked "speedily for intervention in *some form*." In Paris on July 25, Slidell declared himself "more hopeful than I have been at any time since my arrival in Europe."[22] The weight of both the British and French press still leaned strongly toward recognition. And just before he left England in August for a tour of the continent with Queen Victoria, Foreign Secretary Russell arranged with Palmerston for a cabinet meeting when he returned in October to discuss mediation and recognition.

During the next six weeks, prospects for the Confederacy seemed to grow ever brighter. Stonewall Jackson won another victory at Cedar Mountain on August 9. Lincoln and his new general in chief, Henry W. Halleck, decided, over McClellan's protest, to withdraw the Army of the Potomac from the Virginia peninsula southeast of Richmond to reinforce the newly created Army of Virginia under Maj. Gen. John Pope along the Rappahannock River. Lee determined to strike before most of these reinforcements could arrive. In a complicated set of maneuvers, he sent Jackson's corps on a long flanking march to get into Pope's rear, then reunited the army near the Manassas battlefield of the previous year. On August 29–30 the Army of Northern Virginia withstood a series of disjointed attacks by Pope and then counterattacked to win one of the most decisive victories of Lee's career. Lee decided to make this triumph a springboard for an invasion of Maryland to win that state for the Confederacy and perhaps to bring about a peace on previously Union soil. At the same time two Confederate armies were in Kentucky carrying out what appeared to be a successful invasion of that state as well. On September 4 the Army of Northern Virginia began crossing the Potomac River into Maryland.

The news of Second Manassas and of Lee's invasion accelerated the pace of intervention discussions in London and Paris. Benjamin Moran, secretary of the U.S. legation in London, reported that "the rebels here are elated beyond measure" by tidings of Lee's victory. He was disgusted by the "exultation of the British press. . . . I confess to losing my temper when I see my bleeding country wantonly insulted in her hour of disaster." Further word that Lee had invaded Maryland produced in Moran "a sense of mortification. . . . The effect of this news here is to make those who were our friends ashamed to own the fact. . . . The Union is regarded as hopelessly gone."[23] The French foreign secretary told the American minister in Paris that these events proved "the undertaking of conquering the South is impossible." The British chancellor of the exchequer, William Gladstone, said that it was "certain in the opinion of the whole world except one of the parties . . . that the South cannot be conquered. . . . It is our absolute duty to recognize . . . that Southern independence is established."[24]

Gladstone was not a new convert to this position. The real danger to Union interests came from the potential conversion of Palmerston. After Second Manassas he seemed ready to intervene in the American war. "The Federals got a very complete smashing," he wrote to Russell (who was still abroad with the queen), "and it seems not altogether unlikely that still greater disasters await them, and that even Washington or Baltimore might fall into the hands of the Confederates." If something like that happened, "would it not be time for us to consider whether . . . England and France might not address the contending parties and recommend an arrangement on the basis of separation?" Russell needed little persuasion. He concurred and added that if the North refused to accept mediation, "we ought our selves to recognize the Southern States as an independent State.[25]

On September 24 (before news of Antietam arrived in England) Palmerston informed Gladstone of the plan to hold a cabinet meeting on the subject when Russell returned in October. The proposal would be made to both sides: "an Armistice and Cessation of the Blockades with a View to Negotiation on the Basis of Separation," to be followed by diplomatic recognition of the Confederacy.[26] But Palmerston and Russell agreed to take no action "till we see a little more into the results of the Southern invasion. . . . If the Federals sustain a great defeat . . . [their] Cause will be manifestly hopeless . . . and the iron should be struck while it is hot. If, on the other hand, they should have the best of it, we may wait a while and see what may follow."[27]

Little more than a week later, the news of Antietam and of Lee's retreat to Virginia arrived in Europe. These reports came as "a bitter drought and a stunning blow" to friends of the Confederacy in Britain, wrote Secretary of the American legation Benjamin Moran. "They express as much chagrin as if they themselves had been defeated."[28]

The London *Times* certainly was stunned by the "exceedingly remarkable" outcome of Antietam. "An army demoralized by a succession of failures," in the words of a Confederate editorial, "has suddenly proved at least equal, and we may probably say superior, to an army elated with triumph and bent upon a continuation of its conquests." Calling Lee's invasion of Maryland "a failure," the normally pro-southern *Times* admitted that "the Confederates have suffered their first important check exactly at the period when they might have been thought most assured of victory."[29] Other British newspapers expressed similar sentiments. The Union victories at South Mountain (a preliminary battle three days before Antietam) and Antietam restored "our drooping credit here," reported U.S. minister Charles Francis Adams. Most Englishmen had expected the Confederates to capture Washington, and "the surprise" at their retreat "has been quite in proportion. . . . As a consequence, less and less appears to be thought of mediation and intervention."[30]

Adams's prognosis was correct. Palmerston backed away from the idea of intervention. The only favorable condition for mediation "would be the great success of the South against the North," he pointed out to Foreign Secretary Russell on October 2. "That state of things seemed ten days ago to be approaching," but with Antietam "its advance has been lately checked." Thus "the whole matter is full of difficulty," and nothing could be done until the situation became clearer. By October 22 it was apparent to Palmerston that Confederate defeats had ended any chance for successful mediation. "I am therefore inclined to change the opinion I wrote you when the Confederates seemed to be carrying all before them, and I am [convinced] . . . that we must continue merely to be lookers-on till the war shall have taken a more decided turn."[31]

It is quite true, as William Freehling has maintained, that Palmerston was skeptical about British intervention and that such involvement would not occur so long as he remained opposed to it.[32] But as the evidence makes clear, Palmerston was on the verge of committing himself to intervention when Lee invaded Maryland in September 1862. If that campaign had produced another Confederate victory, Palmerston would have joined with a majority of his cabinet and of Parliament in supporting an Anglo-French offer of mediation and recognition of the Confederacy. The carnage at Sharpsburg put an end to that prospect.

Russell and Gladstone, in addition to Napoleon of France, did not give up easily. The French asked Britain to join in a proposal for a six-month armistice in the American war during which the blockade would be lifted, cotton exports would be renewed, and peace negotiations would begin. France also approached Russia, which refused to take part in such an obviously pro-Confederate scheme. On November 12 the British cabinet also rejected it after two days of discussions in which Secretary for War Sir George Cornewall Lewis led the opposition to intervention. In a letter six days later to King Leopold of Belgium, who favored the Confederacy and supported intervention, Palmerston explained the reasons for Britain's refusal to act. "Some months ago," wrote Palmerston, when "the Confederates were gaining ground to the North of Washington, and events seemed to be in their favor," an "opportunity for making some communication" appeared imminent. But "the tide of war changed its course and the opportunity did not arrive."[33]

Most disappointed of all by this outcome was James Mason, who was left cooling his heels by the British refusal to recognize his own diplomatic status as well as that of his government. On the eve of the arrival in London of news about Antietam, Mason had been "much cheered and elated" by initial reports of Lee's invasion. The Earl of Shaftesbury, Prime Minister Palmerston's son-in-law, had told Mason that "the event you so strongly desire," an offer of mediation and recognition, "is very close at hand." Antietam dashed these hopes and soured Mason on the "obdurate" British; he felt "that I should terminate the mission here."[34] He decided to stay on, but never again did his mission come so close to success as it had in September 1862.

Another result of Antietam with an important consequence abroad was Lincoln's issuance of his preliminary Emancipation Proclamation. During the war's first year, the North had professed to fight only for restoration of the Union. Even as late as August 1862, in his famous public letter to *New York Tribune* editor Horace Greeley, Lincoln had said that if he could save the Union without touching slavery he would do it. This position alienated many potential British friends of the Union cause. Since "the North does not proclaim abolition and never pretended to fight for anti-slavery," wrote one of them, "how can we be fairly called upon to sympathize so warmly with the Federal cause? . . . If they would ensure for their struggle the sympathies of Englishmen, they must abolish slavery."[35]

In his letter to Greeley, however, Lincoln had also said that if he could save the Union by freeing some or all of the slaves, he would do that too. In fact he had already decided to take this fateful step and had so informed his cabinet on July 22. Secretary of State Seward persuaded him to withhold the proclamation "until you can give it to the country supported by military success." Otherwise, in this time of northern despair over the military reverses in the Seven Days Battles and elsewhere, the world might view such an edict "as the last measure of an exhausted government, a cry for help . . . , our last *shriek,* on the retreat."[36]

The wait for a military victory to give the proclamation legitimacy and impetus proved to be a long and discouraging one. But Antietam brought the waiting to an end. Five days after the battle, Lincoln issued a proclamation warning Confederate states that unless they returned to the Union by January 1, 1863, their slaves "shall be then, thenceforward, and forever free."[37] Europeans responded to this preliminary proclamation with some skepticism. But when January 1 came and Lincoln fulfilled his promise, a historic shift in European—especially British—opinion took place. "The Emancipation Proclamation has done more for us here than all our former victories and all our diplomacy," wrote Henry Adams from London. "It is creating an almost convulsive reaction in our favor all over this country." Huge mass meetings in every part of Britain—some fifty of them in all—adopted pro-Union resolutions.[38] The largest of these meetings, at Exeter Hall in London, "has had a powerful effect on our newspapers and politicians," wrote Richard Cobden, one of the most pro-Union members of Parliament. "It has closed the mouths of those who have been advocating the side of the South. Recognition of the South, by England, whilst it bases itself on Negro slavery, is an impossibility." Similar reports came from elsewhere in Europe. "The anti-slavery position of the government is at length giving us a substantial foothold in European circles," wrote the U.S. minister to the Netherlands. "Everyone can understand the significance of a war where emancipation is written on one banner and slavery on the other."[39]

Antietam was unquestionably the most important battle of the Civil War in its influence on foreign relations. Never again did Britain and France come so close to intervention; never again did the Confederacy come so close to recognition by foreign governments. In the Revolution the battle of Saratoga brought French intervention, which was the key to ultimate American victory; in the Civil War Antietam turned out to be the Saratoga that failed.

NOTES

1. Quoted in Brian Jenkins, *Britain and the War for the Union,* 2 vols. (Montreal: McGill-Queen's University Press, 1974), 1:104.

2. *Richmond Enquirer,* June 6, 18, 1862; Judah Benjamin to James Mason, Apr.12, July 19, 1862, in Virginia Mason, *The Public Life and Diplomatic Correspondence of James M. Mason* (New York: Neale, 1906), 294, 303.

3. Quoted in Henry Donaldson Jordan and Edwin J. Pratt, *Europe and the American Civil War* (Boston: Houston Mifflin, 1931), 17.

4. Henry Adams to Henry Raymond, Jan. 24, 1862, in *The Letters of Henry Adams,* vol. 1, *1858–1868,* ed. J. C. Levenson (Cambridge, Mass.: Belknap, 1982), 272; *New York Tribune,* Feb. 11, 1862.

5. Mason to Robert M. T. Hunter, Mar. 11, 1862, in Mason, *Public Life and Diplomatic Correspondence,* 266; Charles Francis Adams to William H. Seward, Mar. 13, 1862, *Papers Relating to the Foreign Affairs of the United States, 1862,* pt. 1 (Washington, D.C.: Government Printing Office, 1863), 48; Henry Adams to Charles Francis Adams Jr., Mar. 15, 1862, in Levenson, *Letters of Henry Adams,* 284–85.

6. *Times* (London), Mar. 31, 1862; William L. Dayton to Seward, Apr. 17, 1862, *Papers Relating to Foreign Affairs,* 333.

7. Henry Adams to Charles Francis Adams Jr., May 16, 1862, in Levenson, *Letters of Henry Adams,* 297–98; Mason to Jefferson Davis, May 16, in Mason, *Public Life and Diplomatic Correspondence,* 276.

8. Mason to Lord John Russell, Aug. 2, 1862, and Russell to Mason, Aug. 2, 1862, in Mason, *Public Life and Diplomatic Correspondence,* 327–29; Palmerston to Austen H. Layard, June 19, 1862, in Hubert Du Brulle, "'A War of Wonders': The Battle in Britain over Americanization and the American Civil War" (Ph.D. diss., University of California at Santa Barbara, 1999), 210n.

9. Charles Francis Adams to Seward, June 26, Mar. 13, 1862, *Papers Relating to Foreign Affairs,* 118, 148.

10. *Paris Constitutionnel,* June 7, 1862.

11. *Times* (London), June 23, 1862.

12. Dayton to Seward, June 12, 1862, *Papers Relating to Foreign Affairs,* 349–50.

13. *Richmond Dispatch,* June 16, 1862; *New York Times,* July 10, 11, 12, 1862.

14. *The Diary of Edmund Ruffin,* ed. William Kauffman Scarborough, 3 vols. (Baton Rouge:

Louisiana State University Press, 1972–1989), 2:360 (June 30, 1862); *Richmond Dispatch,* July 4, 1862.

15. *New York Hearld,* July 9, 1862; *New York Evening Post,* quoted in *Richmond Dispatch,* July 15, 1862.

16. *Paris Constitutionnel,* July 19, 1862; Lynn M. Case and Warren F. Spencer, *The United States and France: Civil War Diplomacy* (Philadelphia: University of Pennsylvania Press, 1970), 300–307.

17. *Times* (London), July 17, Aug. 15, 1862; *London Morning Post,* quoted in *New York Tribune,* July 30, 1865.

18. John Bright to Charles Sumner, July 12, 1862, and Richard Cobden to Sumner, July 11, 1862, quoted in James Ford Rhodes, *History of the United States from the Compromise of 1850 to the McKinley-Bryan Campaign of 1896,* 8 vols. (New York: Macmillan, 1920), 4:85n.

19. Agénor-Etienne de Gasparin to Abraham Lincoln, July 18, 1862, and Lincoln to de Gasparin, Aug. 4, 1862, in *The Collected Works of Abraham Lincoln,* ed. Roy P. Basler et al., 9 vols. (New Brunswick, N.J.: Rutgers University Press, 1953–55), 5:355–56.

20. Henry Adams to Charles Francis Adams Jr., July 19, 1862, in *A Cycle of Adams Letters, 1861–1865,* ed. Worthington Chauncey Ford, 2 vols. (Boston: Houghton Mifflin, 1920), 1:166.

21. Ephraim Douglass Adams, *Great Britain and the American Civil War,* 2 vols. (New York: Longmans, Green, 1925), 2:20–23; Howard Jones, *Union in Peril: The Crisis over British Intervention in the Civil War* (Chapel Hill: University of North Carolina Press, 1992), 136.

22. Mason to his wife, July 20, 1862, in Mason, *Public Life and Diplomatic Correspondence,* 281; John Slidell to Benjamin, July 25, 1862, quoted in Case and Spencer, *United States and France,* 310.

23. *The Journal of Benjamin Moran,* ed. Sarah Agnes Wallace and Frances Elma Gillespie, 2 vols. (Chicago: University of Chicago Press, 1948–49), 2:1071–73 (Sept. 13, 15, 17, 20, 1862).

24. Dayton to Seward, Sept. 17, 1862, quoted in Howard Jones, *Abraham Lincoln and a New Birth of Freedom: The Union and Slavery in the Diplomacy of the Civil War* (Lincoln: University of Nebraska Press, 1999), 98; William Gladstone to Lord John Russell, Aug. 30, 1862, and Gladstone to William Stuart, Sept. 8, 1862, Gladstone Letterbook, quoted in ibid., 93.

25. This exchange is conveniently reprinted in James V. Murfin, *The Gleam of Bayonets: The Battle of Antietam and Robert E. Lee's Maryland Campaign, September 1862* (Baton Rouge: Louisiana State University Press, 1965), 394, 396–97.

26. Viscount Palmerston to Gladstone, Sept. 24, 1862, in *Gladstone and Palmerston, Being the Correspondence of Lord Palmerston with Mr. Gladstone, 1861–1865,* ed. Phillip Guedalla (Covent Garden, 1928), 232–33.

27. Russell to Henry R. C. Wellesley, Earl of Cowley [the British ambassador to France], Sept. 26, 1862, in Frank Merli and Theodore A. Wilson, "The British Cabinet and the Confederacy: Autumn, 1862," *Maryland Historical Magazine* 65 (1970): 247n; Palmerston to Russell, Sept. 23, 1862, in Murfin, *Gleam of Bayonets,* 400; Palmerston to Gladstone, Sept. 24, 1862, in Guedalla, *Gladstone and Palmerston,* 233.

28. Wallace and Gillespie, *Journal of Benjamin Moran,* 2:1075 (Sept. 27, 1862). The reports referred to here were of the battles at Turner's Gap and Crampton's Gap on September 14.

29. *Times* (London), Oct. 2, 1862.

30. Charles Francis Adams to Charles Francis Adams Jr., Oct. 17, 1862, in Ford, *Cycle of Adams Letters,* 1:192; Charles Francis Adams to Seward, Oct. 3, 1862, *Papers Relating to Foreign Affairs,* 205.

31. Adams, *Great Britain and the American Civil War,* 2:43–44, 54–55, reprints these two letters.

32. William W. Freehling, *The South vs. the South: How Anti-Confederate Southerners Shaped the Course of the Civil War* (New York: Oxford University Press, 2001).

33. Palmerston to King Leopold, Nov. 18, 1862, quoted in Merli and Wilson, "British Cabinet and the Confederacy," 261.

34. Slidell to Mason, Oct. 2, 1862, enclosing parts of a letter from the Earl of Shaftsbury, quoted in Charles M. Hubbard, *The Failure of Confederate Diplomacy* (Knoxville: University of Tennessee Press, 1998), 117; Mason to Benjamin, Sept. 18, 1862, Mason to his son, Oct. 1, 1862, and Mason to Benjamin, Nov. 7, 1862, in Mason, *Public Life and Diplomatic Correspondence,* 338, 342, 353–54.

35. Lincoln to Horace Greeley, Aug. 22, 1862, in Basler et al., *Collected Works of Abraham Lincoln,* 5:388–89; *Saturday Review,* Sept. 14, 1861, quoted in Adams, *Great Britain and the American Civil War,* 2:181. See also *Economist,* Sept. 1861, quoted in Karl Marx and Friedrich Engels, *The Civil War in the United States,* ed. Richard Enmale (New York: International Publishers, 1937), 12; *Reynolds Weekly Newspaper,* Summer 1861, quoted in G. D. Lillibridge, *Beacon of Freedom: The Impact of American Democracy upon Great Britain, 1830–1870* (Philadelphia: University of Pennsylvania Press, 1955), 115.

36. Basler et al., *Collected Works of Abraham Lincoln,* 5:336–37; Francis B. Carpenter, *Six Months at the White House with Abraham Lincoln* (New York: Hurd and Houghton, 1866), 20–22.

37. Basler et al., *Collected Works of Abraham Lincoln,* 5:434.

38. Henry Adams to Charles Francis Adams Jr., Jan. 23, 1862, in Levenson, *Letters of Henry Adams,* 327; Wallace and Gillespie, *Journal of Benjamin Moran,* 2:1107, 1110, 1115, 1161.

39. Cobden to Sumner, Feb. 13, 1863, in *Europe Looks at the Civil War,* ed. Belle Becker Sideman and Lillian Friedman (New York: Orion, 1960), 222; James Shepherd Pike to Seward, Dec. 31, 1862, quoted in Dean B. Mahin, *One War at a Time: The International Dimensions of the American Civil War* (Washington, D.C.: Brassey's, 1999), 139.

"Witness the Redemption of the Army": Reenlistments in the Confederate Army of Tennessee, January–March 1864

KEITH S. BOHANNON

IN THE SPRING OF 1864, THE THREE-YEAR TERMS OF ENLISTMENT of many soldiers in the Confederate army were set to expire. The question of whether these troops would reenlist voluntarily caused much anxiety in the army and on the southern home front. Although the Confederate Congress passed legislation extending all enlistments for the duration of the war, many army units adopted resolutions prior to the passage of the new law pledging to serve "for the war." These public resolutions, according to historian Gary Gallagher, "ranked among the most dramatic and effective methods of sending a message" from the armies to southern civilians.[1]

Several historians have briefly examined the spring 1864 Confederate army reenlistments. In *Soldiering in the Army of Tennessee,* Larry Daniel quotes soldiers' letters and diaries in his treatment of the subject but offers no substantial analysis of the resolutions published in southern newspapers. Daniel also does not examine closely the reasons why veterans reenlisted. The majority of soldiers reenlisted, he concludes, "simply because they knew the war effort could not continue without them." In his study of the Army of Northern Virginia, J. Tracy Power claims that many soldiers reenlisted out of a sense of patriotism or duty but that some "renewed their terms to avoid criticism from their comrades or the folks at home." Although Power argues that some units "were strongly encouraged, or even forced, to 'voluntarily' renew their enlistments," he quotes only a single source to support this statement. Power, like Daniel, uses primarily letters and diaries to draw his conclusions.[2]

The mass reenlistments in the winter camps of the Confederate Army of Tennessee around Dalton, Georgia, beginning in January 1864 took place only weeks after the army had suffered humiliating defeats in the battles of Lookout Mountain and Missionary Ridge in late November 1863. In the latter engagement victorious Union troops routed a large portion of the southern army, capturing large numbers of prisoners and a staggering forty cannon and sixty-nine limbers and caissons. In the wake of these disasters, many Confederate veterans grew sensitive to reports such as that in a Montgomery newspaper stating that the Army of Tennessee "was so demoralized and reduced by desertion" that it would "be whipped in the next fight."[3]

Dozens of infantry regiments and artillery batteries responded by passing resolutions to reenlist for the duration of the war, demonstrating their continued devotion to the cause of southern independence and nationhood. The resolutions provide revealing commentary from battle-hardened veterans as to why they chose to remain in the ranks: to liberate their homes, to avoid "subjugation" and defend slavery, and to uphold personal honor and the reputation of their units and commanders. While they represent the opinion of many if not the majority of men in the ranks, some private letters and diaries reveal far more ambivalence toward voluntary reenlistment. Some men, particularly those who had joined up in the spring of 1862 to avoid Confederate or state conscription and those who had actually been drafted, remained in the army in part out of fear of punishment at the hands of authorities. When these soldiers reenlisted, they did so to avoid conscription and to possibly obtain a furlough to see their families and homes.

Committees composed of both officers and enlisted men wrote most of the unit resolutions that appeared in southern newspapers. Several such documents reveal a desire to inspire civilian readers. Most soldiers undoubtedly felt like those in Capt. James P. Douglas's Texas Battery, who hoped that their actions would "kindle anew, as from ashes, those fires of patriotism which burned so intensely in the heart of the people . . . during the first few months of this revolution."[4]

The 154th Senior Regiment Tennessee Volunteers is usually ascribed the honor of being the first regiment in the Army of Tennessee to reenlist for the war at Dalton. On January 14, 1864, the men in the 154th held a meeting and formed a committee consisting of one man from each company to draft resolutions expressing the regiment's desires. These stated that the "present exigencies of service render it extremely precarious" to withdraw veteran troops from the army, that the duty of every true man was to participate in the "holy and sacred" struggle "until freedom is won." Thus the 154th's members tendered their services to the Confederacy as long as it needed them.[5]

Over the course of the next eleven days, additional regiments and brigades of Tennesseeans adopted similar declarations. When Gen. Marcus Wright's brigade reenlisted on January 25, its decision nearly completed the enrollment of Maj. Gen. Benjamin F. Cheatham's old all-Tennessee division. The actions of these men inspired troops from other states to emulate their example. Floridian Roderick G. Shaw wrote his sister on January 28 that "the re-enlisting fever is up in our Army," noting that "Tennessee has proven herself to be forward in this most important move." When a member of the 24th Alabama reported his unit's reenlistment to the press, he began by mentioning the resolutions of the Tennessee regiments. "Their action was indeed praiseworthy," he stated, "and justly entitles them to a nation's gratitude."[6]

By the second week of March 1864, evidence suggests that the majority of men in the Army of Tennessee had renewed their service for the duration of the war. In Lt. Gen. William J. Hardee's corps, which comprised half of the army at the time, 79.3 percent of the men had reenlisted by March 10. The highest rates within Hardee's corps were in Cheatham's and Maj. Gen. Patrick R. Cleburne's divisions (88.2 percent and 84.5 percent respectively). Not surprisingly the units that reenlisted first included primarily men who had volunteered for service early in the war.[7]

The Army of Tennessee's high command encouraged the veterans by promising furloughs at the rate of one for every ten men present for duty in those regiments that signed on for the war. Reenlistments, noted a subsequent order, "shall be indicated either by an oath, signing a paper, or some other equivalent act." The furloughs continued until April 3, 1864, when the start of the spring campaign seemed imminent.[8]

The final reenlistments in the army may have been prompted by a threat to take away the furlough system. On March 17 Robert Magill of the 39th Georgia noted in his diary, "Congress passed an act requiring all persons not reenlisted by the 20th to be held during the war under their present organizations, without having the benefit of furlough system." Magill decided that since he did not expect to get out of the army until he either was killed or decided to "go out on my own hook," he reenlisted to try his luck at drawing a furlough.[9]

Similar rationalizations might have motivated other soldiers who served in units like Magill's, which had been organized in the spring of 1862 by men who wished to avoid conscription or who actually entered the army as conscripts.

On March 15, 1864, Joseph Espey of the desertion-plagued 65th Georgia wrote home that reenlistments were "going on but not very fast in our regt." The next day, possibly after the men heard about the furlough-system restrictions after March 20, a diarist in the 65th claimed that "nearly all" of the regiment had reenlisted for the war.[10]

Some officers apparently used alcohol as both an incentive to reenlist and a reward for doing so. In the 18th Alabama men listened to orators who "urged and begged" them to renew their commitment while the soldiers helped themselves to a "barrel of mean whiskey." "After the men were well-drunken," Brig. Gen. Henry D. Clayton called on all those willing to reenlist to march forward. When the soldiers ran forward with a yell, only three of the 18th Alabama remained behind. In Gen. Arthur M. Manigault's brigade, an officer in the 28th Alabama noted that after the men signed up, a wagon stopped in the center of their formation "with a barell of good old whiskey," and "very near all of the men got very near tight."[11]

While published resolutions suggest that most units unanimously reenlisted in a single meeting, such was not always the case. Capt. C. Irvine Walker recorded on January 31 that within Manigault's brigade, "three fourth[s] of the 10th and 19th SC Regts" had stayed on, "more than half" of the 24th Alabama, and "all the 28th Ala., save about 30 men." In the brigade's final regiment, the 34th Alabama, only about half of the men agreed to serve for the duration of the war. Capt. Thomas B. Hampton in the 63rd Virginia wrote home on February 14 that "some of the bravest of our men" are reenlisting, "but the majority hangs back." Artillerist George Grammer noted that his battalion commander "made a few remarks urging . . . the necessity of reenlisting" on January 19 and that two days later nearly all of two batteries had done so. Such was not the case in Grammer's unit, where men reenlisted in small groups over the course of several weeks.[12]

The appointment of Gen. Joseph E. Johnston to command of the Army of Tennessee in mid-December 1863 had a positive effect on morale and was undoubtedly a factor in encouraging reenlistment. Johnston's reputation, his impressive personal appearance, and his efforts to improve physical conditions in the army earned him plaudits from many in the rank and file. Commissary Sgt. Dempsey C. Neal of the 51st Tennessee wrote in his diary on January 20 that Johnston rode through the camps and that "all have the utmost confidence in thare Genl." The resolutions adopted by several units specifically mention their confidence in Johnston. Soldiers in the 16th Tennessee described him as "a commander of vigorous intellect . . . , a strategist of consumate tact and prudence," and "an incorruptable patriot."[13]

The reenlistment resolutions express several common themes. Many regiments, particularly those raised from Tennessee and portions of other states occupied by Union troops, desired to drive the "vandal invaders" from southern soil and liberate their homes and loved ones. Soldiers in the 29th Mississippi pledged never to lay down their arms until their homes and those of their friends "were freed from the polluted occupancy of their now vandal possessors." The men of the 7th Florida despised the "minions of a despotic government" who had laid waste to cities, towns, and villages; imprisoned citizens; and "violently wrested" property from families, leaving wives, mothers, and sisters suffering. When Lt. Col. Christopher C. McKinney ordered the 8th Tennessee Infantry into line to ask the men to reenlist, he exclaimed that the Yankees had been stimulated to fight "by the promise of . . . booty, in the way of confiscated Southern estates." He also reminded his men of reports that black troops garrisoned the Middle Tennessee towns of Shelbyville and Columbia.[14]

Resolutions repeatedly linked Confederate defeat and surrender with the subjugation of white southerners. Confederates fought to show "the country and the world, their right and determination to be freemen," claimed the soldiers in Gen. Otto Strahl's brigade. The men in the 22nd Alabama would never entertain the idea of "base submission" to those who would degrade them "beneath the level of slavery." Soldiers in the 42nd Alabama referred to white southerners as a "respectable minority" who had been "disregarded, insulted and ordered to subserve the purposes and designs of the wicked and Abolitionist majority." When Brig. Gen. States Rights Gist addressed the 46th Georgia on March 19 "he exhorted them to show, by reenlisting, that they did not desire peace so long as the presence of a foe on Southern soil threatened us with chains and slavery."[15]

Some resolutions tied the maintenance of white freedom to the defense of slavery against an "Abolition invasion" of the South. The "vandal hordes" have "armed our slaves," exclaimed the men of the 1st Tennessee Infantry, and "exalted them above their former lords and masters." The resolutions of the 32nd and 45th Mississippi Infantry claimed that the "nefarious purposes" of the foe included the "subjugation, annihilation and eternal degradation of the white race of the South." "They have armed our slaves for our destruction," declared the Mississippians, and are "training them as an instrument for holding our necks more securely under the accursed foot of the detestable tyrant in Washington."[16]

References to personal honor, the sacrifices of fallen comrades, and the record of a unit's service all appear frequently in resolutions. Soldiers in the 5th and 13th Arkansas claimed that abandoning the "glorious cause of constitutional liberty and Southern independence" would "be an act of cowardice beneath the manhood" of men from their state. The resolutions of the 4th Tennessee state that the deaths of the regiment's colonel and "many others of our proud old regiment, call loudly on us to avenge their murders." Veterans in the 47th Tennessee assured readers that the regiment's survivors were "still fired with the same patriotic zeal and fearless devotion" displayed at Shiloh, Perryville, Murfreesboro, Chickamauga, and Missionary Ridge.[17]

Blackened and tattered regimental flags, powerful symbols of Confederate nationalism, appeared in many reenlistment ceremonies. When speaking to his brigade, General Strahl appealed to the men not to forsake their "time-honored colors." Lieutenant Colonel McKinney asked the soldiers in the 8th Tennessee whether they would reenlist or if they would rather "see that battle-flag go down, which, had been proudly upheld over so many bloody fields."[18] General Clayton used flags in a fashion employed by many regimental and brigade commanders. On January 22 he addressed his brigade and planted the flags of the 32nd and 58th Alabama in front of the lines. He then called upon those who would reenlist for the war to rally on the colors. A member of the brigade claimed that the subsequent forward rush by the men "was worthy of Alabamians and the sacred cause in which we are engaged."[19]

The intense loyalty some soldiers felt toward their general officers also inspired reenlistment. Resolutions from Tennessee regiments refer to their "well tried chieftan" General Cheatham, requesting that his old division be reconstituted since it had been broken apart by Gen. Braxton Bragg. When Johnston agreed to give "Old Frank" command of his old division, one Tennesseean noted that the soldiers from the Volunteer State "were again happy and contented." Patrick Cleburne also elicited deep devotion. Although many of his Texans and Arkansans longed to serve closer to home, a temptation some of them could not resist, their loyalty to the talented division commander helped keep the majority of them in the ranks. Capt. George B. Blakemore, a staff officer assigned to one of Cleburne's brigade commanders, noted on February 9 that "the great portion of the Division had reenlisted." He added, "The troops are as much devoted to General Cleburne as Stonewall Jackson's men were to him."[20]

The resolutions passed by Cleburne's regiments and dozens of others in the Army of Tennessee elicited widespread praise from army and government officials. Johnston issued general orders to the army on January 17 praising the reenlistments of the 13th and 154th Tennessee and of Strahl's brigade, noting that their examples were "worthy of being followed by all who love their home and country." Jefferson Davis and the Confederate Congress also lauded these and other units in letters and joint resolutions read to the troops and published in newspapers across the South. In Virginia the Tennessee regiments serving in Lee's army emulated the actions of their brothers in Johnston's command by reenlisting for the war.[21]

Newspaper editors commented at length on the reenlistments in an effort to boost the morale of southerners. The editor of the *Montgomery Weekly Advertiser,* quoting from a piece in the *Huntsville Confederate,* instructed readers not to worry about the fighting condition of the Army of Tennessee. Civilians should instead "render thanks to Almighty God that they have still between them and danger, a living wall of stout hearts and strong arms, animated by the proud spirit of freemen." The editor of the *Mobile Advertiser and Register* drew a direct comparison between the actions of units in the Army of Tennessee and mass meetings in "the old political times." In both instances, he explained, "the minds of the people were being prepared by speeches and resolutions." He concluded, "The soldiers assure us that we need not fear, and we do not fear."[22]

The published resolutions and the accolades offered by President Davis, General Johnston, the Confederate Congress, and newspaper editors give the impression of an army unified in its desire to continue the war. While there was a great deal of truth in this, letters and diaries reveal a more complex portrait of army morale and the attitudes of soldiers toward reenlistment. Despite the efforts of Johnston and his subordinates to quell desertions at Dalton, the problem plagued the army throughout its stay in winter quarters. Johnston admitted in a letter to Davis written January 23, 1864, the same time as the general orders praising reenlistment, that desertion was "becoming more frequent." The general blamed the problem in large part on the inclination of many infantrymen to join the cavalry commands of Nathan Bedford Forrest and John Hunt Morgan, but he admitted that some probably ran away "to avoid the revolunteering which is going on in several divisions."[23]

Some soldiers noticed the slowness of troops from certain states to reenlist for the war. Tennesseean Robert D. Jamison told his wife that men from Alabama and Georgia were reluctant because "the people at home in these states are whipped and write discouraging letters to their friends in the army." Robert McFadden of the 2nd Arkansas Infantry chided the 24th South Carolina and some

Georgia regiments for "not being as lively as ours" to reenlist. "I wish we had some of them in our Brigade," he wrote, "we would manage to arouse them."[24]

The attitudes of several privates exemplify the ambivalent feelings of many of their comrades toward "revolunteering." Bolton Thurmond of the 34th Georgia wrote his sweetheart on March 21 that, although he had reenlisted, it "was very much against my will." He justified his action by saying that nearly everyone else in his company and regiment had already reenlisted, and he did not want to "be by myself." Thurmond remarked that if he had not signed on, he "would hav been conscripted any how and I came in the war as a voluntteer and I want to go out the same."[25] Grant Taylor of the 40th Alabama told his wife on February 9 much the same. Although he was opposed to reenlistment "and am still so . . . , I know I am into it for the war or lifetime." The chance of getting a furlough at some point prior to the spring campaign also motivated Taylor to reenlist, as it did many other desperately homesick soldiers. Mississippian William B. Honnoll told his sister on March 5 that "it seems like there is no chance to get out of the war." His company of the 24th Mississippi had not yet reenlisted, but he acknowledged that they would have to. Despite their reluctance to volunteer, neither Thurmond, Taylor, nor Honnoll suggested that they seriously considered deserting, the only real option to reenlistment or conscription.[26]

Some soldiers privately resented the system of furloughing instituted by Johnston to entice the veterans. Roderick Shaw told his sister on January 28 that though "the re-enlisting fever is up" in the army, none of the Floridians had "made a good start in that direction." "They all want furloughs *now,*" he commented, adding that "they are willing to be kept in service under the Conscription Act rather than go home when they have reenlisted to a man." Pvt. Hezekiah Rabb of the 33rd Alabama felt like many of Shaw's Floridians. Rabb told his wife on February 18 that he was "provoked with the way I have been treated about a furlough." "To think that I have been in the service nearly two years," he continued, "& now they don't want to give me a furlough except [if] I reenlist."[27]

Most soldiers associated reenlistment with the right to reorganize their units also by electing new officers. In December 1861 the Confederate Congress granted troops reenlisting in the Provisional Army the right to vote on their field officers. (Any vacancies afterward would be filled by promotion.) Such elections had been held in the spring of 1862, resulting in the permanent displacement of many unpopular officers. Over the course of several weeks in the winter of 1864, the issues of reorganization and the election of officers were points of heated discussion in the Army of Tennessee, pitting the opinions of generals against those of large numbers of enlisted men.[28]

Twenty-seven of the army's highest-ranking officers (including Lieutenant General Hardee; Major Generals Carter Stevenson, Cheatham, John C. Breckinridge, Cleburne, and Thomas C. Hindman; and twenty-one brigadier generals) made their position on these issues clear in a memorial submitted to the Confederate Congress on December 17, 1863. "In our opinion, it is essential to retain, for the term of during the war, without reorganization, the troops now in service," they advised. The generals also called for placing all white men between fifteen and eighteen and fifty and sixty years of age in military service; the prohibition of any further exemptions, substitutions, or discharges of able-bodied men from service; and the placement of "able-bodied negroes and mulattoes, bond and free," in the army as cooks, laborers, teamsters, and hospital attendants. Enacting these measures as laws, they assured, would "make our armies invincible at the opening of the campaign of next year."[29]

The generals' recommendations elicited harsh criticism from the ranks. Within weeks some enlisted soldiers had sent the document and letters of their own to Congress, "insisting upon securing to the men the right of making a new election of officers, as an indispensable condition of the reorganization of the army for the next active campaign." Others vented their opinions in private correspondence. Floridian Washington Ives claimed that the memorial "might have been dispensed with, as it naturally looks as if our generals were afraid of something." Edward N. Brown of the 45th Alabama told his wife on January 3 that he was "more despondent lately than ever" due to the generals' proposition. "The proposition yet has the garb of secrecy," he wrote, "but it will come to light soon." "Sabine," the pseudonym of a soldier writing to the *Memphis Appeal,* claimed that the generals exaggerated the "disaffection and dejection . . . existing in the ranks" in order to make their case against allowing the enlisted men to elect their officers. What did the "high memorialists fear?" he asked.[30]

The accusations that those who signed the memorial were afraid of something seem unfounded. The generals were not concerned about their own positions since several of them were extremely popular with their men. Although they did not justify their stance on reorganization, they undoubtedly felt that reelections would be detrimental to the army's discipline and morale. Instead the generals probably felt that the selection of regimental officers should be based solely on competence and decided by regularly constituted boards of examination.[31]

Nearly all the reenlistment resolutions that appeared in southern newspapers requested that the soldiers, as volunteers, be allowed the right of reorganization. Several men warned that the failure of the Confederate Congress to abide by these requests could have serious consequences. Joel T. Haley of the 37th Georgia told a friend on January 30 that the "impression prevails that a reorganization will not be allowed." He claimed that "the soldiers demand the privilege as an attribute of a volunteer, and unless it be granted, there will be a great deal of discontent." The resolutions adopted by Company H, 40th Alabama Infantry, asserted that "if the men were only assured that they would be allowed to reorganize, this army would almost unanimously reenlist." The Alabamians stated that it would be a "disastrous blunder on the part of Congress to refuse the men this right."[32] Perhaps the most ominous accusation was that the failure to allow reorganizations would result in a demoralized army during the spring campaign. One soldier correspondent addressed readers of the *Memphis Appeal* by asking, "Is it wise to set our army in battle with purposes crossed, and their cherished hopes defeated?" The editor of the *Appeal* responded several days later when he claimed that the refusal of Congress to allow enlisted men to select their own officers "will have a most depressing effect," while according them the privilege would impart patriotic zeal and devotion "more than equivalent to many thousand new recruits added to the ranks."[33]

Soldiers saw the election of new officers as an exercise of the right to self-government that they had enjoyed as civilians. This right had been "received at the hands of our ancestors as a revolutionary patrimony," proclaimed one correspondent. The resolutions adopted by Gen. Edward C. Walthall's Mississippi brigade stated that reorganization was the "acknowledged privilege of freemen." "Sabine" asked newspaper readers if the soldiers did "not constitute the body of the people when we are at home?" Did the generals who submitted the memorial to Congress "deem republicanism, which draws its breath in a ballot box, a myth?"[34]

A soldier using the pen name "Ike" admitted to *Memphis Appeal* readers that at the beginning of the war, soldiers had "not been capable of making the wisest choice in electing officers" due to a lack of experience in the field. Several years of hard campaigning had changed the men, and "Ike" felt that they were now competent to choose qualified officers. Another soldier elaborated on this point, arguing that "the trials we have seen our officers pass through, are far more scrutinizing and unerring in their developments of fitness and efficiency, than examining boards."[35]

The exercise of voting rights was not the only reason enlisted men desired reorganization. Many hoped to transfer to either artillery or cavalry units, organizations that foot soldiers perceived as enjoying lower casualty rates and less strenuous duty. When Capt. Thomas J. Key received a petition from a "large majority" of the 15th Arkansas Infantry to transfer to his battery, he took the request to Johnston. The general denied the transfer, remarking that "all his army would go into cavalry and batteries if it were allowed." Johnston also touched on this issue in correspondence with Jefferson Davis, requesting that the president deny the request of Kentuckians in the Orphan Brigade to acquire horses. "We want infantry," explained Johnston, "and all our infantry wish to be cavalry."[36]

Some men hoped that reorganization would allow them to vote out officers they did not like, sentiments that not surprisingly appear only in private correspondence. Mississippian Thomas J. Newberry said that most of the men in his regiment did not like the idea of reenlisting without reorganization since they thought there was "some trick in it" and "they dont like the officers." Sgt. Joseph T. Hutcheson of the 37th Georgia told his sister that few men in his regiment "are willing to remain under the command of Col. Rudler . . . while at the same time all are ready to reenlist in the same regiment provided the privilege of reelection is granted."[37]

An Arkansas soldier in Gen. Daniel C. Govan's brigade directed his ire not at field officers, but at the commissary and quartermaster officers whom he believed were not doing their jobs. A quarter of the men in Govan's command were barefooted and thinly clad, he wrote on January 15, 1864, and they frequently had to subsist on nothing but a "bare sufficiency" of bread for periods of twelve hours at a time. "The fault must be somewhere among the stars and bars," complained the soldier, who argued that reorganization would help get rid of incompetent and supernumerary officers.[38]

Little evidence suggests that general officers directly debated the issues of reelection or reorganization with their men. General Hindman touched on reelection in a speech he delivered in late January to Gen. J. Patton Anderson's Mississippi brigade. His "first class oration" discouraged the soldiers from supporting reelections, noting that it "was dangerous to tear down a house for reerection during a storm" and that "it was unadvisable to take the lock of a gun to pieces during a battle." Hindman's speech was probably exceptional, for few generals in the army wanted to address an issue they undoubtedly saw as being divisive and bad for morale.[39]

Despite the misgivings that soldiers had about their generals' memorial, the unit resolutions regarding reenlistment contain *requests* for the reelection of officers, not *demands.* The soldiers saw themselves as citizens in a democracy, and their resolutions clearly state that they would abide by the decisions of the Confederate Congress on the issue. Subsequent developments suggest they did just that.

On February 17, 1864, Congress passed an act stating that all men between the ages of eighteen and forty-five serving in the Confederate army "shall be retained, during the present war ... in the same regiments, battalions and companies to which they belong ... with the same organization and officers, unless regularly transferred or discharged, in accordance with the laws and regulations for the government of the army." This action ended the internal debate within the Army of Tennessee over the question of reorganization and the reelection of officers, judging from the absence of any subsequent comments on the issues in letters and diaries or in soldiers' correspondence with newspapers. The men accepted the decision of Congress and turned their attention to other matters, including preparation for the upcoming spring campaign. They clearly realized what historian David Potter has written about the survival of the state, that it may depend upon the government's power "to override divisive impulses and to control an aggregation of people, as if they were one, even despite a significant degree of reluctance on the part of some of those who are being thus united."[40]

The reenlistments that took place in the Army of Tennessee in the months of January through March 1864 suggest that the majority of men retained a high level of morale and confidence in their leadership. "There is some that are willing to give it up," admitted Mississippian Sam Settle on January 24, "but the majority are in favor of continuing the war for a while longer yet." Reenlistment was important to men who wished to retain the "proud character of volunteers" in the face of laws that would have branded them with the odious title of conscripts. "We are not here as dumb, driven cattle, unwilling slaves to the conscription," wrote a Texan in Douglas's Battery, but as "cheerful and hopeful soldiers."[41]

The pageantry and oratory surrounding the reenlistment meetings elicited strong emotions. An orderly in the 37th Georgia saw "brave men, battle worn and bullet-scarred, weep as children" as they listened to the appeal of Maj. Gen. William Bate to reenlist. A member of Govan's brigade remembered years later a spontaneous reenlistment meeting in Cleburne's division. Some soldiers "grasped each other's hands," he recalled, while others laughed, cried, and shouted "Hurrah for Jeff Davis." Staff officer Walker Anderson expressed the feelings of many men when he wrote that the reenlistment of his old brigade was "a glorious action, and makes my heart swell with pride and fills me with enthusiasm."[42]

Some soldiers saw reenlistment as not only a reaffirmation of their loyalty to the Confederacy but also a public statement to southern civilians and the enemy. The men of the 29th Mississippi "confidently believed that our army, if cheerfully made by its own election, an army of volunteers, would do more than all else to disconcert the enemy." C. Irvine Walker voiced similar sentiments, claiming that "the army is the life and soul of the Confederacy," and that if it rededicated itself, "the movement will be equal to victory and ensure a glorious spring campaign."[43]

The reenlistment resolutions are valuable in revealing why Confederate soldiers in the hard-luck Army of Tennessee remained in service during the months prior to the 1864 Atlanta campaign. The resolutions confirm the conclusions of James M. McPherson, who has argued that most Civil War soldiers "were intensely aware of the issues at stake and passionately concerned about them." Yet private correspondence shows a reluctance on the part of some men to reenlist voluntarily for the duration of the war. For many of these soldiers, the intimidation instilled by witnessing the executions of deserters was probably as important a factor in keeping them in the ranks as any loyalty to the Confederacy. Ongoing problems with desertion in the Army of Tennessee during the winter at Dalton and throughout the Atlanta campaign, as well as the poor performance of some units on the battlefield during the summer and fall of 1864, suggest that some soldiers did not share the same level of ideological commitment as the majority of their comrades.[44]

In the twilight of their lives, many veterans of the Army of Tennessee looked back on their reenlistments with pride. Veterans hotly debated the question of which unit was the first to reenlist. The pages of the *Confederate Veteran* magazine suggest that the survivors of the 154th Senior Regiment Tennessee Volunteers rightfully won the contest, citing as evidence Joe Johnston's General Order No. 10, dated January 17, 1864. In their musings on the subject, veterans made no mention of the reluctance of some comrades to reenlist or the problems of desertion that plagued the army. Instead many undoubtedly agreed with Philip D. Stephenson, who recalled the reenlistment of the soldiers at Dalton as "one of the most extraordinary and phenomenal manifestations of human spirit ever among men."[45]

NOTES

1. Accounts by several soldiers from the fall of 1863 suggest that the reenlistment question had been discussed during the siege of Chattanooga. See William L. Roberts Diary, Nov. 20, 1863, Alabama Room, Anniston, Ala., Public Library; John M. Coski, ed., "I Am in for Anything for Success," *North & South* 6 (2003): 79; and Gary W. Gallagher, *The Confederate War: How Popular Will, Nationalism, and Military Strategy Could Not Stave Off Defeat* (Cambridge, Mass.: Harvard University Press, 1997), 93. The author would like to thank the following individuals for assisting with this essay: Michael Musick, Kenneth Noe, James Ogden III, Richard Sommers, Zack Waters, and Lee White.

2. Larry Daniel, *Soldiering in the Army of Tennessee: A Portrait of Life in the Confederate Army* (Chapel Hill: University of North Carolina Press, 1991), 140; J. Tracy Power, *Lee's Miserables: Life in the Army of Northern Virginia from the Wilderness to Appomattox* (Chapel Hill: University of North Carolina Press, 1998), 3–4.

3. Peter Cozzens, *The Shipwreck of Their Hopes: The Battles for Chattanooga* (Urbana: University of Illinois Press, 1994), 389; "The Morale of the Army of Tennessee," *Montgomery Weekly Advertiser,* Jan. 29, 1864.

4. Texas, "Douglas' (Texas) Battery," *Memphis Appeal,* Jan. 21, 1864.

5. "A Voice from the Army," ibid., Jan. 18, 1864; Lambda Tau, "Letter from Dalton," ibid., Jan. 20, 1864.

6. "Wright's Brigade," ibid., Jan. 25, 1864; Roderick G. Shaw to sister, Jan. 28, 1864, Shaw Collection, Special Collections, Florida State University Library, Tallahassee (hereinafter cited as FSU); Soldier, "From the Army of Tennessee," *Mobile Daily Advertiser and Register,* Feb. 14, 1864.

7. The author found that by mid-February 1864 at least sixteen out of twenty-six infantry brigades and numerous additional regiments and artillery batteries had composed reenlistment resolutions or held ceremonies in which the men swore to reenlist at the expiration of their service. These incomplete figures come from resolutions printed in newspapers and statements made in letters and diaries. Some regiments undoubtedly endorsed declarations that the author did not locate, while other units might have reenlisted without adopting any formal resolutions. The majority of men in some regiments may have refused to reenlist and subsequently been conscripted, but the author found no evidence of this. "Thirty-Seventh Alabama," *Memphis Appeal,* Feb. 16, 1864; Cassius, "Re-enlistment," ibid., Feb. 5, 1864; "42d Alabama Volunteers," ibid., Feb. 20, 1864; U.S. War Department, *The War of the Rebellion: A Compilation of the Union and Confederate Armies,* 128 vols. (Washington D.C.: Government Printing Office, 1880–1901), ser. 1, 32(3):670 (hereinafter cited as *OR;* all references to ser. 1).

8. *OR,* 32(2):582, 630; General Orders No. 30, Apr. 3, 1864, "Johnston—Army of Tenn—General Orders 1863–1864," RG 109, War Dept. Coll. of Confederate Records, Records of the Army and Dept. of Tennessee, Dept. of Tennessee, Orders and Circulars, 1862–65, National Archives, Washington, D.C.

9. Robert M. Magill, *Personal Reminiscences of a Confederate Soldier Boy,* ed. Brenda D. Phillips (Repr., Milledgeville, Ga.: Boyd, 1993), 46.

10. Joseph S. Espey to family, Mar. 15, 1864, Joseph Espey Papers, Southern Historical Collection,

University of North Carolina, Chapel Hill; Diary of an unidentified member of Co. B, 65th Georgia Infantry, Mar. 16, 1864, Kennesaw Mountain National Battlefield Park Library (hereinafter cited as KEMO).

11. Edgar W. Jones, "History of the 18th Alabama Infantry Regiment," 18th Alabama Unit File, Chickamauga-Chattanooga National Military Park Library (hereinafter cited as CCNMP), typescript; M. A. Cameron to brother, Jan. 24, 1864, M. A. Cameron Letters, box 1548, Special Collections, University of Alabama Library, Tuscaloosa.

12. C. Irvine Walker to wife, Jan. 31, 1864, letter in private possession, transcript provided by Lee White, CCNMP; Thomas B. Hampton to wife, Feb. 14, 1864, Thomas B. Hampton Letters, Center for American History, University of Texas, Austin; George Grammer Diary, Jan. 19, 21, Mar. 6, 8, 20, 24, 25, 1864, Warren Light Artillery File, CCNMP. As late as February 21, John Crittenden noted that while thirty men in his company of the 34th Alabama had reenlisted, "the balance still stand out that they will be conscripted first." John Crittenden to wife, Feb. 21, 1864, John Crittenden Letters, Center for American History.

13. Albert Castel, *Decision in the West: The Atlanta Campaign of 1864* (Lawrence: University Press of Kansas, 1992), 31; Dempsey C. Neal Diary, Jan. 20, 1864, typescript in possession of author; "Sixteenth Tennessee Regiment," *Memphis Appeal,* Jan. 26, 1864. See also Daniel, *Soldiering in the Army of Tennessee,* 138–39.

14. "The 29th Mississippi," *Memphis Appeal,* Feb. 12, 1864; Robert Watson Diary, Feb. 8, 1864, 7th Florida File, CCNMP; Lambda Tau, "Letter from Dalton," *Memphis Appeal,* Jan. 20, 1864.

15. James McPherson has noted that Confederates frequently used the words "subjugated" and "enslaved" to describe the fate that white southerners would face if they lost the war. "Strahl's Brigade Volunteers for the War," *Memphis Appeal,* Jan. 19, 1864; "22d Alabama Regiment," ibid., Feb. 2, 1864; "42d Alabama Volunteers," ibid., Feb. 20, 1864; Willis P. Burt Reminiscences, Laura Burt Brantley Papers, Georgia Historical Society, Savannah; James M. McPherson, *What They Fought For, 1861–1865* (Baton Rouge: Louisiana State University Press, 1994), 12.

16. "Sixteenth Tennessee," *Memphis Appeal,* Jan. 26, 1864; "First Tennessee Regiment," ibid., Jan. 29, 1864; "32d and 45th Mississippi Regiments," ibid., Feb. 16, 1864.

17. "5th and 13th Arkansas Regiments," ibid., Jan. 31, 1864; "The 4th Confederate Tennessee Regiment," ibid., Mar. 1, 1864; Sampson, "Re-enlisting," ibid., Jan. 20, 1864.

18. "Strahl's Brigade," ibid., Jan. 20, 1864; Lamda Tau, "Letter from Dalton," ibid., Jan. 19, 1864.

19. Pedes, "The Re-enlistment of Clayton's Brigade," *Montgomery Weekly Advertiser,* Jan. 29, 1864.

20. "1st Tennessee Regiment," *Memphis Appeal,* Jan. 29, 1864; "The 4th Confederate Tennessee Regiment," ibid., Mar. 1, 1864; "6th and 9th Tennessee Regiments," ibid., Jan. 28, 1864; Christopher Losson, *Tennessee's Forgotten Warriors: Frank Cheatham and His Confederate Division* (Knoxville: University of Tennessee Press, 1989), 133, 135, 143; *Isaiah Harlan's Civil War Letters* (n.p., n.d.; transcript in possession of author), 53; George T. Blakemore letter, Jan. 23, 1864, MC-5 File, KEMO.

21. Johnston issued at least three subsequent general orders praising the reenlistment of specific units. *OR,* 32(2):571, 573, 574, 579, 665–67, 686, 735–36, 750, 754; "Confederate States Congress," *Memphis Appeal,* Feb. 1, 1864.

22. "The Morale of the Army of Tennessee," *Montgomery Weekly Advertiser,* Jan. 29, 1864; "The

Army," *Mobile Advertiser and Register,* Jan. 20, 1864. See also "Congress and the Re-enlisting Troops," *Richmond Sentinel,* republished in *Mobile Advertiser and Register,* Feb. 3, 1864; and "Continued Re-enlistments," *Memphis Appeal,* Jan. 27, 1864.

23. While little evidence exists regarding reenlistments in the Army of Tennessee's cavalry corps, a Union intelligence report dated February 8, 1864, claims that one southern cavalry regiment fired on another unit when it "refused to reenlist as ordered." *OR,* 32(2):353, 604.

24. The first Georgia unit in the Army of Tennessee to reenlist for the war was the 1st Georgia Sharpshooter Battalion, the adjutant of which reported the unit's action in a dispatch dated February 17. Henry D. Jamison, comp., *Letters and Recollections of a Confederate Soldier, 1861–1865* (Nashville, 1964), 88; Robert J. Stevens, *Captain Bill, Book Two* (Richburg, S.C.: Chester District Genealogical Society, 1985), 53; George H. Johnston to editor, *Savannah Republican,* Feb. 22, 1864.

25. Bolton Thurmond to Miss S. F. Porterfield, Mar. 21, 1864, Bolton Thurmond Letters (microfilm), Georgia Department of Archives and History, Atlanta.

26. Ann K. Blomquist and Robert A. Taylor, eds., *This Cruel War: The Civil War Letters of Grant and Malinda Taylor, 1862–1865* (Macon, Ga.: Mercer University Press, 2000), 222; W. B. Honnoll to sister, Mar. 5, 1864, Honnoll Family Papers, Special Collections, Emory University Library, Atlanta.

27. Roderick G. Shaw to sister, Jan. 28, 1864, Shaw Collection, FSU; Hezekiah Rabb to wife, Feb. 18, 1864, Michael P. Musick Collection, U.S. Army Military History Institute, Carlisle Barracks, Pa.

28. "Tenth Mississippi Regiment," *Memphis Appeal,* Jan. 26, 1864.

29. "Confederate States Congress," ibid., Jan. 4, 1864.

30. "Reorganization of the Army," *Augusta Weekly Chronicle and Sentinel,* Feb. 10, 1864; Washington Ives letter, Jan. 5, 1864, Washington Ives Papers, FSU; Edward N. Brown to wife, Jan. 3, 1864, Edward N. Brown Papers, Alabama Department of Archives and History, Montgomery; Sabine, "From the Army," *Memphis Appeal,* Jan. 18, 1864.

31. The memorial undoubtedly reflects in part the professional attitudes of old-army officers. Three of the thirteen known signers attended West Point and served in the antebellum U.S. Army, and one (Patrick Cleburne) had served in the British army.

32. Joel T. Haley to Enoch Faw, Jan. 30, 1864, Enoch Faw Letters (microfilm), Confederate Collection, Tennessee State Library and Archives, Nashville; "Reenlistment," *Memphis Appeal,* Feb. 5, 1864. See also One of the Arkansas Volunteers, "Govan's Brigade," ibid., Jan. 21, 1864.

33. P. R., "Reorganization of the Army," ibid., Jan. 29, 1864; "Army Reorganization," ibid., Feb. 2, 1864.

34. "Walthall's Brigade," ibid., Jan. 23, 1864; Sabine, "From the Army," ibid., Jan. 18, 1864.

35. Sabine, "From the Army," ibid., Jan. 18, 1864. "Ike" countered the argument that elected officers would be too indulgent with the men by claiming that those "who deal impartial justice to all will never be unpopular" as military commanders. Ike, "Reorganization," ibid., Jan. 18, 1864. See also A Private, "Reorganizing the Army," ibid., Jan. 21, 1864.

36. Wirt A. Cate, ed., *Two Soldiers: The Campaign Diaries of Thomas J. Key C.S.A. and Robert J. Campbell U.S.A.* (Chapel Hill: University of North Carolina Press, 1941), 28, 64; *OR,* 32(2):621.

37. Enoch L. Mitchell, ed., "The Civil War Letters of Thomas Jefferson Newberry," *Journal of Mississippi History* 10 (Jan. 1948): 76; Joseph Hutcheson to sister, Jan. 25, 1864, Hutcheson Family Papers, State University of West Georgia Library, Carrollton.

38. One of the Arkansas Volunteers, "Govan's Brigade," *Memphis Appeal,* Jan. 21, 1864.

39. "Our Army Correspondence, Letter from North Georgia," *Mobile Advertiser & Register,* Feb. 5, 1864. Lt. Joseph M. Rand of the 41st Mississippi noted Hindman's speech in his diary but recorded that the next day only a portion of the regiment reenlisted. Joseph M. Rand Diary, Jan. 27, 28, 1864, Mississippi Department of Archives and History, Jackson.

40. James M. Matthews, ed., *The Statutes at Large of the Provisional Government of the Confederate States of America* (Richmond: R. M. Smith, Printer to Congress, 1864), 211; David M. Potter, *The South and the Sectional Conflict* (Baton Rouge: Louisiana State University Press, 1968), 41. For an example of a unit resolution in which the men were "willing to abide the action of Congress" regarding reorganization, see "Thirty-Seventh Alabama," *Memphis Appeal,* Feb. 16, 1864.

41. Sam Settle to father, Jan. 24, 1864, MI-9 File, KEMO; "51st and 52d Tennessee Regiments," *Memphis Appeal,* Jan. 26, 1864; Texas, "Douglas' (Texas) Battery," ibid., Jan. 21, 1864.

42. Orderly, "Correspondence of the Columbus Times," *Macon Telegraph,* Jan. 29, 1864; Nathaniel C. Hughes, ed., *The Civil War Memoir of Philip Daingerfield Stephenson, D.D.* (Conway: University of Central Arkansas Press, 1995), 159; Walker Anderson to sister, Feb. 9, 1864, E. E. Kimbrough Collection (microfilm), Georgia Department of Archives and History, Atlanta.

43. "The 29th Mississippi," *Memphis Appeal,* Feb. 12, 1864; Walker to wife, Jan. 24, 1864, letter in private possession, transcript provided by Lee White, CCNMP.

44. McPherson, *What They Fought For,* 4. On desertion in the Army of Tennessee during this time, see Daniel, *Soldiering in the Army of Tennessee,* 107, 114, 136–38; and Mark A. Weitz, *A Higher Duty: Desertion among Georgia Troops during the Civil War* (Lincoln: University of Nebraska Press, 2000).

45. *Confederate Veteran* 8 (1900): 528; 9 (1901): 53; 10 (1902): 171; and 10 (1902): 259; Hughes, *Memoir of Philip Daingerfield Stephenson,* 158.

The Essential Nationalism of the People: Georgia's Confederate Congressional Election of 1863

ROD ANDREW JR.

MANY YEARS AFTER THE CIVIL WAR, EX-CONFEDERATE CONgressman Hiram P. Bell recalled an amendment he had offered on the floor of the Confederate House of Representatives, probably in the spring of 1864. He remembered attempting in a night session to exempt "the products of the garden, orchard and dairy, when used for the support of the family, and not for sale," from taxation by the Confederate government.[1] Bell was a rookie congressman from Georgia and a veteran of the battle of Second Manassas and fighting around Vicksburg, Mississippi, where he was seriously wounded. He had taken his seat in Richmond after the 1863 congressional election, the results of which many historians have interpreted as a sign of rising opposition to the administration of Pres. Jefferson Davis and therefore faltering Confederate nationalism. Some southern congressmen indeed suspected that members of the Georgia delegation were Davis opponents and tools of Georgia governor Joseph E. Brown. Brown had consistently opposed the centralizing, nationalistic measures of the Davis administration as a threat to individual liberties and states' rights.[2]

Bell was indignant at the initial reaction his amendment provoked. Rep. Charles M. Conrad of Louisiana derided the proposal, perhaps reading it as a tacit rebuke of Davis's policies and an attempt to check the authority of the Richmond government. Bell later explained that Conrad "by way of ridicule proposed to amend my amendment by adding 'butter and eggs.'" Another congressman moved to add "bees-wax and tallow," and a "ripple of amusement" passed through the chamber. Bell then stood up and answered: "I accept both amendments, for the reason that they extend the aid which my amendment is designed to give to the toiling women and children of the country, to prevent their starvation. I apprehend that their gallant husbands and fathers in the trenches around this beleaguered capitol, will not appreciate the statesmanship that would deride by ridicule, an effort to help those dearer to their hearts than the blood they so freely give for our protection. Nor will their respect be increased for the wisdom and gravity of legislators who can derive amusement from such derision. I confess my surprise at this feeble effort at wit."[3]

Who was striking the more nationalistic pose, those who defended the government's centralizing tendencies and stringent war measures in its attempts to fight for the survival of the Confederacy, or those who, like Bell, occasionally resisted government policies by expressing admiration for the gallant soldier and compassion for his "toiling" and suffering family?

There is a long historical tradition that asserts that states' rights, internal dissent, and class conflict undermined the Confederacy from within, an internal decay that was more debilitating than the advance of Union armies. Several scholars have used the 1863 elections as a gauge to measure popular discontent within the Confederacy, resentment of governmental authority, and crumbling nationalism. Along with North Carolina, they have singled out Georgia as a state in which the election represented a repudiation of the Davis administration and the "big government" policies emerging from Richmond. W. Buck Yearns makes this argument most clearly in *The Confederate Congress,* noting that "only one Georgian in the First Congress had consistently opposed the administration; six of these sought reelection, all were defeated, and eight of the new representatives were anti-Davis."[4] The Georgia elections have thus provided ammunition for those who seek to explain Confederate defeat with the "loss of will" thesis—the argument that weak or crumbling nationalism sealed the Confederacy's fate long before Appomattox.[5]

The "loss of will" thesis survives despite the fact that scholars over the last quarter century have done much to enrich our understanding of Confederate nationalism, often in ways that challenge the former argument. In the 1970s Emory Thomas explained that Confederate nationalism was neither static nor a direct reflection of Old South society. "Southern nationalism" evolved into Confederate nationalism, which in turn underwent drastic transformations in the crucible of war and political revolution. Thomas repeated the shibboleth that the elections of 1863 "reflected a decline in national morale and less than confidence in the Davis administration's ability," but he made it possible for historians to unshackle Confederate nationalism from rigid conformity to states' rights ideology and unbridled individualism. Patriotic Confederates, Thomas showed, conceded much of both to keep the war effort going.[6]

Several historians have since drawn on these insights to demonstrate that Confederate nationalism ultimately could exist with only a tenuous attachment to states' rights ideology and even without deep emotional attachments to the government in Richmond. Drew Gilpin Faust has amplified Thomas's points on the contingency and adaptability of Confederate nationalism by remarking that its creation was a process, that "[t]he struggle for nationalism often becomes itself the occasion for its fullest realization." While acknowledging that the pressures of war often unleashed class antagonism, both Faust and George C. Rable have noted that internal dissent in the Confederacy often represented the strength or the construction of nationalism rather than the reverse. Faust has argued that Confederate nationalism could serve "at once" as "critique and defense of the South."[7] Rable has shown that there were serious political controversies within the Confederacy but that leaders and people continued to condemn partisanship and clung tenaciously to a "political culture of national unity."[8] Other historians who have stressed the durability of the white southern struggle for independence, including Gary Gallagher and William Blair, have also noted that nationalism did not necessarily mean loyalty or attachment to the Confederate government or to a particular political ideology. Nationalism was grounded and often intertwined with local and individual concerns, according to Blair. Gallagher has convincingly argued that for much of the war nationalism focused on and drew its strength from the military, particularly Robert E. Lee's Army of Northern Virginia.[9]

Nationalism, then, is very complex—and it is a process as much as it is a fixed quotient of patriotic feeling at a given point in time. A simple yardstick, such as a midterm election, then, may not adequately assess the strength or character of Confederate nationalism over time, but it can provide a useful window for observing it at a given moment as well as clues about its essential character. While it is true, for example, that nine of Georgia's ten Confederate representatives either declined to run for reelection or were defeated in 1863, this did not necessarily imply a rebuke to the Davis administration, much less the disintegration of nationalism. A district-by-district, case-by-case examination of voting results does not reveal a clear repudiation of Confederate authority. The election was a critique, not a rejection, of the Davis government.

More fundamentally the election was a critique of the flaws and strengths within a society at war. Rather than indicating alienation from the cause of independence or from the nation itself, it illustrates a recommitment to both. The results of each race illuminate central features of Confederate nationalism as it existed by the third year of the war, a nationalism grounded more in shared sacrifice at home and martial valor at the front than in states' rights ideology or loyalty to Jefferson Davis. Put another way, the central concern of Georgia voters was not Davis himself or a Milledgeville-versus-Richmond referendum, but rather who was and was not doing his share to save the homeland from disaster and the people from suffering. Georgians expressed far less resentment for a central government that demanded too much than they did for individuals who were giving far too little. Their nationalism in 1863 constituted patriotic devotion that demanded collective and universal sacrifice to achieve the goals of military victory, national independence, and the welfare of the people. In many ways the army and individual soldiers had become the tangible symbols of that emerging, almost mystical, sense of devotion. Wounded veterans, therefore, rather than congressional incumbents became extremely attractive candidates. Votes for men with empty sleeves, wooden legs, and honorable war records were affirmations of this evolving Confederate nationalism.[10]

By the fall of 1863, voters in Georgia had lost loved ones on the battlefield and seen plenty of economic hardship. While some shirked their duties or profited at the expense of their fellow citizens, the enemy was poised just off the Atlantic coastline. Meanwhile a Union army held Chattanooga, just beyond Georgia's northern border. With these facts in mind, voters in the state faced several controversial issues in 1863. One of the most important of course was conscription. In March 1862 President Davis asked the Confederate Congress to pass a conscription law. On April 16 Congress complied and passed a measure making men in the eighteen-to-thirty-five age group eligible to be drafted into military service. In September congressmen raised the age limit to forty-five. There were several features of the conscription law that made it particularly onerous. First, it was legal for those who could afford it to hire a substitute if they were drafted. Second, the law also exempted men in certain occupations and planters or overseers who were responsible for the labor of twenty or more slaves. Finally, conscription placed the authority to raise armies in the hands of the government in Richmond rather than the states.[11]

In Georgia, as in other states, conscription was one of the most controversial issues of the day. Governor Brown argued that the law was unconstitutional and that it was a gross encroachment on state sovereignty by the central government. He told President Davis that the measure was also unnecessary. Brown did much to hinder the national government's conscription efforts in Georgia.[12]

Most of the state's newspapers, however, favored conscription and censured the governor for his obstruction. An editorial in the *Columbus Daily Sun* ridiculed his "insane crusade against the Confederate authorities" and his opposition to the Conscription Act. An editorial in the *Milledgeville Southern Recorder* in 1863 opposed Brown's reelection as governor principally because of his resistance to the draft. The needs of the hour, said the article, were far more important than a constitutional "abstraction."[13]

Probably the most troubling thing about conscription to most citizens, however, was that some men could avoid military service, whereas others could not. While some were giving their all for their country, others, including civilian officials, appeared cowardly by hiring substitutes or hiding behind exemptions. A public meeting held in Jonesboro in July 1863 called for an end to all exemptions and for all government officials, except the president and the cabinet, to join the army and be replaced by wounded veterans. In August citizens of Groomsville, in Brooks County, indignantly petitioned Governor Brown to ignore Dr. W. R. Joiner's request for exemption from the draft "by Reson of his being a Phisisian." Joiner's neighbors insisted that they held no animosity against him, but they "did not like to see and [*sic*] able and hearty man to take so low down a trick to forsake his country in its dark Hour of Trial."[14]

Indeed, throughout 1862, 1863, and 1864, Brown continually received letters from citizens and even troops in the field protesting that draft dodgers were not doing their share and that not enough was being done to press them into service. Others, like the citizens of Groomsville, provided lists of names of physically able men in their communities who they thought should be at the front but were not.[15] Undoubtedly there were overtones of class resentment in these protests. One letter from "the ladies of Spaulding County" insisted that the governor ensure that "the rich" and even the "old men" be called to active duty: "[We] want to see these old men shoulder their musket now the crops are all layed bye wheat all cut & I think the women can gather the corn now you go & take all the rest of the men & whip them at once & then we will have peace."[16] Several congressional candidates addressed the conscription issue in 1863, including three incumbents who lost their bids for reelection. Clearly many Georgians believed that the time had come for all men—rich, poor, old, and young—to do their time at the front.[17]

Another searing issue was the Confederate government's impressment policies. As early as 1861 Confederate military officers had informally confiscated the property and produce of citizens for the use of the army. In early 1862 Congress passed a law to regulate the means of doing so. While this act was an admission that impressment was a necessary and legal practice, it also fixed prices for goods taken in an unsuccessful attempt to ensure that citizens would receive just compensation.[18]

Impressment was a volatile issue in Georgia, particularly since some citizens were suffering more than others. Those who did not receive a fair price for goods taken from them despised the policy. Impressment agents worked over some areas far more thoroughly than others. Also many citizens suffered robbery at the hands of dishonest men pretending to represent the Confederate government. There was a widespread feeling that impressment agents, both legitimate and fraudulent, were suspicious characters who were not contributing their fair share toward victory. Governor Brown urged the legislature in 1863 to pass a bill that would make unauthorized impressment a felony, punishable by ten years in prison and thirty-nine lashes on the bare back. This never became law, but legislators did try to make sure that impressment agents were not mere shirkers from the army. They mandated that all officers who were subject to conscription should be removed by the secretary of war and replaced by men who were not affected.[19]

A review of Georgia newspapers during the 1863 election campaign shows that citizens were also extremely concerned about soaring inflation and the depreciation of the Confederate currency. Nearly every candidate and newspaper addressed this subject, which may have been discussed even more than conscription or impressment. Georgians blamed the depreciation of the currency on a number of factors but especially on speculators and blockade runners, whose activities drove up the rate of inflation. Citizens frequently expressed anger at those who refused to accept Confederate notes as payment for goods and debts. For instance, in Putnam County a group of citizens held a public meeting in which they resolved that anyone who debased the currency by refusing to accept Confederate Treasury notes should be conscripted into the army and that a grand jury would record their names on a "Black Roll . . . as an everlasting record of their defection to their country in the hour of her peril."[20] Residents of Stewart County passed a similar resolution. Again greedy or selfish persons were thought to be at the heart of the Confederacy's problems.[21]

Taxation affected the currency issue. Confederate Treasury secretary Christopher Memminger had continued to plead for increased taxes as a means to raise government revenue and stabilize the currency. In April 1863 Congress complied and passed a comprehensive levy that became known as the "tax in kind." This law included a license tax on certain occupations, a graduated income tax, and a tithe (10 percent) on all agricultural produce and livestock.[22]

Many Georgians bitterly resented the tax in kind, though others understood that it was vital for national survival. For instance, the *Sandersville Central Georgian* stated that it was foolish to complain about the government taking one-tenth of one's wealth—if the Yankees came to occupy the country, they would spare one-tenth and take the other nine. Others argued that Congress's sin was not having the courage to resort to taxation before it was too late. A congressional convention in Blackshear, Georgia, declared that the Richmond government should have implemented a moderate system of taxation immediately upon its decision to issue paper money; instead it had procrastinated, and in the meantime the currency collapsed. Thus the crux of the problem was not that the government was making unreasonable demands, but that these demands had only been made necessary by Congress's incompetence and failure to do its job in the beginning.[23]

A number of other points shaped the elections in Georgia. First, a review of extant newspapers from the summer and fall of 1863 reveals only moderate interest in the congressional races. Several newspapers expressed satisfaction that candidates were refraining from active campaigning, saying it was no time for disunity, party divisions, or stump speaking. Others commented on the low turnout or lack of excitement on election day. Papers devoted more editorial space to the gubernatorial election, and editors and correspondents saved their most angry and strident arguments for that race.[24]

Second, the weakness of the currency appeared to be the most thoroughly discussed issue. Editors, candidates, and citizens in public meetings usually blamed this problem on speculators, extortionists, blockade runners, and other unpatriotic citizens. Newspapers and candidates also discussed conscription, though usually only as it had to do with exemptions and substitutions—those elements of the law that suggested favoritism or inequality of sacrifice. Almost no one wished to curtail or eliminate conscription altogether, and some called for more stringent measures to ensure that all able-bodied men served in the army.

Finally, nearly every newspaper and several candidates came out in open opposition to peace negotiations with the Union, or "reconstruction." Candidate James M. Smith, winner in the Seventh District, made much political capital out of this issue by publishing a letter written to him by a peace advocate along with his indignant reply.[25]

In Georgia's Second Congressional District, in the southwestern corner of the state, the incumbent Charles J. Munnerlyn squared off against challengers William E. Smith and James L. Seward. Munnerlyn had been a planter and a secessionist before the war. He had served briefly as a private in the 1st Georgia Volunteers but left the service due to poor health in November 1861.[26]

Munnerlyn was definitely a pro-Davis candidate, having been a strong supporter of the administration's measures in the First Congress. In his letter "To the Voters of the Second Congressional District" in the *Milledgeville Southern Recorder*, Munnerlyn defended most of Congress's actions. He said that the conscription law was a harsh but essential measure that had saved the army. He added that Congress had well provided for the soldiers. Munnerlyn defended his votes for revenue bills, including the "Tax Law," which he admitted was imperfect and burdensome but necessary. He then denied the charge that he had voted to increase his own salary or that he had voted against increasing the soldiers' pay. As for conscription the congressman said that he believed some exemptions were necessary but supported the repeal of the "Twenty Negro feature." Thus Munnerlyn generally defended his pro-administration stance, with the possible exception of exemptions and the embarrassing matter of Congress's voting to raise its own pay without raising that of the soldiers.[27]

Despite the *Southern Recorder*'s endorsement of Munnerlyn, he lost, though not because of the policies of the Confederate government or his own voting record. His weaker challenger, James Seward, had also been in favor of further strong measures by the national government. In fact he expressed his support of "a suitable tax" based on principles of equality and justice to restore confidence in Treasury notes. Seward appealed for more-stringent government measures against speculators and blockade runners and also endorsed Congress's impressment and taxation measures while addressing the voters' concerns about dishonest impressment agents and tax collectors. He did not mention conscription or exemptions.[28]

Seward received more votes than Munnerlyn but not as many as the election's winner, William E. Smith of Albany. Smith was a lawyer and planter who had held several county offices before the war, none of which had been elective. He had served as a first lieutenant and then a captain in the 1st Georgia Infantry until he lost a leg in a charge during the 1862 Peninsula campaign.[29]

Smith received 2,820 votes, almost equaling the combined totals of Seward's 1,618, and Munnerlyn's 1,220. Obviously Smith was a clear favorite, though not because of any attack on the policies emerging from Richmond. He did not sound like a Davis administration opponent during the campaign of 1863. His address to the voters in the *Southern Recorder,* though lacking specifics, was a call for national unity and a plea to support the national government. He dismissed the "reconstruction" idea by saying that the only way to obtain peace was through national unity and by driving every last Yankee from the South's soil. Smith admitted that the Confederate government, like all human institutions, was not infallible, but with stirring platitudes he skillfully linked patriotism to support of the national authority: "If the Confederate Government fails, either through the want of support of those whose interest it is to support it, or from the attacks of [the enemy], we may safely conclude that our subjugation is at hand. . . . If we but sustain with enthusiasm our Government, by sustaining the army, navy, and the currency, and becoming ourselves a unit in action, having always in view the general welfare, the smiles of a genial peace will soon be upon us."[30]

With all three candidates refusing to condemn the big-government measures of Davis and Congress, what could explain Smith's victory? There is evidence that the voters saw Smith as the candidate who had already proven his patriotism on the battlefield. One citizen wrote to the *Milledgeville Confederate Union* that he supported Smith because that candidate had forsaken a thriving practice and a judgeship in Georgia's southwestern circuit to serve his country. His leg had been "torn to pieces" while leading a charge. When Smith recovered, he sought a position in the cavalry or the navy—"no quartermaster's or any such position would he have." The same writer urged the voters to elect congressmen who would "stop this Nassau blockade running, of yankee notions—build up our depreciated currency—put a check on extortion—stop the substituting system—do away with exemptions—raise the poor soldiers' pay . . . let this war no longer be a poor man's war."[31] Apparently Smith's election represented the people's perception that the war's burdens were falling more heavily on some than others, and they therefore sought to reward a candidate who had already given much to his country. They turned not to a peace-seeking candidate or opponent of the war effort but to a combat hero who demanded greater sacrifices from slackers.

If the people regarded Smith as a leader who would work to make the burdens of war more equitable, his actions in Congress proved them correct.

He opposed the Davis administration's economic policies, though mainly in an effort to eliminate inequalities in the tax and impressment laws. He also worked to maximize the use of the South's military manpower. In May 1864, for example, he proposed placing all able-bodied men in the army and assigning all others to civilian activities. To make sure that no one shirked his duties while others sacrificed, he requested a heavy penalty for those conscripted who refused to serve. Additionally he opposed the clause of the 1864 Conscription Act that allowed exemptions for slaveholders who owned fifteen or more slaves. He also wanted the government to authorize labor details for "large and helpless families" without property.[32] While he did vote during the second session of 1864 against the administration's suspension of the writ of habeas corpus, it did not contradict his belief in shared sacrifice. His other votes during the same session, for example, indicate high support for conscription and the right of the government to impress needed supplies from civilians. Given this, one should regard Smith's election less as a rebuke of the Davis government's centralizing policies than as a sign of frustration that some citizens were having it harder than others. That frustration in turn rested on the assumption that all the nation's citizens should be willing to bear their share of the burden and sacrifice to save the South.[33]

The story was similar in the Third Congressional District, composed of Columbus and other parts of west central Georgia. The Third District has received close attention in David Williams's *Rich Man's War,* which blames class antagonisms for alienating citizens from the Richmond government and the war effort. As in the Second District, the pro-Davis incumbent, Hines Holt, lost his reelection bid to a disabled veteran, Mark H. Blandford. But alienation of the lower classes cannot adequately explain the incumbent's defeat.[34]

Holt had been a planter and attorney before the war. In 1860 he was still a cooperationist, but after being elected to the First Confederate Congress, he found himself a supporter of most of the Davis administration's measures. Holt cosponsored the first peace proposal in Congress in September 1861, calling for a delegation to go to Washington to negotiate a just and honorable peace. But he had no patience with halfway wartime measures in Congress, and Holt's solutions were most likely to meet the approval of poorer citizens of his district. While many claimed that planters greedily continued to grow cotton instead of crops that could feed their starving neighbors, the congressman once proposed that the Confederate government buy all cotton at four cents a pound (a very low price) and withhold it from the market until Britain broke the

Union blockade. He also called for an end to all exemptions from conscription. During the 1863 campaign Holt answered a query from a constituent in the *Columbus Enquirer* as to what position he had taken on raising congressional salaries. He replied that there had been three positions on Congress's pay: one, pay congressmen three thousand dollars a year; two, pay them two thousand dollars a year; and three, provide a small per-diem compensation for their time actually spent in session. Holt said he had belonged to the third and smallest group. He also reminded voters that he had supported an end to all military exemptions. In several ways, then, Holt effectively answered the frustrations of his constituents who thought the war had become a "poor man's fight."[35]

The *Columbus Enquirer* endorsed the congressman for reelection. An editorial on September 3 pointed out that although Holt originally had been a Unionist and Blandford a secessionist, this did not make Holt any less of a patriot; in fact the paper said he had wholeheartedly and diligently supported the Confederacy. This was no time to change public servants who were directing the affairs of the country unless it was for unfaithfulness or incompetence.[36]

The challenger, Mark Blandford, had been a lawyer and a merchant before the war and had also served as a sergeant in the 1st Georgia Infantry during the Mexican War. In 1861 he raised and commanded a company in the 12th Georgia. Severely wounded the following year during the battle of McDowell in Stonewall Jackson's Shenandoah Valley campaign, Blandford had his right arm amputated, and he returned home. President Davis soon appointed him as a judge in a military court in A. P. Hill's Corps with the rank of lieutenant colonel.[37]

It may be impossible to find a record of anything Blandford had to say on political issues before the election. Perhaps his military duties in Virginia prevented him from campaigning. Nor was there much said about him in the Georgia press. The *Columbus Enquirer* raised the question of whether or not Blandford was eligible for office under the Confederate Constitution, since he already held another government post as president of the military court in Hill's Corps. The paper conceded that Blandford was a worthy man and deserving of a high post of honor for his services but remarked that he already had such a post.[38] In the end the people of the Third District ignored their newspaper's constitutional objections as well as its endorsement of Holt. Blandford won the election rather handily by a vote of 3,429 to 2,322.

Because of the lack of coverage of the election by the Columbus papers, it is difficult to pinpoint the reasons for Holt's defeat. Perhaps local cotton growers or merchants resented his effort to have the government buy all cotton at a fixed price and remove it from the market. His stand on this issue may explain the *Enquirer*'s editorial on September 7, claiming that it was perfectly all right for the government to seize produce that speculators were attempting to sell at exorbitant prices that would therefore drive up inflation.[39]

Given Blandford's nonexistent platform, there is simply not enough evidence to conclude that Holt's defeat was another example of Georgians rejecting a pro-Davis, pro-big-government Congress for an anti-Davis one. Nor does the anger and supposed alienation of non-elites provide a sufficient explanation. After his election Blandford did oppose the administration's stringent control over the economy. But he supported Davis's efforts to end all exemptions from military service and proposed that the president be given complete control over all manpower, raising a howl of protest from states' rights advocates. Nor was he inclined to limit the president's authority in other executive matters.[40]

Buck Yearns and Ezra Warner may have come closer to the real explanation when they wrote that Holt lost to Blandford "in a battle of personalities."[41] Perhaps a majority of the Third District's voters simply saw the election as a race between a wounded hero and veteran who had given his arm to the cause and a politician who had done little more than politic in Richmond.

Like the Second and Third Districts, the congressional race in the Fourth District, covering central Georgia (including the state capital, Milledgeville, and the city of Macon), does not provide a clear example of citizens rejecting the Davis program. The race began as a four-way contest between the pro-Davis incumbent, Augustus Holmes Kenan, and his challengers, Wilde C. Cleaveland, Dr. Edmund J. McGehee, and Capt. Clifford Anderson of the Army of Northern Virginia.

Kenan was a well-known Milledgeville lawyer who had opposed secession. In Congress he was a strong Davis supporter, so much so that Governor Brown called him Davis's stooge. He believed in the wartime necessity of a strong central government, once arguing that "states Rights will be easily adjusted when we establish the right to have states."[42] In August 1863 both the *Confederate Union* and the *Southern Recorder* published a letter from eight citizens asking Kenan to run for reelection: "It is the warm and manly support which you have uniformly given the Administration, that commands our highest approbation."[43] Kenan replied, "I felt it to be the duty of all to stand by the Government and its measures in war. The mighty conflict in which our country is involved should silence for the present at least, the opposition of factious ambition and State Rights' jealousies. The public peril demands that we have union and concert of action—prompt, cordial, and subordinate cooperation between State and Confederate rulers."[44]

Kenan's stance left the door wide open for opponents to campaign on an antigovernment or states' rights program if they thought it would be advantageous to do so. They did not. Both Cleaveland and McGehee proclaimed themselves supporters of the strong national government erected under the Davis administration. Cleaveland also harangued those perceived to have profited from the war, including blockade runners; those who traded with the enemy; factory owners who had profited from the war but contributed little to the war effort; and those who owned enough slaves to avoid conscription. Cleaveland advocated conscripting all these classes of citizens as well as those who refused to accept Confederate currency.[45]

For unknown reasons both Cleaveland and McGehee withdrew from the contest by September 29, leaving Kenan and the eventual winner, Clifford Anderson. Anderson had been a lawyer, a Macon city-court judge, and an ardent secessionist before the war. He enlisted in the army as a private and distinguished himself in combat, gaining an appointment to Brig. Gen. A. R. Wright's staff. He later won promotion to the rank of captain for his heroism at the battle of Gettysburg. An editorial in the *Confederate Union* endorsed Anderson, based on his character, his lack of association with political intrigue, and his concern for the welfare of his district's residents. The editor believed that the officer would help wounded veterans and indigent families.[46]

Anderson himself addressed his future constituents in a short letter postmarked "Hqtrs., Wright's Brigade," and published in the *Southern Recorder.* He mentioned few specifics but did promise to work to get aid from friendly foreign powers, provide for the welfare of the troops, and labor to "improve the currency and keep the public debt within safe and legitimate bounds." He added that he would not forget "the interests of the industrial and producing classes of our people, upon whose skill and labor our success so largely depends."[47]

Did Anderson's defeat of Kenan (2,478 votes to 1,932) represent a repudiation of the pro-Davis candidate in favor of the anti-Davis, states' rights, or "moderate" candidate? Once again the campaign rhetoric does not offer a conclusive answer to this question. In its absence one may turn to a summary of Anderson's record in the Second Congress, where he became a loyal supporter of Davis and an opponent of Governor Brown's obstructionist policies. Thus in Georgia's Fourth District, the voters simply exchanged one pro-Davis representative for another. Again it is impossible to sustain the generalization of

Yearns and others that the 1863 congressional elections in Georgia represented a repudiation of the Davis administration. (Notably Representative Anderson did frequently call for relief efforts for the families of Confederate soldiers and impoverished civilians.)[48]

A few patterns emerge from the results of these three congressional races. In all three the incumbents frankly defended their pro-administration, nationalist stances, and all three lost. Despite that fact, none of the challengers offered anti-Davis agendas. Those of the successful challengers were either vaguely supportive of the Confederate government or not made public. Of the three victors, Smith and Blandford may be said to have a mixed record on the Davis agenda once in office, while Anderson was a firm Davis supporter. Finally and perhaps most importantly, in all three cases incumbent politicians lost to men the public perceived as valiant soldiers.

Results of the other seven races suggest a strong current of nationalism, indicating neither was especially pro- nor anti-Davis. The exception was the First District, which included the coastal area around Savannah, where the pro-Davis incumbent actually defeated a challenger who clearly opposed the president. Unlike other Georgians in the fall of 1863, citizens in the eastern part of this district had some experience with Federal occupation. The Union blockade had affected them more directly than others in the state, and Union forces had captured Tybee Island and Cockspur Island, only a few miles from Savannah itself. These areas in the First District gave a heavy majority to the incumbent, Julian Hartridge, who frankly defended Davis's and Congress's stringent war measures. Challenger Thomas Butler King, who "arraigned the government severely on almost everything," including "centralized despotism which was abusing the states," lost by a count of 3,077 to 2,319, while a third candidate received 766 votes.[49]

In the Fifth and Sixth Districts, pro-Davis incumbents lost to candidates whose platforms are no longer extant but who later had a mixed voting record on administration measures. In the northwestern Tenth District, which bordered Tennessee and Alabama, the pro-Davis incumbent, Augustus R. Wright, declined to run again. His replacement was lawyer Warren Akin, who had campaigned against Brown for governor and who took a strong pro-administration stance. Akin received the endorsement of the *Rome Tri-Weekly Courier*, a pro-Davis newspaper.[50]

In the Seventh, Eighth, and Ninth Districts, the story was similar to that of the Second, Third, and Fourth—veterans replaced incumbent politicians.

The incumbent did not run in the Seventh District. There James M. Smith, a wounded veteran, defeated a Confederate tax collector, a Mr. Cabaniss. In the Eighth incumbent Lucius Gartrell declined to run. Three active army officers or former officers entered the contest. As in other races, the newspapers reported little debate on the issues in this district, but the election went to Capt. George N. Lester, who had lost his right arm at Perryville. The Ninth District's choice was Hiram P. Bell, an officer whose leg had been shattered at Vicksburg.[51]

Bell presumably was one of the winners during the 1863 contests whose election has represented for Yearns and other historians the rise of antigovernment sentiment and failing nationalism. In reality he is a clear example of the style of nationalism that glorified heroic soldiers and their families. When Bell published his memoirs four decades later, he praised the abilities of Jefferson Davis and his secretary of war John C. Breckenridge. It is possible of course that his feelings toward the Confederate president had mellowed as the years passed—and as Lost Cause mythology elevated Davis's standing in the eyes of southerners. As a congressman Bell had voted with the administration on some matters and against it on others, particularly on the issue of habeas corpus. The clearest trend in his legislative record, though, seems to have been concern for the troops at the front and poverty back home. Despite his kind comments regarding Davis and Breckenridge, the real heroes in Bell's memoirs are the soldiers and their families, just as they had been during his tenure in the Confederate Congress. Commenting on the food shortages in Lee's army, Bell writes: "This was not the fault of the Government, nor its officials. . . . The government exhausted all its powers and resources, in the effort to provide for the necessities and comforts of its heroic defenders, yet these brave men stood by their flag and defended their convictions with a valor never surpassed, under the leadership of a General without an equal."[52] This glorification of martial valor and recognition of sacrifice is remarkably consistent with the attitudes of Georgians in the 1863 congressional campaigns.

The predominant pattern in the ten congressional races in Georgia was not the replacement of pro-administration incumbents with anti-Davis challengers. Only one candidate, Thomas Butler King, stood on a strong states' rights platform, and he lost handily. Nor did the voters send a corps of peace activists or war opponents to Richmond. No one called for "peace at any cost" or suggested compromising on the goal of independence. Where their platforms are extant, one can see that both incumbents and challengers tended to attack extortionists, speculators, and draft dodgers much more than they criticized the government in Richmond, and they certainly did not turn against the war. Instead the predominant pattern was of voters replacing incumbents with men who had served at the front and been wounded in combat and now called for greater commitment to the war effort and the cause of independence. Clearly voting for veterans was an expression of evolving Confederate nationalism.

Confederate nationalism evolved over time. The Georgia congressional elections of 1863 represent only a window into the state of Confederate nationalism and popular will at a particular place and time. But it provides important clues about the nature of that nationalism and how it evolved throughout the war. Georgians in 1863 were reacting to hardship not with resignation, but with frustration mingled with renewed determination. It is unwise to define Confederate nationalism rigidly in terms of commitment to the original states' rights doctrine, which was so essential to southern and Confederate political ideology in 1860–61. Certainly this was still important, and it continued to shape internal political debates throughout the history of the Confederacy. But in the national crisis of late 1863, it appeared as a secondary concern to most voters and congressional candidates.

Neither did Confederate nationalism in late 1863 necessarily imply loyalty to an impersonal central government. It rested more often on an almost mystical sense of country defined by individual and collective sacrifice and, most importantly, martial valor. And as candidates, editors, and citizens made clear, the ultimate goal of that nationalism was to win the war and achieve national independence. While civilians suffered and sacrificed at home, an even more visible and concrete manifestation of that sacrifice in the public mind was military service at the front. For a nation born in war, the army is often the focus of nationalism. The election of wounded veterans to Congress, then, was an expression not of faltering nationalism or national will, but of the essential nationalism of the people. In a society that prided itself on its supposed martial traditions, this should not be surprising, particularly in wartime. And it should not perplex historians that Confederate nationalism could exist independently of love for government authorities. If the Davis administration never ultimately became the focus of Confederate nationalism, perhaps it was because it failed effectively to tap into the essential and undeniable fervor of white southerners—a militaristic and public-spirited patriotism born of suffering, hardship, and fear.[53]

NOTES

1. Hiram Parks Bell, *Of Men and Things: Being Reminiscent, Biographical, and Historical* (Atlanta: Foote & Davis, 1907), 98. The author would like to thank Kyle Sinisi and Paul Anderson for their comments on earlier drafts of this essay. He also thanks Emory Thomas, in whose graduate seminar this essay originated in 1994.

2. Jon L. Wakelyn, ed., *Biographical Dictionary of the Confederacy* (Westport, Conn.: Greenwood, 1977), 97. Bell commented on these suspicions toward the Georgia delegation; see *Of Men and Things,* 110.

3. Bell, *Of Men and Things,* 98. This brief moment of frivolity was not recorded in the official journal of the Confederate Congress. Bell's efforts may have resulted in the House amending the tax law on June 2, 1864, to exempt from "the assessed value of property . . . the products of gardens intended for the use of the family of the owner, [and] . . . fruit raised from domestic use and not for sale." *Journal of the Congress of the Confederate States,* vol. 7 (Washington, D.C.: Government Printing Office, 1905), 149–50.

4. Wilfred Buck Yearns, *The Confederate Congress* (Athens: University of Georgia Press, 1960), 55.

5. Older works that posit the weakness of Confederate nationalism include Frank L. Owsley, *State Rights in the Confederacy* (Chicago: University of Chicago Press, 1925); David Herbert Donald, "Died of Democracy," in *Why the North Won the Civil War* (Baton Rouge: Louisiana State University Press, 1960), 77–90; and Bell I. Wiley, *The Road to Appomattox* (Memphis: Memphis State College Press, 1956). More-recent works include Richard E. Beringer, Herman Hattaway, Archer Jones, and William N. Still Jr., *Why the South Lost the Civil War* (Athens: University of Georgia Press, 1986); and Paul D. Escott, *After Secession: Jefferson Davis and the Failure of Confederate Nationalism* (Baton Rouge: Louisiana State University Press, 1978). For the weakness of nationalism in Georgia, see T. Conn Bryan, *Confederate Georgia* (Athens: University of Georgia Press, 1953), 80–100; Mark A. Weitz, *A Higher Duty: Desertion among Georgia Troops during the Civil War* (Lincoln: University of Nebraska Press, 2000); and David Williams, *Rich Man's War: Class, Caste, and Confederate Defeat in the Lower Chattahoochee Valley* (Athens: University of Georgia Press, 1998). Emory Thomas has argued that the 1863 elections represented weakening support for the Davis administration, which "did not necessarily go with defeatism, although sometimes it did." Thomas, *The Confederate Nation: 1861–1865* (New York: Harper & Row, 1979), 258.

6. Thomas, *Confederate Nation,* esp. 3–4, 224–35. See also Thomas, *The Confederacy as a Revolutionary Experience* (Englewood Cliffs, N.J.: Prentice-Hall, 1971), esp. chap. 4.

7. Drew Gilpin Faust, *The Creation of Confederate Nationalism: Ideology and Identity in the Civil War South* (Baton Rouge: Louisiana State University Press, 1988), 6.

8. George C. Rable, *The Confederate Republic: A Revolution against Politics* (Chapel Hill: University of North Carolina Press, 1994), 300.

9. Gary W. Gallagher, *The Confederate War: How Popular Will, Nationalism, and Military Strategy Could Not Stave Off Defeat* (Cambridge, Mass.: Harvard University Press, 1997), 8, 12, 63–71; William Blair, *Virginia's Private War: Feeding Body and Soul in the Confederacy, 1861–1865* (New York: Oxford University Press, 1998). Paul Escott also uses an expanded definition of Confederate

nationalism that includes not only a "unifying ideology" but also social cohesion and "enthusiasm and patriotic dedication based on a feeling of regional identity." Yet he seems to measure all these indices primarily in terms of loyalty to the Davis administration or the national government in Richmond. *After Secession,* ix–x.

10. George C. Rable has questioned the traditional interpretation of the 1863 elections. *Confederate Republic,* 215, 232, 235. William Blair has demonstrated convincingly the distinction between opposition to Confederate national policies and faltering nationalism—Virginians, for example, often pushed for changes in national policy while wholeheartedly supporting the Confederate cause. Both Blair and Drew Gilpin Faust have suggested that disgust with greed, extortion, and speculation, and the way in which the burdens of wartime sacrifice fell unevenly on the population, was linked to the development of Confederate nationalism and not necessarily the decline of it. Blair, *Virginia's Private War,* 4–7; Faust, *Creation of Confederate Nationalism,* 41–57.

11. Thomas, *Confederate Nation,* 152–55.

12. Ibid.

13. *Milledgeville Southern Recorder,* Sept. 1, 1863.

14. Petition to Gov. Joseph E. Brown in regard to Dr. W. R. Joiner, Brooks County folder, box 51D, Petitions, Governor's Subject File, Joseph E. Brown Correspondence, Georgia State Archives, Atlanta.

15. See approximately a dozen anonymous letters on this topic in "Anonymous" folder, box 22, Governor's Incoming Correspondence, Series 1-1-5, Georgia State Archives. Also see the petition to Governor Brown from the men of Companies C and K, 47th Regiment Georgia Infantry, Sept. 29, 1864, in Bullock County folder, Petitions, Governor's Subject File, Joseph E. Brown Correspondence.

16. Anonymous petition from Griffin, Ga., June 25, 1864, "Anonymous" folder, box 22, Governor's Incoming Correspondence, Series 1-1-5.

17. *Milledgeville Southern Recorder,* Aug. 11, 1863.

18. Escott, *After Secession,* 66–67.

19. Bryan, *Confederate Georgia,* 90–93.

20. *Milledgeville Southern Recorder,* Aug. 11, 1863.

21. *Columbus Southern Enquirer,* Sept. 9, 1863.

22. Escott, *After Secession,* 67–68; Thomas, *Confederate Nation,* 197–98.

23. *Sandersonville Central Georgian,* Aug. 26, 1863; *Milledgeville Confederate Union,* Sept. 1, 1863.

24. *Milledgeville Confederate Union,* July 7, 1863; *Augusta Daily Constitutionalist,* Aug. 18, Oct. 8, 1863; *Columbus Daily Sun,* Sept. 12, 1863.

25. On this particular incident see *Atlanta Daily Intelligencer,* Aug. 28, 1863; and *Milledgeville Confederate Union,* Sept. 8, 1863.

26. Richard N. Current et al., eds., *Encyclopedia of the Confederacy,* 4 vols. (New York: Simon & Schuster, 1993), 3:1093.

27. *Milledgeville Southern Recorder,* Aug. 4, 1863.

28. Ibid., Sept. 1, 1863.

29. Current et al., *Encyclopedia of the Confederacy,* 4:1479; Wakelyn, *Biographical Dictionary of the Confederacy,* 393.

30. *Milledgeville Southern Recorder,* Aug. 25, 1863. Jon Wakelyn describes Smith as an opponent

of the Davis administration. *Biographical Dictionary of the Confederacy,* 393. But see also Rable, *Confederate Republic,* 231.

31. *Milledgeville Confederate Union,* July 18, 1863.

32. *Journal of the Congress of the Confederate States,* 107.

33. Ibid., 54, 65, 80, 106–7; Ezra J. Warner and W. Buck Yearns, *Biographical Register of the Confederate Congress* (Baton Rouge: Louisiana State University Press, 1975), 226.

34. Williams, *Rich Man's War,* 2, 135–37. Williams's interesting work pays little detailed attention to the 1863 election itself.

35. Holt resigned his seat for unknown reasons in 1862 only to seek reelection the following year. His replacement in 1862, Porter Ingram, did not run in 1863. Ingram apparently made little impression on the voters either way. The *Columbus Enquirer* of August 29, 1863, referred to Holt as the incumbent. It mentioned Blandford and William M. Brown as other possible candidates, though not Ingram. Yearns, *Confederate Congress,* 240; Warner and Yearns, *Biographical Register of the Confederate Congress,* 125–26; Current et al., *Encyclopedia of the Confederacy,* 2:786; *Columbus Enquirer,* Sept. 2, 1863.

36. *Columbus Enquirer,* Sept. 3, 1863.

37. Current et al., *Encyclopedia of the Confederacy,* 1:174; Wakelyn, *Biographical Dictionary of the Confederacy,* 98–99.

38. *Columbus Enquirer,* Sept. 25, 1863.

39. Ibid., Sept. 7, 1863.

40. Current et al., *Encyclopedia of the Confederacy,* 1:174; Warner and Yearns, *Biographical Register of the Confederate Congress,* 23; Wakelyn, *Biographical Dictionary of the Confederacy,* 99.

41. Warner and Yearns, *Biographical Register of the Confederate Congress,* 126.

42. Ibid., 143.

43. *Milledgeville Confederate Union,* Aug. 18, 1863; *Milledgeville Southern Recorder,* Aug. 11, 1863.

44. Ibid.

45. *Milledgeville Confederate Union,* Sept. 1, 15, 1863.

46. Ibid., Sept. 29, 1863.

47. Ibid., Sept. 22, 1863.

48. Current et al., *Encyclopedia of the Confederacy,* 1:29; Wakelyn, *Biographical Dictionary of the Confederacy,* 72–73; Rable, *Confederate Republic,* 232.

49. William Alexander Percy, "Localizing the Context of Confederate Politics," *Georgia Historical Quarterly* 79 (Spring 1995): 192–209.

50. *Augusta Daily Chronicle and Sentinel,* Oct. 6, 1863; *Daily Constitutionalist,* Oct. 6, 1863; *Milledgeville Southern Recorder,* July 7, Sept. 8, 1863; *Rome Tri-Weekly Courier,* Aug. 29, Sept. 3, 1863.

51. Wakelyn, *Biographical Dictionary of the Confederacy,* 97, 283, 391; Warner and Yearns, *Biographical Register of the Confederate Congress,* 223, 149, 22; Current et al., *Encyclopedia of the Confederacy,* 2:665.

52. Bell, *Of Men and Things,* 95–96.

53. Escott's *After Secession* also emphasizes the failure of Davis's government to win the loyalty and affections of Confederate citizens but arrives at different conclusions than those offered here.

“The Chrysalis State”: Slavery, Confederate Identity, and the Creation of the Border South

CHRISTOPHER PHILLIPS

ON JANUARY 1, 1862, COL. CHARLES WHITTLESEY OF THE 20TH Ohio Infantry and commander of what later archivists denoted as “counter-insurgency” in and around the Ohio River town of Warsaw, Kentucky, forty-five miles downstream from Cincinnati, received a short letter from James M. Vanice, a nonslaveholding house painter living there. In it Vanice “*pledge[d] my word* that I will neither aid nor take up Arms for the South, so long as the thing remains as it is, that is so long as the Government is not for the Freedom of Slaves.”[1] At first glance this revealing entreaty is hardly surprising, given that historians for the past half century have done all in their power to interpret the Civil War as one that in its barest essence was waged for and against the continuation of chattel slavery. Yet Vanice’s missive does become a clarion when one considers that the author lived in one of four slaveholding states that maintained their neutrality in the conflict, pledging allegiance to the Federal government and its president, Abraham Lincoln (himself a native Kentuckian and lifelong border resident), who had heretofore done all in his power to exclude emancipation from the Union war aims. Moreover Vanice’s 1862 reference to the South as an external entity suggests much about the transformation of these border residents’ regional affiliation as well as their own unique sectional identity.

Historians find the border slave states, especially Kentucky and Missouri, difficult to categorize in their various studies of the American past. Routinely they consider them as part of the South, largely from the mistaken perception of a fixed early American boundary between freedom and slavery. In this they merely project the traditional interpretations by these states' histories and historians who, often products of the very states they study, seek to define their subjects' experiences alongside the histories in which they themselves were raised and which often actuated their interest in history. Most assume the existence of a clearly defined and static geographical line between the North and South, mirroring (or so we think) the cultural and political divide that led to the Civil War itself. Of course such a view of the war and of American regionalism is both simplistic and inaccurate. It ignores the nature and, more important, the lasting regional consequences of the Civil War, particularly in its most contested space: the western border states. One of the war's greatest and most overlooked ironies is that while the border slave states east of Appalachia grew more northern after the war, the same such states west of the mountains, Kentucky and Missouri, became decidedly southern. Thus in the end the victorious North created a larger South than the defeated Confederacy could accomplish for itself. In the process of coming to the support of the Union, the border West in the end actually became the border South.

In fact nowhere do we see more clearly the emerging reasons for the Civil War, or why it was so staggeringly bitter, than in the lives of people who lived along the Ohio and Missouri rivers. If the nature of the American Civil War can best be gauged by the experience of the complex and fragile border (or "North of South," as one Ohio observer aptly described the region in 1861),[2] then perhaps more intriguing is that the war along the middle border cast long shadows, offering the stark outline of an intrasectional crisis—one largely subsumed by the national sectional crisis—by which the middle border itself cleaved, with the Ohio and Missouri rivers assuming their present status as cultural and political boundaries between North and South. This regional alpha-omega created in large part the dual identity of the border, one lost and one found, one western and one southern.

More to the point, the unique experience of the western border slave states during the Civil War and their equally anomalous place within and without the Confederacy set the stage for residents of the states below the Ohio and Missouri rivers defining themselves as "southern" specifically as a result of their war experience and their ensuing postwar racial experience. Identity politics surrounding the memory of the Confederate nation, most attributable to these states' tenuous places within it, offered the vehicle by which the border slave states became part of the South, a section that but few claimed for themselves prior to the war.

Antebellum white border residents believed themselves to be neither southern nor northern but something better than either. If anything regional, they considered themselves westerners. In 1844, Louisville's *Western Monthly Magazine* trumpeted the "Democratic Principle" of "what is now called the West—the Great Valley," while the title of Lexington's *Western Review and Miscellaneous Magazine* sounded remarkably like that of the *Western Monthly Review,* the *Western Spy,* and the *Western Monthly Magazine,* all published just over the Ohio River in Cincinnati.[3] This conscious western identity was articulated best by Missouri proslavery politico James S. Rollins, who cautioned his son, a cadet at the U.S. Military Institute at West Point, to "say to the Northern and Southern cadets—that you belong to *neither section*—that you are a true son of the great West."[4] Indeed one Bluegrass resident, Henry M. Duncan Jr., who had attended Harvard before leaving in 1859 to study law in his home state, took great pains to convince his former New England mates that those from "old fashioned Kentuck . . . , this Athens of the New World . . . , [were] the greatest people in the world." Duncan appears to have succeeded, at least in part; in his honor his Cambridge correspondents took care to distinguish Kentuckians from those of the "more Southern states" but clearly continued to hold that slaveholders, regardless of their region, were southerners. In November 1860, just after Abraham Lincoln's fateful election, Duncan playfully turned the tables on one of his former mates, asking, "If it is safe for a 'Southerner' to visit New England?" By his jovial response, the Massachusetts correspondent at least clearly got the joke.[5]

The case of Missouri's proslavery star—Kentucky-born David Rice Atchison—is instructive of border residents' ability to separate slaveholding from any peculiarly southern status. An able ally of John C. Calhoun, Atchison claimed that "as a Senator from Missouri and as a citizen of a Slave State, it is my duty to resist every attempt to change her institutions, and every assault upon her rights . . . by a series of measures to reduce the latter to a state of *helpless inferiority,* and to subject them and their institutions to the mercy of Abolitionism."[6] However fire-eating his words, Atchison was no planter, not even in Missouri's reckoning (much less in that of the cotton states). He was not even a farmer but a bachelor lawyer and circuit court judge prior to attaining the Senate. Son of a small slaveholder from Kentucky, Atchison had removed to western Missouri and become leader of the region's common whites by not assuming the part of any cotton-state planter; indeed he owned at most one bondsman.[7]

Atchison was anything but alone as a border state resident who owned few if any slaves. In 1860, Missouri's 115,000 slaves accounted for just 9.6 percent of its residents, the smallest of the slave states save elfin Delaware, while its 24,000-odd slaveholders comprised just 2.3 percent of its total free population.[8] And while Kentucky's 225,500 slaves in 1860 constituted 20 percent of Kentucky's overall population, significantly higher than in Missouri, the Bluegrass State ranked only ninth among all states then holding slaves. This percentage of Kentucky's population proved a far cry from Deep South states like Mississippi and Louisiana, where nearly half of their populations were slaves.[9] The border was preeminently a land of small slaveholders. No Kentuckian or Missourian owned more than three hundred slaves; in Kentucky only seven men owned over one hundred and but seventy held fifty or more.[10] The average Missourian owned fewer than five slaves. Characteristic of the upcountry portions of the Lower South, planters did not enjoy hegemony on the border; the yeomanry made up the backbone of the states' leadership even compared with other border slave states, a distinction that antebellum newspaper titles reflect. While southern Marylanders boasted the *Planter's Advocate,* Kentuckians read the *Kentucky Yeoman.*

The vigor with which both simple border residents like James Vanice and political leaders like David Rice Atchison reacted to the abolitionists' assaults on the peculiar institution grew more from roots sunk firmly into a western bedrock of individual liberties and democratic rights than any defense of material interests that might have reigned in cotton's kingdom. More than anywhere in the nation, these westerners suffered through the Lockean conundrum of supporting limited government, though only so far as it protected individual rights, while considering governmental power as the greatest threat to those same rights. Such logic moved Howard County, Missouri, politico Duff Green in 1819 to offer a biting toast, ironically just as he called for an unrestricted statehood for his by then controversial home territory: "The Union—It is dear to us, but liberty is dearer."[11]

And among those liberties that Green and other border residents (or "borderites") held so dear, few were more sacred than slavery. Hundreds of thousands of westerners, from the Bluegrass of Kentucky to the Boon's Lick of Missouri, embraced slavery as perfectly consistent with the egalitarian social progress they associated implicitly with national growth. While free-labor ideologues, eschewing moral pronouncements, would condemn the nation's slave-based society as socially stagnant, economically irrational, and thoroughly undemocratic, early slaveholding westerners beat them to the proverbial punch. For them slavery was a perfectly democratic institution, consistent with the promise of western expansion.[12] Slaveholding, more widely dispersed over the border region than in any other slaveholding area, proved consistent with these residents' traditional frontier commitment to personal liberties and congruent with democratic ascendance.

Yet unlike the Deep South, where the tie between slavery and economic fortune honed a much sharper edge to its populace's commitment to personal liberties, border people convinced themselves that they could discern the possibility of the simultaneous maintenance of slavery and continued loyalty to the Union. As such they rejected secession, taking great pride in their traditional roles as mediators, both geographical and political, between the extremists of both the North and the South. "Kentuckians," noted one observer after touring the state in the spring of 1861, "have always been 'Union Men' in principle & deed. They have not yet departed from the Union loving & patriotic sentiment & teachings of Clay, Crittenden, . . . & a host of others."[13] Another border resident wrote to kin in southern Indiana: "If God should tell me I had either to go to Hell or the Southern Confederacy I should ask a week for deliberation. . . . I would a thousand times rather be where we are, and that's where [we are] going to stick."[14]

True to their western identity, neither Missouri nor Kentucky sent representatives to a "southern convention" held at Nashville in 1850; yet when a border state conference was held in Frankfort, Kentucky, in May 1861, only those states' representatives were in attendance.[15] In an attempt to keep their footing as slaveholders and Unionists, borderites sought to convince the nation that a fourth section of the country existed apart from the North, South, and West, one that ameliorated the antagonistic influences in the nation. The concept of a middle confederacy of sorts as healer to the ailing nation vindicated their place as virtuous slaveholders within the Republic.[16] Indeed both states opted for armed neutrality when the cotton states withdrew from the Union and even as the neighboring Upper South states seceded after Lincoln's call for volunteers following Fort Sumter. Ultimately Kentuckians did not call a secession convention, and Missouri was the only state whose residents called a convention and then voted *against* leaving the Union.

Yet clearly borderites maintained a jittery fidelity. Holding no faith in the "Black Republican" Party, Kentucky's voters had shown for Constitutional Unionist John Bell in the 1860 presidential election over even their native son, Southern Democrat John C. Breckinridge, while Missouri went for the Northern Democratic candidate, Stephen A. Douglas. Kentucky-born Lincoln received scant votes outside the city of St. Louis, where antislavery Germans flocked to the polls.[17] White borderites, insisting upon the Federal government's protection of the rights to slave property, assumed the curiously incongruous position of disavowing the constitutional right of secession while "recogniz[ing] the right of revolution," thus producing, in the historian Carl Degler's words, "a peculiar Unionism," a curious hybrid that at once espoused steadfast loyalty to the Union while supporting slavery as the foundation of liberty.[18] A Union meeting in Louisville put the matter more directly when it declared in 1861 that although Kentucky acknowledged "her loyalty and fealty to the Government of the United States, . . . [which] she will cheerfully render until that Government becomes aggressive, tyrannical, and regardless of our rights in slave property," and that the state would hold that government to "rigid accountability."[19] Although Missourian John A. Hockaday wrote passionately in 1861, "Father informs us that you had heard I had bolted my position as an advocate of the Union. My Answer to the report is *never, never never,*" he attached an ominous declaimer: "Yet whilst there is a possibility of [Missouri] maintaining her position as one of the Sovereign states of this Union, I shall as ever be found battling in my humble way to Secure a *continued* and *perpetual* Existence of her present relations to our once happy government." While the infant Confederate States might have held forth state sovereignty as the constitutional cornerstone of secession, border state residents believed their duty lay in defending state sovereignty only against extremism within the Union. Until the national government attempted to make war upon a sovereign state, or to coerce one of the loyal states to make war upon the seceded states, neutrality was anything but secession.[20]

A year into the future witnessed a sea change in the border experience and in its residents' attitudes toward the Union. Although Lincoln, who purportedly claimed that while he would like God on his side, he must have Kentucky, excluded it and the other border slave states from his Emancipation Proclamation, white residents by that time had seen widespread violations of their personal liberties brought by Union occupation. Widespread military arrests, often arbitrary, caused even William T. Sherman, then military commander in Kentucky and no advocate of "soft" war, to remark, "So many improper arrests were made by self-constituted authorities that there was a physical impossibility of keeping them."[21] Indeed, in the summer of 1862, Burksville, Kentucky, resident Otho Miller condemned the conduct of Indiana and Pennsylvania troops near his home: "These Federal troops have disgraced themselves and the Cause and have mortified the union men here besides." Such behaviors, along with the proclamation, contributed directly to the emergence of the guerrilla warfare that would ultimately plague the border states (and define the wartime border experience) than would any conventional military campaigns.[22]

The irony of this identity shift is that among the first to label border residents as southerners were those Union soldiers who occupied the region. As early as November 1861, one southwestern Illinoisan wrote home upon his regiment's arrival in Louisville, "We have at last got into 'Dixie's Land.'" No more clear demonstration of the conviction held by many Federal soldiers that the presence of slavery (and of slaves) was the singular barometer of the physical South came from one Iowan, Lot Abraham, who in November 1862 sent a "contraband" freedman from Louisville to his home in Mount Pleasant, bearing a message for his family. "Before you now appears *a man of the South*," Abraham wrote to his kin, "take a good look at him & tell me what you think—*hes black but thats no matter.*"[23]

As this episode reveals, the wartime liberation of bondspeople on the border began well before and despite the Emancipation Proclamation, notwithstanding widespread governmental disavowals. As early as May 1861, conservative St. Louis Unionist Thomas T. Gantt wrote to then–department commander William S. Harney of a conversation with a Greene County resident who "asked me whether I supposed it was the intention of the United States Government to interfere with the institution of negro slavery in Missouri or any Slave State, or impair the security of that description of property." "Of course," Gantt averred, "my answer was most unqualifiedly, and almost indignantly in the negative. I told him that . . . I felt certain that the force of the United States, would, if necessary, be exerted for the protection of this, as well as any other kind of property." Yet Gantt, noticeably anxious, saw fit to query the department commander, himself a slaveholding Tennesseean, whether he had answered correctly. Harney responded that he would have answered the same but noted: "I am not a little astonished that such a question could be seriously put. . . . I should as soon expect to hear that the orders of the Government were directed towards the overthrow of any other kind of property as of this in negro slaves." Harney's naïveté matched those of slaveholders such as Gantt; both were convinced that their loyalty to the Union would forestall such an abomination.[24]

Other border residents actually seemed to accept the inevitability of slavery's end. One Unionist woman in Kentucky wrote to her brother early in 1862, "I sometimes think that God is now punishing our whole count[r]y for its sins, more especially for the sin of human slavery and that sweet Peace will never more hover over us until the oppressed go free."[25] But all were clear that emancipation by presidential fiat was not welcome. Another Kentuckian was just as direct on the issue of sovereignty, if less supportive of slavery: "I believe it is to the interest of Ky to get clear of the negro institution; and shall go with the party which will go for that in a proper way: but I want this done by her own people, in her own way, gradually and in her own time & not by outside pressure from people of other states, or the power of the Federal Gov. and I want that done in pursuance of her own laws & Constitution."[26]

For more residents the border states' exclusion from the proclamation did little to allay their fears that the war would ultimately end slavery in the states. Many borderites, convinced that the president would not prove true to his word regarding the proclamation's exclusions, lashed out against those whom they perceived either to represent or support Federal authority. One Union commander wrote to the new Kentucky governor, James F. Robinson, late in 1862 that "persons of seeming loyalty, on the street corners and upon the public highways; at their tables at home; and in their public prints, are daily announcing that this war is being now conducted by abolitionists; that it is against the institutions of the south, and waged solely to free the negroes."[27] J. P. Lancaster of Missouri complained: "I am in a Slave State. I have no slaves. I do not want to fight. I love the Union, and beg and plead for peace—and for all these things I am charged with being a Submissionist, a Black-Republickan—a friend of the North and an enemy to the South, . . . & if I do not fight for the South I will be hanged."[28] Another Kentuckian, touring fourteen counties of the state, concluded that "halfway conditional men have become advocates of the South, and secessionists have broken their silence with traitorous speeches."[29] The entire border suffered a war within a war as its residents divided despite their states' pledge of neutrality, engulfed in a partisan conflict that erupted with a fury beyond that found elsewhere in the nation.

Once issued, the Emancipation Proclamation's effect upon Kentucky was electrifying and immediate. One woman wrote that "the land I gaze upon is ours by the laws of all countries, yet it is in the hands of hirelings brought from other states by an Abolition president, to wrest from white Kentuckians their lawful rights in property, freedom of speech, and all else a brave and free people hold dear."[30] Another was more blunt: "It is 'Nigger' morning, noon & night at home, abroad, in the pulpit and every where else all [the abolitionists] want is the extinction of slavery and they care not by what means it is accomplished."[31] Most affected were the loyal Unionists, whose faith in the government the proclamation sorely shook. Kentuckian T. S. Bell reported to the judge advocate general, Joseph Holt (himself a Kentuckian), that "many of . . . the most faithful men [were] expressing doubts as to Lincoln's ability."[32] Samuel Haycraft, a Unionist state legislator from Elizabethtown, wrote in his diary in 1863: "The Radicals & abolitionists have taken new life & courage to put their diabolical plans into execution under cover of the sins of the South. Both [are] wrong & their sins cry to Heaven."[33]

Even the Union army of occupation was affected, perhaps more so than in other regions of the war since it was composed of many Kentucky regiments. One officer serving with an Illinois battery wrote in late 1862 that the Kentuckians in the army were "more than half opposed to the North, and in sympathy now with the South" and that the officers were "more than half Rebels," despite holding most of the highest ranks.[34] Kentuckian Thomas Gunn, serving in Tennessee, wrote home to his mother that "many of our officers have been complaining and murmuring during the past few days on account of alleged interferences in Ky with private property (niggers) on the part of some northern Regts."[35] Hundreds of officers and many more enlisted men tendered their resignations from the Federal army.

Rather than accept the inevitability of black liberation, many white borderites resisted the revolutionary social change with fear and anger, nowhere earlier or more apparent than in Missouri. "Our wives and daughters are panic stricken," wrote one Lafayette County resident, "and a reign of terror as black as hell itself envelops our county."[36] Many who had once believed that their state's stand for the Union would protect the peculiar institution within its borders now unleashed their fury by joining in the partisan warfare that exploded with the coming of emancipation. The provost marshal at Lexington had captured the contagion of Missourians' bitterness over emancipation when he wrote in August 1863: "The Negro in this County is the all 'inspiring theme' with many of the people. It is not the 'Rebellion, the Bushwhackers or the Rebel Sympathisers['] in Mo. but the Negro is the source of all our trouble, and the great question that divides the people Hundreds of men who[,] were it not for the negro[,] would be union men are now very doubtful. Many of them make the preservation of the institution of slavery a 'condition predicent' [*sic*] to the Union thereby effectually identifying their interests with the rebellion."

Perhaps more important, Union troops and loyalist citizens were not their only target; former and current slaves bore the brunt of this reign of terror. One bushwhacker claimed that he had been "instigated by the late slave owners to hang and shoot every negro he can find absent from the old plantation."[37] This extension of violence to black and Unionist Missourians reflects more than a broadening of the war's scope; symbolically, rural borderites linked slavery's death with the tyranny of the national government and lashed out at both progenitor and progeny. Statutory emancipation did little to stem either the violence or the resultant resentment. As a Union general commanding the Boon's Lick region, where slaveholding was most dense in Missouri, wrote in March 1865: "Slavery dies hard. I hear its expiring agonies and witness its contortions in death in every quarter of my district. In Boone, Howard, Randolph, and Callaway the emancipation ordinance has caused disruption of society equal to anything I saw in Arkansas or Mississippi in the year 1863."[38]

Although guerrilla activity of all kinds increased precipitously after Lincoln issued the proclamation, especially in Missouri, Kentucky's disaffected white residents unleashed their full fury only after the Enrollment Act of July 4, 1864, when enlistment of black troops began there, a year after such actions had begun in all other slave states. While loyal Kentucky masters could apply for a three-hundred-dollar compensation for each slave who enlisted, they were hardly appeased (and rarely paid), much less those owners judged disloyal by local boards of trade and provost marshals, who were not to be compensated in any way for the loss of their slave property. One Brandenburg resident warned Union authorities of "a general uprising to the rebelious portion of the population of Ky.," including an attempt on Louisville and a "masacree [of] all the negro troops. . . . I am decidedly of the opinion that at no period since the inauguration of this hellish rebelion has there been more energy & industry employed by the rebels than now."[39]

Outraged white Kentuckians threatened blacks and often apprehended them on their way to enlist, sometimes beating, maiming, and even murdering them. Between mid-May and July 1864, eight slaves were killed in Nelson County for attempting to volunteer. In Marion County slaveholders caught two former slaves attempting to enlist and cut off their left ears. Local military and government authorities, particularly provost marshals, charged with coordinating slave enlistments, were not exempt from such punishment: a Green

County officer reported that provost marshals there were flogged; in Larue County a special agent was stripped, tied to a tree, and cowhided; and James Fidler, provost marshal in Lebanon, was shot at twice in one day by Kentucky Union troops while walking the town's streets. During the course of the war, seven provost marshals in the state were slain either directly or indirectly as a result of the agitation.[40]

This trend only continued into the postwar period. Unlike Maryland and Missouri, Kentucky failed to move along a path that had been cleared in the border states by abolishing slavery voluntarily. When Congress adopted the Thirteenth Amendment, legal slavery existed only in Kentucky and Delaware.[41] In deliberating the ratification of the amendment, the Bluegrass State burst again into widespread violence. The former wartime divisions blurred, even galvanized, in opposition to the amendment, and political candidates were identified by their stance on the issue. In Grayson County a pro-amendment candidate for the state legislature was gunned down by an assassin in August 1865 after a stump speech in Millerstown, prompting one witness to quip, "I suppose you know now that old Grayson stands right on the question."[42] In Danville on the day of the election, locals rioted, firing on Union troops (some of whom were black), and the commanding general was nearly killed while on duty at the polling place.[43] The state rejected the amendment, and even after the other states had ratified, the Kentucky legislature stood "sullen and defiant," insisting that their voters' will was final. Many masters held on to their slaves as long as possible; as late as Christmas 1865 Orlando Brown wrote from Frankfort to his son, a U.S. officer: "I am daily looking for the Authentic announcement of the adoption of the Amendment. When it comes I will let our Servants know that they are free. What they intend to do and what we intend to do is equally unknown."[44]

In January 1866 the legislature issued a public address stating emphatically that Congress had no power "to pass any law granting the right of suffrage in the States to persons of African descent."[45] (Indeed Kentucky did not ratify the Thirteenth Amendment until 1876, only some twenty years sooner than Mississippi, and then by legislative act rather than popular vote). The mistreatment of former slaves in Kentucky and Missouri caused the U.S. government to assign Freedmen's Bureau agents to both states—the only such loyal slave states to have the bureau operate within their borders during the postwar period—though they were governed by no other legislative mandates associated with Reconstruction.[46]

Evidence suggests that this defiance turned quickly into a collective Confederate memory and social identity in which border state residents claimed that they and their culture were and always had been southern. Within a few years of the war's end, small towns and cities throughout the border began erecting monuments honoring their Confederate dead. Indeed, of the sixty-eight Civil War monuments standing today in Kentucky, all but twelve celebrate its Confederate heritage, despite the state's Union enlistments having outnumbered Confederate enlistments two to one. Missouri's troop spread was even more lopsided, where three times as many soldiers fought with the Union as with the Confederacy.[47] That a third of Kentucky's roughly seventy-five thousand Union enlistments were African Americans only intensified white borderites' postwar fever to construct a southern past, one that led to Kentucky's 1928 adoption of the paternalistic Stephen Foster "plantation" song, "My Old Kentucky Home," as its state song, still sung proudly, though with only slightly revised apologist language that proves nonsensical, given the song's true meaning (a slave who was sold south sings of his former home in Kentucky). In Louisville the Lost Cause periodicals *Southern Bivouac* and *Lost Cause,* established in 1882 and 1898 respectively, called for white Kentuckians to "cherish the memory of their Confederate elders, and the heritage and cause which her people fought and died for—the South."[48] In Missouri former Confederates such as Daniel M. Frost plied the state and private benefactors to establish the Confederate Veterans Home in Higginsville as well as an accompanying Veterans Cemetery.

Such memorials served not just to honor the valiant dead but also as counterweight to charges of these soldiers' unpatriotic and traitorous behavior. Indeed Missourians—like their Kentucky counterparts—sought to preserve the memory of those who sacrificed their lives resisting Federal invaders from their loyal states. One can see such defiance nowhere better than in Palmyra, Missouri, where a granite obelisk on the courthouse lawn stands silent vigil, a reminder of the atrocity the community suffered at the hands of Federal troops.[49] The act of memorialization bound Missourians and Kentuckians with the former Confederate states, not only in the replication of such activities, as was occurring throughout the South, but also by entwining their shared experience of war. Because borderites' version of the conflict was different than that of most of the South, the prism of their collective memory tilted slightly.

Once complete this Confederate mystique in the border states capped a process that had spanned decades, gradually assuming a shape that residents had until the postwar years limited to the political realm. People in these former slave states now articulated a southern identity—itself a political entity in that it derived from their frustration with government—that transcended the immediate celebration of a Confederate heritage or even the Lost Cause. Perhaps the most lasting symbol of Missouri's Confederate heritage—which at the same time served as a bridge to the adoption of a southern identity in at least one portion of the state—was the adoption of the term "Little Dixie" as a moniker for the former slaveholding center along the Missouri River. Unknown before and during the war itself, the origin of Little Dixie approximates former Confederate John S. Marmaduke's ascendance to governor. A Kansas City newspaperman in 1941 traced the term to the congressional candidacy of John B. Hale, who popularized it as a description for the central river counties while campaigning in the Second Congressional District in 1887. The common sobriquet reflects more than past and current voting trends; it stands as a distorted symbol of what Missourians believed they were culturally, yet never were, and what they were never politically, yet would not now believe.[50]

The apotheosis of the border's construction of southern memory was the 1924 erection of the Jefferson Davis Birthplace Memorial near Fairview, Kentucky, an obelisk that stands 351 feet tall (reputedly the tallest freestanding concrete structure in the world) and honors the president of a nation to which the state never swore allegiance. The Abraham Lincoln Birth Shrine in nearby Hodgenville, a granite structure built to house the cabin in which, as the curators freely admit, Lincoln probably was not born, pales in comparison. Kentucky state highways now proudly bear the names "Dixie" and "Jeff Davis," the entirety of middle Missouri is now known as Little Dixie, and schools throughout the region boast such mascots as the Rebels and Colonels, all delineated in the twentieth rather than the nineteenth century. Indeed the historian E. Merton Coulter's ageless adage that (despite the Confederacy having placed stars on its flag for the western border states) "Kentucky waited until after the war to secede from the Union" bears merit not only for that state but also for the entire border region.[51]

In thousands of households in postwar Missouri and Kentucky in general, the politics of memory placed the antebellum border states firmly in the South, thus accomplishing what their wartime governments had not. In both, postwar leaders recognized the necessity of assuaging their constituents' nagging insecurity of their collateral place in the Confederacy just as they appeased a deep-seated anger among them born of the resentment of the experience and outcome of the war in Missouri and Kentucky. Where the former Confederate states benefited from the inclusive wartime cultivation of Confederate nationalism and the ensuing postwar Lost Cause mythology, thus appeasing the bitterness attendant with their defeat at the hands of a nonvirtuous and foreign government by assessing the war as a noble cause that might have been lost but was not wrong, borderites faced the grim reality of exclusion by all sides. Their respective political alignments, driven by the then-Unionist loyalty of the largest portion of their populations, now exposed them as having chosen the wrong side based upon the prevailing assumption of the war as being waged against slavery.[52] For many of the border's white residents, the course of the Civil War pointed out clearly that a new alliance had emerged, one in which the northern and northwestern states had united in their conspiracy against slavery. No longer was the West a place of liberty; the democratic process that had once buttressed westerners' belief in independence now threatened the institution that to them embodied those liberties, not only in the territories but in the existing states as well. Angry and disillusioned, many white Kentuckians and Missourians questioned and even withdrew their loyalty to the federal government and the Union itself. These one-time westerners now looked to the region that embodied their sense of betrayal and victimization—the beleaguered South—for more than comfort.

As the border experience suggests, regional identity fits best within the political (or as historian Drew Gilpin Faust has termed it, "metapolitical") rather than the cultural realm, where in the border South it developed in its unique historical context as an antebellum defense against the North's political threat to the institution of slavery and the U.S. government's direct attacks on slaveholding residents in the ensuing civil war. In the postwar period southern identity became a means by which residents of former slave states sought to reestablish hegemony in defiance of federal authority during and after Reconstruction. Southern identity in the former Confederacy, in C. Vann Woodward's and others' time-honored arguments, stemmed directly from a post–Civil War experience of "frustration, failure, and defeat."[53] By 1865, even before the war had concluded, many in the border slave states had begun scripting their southern identity, centering it largely upon the destruction of the peculiar institution and their respective state's own ill-fated stances within rather than without the Union.[54]

A Federal officer stationed in Kentucky in September 1865 wrote that the state was "as yet in the chrysilis [*sic*] state, somewhere between the grub and the butterfly," referring immediately to the adjustment that white border residents were forced to make as a result of slavery's extinction.[55] The metamorphosis characterized the war experience of the border as a whole as these new southerners turned their collective backs on the remade Midwest and claimed their place within the anything-but-dead Confederate nation. While the former seceded states undertook the process of constructing Wilbur J. Cash's "frontier the Yankee created," many displaced borderites, marginalized by the North, the South, and even the West, forged a new place in this grim new world. Those who had once conflated liberty, democracy, and slavery now linked themselves and their future to the past of a free and brave yet wronged slaveholding nation, whose cause, though defeated, had been just. More even than postwar southerners as a whole, border residents invoked "a consciousness of change, of suspension between two worlds, a double focus looking both backward and forward," as yet another historian has written of the embittered historical consciousness that acted as a wellspring for the political process of southernization.[56] Indeed, almost as northerners had expected, even decreed, through the maelstrom of civil war, these Confederates in Kentucky and Missouri had become southerners.

NOTES

1. James M. Vanice to Charles Whittlesey, Jan. 1, 1862, Charles Whittlesey Papers (microfilm), Western Reserve Historical Society, Cleveland, Ohio (hereinafter cited as WRHS); Seventh U.S. Census, 1850, Population Schedule, Gallatin County, Ky., National Archives, Washington, D.C. (hereinafter cited as NA).

2. S. B. Axtell to L. Kerr, Apr. 5, 1861, WRHS.

3. *Western Monthly Magazine,* June 1844, 196; Richard Wade, *The Urban Frontier: Pioneer Life in Early Pittsburgh, Cincinnati, Lexington, Louisville, and St. Louis* (1959; repr., University of Chicago Press, 1964), 99, 253–54.

4. James S. Rollins to "My Dear Son," Nov. 14, 1858, James S. Rollins Papers, Western Historical Manuscripts Collection, Joint Collection—State Historical Society of Missouri/University of Missouri, Columbia (hereinafter cited as SHSM).

5. F[rank] R. Matthews to Henry T. Duncan Jr., Apr. 29, 1858, Henry M. Bond to Duncan, n.d. [1859], and C. J. Wilby to Duncan, Nov. 25, 1860, Duncan Family Papers, Special Collections and Archives, Margaret I. King Library, University of Kentucky, Lexington (hereinafter cited as UK).

6. *Liberty Tribune,* June 29, 1849, quoted in William E. Parrish, *David Rice Atchison, Border Politician* (Columbia: University of Missouri Press, 1961), 73, 79–80.

7. Paul C. Nagel, *Missouri: A Bicentennial History* (New York: W. W. Norton, 1977), 126; Parrish, *David Rice Atchison,* 1–5; Harrison A. Trexler, *Slavery in Missouri* (Baltimore: Johns Hopkins Press, 1914), 43–44; Sixth U.S. Census, 1840, Population Schedule, Clay County, Mo., NA; Seventh U.S.

Census, 1850, Population and Slave Schedules, Platte County, Mo., NA; Eighth U.S. Census, 1860, Population and Slave Schedules, Clinton County, Mo., NA; William W. Freehling, *The Road to Disunion,* vol. 1, *Secessionists at Bay, 1776–1854* (New York: Oxford University Press, 1990), 550; A[ndrew] P. Butler to Atchison, Mar. 5, 1856, David Rice Atchison Papers, SHSM; D. R. Atchison to William Atchison, Aug. 12, 1865, ibid., quoted in Parrish, *David Rice Atchison,* 115, 220–21.

8. Lewis C. Gray, *History of Agriculture in the Southern United States to 1860,* vol. 1 (1932; repr., Gloucester, Mass.: Peter Smith, 1958), 482; Perry McCandless, *A History of Missouri,* vol. 2, *1820 to 1860* (Columbia: University of Missouri Press, 1971), 35–36, 59–60; R. Douglas Hurt, *Agriculture and Slavery in Missouri's Little Dixie* (Columbia: University of Missouri Press, 1992), 219–23; Nagel, *Missouri,* 128.

9. Figures drawn from Ira Berlin, *Slaves without Masters: The Free Negro in the Antebellum South* (New York: Oxford University Press, 1974), 396–401.

10. E. Merton Coulter, *Civil War and Readjustment in Kentucky* (1926; repr., Gloucester, Mass.: Peter Smith, 1966), 7–8.

11. McCandless, *History of Missouri,* 6.

12. Marvin Meyers, *The Jacksonian Persuasion: Politics and Belief* (Stanford, Calif.: Stanford University Press, 1957), 49–50. For a full discussion of the free-labor ideology, see Eric Foner, *Free Soil, Free Labor, Free Men: The Ideology of the Republican Party before the Civil War* (New York: Oxford University Press, 1970), 11–72.

13. James M. McPherson, *Battle Cry of Freedom: The Civil War Era* (New York: Oxford University Press, 1985), 293; S. B. Axtell to L. Kerr, Apr. 5, 1861, WRHS.

14. R. M. Fairleigh to Dr. Galt Booth, May 8, 1861, Beall-Booth Family Papers, Filson Historical Society, Louisville, Ky. (hereinafter cited as FHS).

15. Ibid; *Appendix to the Congressional Globe,* 33rd Cong., 1st sess. (Washington, D.C.: Office of the Globe, 1855), 301; Thelma Jennings, *The Nashville Convention: Southern Movement for Unity, 1848–1851* (Memphis: Memphis State University Press, 1980), 187–211; Parrish, *David Rice Atchison,* 101; Coulter, *Civil War and Readjustment in Kentucky,* 81–82.

16. *Appendix to the Congressional Globe,* 34th Cong., 1st sess. (Washington, D.C.: Office of the Globe, 1856), 465 *Missouri Statesman* (Columbia), Mar. 9, 1849.

17. Coulter, *Civil War and Readjustment in Kentucky,* 24.

18. Carl N. Degler, *The Other South: Southern Dissenters in the Nineteenth Century* (New York: Harper & Row, 1974), 116.

19. *Congressional Globe,* pt. 4 and app., 37th Cong., 2nd sess., 81.

20. McPherson, *Battle Cry of Freedom,* 294–95; John A. Hockaday to Rollins, May 6, 1861, Rollins Papers; Daniel W. Crofts, *Reluctant Confederates: Upper South Unionists in the Secession Crisis* (Chapel Hill: University of North Carolina Press, 1989), 195–214.

21. William T. Sherman to W. T. Ward, Nov. 2, 1861, in U.S. War Department, *The War of the Rebellion: A Compilation of the Official Records of the Union and Confederate Armies,* 128 vols. (Washington, D.C.: Government Printing Office, 1880–1901), ser. 1, 4:327 (hereinafter cited as *OR;* all references to ser. 1).

22. D. C. Wickliffe to Orlando Brown, Dec. 20, 1862, and Otho Miller to Orlando Brown, July 13, 1862, Orlando Brown Papers, FHS.

23. Watson Goodrich to Alvin C. Woolfolk, Nov. 26, 1861, Watson Goodrich Letters, FHS; Aaron Harding to "Dear Sons," Nov. 7, 1862, John Harding Collection, FHS.

24. Thomas T. Gantt to William S. Harney, May 14, 1861, and Harney to Gantt, May 14, 1861, in Ira Berlin et al., eds., *Freedom: A Documentary History of Emancipation, 1861–1867* (Cambridge: Cambridge University Press, 1982–93), ser. 1, 1:413–14.

25. Mary Gunn to Thomas M. Gunn, n.d. [1862], Gunn Family Papers, UK.

26. Ed F. Dulin to E. Hubbard Smith, Apr. 5, 1864, E. Hubbard Smith Papers, Mss. C/S, FHS.

27. Gordon Granger to James F. Robinson, Nov. 22, 1862, box 1, ser. 2173, Letters Received, Dept. of Kentucky, 1862–69, Records of the U.S. Army Continental Commands, 1821–1920, pt. 1, RG 393, NA.

28. J. P. Lancaster to J. O. Broadhead, May 9, 1861, James O. Broadhead Papers, Missouri Historical Society, St. Louis (hereinafter cited as MHS).

29. T. H. Bell to Joseph Holt, Dec. 22, 1862, Joseph Holt Papers, Library of Congress, Washington, D.C.

30. Mary E. Van Meter Diary, Feb. 25, 1863, UK.

31. Jane Phillips to Annie Gratz Cooper, Feb. 25, 1862, Cooper-Phillips Family Papers, UK.

32. Bell to Holt, Dec. 22, 1862.

33. Samuel Haycraft Journal (transcribed and extracted), 1849–73, Sept. 27, 1863, FHS.

34. Jac[ob] H. Stokes to Lyman Trumbull, Nov. 17, 1862, Lyman Trumbull Papers, Library of Congress, Washington, D.C.

35. Thomas M Gunn to Mother, Dec. 3, 1862, Gunn Family Papers.

36. Michael Fellman, *Inside War: The Guerrilla War in Missouri during the American Civil War* (New York: Oxford University Press, 1989), 70.

37. H. B. Johnson to "General," Aug. 14, 1863, in Berlin et al, *Freedom,* ser. 1, 2:577–78, 558–61, 562.

38. Michael Fellman, "Emancipation in Missouri," *Missouri Historical Review* 83 (Oct. 1988): 50–56; Clinton B. Fisk to James E. Yeatman, Mar. 25, 1865, *OR,* 48:1257.

39. William Alexander to Thomas B. Fairleigh, June 16, 1864, box 3, ser. 2173, Letters Received, Dept. of Kentucky, 1862–69, RG 393; Salmon P. Chase to William P. Mellen, July 4, 1863, entry 3/6, bk. 13, pp. 321, 362–64, box 60, ser. 40, Letters Sent Related to Restricted Commercial Intercourse, 1861–68, Dept. of the Treasury Records, pt. 56, RG 56, NA.

40. Victor B. Howard, *Black Liberation in Kentucky: Emancipation and Freedom, 1862–1884* (Lexington: University Press of Kentucky, 1983), 63–64; William H. Sidell to James B. Fry, June 25, 1864, box 4, ser. 2173, Letters Received, Dept. of Kentucky, 1862–69, RG 393.

41. Howard, *Black Liberation,* 2.

42. David C. Phillips to Bird Willis, Aug. 1865, Phillips Family Letters, Kentucky Historical Society, Frankfort.

43. M. D. Rodocker to John M. Palmer, Aug. 12, 1865, box 5, ser. 2173, Letters Received, Dept. of Kentucky, 1862–69, RG 393.

44. Orlando Brown Sr. to Orlando Brown Jr., Dec. 25, 1865, Orlando Brown Papers.

45. *Union Standard,* Jan. 17, 1866, quoted in Howard, *Black Liberation,* 89.

46. George C. Wright, *Racial Violence in Kentucky, 1865–1940: Lynchings, Mob Rule, and "Legal Lynchings"* (Baton Rouge: Louisiana State University Press, 1990), 2.

47. McPherson, *Battle Cry of Freedom,* 293.

48. *Southern Bivouac,* July 19, 1882.

49. Gaines M. Foster, *Ghosts of the Confederacy: Defeat, the Lost Cause, and the Emergence of the New South, 1865 to 1913* (New York: Oxford University Press, 1987), 127–44; Ralph W. Widener, *Confederate Monuments: Enduring Symbols of the South and the War between the States* (Washington, D.C.: Andromeda Associates, 1982), 132–36; Stephen Davis, "Empty Eyes, Marble Hand: The Confederate Monument and the South," *Journal of Popular Culture* 16 (Winter 1982): 2–8, 16–19; Robert E. Miller, "Daniel Marsh Frost, C.S.A.," *Missouri Historical Review* 85 (July 1991): 398. My thanks to Fitzhugh Brundage for pointing me to sources on Confederate monuments.

50. *Kansas City Times,* Dec. 5, 1941, cited in Daniel Joseph Conoyer, "Missouri's Little Dixie: A Geographical Delineation" (Ph.D. diss., Saint Louis University, 1973), 1–3, 224–314 passim; Robert M. Crisler, "Missouri's Little Dixie," *Missouri Historical Review* 42 (Jan. 1948): 130–39; John H. Fenton, *Politics in the Border States* (New Orleans: Hauser, 1957), 156–57; Albert E. Twombly, *Little Dixie* (Columbia: University of Missouri Press, 1955). Conoyer concluded after only a two-week field observation in 1971 that little remained in Little Dixie of what he assumed was a once-southern cultural heritage. He delimits the region with such evidence as surnames, speech patterns, food preferences, farm acreage, and agricultural products.

51. Coulter, *Civil War and Readjustment in Kentucky,* 329.

52. Drew Gilpin Faust, *The Creation of Confederate Nationalism: Ideology and Identity in the Civil War South* (Baton Rouge: Louisiana State University Press, 1988), 14–16 and passim; Emory M. Thomas, *The Confederate Nation: 1860–1865* (New York: Harper & Row), 67–119 and passim; David W. Blight, *Race and Reunion: The Civil War in American Memory* (Cambridge, Mass.: Harvard University Press, 2001), 255–99.

53. Paul M. Gaston, *The New South Creed: A Study in Southern Mythmaking* (New York: Alfred A. Knopf, 1970), 4–13; C. Vann Woodward, *The Burden of Southern History* (1960; repr., New York: Mentor, 1969), 27.

54. Gaston, *New South Creed,* 4–13; Woodward, *Burden,* 27.

55. Ira Delano to John M. Palmer, Sept. 29, 1865, box 5, ser. 2173, Letters Received, Dept. of Kentucky, 1862–69, RG 393.

56. Wilbur J. Cash, *The Mind of the South* (New York: Vintage Books, 1941), 105; George B. Tindall, "Mythology: A New Frontier in Southern History," in *The Idea of the South: In Pursuit of a Central Theme,* ed. Frank E. Vandiver (Chicago: University of Chicago Press, 1964), 12.

FAMILY AND GENDER

The Moral Imagination of Confederate Family Politics

JEAN E. FRIEDMAN

I could not love thee, Dear, so much,
Loved I not honour more.
RICHARD LOVELACE, "To Lucasta"

TRADITIONAL SENTIMENTS OF HONOR RESONATED WITH MID-nineteenth-century southern notions of virtue even though, as noted by historian Bertram Wyatt-Brown, the ethics of honor competed with evangelical and Primitive Baptist moral norms until the Civil War. Old South honor referred to the ritual defense of personal, familial, racial, and sectional pride against the fear of public humiliation. The code of honor in effect ranked men in the social hierarchy. In contrast, obedience to God in the formation of conscience and consequent guilt ensured a holy life of Christian self-discipline. Thus Wyatt-Brown concludes that the Civil War compelled an uneasy merger of Christian and secular ethics that yielded a pious code of honor as southerners reacted violently to northern moral criticism of slavery. He argues that the code of honor cut a broad swath across class, generation, and religion.[1]

Yet Wyatt-Brown's path-breaking work fails to answer a key question: If honor ultimately subsumed all ethical persuasions, then why and how did an individual develop the moral imagination to challenge or subvert that largely masculine code?[2] Perhaps one's perception of oneself within the various southern family patterns shaped one's ethical choices. Close analysis of family styles of harmony and conflict, in addition to questions important to the individual,[3] reveals broader categories of ethical norms than recent studies of the code of honor may indicate. For instance, a Confederate family's moral vision, whether enlightened Jewish Orthodox, traditional Roman Catholic, Protestant Baptist, or morally ambivalent, also determined southern ethics regarding the war.

For southerners the choice for or against war with the North involved an individual's peculiar relationship with the family's moral vision. Indeed the very development of selfhood engaged this outlook.[4] That moral imagination applied to one's choice for war or peace involved not only political and social influences but also an internal moral process that turned back upon itself to its origin—the family. Although one member might deviate from an otherwise harmonious family's wishes, the web of dependence exerted a powerful influence nonetheless, with a language all its own that invited deeper investigations of shared values and moral assumptions.[5] In the case of internal family conflict, of generational friction, the Civil War politicized personal issues. Ideology, sectional interests, and politics played out publicly in a contest already privately debated. That does not make the political stakes in the Civil War reducible to petty personal squabbles or Freudian narratives. But it does emphasize the way in which conflict and values within a particular family structure raised the moral stakes and demanded the definition of moral direction and sense of justice.

Moral culture may be understood not simply in terms of ritual and behavior but also, according to philosopher Charles Taylor, in terms of the object of one's love.[6] What moves an individual, what constitutes notions of respect, dignity, and the meaning of a full life, are the questions that help an individual develop an identity by deciding what is important. That identity then calls for a commitment to the chosen good. The development of self in tandem with moral vision assumes that one is a self only among other selves. And the sense of self is always changing according to the narrative of the life lived. That is, one exists within a context of questions, and the questions determine the direction of the life.[7]

Consider what this meant in the lives of Maj. Alfred Mordecai of North Carolina and Dr. George William Bagby of Virginia. These men represent two different moral perspectives and therefore two distinct processes of moral imagination. Yet the wartime decisions of both ultimately rested upon their family's moral culture. Major Mordecai, a favored son in a harmonious family, assimilated its enlightened Orthodox Jewish ethics. As an observant Jew, the question of how to live a righteous life defined him. A distinguished U.S. Army ordnance officer, international consultant on weapons technology, and commander of the New York Watervliet Arsenal, he faced a crucial decision in 1861: Should he retain his army post and fight against his southern homeland or resign and join the Confederacy? When he resigned from the U.S. Army and retired to private life, his southern family reviled his choice and pitied his fate. Yet Alfred Mordecai placed the family's moral standards both above family interest and his own military sense of honor.

George William Bagby, anything but a favored son, lived with a domineering father in a fractured family and developed an ambiguous set of values. The Civil War only exacerbated his moral uncertainty. A medical doctor by training, he nonetheless had great ambitions for a journalistic career. The Civil War forced him to choose between honest coverage of dramatic political events and the fire-eating brand of incendiary journalism. He wrote in both veins: polemical fodder that inflamed the South's decision for war against the North, and objective criticism that contributed to the South's dissatisfaction with the administration of Jefferson Davis. The contrast in moral choices between the two men reveals a difference in individual perceptions of family moral patterns, righteousness versus rigidity, that enabled them to challenge or undermine the prevalent southern code of honor.

Alfred Mordecai, born in 1804 in Warrenton, North Carolina, the son of Jacob and Rebecca Myers Mordecai, early proved himself a scholar in a scholarly family. In 1808 his father founded the Warrenton Female Academy, a renowned institution that emphasized progressive education in the classics and sciences for young women. Five of the eldest children from Jacob's first marriage to Rebecca's sister, Judith Myers, contributed to the success of the school, which lasted a prosperous decade until the family moved to Spring Farm outside of Richmond, Virginia.[8] The academy proved a key element in the formation of family unity.

Jacob and especially his eldest daughter, Rachel, taught according to an enlightened Anglo-Irish guide, *Practical Education,* based on Enlightenment principles. This educational text was written by the celebrated Richard Lovell Edgeworth and his novelist daughter, Maria.[9] A correspondence initiated by Rachel Mordecai with Maria Edgeworth in Edgeworthstown, Ireland, opened a half century of communication between the families, including a visit by Alfred in 1833 to the Edgeworths.[10] Alfred and all the younger children from Jacob's second marriage experienced this progressive home schooling, which demanded moral patterning, dialogic method, and a liberal ideology.

The Edgeworths counseled the "education of the heart," the inducement of "useful and agreeable habits, well regulated sympathy and benevolent affections," that is, a warm yet disciplined heart devoted to the practice of virtue.[11] Such practice instilled virtues of benevolence, honesty, self-reliance, self-control, and industry. The Enlightenment virtue of benevolence fostered an obligation to the broader social order. Family members practiced charity and retained a patriotic loyalty to the nation. Instruction in science and mathematics honed observation and enhanced inductive skills. Moreover scientific methods also guided a rational approach to experience that proved invaluable in training the emotions. Nonetheless the Edgeworth family remained a benevolent patriarchy that involved paternal control over sons' and daughters' careers and marriage choices.

The Mordecai family revered egalitarian values by educating both women and men. In addition they respected individual rights by holding democratic family conferences. Yet the Mordecai siblings honored traditional patriarchal values and sought their father's permission to marry. The father also remained the authority on matters of religion and morals. As a family the Mordecais easily absorbed the democratic ideology of the early nineteenth century "Republic of Men" that obscured a paternal hegemony. Enlightened ethics and Orthodox Judaism thus contained assumptions of hierarchy that contradicted democratic principles.

As Orthodox Jews, the Mordecais kept a kosher household, observed the High Holidays, reverenced the *hashem* (the name of God), and maintained a faith in Providence. Orthodox notions of holiness or perfection far exceeded the demands of republican virtue. The Hebrew belief in a transcendent, holy God, whose ways could not be known or understood, demanded obedience and called all believers to holiness. The people covenanted to God followed his way and not the ways of the idolatrous. The covenant promised God's providential care in return for his people's total giving. Moreover the prophetic tradition demanded a high ethical standard of righteousness: justice, humility, and service to the poor. Following the precepts of the Torah required a sanctified life.[12]

Mordecai biographer Emily Bingham has noted that the family defined themselves in terms of a covenant, as a "'little faithful band of love and duty,'" devoted to mutual protection, religious and intellectual liberalism, and bourgeois domesticity. Only later in mature years, according to Bingham, did individual members, pressured by issues of class and religious assimilation, challenge family cohesion.[13] Inner-family contradictions notwithstanding, they retained the principled ethic of enlightened Jewish Orthodoxy.

Alfred Mordecai, a talented scientist and technician, demonstrated an integrity woven of the two strands of objectivity and Orthodox Jewish self-giving. His principles can only be understood by his interpretation of the resources found in his upbringing. But the Mordecai family did not share his interpretation. In 1861 Alfred resigned his commission in the U.S. Army but refused his family's and the Confederate government's pleas to take up the South's cause.

The family's moral vision shaped Alfred's education and character. His father and elder brothers and sisters favored Alfred among the six young children of Jacob Mordecai's second marriage. Alfred's sister Ellen, fourteen years his senior, who taught him, considered him one of the best students in the school and believed that the boy would be conscientious "when he [got] over his foolishness."[14] The family evidently had a disciplinary problem with the young teenager. Alfred later apologized to his brother Solomon, who also trained him, writing, "How ungrateful I have been to be the means of knowingly inflicting pain on you instead of endeavoring by all means in my power to relieve you from the cares and anxieties with which you have been perplexed on my account."[15] Ellen expected Alfred to learn sympathetic understanding. He did so later in the context of self-criticism.

Alfred's brothers and sisters instructed him in the classics, French, mathematics, science, history, literature, and geography. His education included the Jewish catechism and Maria Edgeworth's *Moral Stories.* As a boy Alfred enthusiastically followed the campaigns of the War of 1812; the war had a special significance since Mordecai and Myers family members in Norfolk refugeed with Jacob's family during the British blockade of the Virginia coast. Alfred then followed Napoleon's exploits in Europe. Appraising his son's talents and interests, Jacob decided to send him in 1819 to the fledgling West Point for a scientific education.[16] He may also have been encouraged to do so since a Jewish cadet had graduated in the academy's first class in 1802.[17]

Reorganized in 1817 by Superintendent Sylvanus Thayer, West Point emerged as a premier scientific and technological institute. There Alfred's growth clearly showed that the development of self and moral vision were clearly intertwined.[18] Inspired by Thayer's vision, the young Mordecai applied himself assiduously to his engineering studies, embraced Thayer's concern with international military and technological developments, and imitated his values of rectitude and honor. During his first year of study, he placed second (out of ninety-one students) in mathematics, studied French in his spare time in order to read French military texts, and followed the academy's honor code that one's word was one's bond. Distinguished as first in his graduating class, Mordecai earned Thayer's invitation to teach at the academy. His outstanding scholastic record determined his course as an engineering officer.[19]

Alfred rose steadily in the military as an ordnance officer. He commanded arsenals at Frankford, Pennsylvania; Washington, D.C.; and Watervliet, New York, and served as assistant to the secretary of war and to the chief of ordnance. He published the *Digest of Military Laws* (1833) and served on the Ordnance Board, which contributed to the antebellum technological revolution in the U.S. military. And like his mentor Thayer, Mordecai was sent to Europe and the Crimea to study European weapons systems. His reports and his experiments that resulted in publications for the Ordnance Board proved invaluable in the improvement of weapons technology. Through this work he earned an international reputation.[20]

The Mordecai family took pride not only in Alfred's academic achievements but especially in his character. Ellen remarked, "He surpasses my highest expectations . . . ; he is the pride of our father's heart."[21] Rachel wrote, "Alfred always reminds me of Miss E[dgeworth]'s Orlando—so wise, steady and sedate."[22] His mother, Rebecca, likewise approved: "His mother's Blessing ever rests on his head; and like the patriarchs would extend to the utmost bounds of everlasting Hills."[23] With Alfred's marriage to Sara Hays in 1836, he entered into an observant, well-integrated Philadelphia Orthodox family. Sara's mother, Richea Gratz Hays, was the sister of Rebecca Gratz, a celebrated philanthropist and activist in the Philadelphia Orphan Society.[24] Although Alfred did not remain an observant Jew, he retained the meaning, value, and intent of his early practice, even when he found himself far from his family.[25]

Stationed in the North, the young officer still remained connected with his family. One summer moonlit night in 1836 as he sat by an open window, Alfred wrote to his young niece that he was thinking "how each of the widely scattered family was spending this same lovely evening."[26] Later he urgently requested aid from his sister when he was recalled to active duty soon after his daughter, Emma, died and his wife lay ill. He felt a special spiritual bond to his younger sister, also named Emma. "I read God's blessing in all and felt that I was leaning on no broken reed when I committed all to his care," he wrote. "I got your last dear letter the day before I left, and more than ever if possible my darling I was struck with the perfect harmony of our spirits the similarity of our hidden experience."[27] Alfred thus expressed a faith in God and clung to a Jewish notion of the importance of family. The Civil War, however, tried both his faith and his commitment to family.

Prior to the war Alfred kept to northern conservative opinion and company. He supported the Whiggish *Boston Courier* and hoped the *Albany Argus* would condemn abolitionist John Brown's Harpers Ferry raid. He believed a Republican defeat necessary to "save our goodly fabric [nation] from ruin."[28] Alfred saw no security in a united South; rather he supported a politically untenable alternative, a reconstructed Union without resorting to war. His thoughts went back to his family's classical training as he recalled a conversation between Pyrrhus and his counselor before the Roman campaign: "How much easier and better it would be to sit down now in peace, than to purchase it with the horrors of revolution and civil war!"[29]

In January 1861 Alfred still disdained any "extreme course" by the South. Amid the rising tensions, however, his concern lay with his family, and he discussed with his brother Samuel the possibility of a journey south to visit them. In April he did reach Richmond and visited his mother, but he apologized to his brother George for not stopping in Raleigh to visit him because a storm delayed the trip, and in any case the shelling of Fort Sumter prompted his immediate recall to the New York arsenal. Even after Sumter, Alfred considered wise North Carolina's cautious approach to secession.[30]

His conservative views precluded any abolitionist sympathy. He could hold stringent moral principles yet support the institution of slavery because Enlightenment ethics and Jewish Orthodoxy maintained a paternal hierarchy. Jacob Mordecai's family owned a few slaves, and Alfred once commented to his niece as he observed a "nigger gal" who just scoured his room at the Frankford Arsenal in Pennsylvania, "Don't you know how much I enjoy the sight of her in this land of white niggers."[31] He criticized peace plans that he felt undermined slavery and feared that in Lincoln's cabinet "unmixed abolitionism will rule."[32] Given Alfred's sympathies, the Mordecai family hoped he would join the Confederate army. As his brother's confidante, Samuel explained to the family, "Under no circumstances will [Alfred] be placed in conflict with his native land and that of his dearest connections."[33] At the same time, the Mordecais worried about Alfred's domination by his northern wife's "petticoat appeals."[34] Certainly Alfred's long-term residence in the North and his wife's influence contributed to his refusal of offers from President Davis and other high-level officials to join the Confederacy.[35] Nonetheless such influences played upon deeper religious and Enlightenment ethical sentiments.

The Mordecais realized their worst fears when Alfred resigned his commission and vowed to retire to private life in Philadelphia. They received the news just as Alfred's nephew, Edmund Myers, and a number of other nephews joined Confederate ranks and seventeen-year-old Alfred Mordecai Jr. of West

Point joined the Union army. Samuel blamed Alfred's "weakness" in submitting to pressure from his in-laws.[36] Rebecca attempted to appeal to her son's family loyalty: "Be still useful to yourself, to your family and to your native state," she wrote, while assuring him that the family neither judged him harshly nor felt alienated from him. She knew how to twist the arrow in the heart, however, when she implored Alfred to withdraw his son from active combat. "Let it not be said that he applied a torch to your mother's habitation."[37]

The family's deep disappointment, however, never equaled the vehement criticism directed at Alfred in New York. The *Troy Daily Times* doubted his loyalty and argued that all military personnel who resign ought to be arrested and then placed on parole. In Major Mordecai's case the paper insinuated that he transferred designs for a "bullet machine" to the Confederacy when he visited Richmond in April.[38] Alfred wrote a defense of his conduct that accounted for all of his time in the South, including the visit to his mother in Richmond. Furthermore he argued that his identity as a southerner compromised his position as commander of the Watervliet Arsenal. Therefore, instead of resigning, he had requested a less active duty. In the most forceful terms he argued, "If any one imagines that I could persevere, for an indefinite time, in forwarding warlike preparations which were intended to be used against the homes of my mother, brothers and numerous relatives in the South, he gives me too much credit for philosophy."[39] The *Daily Times* called him a traitor for requesting lesser duties, thus deserting his country in its hour of need. It claimed that true patriotism held country above family.[40]

A career soldier, Alfred invested mightily in advancement and promotion. His identity rested in his honor as a U.S. military officer; Alfred swore he never betrayed that trust. Given his untenable dilemma, he made a rational choice to resign. Enlightenment Jewish Orthodoxy informed his course of action neither to betray his office nor fight against his family. In the *Daily Whig* he argued his case as a southerner and a family man. Alfred's decision rested solidly on his family's basic moral directive, namely enlightened self-discipline applied to total self-giving. Yet the Civil War revealed contradictory tendencies within the family ethos. Democratic principles of equality and independence imbibed in his family clashed with the close-knit style of his Orthodox kin. Alfred emerged as a singular individual, apart from his family's interest but not from its ethical core.

For Alfred the military code of honor rested upon Jewish righteousness. He could not give up either his military honor or his family honor unless he served a higher purpose. His was a primal ethic, the Jewish spirit of righteousness that existed before Indo-European notions of honor.[41] Confronted with the choice between honor as community derived and honor as God directed, Alfred chose the traditional path of justice and humility, leaving all to the Divine will. He considered it just to reject betrayal of his southern family and his military commission. Initially he gained nothing but poverty. From 1861 to 1864 he tutored a few students in mathematics. Alfred's moral code went beyond the strict military ethic of honor that demanded duty to nation above family. Rather, he observed the Orthodox way, which demanded everything. Toward the end of the war his prospects brightened. From 1864 to 1866 he worked in Mexico as assistant engineer of the Mexico and Pacific Railroad. Thereafter his friends obtained for him an appointment as secretary of the Pennsylvania Canal Company, a subsidiary of the Pennsylvania Railroad Company.[42] Upon Alfred's death in 1887 at the age of eighty-three, his eulogist acclaimed his righteousness: "The name and character of Major Alfred Mordecai should be deemed worthy of mention and regard; for the lessons of the youth were the source of strength in the man, and in old age gave that peace of conscience, which made his simple greeting almost a benediction."[43]

In sum, Mordecai exemplified the early-nineteenth-century enlightened family norms that supported "rational orthodoxy."[44] Such standards survived into the Civil War era. A product of a small town, Alfred's career afforded him the initiative to shed his provincialism and with it a narrow sense of community and honor. Rather, his habit of "well-regulated sympathy," benevolence, and dependence upon Divine Providence conditioned him for the sacrifice of his honor. But the rational and religious ethic that guided Alfred Mordecai's family norms unraveled in the later Victorian decades, replaced by evangelical enthusiasm and romantic idealism.

Nonetheless the growth of southern towns and urban culture spawned a skepticism that competed with waves of evangelicalism. George William Bagby, born in 1828 in the vital market town of Lynchburg, Virginia, was raised among a new generation of educated men for whom money and ambition vied with piety and honor.[45]

Bagby earned a medical degree but abandoned his practice for a journalistic career. Hired by the polemical newspapers *Charleston Mercury* and *New Orleans Crescent* as a Washington and Richmond correspondent before and during the Civil War, Bagby found it increasingly difficult to make a living without bending to distorted notions of truth. On the eve of the Civil War, he joined the community of fire-eaters who felt the South's honor at stake. Yet he went against the code of honor in criticizing the Davis administration. His diatribes against both the North and the Confederate government arose from an inchoate anger, given vent without a well-defined moral framework.

The genial writer-physician and politician, known as "a Virginia Realist,"[46] produced romantic views of the past and had little faith in large systems, whether of religion or government. Trained in scientific rationality, he very nearly came undone through his passionate prejudices. Although he tried desperately to mold his life to his will, his life often demonstrated a depressed passivity.[47] After the Civil War his curious mix of verisimilitude and myth found a loyal Virginia audience with his popular Old South essays. Until then he had not found himself.

George William Bagby, the only son of merchant George Bagby, never felt himself to be a favored son. On the contrary, after the death of his mother, Virginia, when he was eight years old, his father sent him to a series of "old field schools" in Buckingham and Prince Edward counties and to the plantation of his uncle, James Evan, in Prince Edward County.[48] The plantation served as a refuge, and the schools proved a beneficial separation since his father had an "evil temper" and berated the boy for his less than stringent morals. This attitude may have had some effect on the ambivalent moral values young George developed.[49] His father held to a fierce evangelicalism with an emphasis upon sin, repentance, and a strict moral code. Although he loved his children and wrote affectionate letters, his insistence that his son imagine the horrors of martyrdom and the death of sinners must have frightened the child. The elder Bagby wrote to his six-year-old son of the martyrdom of a little girl who refused to recant her Christianity before Roman officials, explaining: "They drove a stake in the ground and chained her little hands and feet to it and then built a great fire to burn her up." Moreover he wrote that two wicked boys drowned in a millpond.[50] Wicked children were those who did not love their father: "You are in danger every day. You may soon die,"[51] he threatened. George Bagby presented a cruel and punishing image of God and of paternal authority. It is no wonder his son developed habits of deception and deviousness.

Letters from the master at Edgehill Academy in Princeton, New Jersey, where the teenage George attended school, noted the boy's evasion or subversion of the rules. He did not speak the truth, his teachers complained.[52] George's actions pained his father, who warned: "No son prospers who insults authority of Father and Mother. God has inseparably connected the happiness of the child with his obedience to his parents."[53] Secretly young George indulged in sexual fantasies tinged with guilt. He drew caricatures of himself as a demon racing toward a young woman. He depicted priapic demons boiling a man in a pot.[54] His father only saw his son's laziness, his lack of gratitude. Gradually young George fell into depression. Despite his unhappiness, he excelled in school so much so that his father cautioned that he placed too much trust in his intellectual powers, offering constructive advice to think through and not parrot his studies.[55] George William Bagby inherited a legacy of love and fear, and this ambiguity propelled him into adulthood.[56]

In 1846, soon after his father remarried, George entered the University of Pennsylvania Medical School, where he gained a reputation for skill and accuracy.[57] The bouts with depression continued, however, and his father noted, "You are your own tormentor," and advised him to seek divine help.[58] Despite the young medical student's moods, he graduated and set up a practice in Lynchburg. Four years later James McDonald, the editor of the *Lynchburg Virginian,* encouraged him to start a new career in journalism because the physician loved words, reading, and writing and claimed reporters as his closest friends.[59]

Bagby's journalistic apprenticeship in Lynchburg included more than professional training. Fellow newspaperman Thomas Jellis Kirkpatrick endeavored to help him sort through the questions the physician-journalist entertained concerning a moral life. Between 1850 and 1853 they corresponded and wrestled with the larger questions of God, sin, and moral responsibility. When Bagby became a writer, Kirkpatrick worried that now he had "unwholesome influences to create prejudices which are unreasonable and highly injurious."[60] He sympathized with Bagby's aspirations but likened them to his own vainglorious desires, warning, "We must have fixed, enduring and long-cherished aims."[61] Despite his qualms, Kirkpatrick several times offered to help Bagby obtain a post in his hometown or publish in his columns. The two bachelors probably lived together until Kirkpatrick married. Kirkpatrick observed that denial of secret depravity leads to pride and criticism of others.[62] Friendship and an evangelical conversion emboldened him to offer guidance to Bagby and provide honest criticism of his moral ideology. Kirkpatrick sensed that his friend was morally adrift.

Bagby insisted that moral evil did not exist, that it proved inconsistent with God's perfection. Kirkpatrick replied that God's justice demanded that hell existed as an answer to the consequences of moral evil: if hell did not exist, then neither did the difference between good and evil. According to Kirkpatrick, lusty desires corrupted the body, and only a force of will could prevent the disastrous consequences. He believed that Bagby's denial of sin was the result of a "lazy, voluptuous idealism" that led to deceitfulness.[63] Bagby's notion of manliness did not include powerlessness, and he believed that Christian notions of God's justice included a wretched notion of the moral order. In his view the idea of justice condemning people to hell was repugnant. Kirkpatrick reminded him that human beings existed as free agents and could not exist as such without the choice between good and evil. But in the end where did truth reside? What beliefs could these two men share? Kirkpatrick suggested, "There is truth in love."[64]

Clearly Bagby entertained ambiguous moral assumptions in direct opposition to his father's rigid moral theology. Kirkpatrick's fears that such indifference to right and wrong would open his friend to all the vicissitudes of passion and prejudice proved prophetic. On the eve of the Civil War, George Bagby faced challenges that tested his moral strength.

The Civil War set families and generations apart, including the Bagbys, father and son. Their differences had increased as the younger man matured politically. The father remained a steadfast Whig in a Whig town, his party loyalty determined by his business and religion. As a merchant and trader in Lynchburg, an urban-commercial center fueled by the canal and railroad arteries that stimulated manufacturing and a dynamic market system in western Virginia, the senior Bagby honored Henry Clay's American System, which supported such economic growth. As a Presbyterian, his Puritan ethic of hard work and conversion of heart spurred his quest for financial security and peace of mind.[65] The younger Bagby first intimated his father's interest in anti-mercantilist, strict-constructionist, states' rights ideology when he attended the Democratic convention in Baltimore in 1844. His visit coincided with his first taste of freedom before entering medical school. His father, meanwhile, cheered the Virginia Whig partisan John Minor Botts and glowed at the defeat of "locofocos," the hard money Democrats, in 1848. He later decried the decline of the Whigs in 1857 when party losses began to mount in local elections. His Whig loyalty remained on the eve of the Civil War as he gathered with fellow Presbyterians in January 1861 in a prayer for the Union and the success of reconciliation with the North through the Crittenden Compromise.[66] Only the outbreak of hostilities forced him to change his mind. The elder Bagby's faithful partisanship made him fearful for his son's association with Democrats. In 1859 the father remarked that he knew "not how an honest true hearted man could be a Democrat."[67] Democrats, he believed, reveled in corruption as spoilsmen.[68]

As the political scene darkened in the late 1850s, the younger Bagby's newspaper, the *Lynchburg Express*, folded because it could not rival the influential Whig paper, the *Lynchburg Gazette*. He then moved to Washington in 1857 as a correspondent for the *New Orleans Crescent*. While there, he observed the Democrats flounder and the Republicans gain strength. In 1859 he moved to Richmond, where a more financially secure opportunity opened as librarian of both the Richmond Library Association and the Virginia Historical Society. But he also continued to pursue journalism as a freelance writer for local newspapers and for the *Charleston Mercury* and *New Orleans Crescent*, both highly partisan secessionist papers. In 1860 he served as the editor of the *Southern Literary Messenger* in Richmond and ventured out on the lecture circuit.[69]

George William Bagby represented the new generation of politically minded men who emerged in Virginia at the time of the constitutional convention of 1851. During the decade preceding the Civil War, they paid no attention to the nuances of Madisonian nationalism and increasingly pitched everything into the yaw of states' rights.[70] Bagby's correspondence, both personal and political, took on the same heedless cast. For example, John Hampton Chamberlayne, Bagby's future brother-in-law who later joined the Confederate army as an artillery captain, railed against Kentucky senator John J. Crittenden's peace efforts in Congress, saying that Crittenden and his like should be banished from this generation: "Gray heads are good when things are as they have been; but they cannot direct revolutions."[71] Stephen Davenport Yancy wrote to Bagby in January 1861: "I am emphatically opposed to any disgraceful compromise. . . . I would prefer to see blood flow like the cataract of Niagara and chaos reign supreme over this once happy and prosperous country."[72] Bagby himself wrote to Virginia congressman John Esten Cooke, with whom he remained on friendly terms, remarking, "If you . . . let Virginia stay in this Abolition hole of a Union, I'll disembowel you on sight."[73] The congressional delegation wavered on secession until the state constitutional convention of April 1861, when Virginia joined the Confederacy.

The South resisted the intemperate call for disunion in 1828, 1833, and 1844. In those years Robert Barnwell Rhett Sr. emerged as a leading secessionist orator, and he later inspired his son, the editor of the *Charleston Mercury*, as well as a radical journalistic cadre.[74] When Robert Barnwell Rhett Jr. took over the

Mercury and pursued a temperate climate of unbiased journalism, the South embraced his editorship. But with the outbreak of hostilities, Rhett's paper reverted to vituperation, lies, and distortion. This fueled Bagby's polemics in the early years of the war. In print he surmised that it would fall to South Carolina to make the state "fatter with Yankee gore than the plains of Manassas."[75] He dismissed Lincoln as "a poor dirty stick" and purported to demonstrate that Yankee newspapers showed the "unutterable depravity of the Northern people."[76] In addition to such "patriotic gore," Bagby traded in rumor and innuendo. He conspired with Rhett in January 1861 to supply the *Mercury* with a letter from a "gentleman" who attested to the claim that Hannibal Hamlin, Lincoln's vice president, was a descendent of a mulatto.[77] The claim, wholly fictitious, raised a firestorm of racial hatred in the South.

Yet when Bagby joined the Confederate army in 1862, serving for a year until poor health forced him to resign, he observed favoritism, inefficiency, and incompetence. During this time he wrote sporadically for newspapers, but afterward he emerged as an unreserved critic of the Davis administration and army field operations.

Bagby's open criticism of the government proved too much even for the hard-hitting *Mercury*. Rhett censored Bagby's correspondence and advised him that criticism was a casualty of war. Rhett acknowledged, "Truth is hard to get."[78] Nonetheless, he said: "Our affairs are now in such a condition that it is necessary to *sustain* the courage of the people; and criticism, unless plainly and palpably beneficial, does more harm than good. . . . People cannot always stand too much truth." To make the point even plainer, Rhett asked Bagby to "try and shape your correspondence in accordance with these views, the truth but not all the truth at present."[79] Again the editor negated many of his writer's criticisms of the president. "I would never attack him [Davis] except upon public matters and with infallible proofs," said Rhett.[80] Chastened but not silenced, Bagby persisted in telling the truth in the *Mercury* and in other newspapers. He excoriated rich millers who monopolized transportation and profited handsomely from the war, kept a close eye on rumors of European loans for the Confederacy, criticized Davis's favoritism in his military appointments, and pleaded for the relief of black refugees.[81] In one unfortunate incident he accused an officer of financial fraud but later, to avoid a duel, recanted his allegations.[82] Bagby felt compelled to report unvarnished truth. Yet his prejudice against the South's enemies would not allow complete objectivity.

Since Bagby held an ambiguous code of ethics, his ambition and determination made him prey to duplicity and falsehood. He joined the *Mercury*'s reckless course on the eve of war and painted Northern opposition in exaggerated and distorted poses. He conspired with Rhett to play the race card and further embittered sectional hatred. As a radical journalist he seized the moment and joined forces with the fire-eaters who used the code of honor as a cover for a weak administration, a secessionist administration that radicals upheld at any cost. The *Mercury*'s anxiety stemmed from the dubious image of the newspaper in Southern minds. Southerners only succumbed to the Rhetts' extremism during the Civil War. Earlier the Southern population was not so taken with their brand of secessionist rhetoric. The newspaper quickly folded after the war. Bagby himself came to rebel against the extremism of the *Mercury.* His brief war experience allowed him to distance himself from Rhett's yellow journalism. In the course of distancing himself from polemical journalism he attained a degree of emotional maturity, individuation, a separation from the destructiveness of his earlier connections.

As he struggled with the truth and slowly began to grasp it, there was one person who understood his anguish. Lucy Parke Chamberlayne, daughter of the distinguished physician Dr. Lewis Webb Chamberlayne, founder of the Medical College of Virginia, and Martha Burwell Dabney Chamberlayne, embodied character, strength, perseverance, and an intelligent insight into politics. Dr. Chamberlayne died in 1854, and the family sold their estate, Montrose, in the first year of the Civil War. Lucy ensured a family income by enlisting in the Confederate Civil Service as a clerk in the Treasury Department, where she was celebrated for her savvy understanding of bureaucratic personnel.[83] When Bagby courted Chamberlayne in Richmond during the fall of 1862, she wrote, "I hope ever to remain pure and loyal—wanting to be your wife—the keeper of your honor and your love."[84] They married in February 1863. Lucy Chamberlayne provided the moral framework, the emotional harbor for the critical and impulsive writer. Their marriage proved happy, and they raised a large family. Nonetheless their postwar separation due to Bagby's job search took a toll on the couple's well being.

Hard times came after the war and prevented Bagby from obtaining a correspondent's post in Washington. He could not earn a living even as both associate editor of the *Richmond Whig* and contributing editor of the *Richmond Examiner.* Moreover the *Southern Literary Messenger,* which he edited, paid only $300 a year. So in May 1865 Bagby went to New York looking for a newspaper that would hire him. But he received a cold reception from former northern friends, and when his hardships continued, he fell into depression and despair. Desperately he wrote his wife: "Mother, you have spoiled me and I feel lost without you. There is no [world] away from you . . . and no friend but you. Pray always for me that I may be guided aright. . . . I am crying."[85] The very next day he wrote again in the same anguished tone: "I think of Virginia [their daughter] as I lay up here alone with the bible. . . . Truly you are my mother the only mother I ever knew and I honor you as such.[86] Later he admitted he cried on his sofa and pleaded, "Come to me mother."[87] By the end of July, Bagby had only $1.25 in his pocket. After his emotional breakdown in New York, he retreated to Richmond and the safer realm of domestic care and pleasant memory. By Christmas he was able to launch a southern lecture tour redolent of Old South memories.[88] Thus began a new writing career.

For two men the decision for or against war played out in family dynamics, the individual's interpretation of his inherited moral vision. Alfred Mordecai, an esteemed son in a warm, cohesive family, practiced the precepts of enlightened virtue and Jewish Orthodoxy. His "education of the heart," which resulted in disciplined character and habitual virtue, prepared him for his critical trial, submission to a higher purpose. Mordecai remained loyal to the values that structured his family's cohesion. Faced with the dilemma of acting in accord with military honor or personal integrity, he chose the latter, not to fight. Justice, according to the Mordecais, demanded that he fight for the Confederacy. But Alfred upheld the family principle of sacrificial trust in Divine Providence against immediate family interest.

George William Bagby fashioned himself in conflict with his father. He rebelled against his father's strict moral standard, which demanded submission to an all-powerful God and an overweening parental authority. Yet Bagby never developed a consistent alternative set of values. Although he joined the radicals in defending the South's conception of honor against northern criticism of slavery, he came to undermine wartime yellow journalism by attacking the Davis administration. Bitterness and rage filled the hollows of his heart. Until Lucy Chamberlayne promised to keep his honor and he discovered in his emotional breakdown in New York that he needed her for stability, Bagby could not love "honor more." With her support he then continued with greater confidence to present his ambiguous vision of fact and myth, heartily approved by his Virginia audience.

These two case studies only suggest a course of investigation into the complex pattern of Confederate moral culture, which included a pattern woven of Enlightenment ethics, skepticism, and Jewish Orthodoxy along with traditional notions of honor and evangelicalism. While historians point to the wealth of family narratives that influence partisan identities, they do not acknowledge the role of the family's moral vision in the development of the Confederate self. And the individual's interpretation of that moral vision undeniably played a crucial role in secession and war.

NOTES

1. Bertram Wyatt-Brown, *The Shaping of Southern Culture: Honor, Grace, and War, 1760s–1880s* (Chapel Hill: University of North Carolina Press, 2001), xii, xiv, 85, 104, 133, 214; Wyatt-Brown, *Southern Honor: Ethics and Behavior in the Old South* (New York: Oxford University Press, 1982), xv, 26–27, 114; Wyatt-Brown, *Honor and Violence in the Old South* (New York: Oxford University Press, 1986), viii, 4, 14, 22, 39.

2. Edward Tivnan uses the term "moral imagination" as an attempt to debate moral convictions in a confusing contemporary moral environment where no consensus exists on what is right or wrong. *The Moral Imagination: Confronting the Ethical Issues of Our Day* (New York: Simon & Schuster, 1995). My view of moral imagination implies the capacity of individuals to confront or challenge a moral consensus, such as the code of honor during the Civil War.

3. James Q. Wilson, *The Moral Sense* (New York: Free Press, 1993), 144.

4. See Charles Taylor, *Sources of the Self: The Making of the Modern Identity* (Cambridge, Mass.: Harvard University Press, 1989), x.

5. For the argument that "personal history determines partisan course," see Jean H. Baker, *Affairs of Party: The Political Culture of Democrats in the Mid-Nineteenth Century* (Ithaca, N.Y.: Cornell University Press, 1983): 66. For other works that analyze the role of family upon morality and politics, see Kimberly K. Smith, *The Dominion of Voice: Riot, Reason, and Romance in Antebellum Politics* (Lawrence: University Press of Kansas, 1999); Daniel J. Elazar, *Building toward Civil War: Generational Rhythms in American Politics* (New York: Madison Books, 1992); George C. Rable, *The Confederate Republic: A Revolution against Politics* (Chapel Hill: University of North Carolina Press, 1994); Emory M. Thomas, *The Confederate Nation: 1861–1865* (New York: Harper & Row, 1979), 19–28; and John C. Inscoe and Gordon B. McKinney, "Highland Households Divided: Family Deceptions, Diversions, and Divisions in Southern Appalachia's Inner Civil War," in *Enemies of the Country: New Perspectives on Unionists in the Civil War South,* ed. John C. Inscoe and Robert C. Kenzer (Athens: University of Georgia Press, 2001), 54–72. For arguments on the interactions of gender and moral issues, see Stephen W. Berry, *All That Makes a Man: Love and Ambition in the Civil War South* (New York: Oxford University Press, 2003); Stephanie McCurry, "The Politics of Yeoman Households in South Carolina," in *Divided Houses: Gender and the Civil War,* ed. Catherine Clinton and Nina Silber (New York: Oxford University Press, 1992), 22–42; Reid Mitchell, "Soldering, Manhood, and Coming of Age: A Northern Volunteer," ibid., 43–54; and Drew Gilpin

Faust, "Altars of Sacrifice: Confederate Women and the Narratives of War," ibid., 171–99. Although scholars might agree that varied cultural factors weighed upon the attitudes toward war, they disagree upon how moral conflict within the family led to the support or nonsupport of war.

6. Wyatt-Brown, *Southern Honor,* 33, 55, 57, 93, 95, 166–67, 328, 330–31, 349–61, 365, 406; Steven M. Stowe, *Intimacy and Power in the Old South: Ritual in the Lives of the Planters* (Baltimore: Johns Hopkins University Press, 1987), 1–4, 24–49.

7. Taylor, *Sources of the Self,* x, 14, 27–35, 47.

8. For a history of the Mordecai family and their educational experiments, see Jean Friedman, *Ways of Wisdom: Moral Education in the Early National Republic* (Athens: University of Georgia Press, 2001). See also Emily Bingham, *Mordecai: An Early American Family* (New York: Hill and Wang, 2003); Edgar E. MacDonald, ed., *The Education of the Heart: The Correspondence of Rachel Mordecai Lazarus and Maria Edgeworth* (Chapel Hill: University of North Carolina Press, 1977); and Myron Berman, *Richmond's Jewry, 1769–1976: Shabbat in Shockoe* (Charlottesville: University of Virginia Press, 1979).

9. Richard Lovell Edgeworth and Maria Edgeworth, *Practical Education,* 2 vols., 2nd ed. (Boston: T. B. Wait & Sons, 1815).

10. Friedman, *Ways of Wisdom,* 11–22; MacDonald, *Education of the Heart,* 107, 124, 251.

11. Edgeworth and Edgeworth, *Practical Education,* 1:4.

12. Friedman, *Ways of Wisdom,* 22–26, 84–88; Taylor, *Sources of the Self,* 268–70.

13. Bingham, *Mordecai,* 5.

14. Ellen Mordecai to Solomon Mordecai, July 31, 1817, Jacob Mordecai Papers, Duke University, Durham, N.C.

15. Alfred Mordecai to Solomon Mordecai, Feb. 24, 1819, Mordecai Family Papers, Southern Historical Collection, University of North Carolina, Chapel Hill.

16. Alfred Mordecai, "Memoirs," in *Memoirs of American Jews, 1775–1865,* ed. Jacob Radar Marcus, 3 vols. (Philadelphia: Jewish Publication Society of America, 1955–56), 3:219–21; Stanley L. Falk, "Major Alfred Mordecai: First Ordnance Officer to Apply Scientific Methods to Armament," *Nearprint* (Nov.–Dec. 1959): 396.

17. James R. Endler, *Other Leaders, Other Heroes: West Point's Legacy to America and beyond the Field of Battle* (Westport, Conn.: Praeger, 1998), 6.

18. Taylor, *Sources of the Self,* x.

19. Stephen E. Ambrose, *Duty, Honor, Country: A History of West Point* (Baltimore: Johns Hopkins University Press, 1966): 62–68, 73–74, 87–90, 104; George S. Pappas, *To the Point: The United States Military Academy, 1802–1902* (Westport, Conn.: Praeger, 1993), 114.

20. Falk, "Major Alfred Mordecai," 395–97.

21. Ellen Mordecai to Solomon Mordecai, July 12, 1821, Mordecai Family Papers.

22. Rachel Mordecai Lazarus to Ellen Mordecai, Dec. 6, 1821, ibid. Orlando is a reference to the older brother of Rosamond in Maria Edgeworth's collection of popular children's stories, *Early Lessons.* He is the very model of an enlightened, scientifically minded young man who leads his sister toward moral reasoning. See "Rosamond," *Early Lessons* (London: George Routledge & Sons, 1856), 42–61.

23. Rebecca Mordecai to Jacob Mordecai, Sept. 6, 1825, Mordecai Family Papers.

24. MacDonald, *Education of the Heart,* 28n, 289, 332.

25. Bingham, *Mordecai,* 236–37. Prophets and psalmists regarded an upright man as one who loves justice, practices beneficence and humility, and thus "is not afraid of evil tidings; his heart is firm, he trusts in the Lord." See Micah 6 and Psalm 112 for an expression and definition of the righteous man. Adele Berlin and Marc Zvi Brettler, eds., *The Jewish Study Bible* (New York: Oxford University Press, 2004), 1215, 1409–10.

26. Alfred Mordecai to Little Ellen Mordecai, c/o George Mordecai, July 21, 1836, Mordecai Family Papers.

27. Emma Mordecai to Ellen Mordecai, Mar. 15, 1845, ibid.

28. Alfred Mordecai to Samuel Mordecai, Dec. 7, 1859, Jacob Mordecai Papers; Alfred Mordecai to George Mordecai, Aug. 29, 1860, George Mordecai Papers, Southern Historical Collection, University of North Carolina, Chapel Hill.

29. Alfred Mordecai to George Mordecai, Jan. 6, 1861, George Mordecai Papers.

30. Alfred Mordecai to George Mordecai, Aug. 29, 1860, Jan. 9, 1861, ibid.; Alfred Mordecai to Samuel Mordecai, Dec. 10, 1860, Mordecai Family Papers.

31. Alfred Mordecai to Little Ellen Mordecai, c/o George Mordecai, July 21, 1836. Alfred applied the derisive term "white nigger" to abolitionist sympathizers and by extension to white northerners. He meant to reduce them to the social level of the most common African American. See Eugene D. Genovese, *Roll, Jordan, Roll: The World the Slaves Made* (1974; New York: Vintage Books, 1976), 438; and Eric Foner, *Free Soil, Free Labor, Free Men: The Ideology of the Republican Party before the Civil War* (New York: Oxford University Press, 1970), 263–64.

32. Alfred Mordecai to George Mordecai, Jan. 20, 1861, George Mordecai Papers.

33. Samuel Mordecai to George Mordecai, Mar. 26, 1861, ibid.

34. Samuel Mordecai to George Mordecai, Apr. 23, 1861, ibid.

35. Alfred Mordecai to George Mordecai, Jan. 20, 1861, ibid.

36. Samuel Mordecai to George Mordecai, Apr. 22, June 9, 1861, ibid.

37. Rebecca Mordecai to Alfred Mordecai, Aug. 25, 1861, Mordecai Family Papers.

38. *Troy (N.Y.) Daily Times,* May 8, 1861.

39. *Daily Whig,* May 9, 1861.

40. *Troy (N.Y.) Daily Times,* May 10, 1861.

41. See Wyatt-Brown, *Southern Honor,* 33.

42. Obituary, "Major Alfred Mordecai," *The Jewish Exponent,* Nov. 25, 1887.

43. Ibid.

44. E. Brooks Holifield, *The Gentlemen Theologians: American Theology in Southern Culture, 1795–1860* (Durham, N.C.: Duke University Press, 1978), ix. Holifield notes the English and Scottish enlightened influences upon American Christian "rational orthodoxy," but the same might apply to Jewish Orthodoxy as shaped by Moses Mendelssohn and the German Enlightenment.

45. William G. Shade, *Democratizing the Old Dominion: Virginia and the Second Party System, 1824–1861* (Charlottesville: University Press of Virginia, 1996), 10; Christine Leigh Heyrman, *Southern Cross: The Beginnings of the Bible Belt* (Chapel Hill: University of North Carolina Press,

1997), 8; Steven Elliott Tripp, *Yankee Town, Southern City: Race and Class Relations in Civil War Lynchburg* (New York: New York University Press, 1997), 8–9, 34–35; F. N. Boney, *John Letcher of Virginia: The Story of Virginia's Civil War Governor* (Tuscaloosa: University of Alabama Press, 1966).

46. La Salle Corbell Pickett, *Literary Hearthstones of Dixie* (Philadelphia: J. B. Lippincott, 1912), 230.

47. For a discussion of Romantic sensibility, see Lawrence S. Lockridge, *The Ethics of Romanticism* (New York: Cambridge University Press, 1989), 51; Alex Comfort, "The Ideology of Romanticism," in *Romanticism: Points of View,* ed. Robert F. Gleckner and Gerald E. Enscoe (Englewood Cliffs, N.J.: Prentice-Hall, 1970), 165–80; and Morse Peckham, *Romanticism and Behavior: Collected Essays II* (Columbia: University of South Carolina Press, 1976), 21.

48. George W. Bagby, *The Old Virginia Gentleman and Other Sketches,* ed. Ellen M. Bagby (Richmond, Va.: Dietz, 1943), xviii–xix.

49. George Bagby to Ellen Matthews, Dec. 22, 1853, George Bagby Papers, Virginia Historical Society, Richmond. For a discussion of the effect of paternal aggression upon sons' moral development, see Wilson, *Moral Sense,* 105; and Justin Aronfreed, *Conscience and Conduct* (New York: Academic Press, 1968): 308–9.

50. George Bagby to George William Bagby, Nov. 21, 1835, George W. Bagby Papers, Virginia Historical Society (hereinafter cited as GWB Papers).

51. George Bagby to George William Bagby, Sept. 11, 1834, ibid.

52. George Bagby to George William Bagby, May 3, 1842, ibid.

53. George Bagby to George William Bagby, Jan. 10, 1843, ibid.

54. "Private Bagby Book," ibid.

55. Edgehill School Report Card, Apr. 30, 1841, ibid.; George Bagby to George William Bagby, Jan. 10, 1843, Mar. 18, 1844, ibid.

56. For Wilson's argument that lack of attachment hinders moral development, see *Moral Sense,* 105.

57. George William Bagby to Ellen Bagby, Dec. 8, 1846, and Thomas Jellis Kirkpatrick to George William Bagby, Aug. 13, 1850, GWB Papers.

58. George Bagby to George William Bagby, Dec. 28, 1848, ibid.

59. Pickett, *Literary Hearthstones,* 236–38; Bagby, *Old Virginia Gentleman,* xix, 173, 176.

60. Kirkpatrick to George William Bagby, Aug. 22, 1850, GWB Papers.

61. Ibid.

62. Kirkpatrick to George William Bagby, Nov. 16, 1851, ibid.

63. Kirkpatrick to George William Bagby, Feb. 10, 1852, ibid.

64. Kirkpatrick to George William Bagby, Apr. 29, 1859, ibid.

65. Shade, *Democratizing the Old Dominion,* 10, 14, 25–40; George S. Morris and Susan L. Foutz, *Lynchburg in the Civil War: The City—the People—the Battle,* 2nd ed. (Lynchburg, Va.: H. E. Howard, 1984), 1–7.

66. George Bagby to George William Bagby, Feb. 4, 29, 27, 1856, Jan. 5, May 27, Sept. 3, 1857, GWB Papers.

67. George Bagby to George William Bagby, Jan. 28, 1859, ibid.

68. George Bagby to George William Bagby, Feb. 9, 1859, ibid.

69. Allen Johnson, ed., *Dictionary of American Biography* (New York: Charles Scribner's Sons, 1928), 492; Bagby, *Old Virginia Gentleman*, xxi.

70. Shade, *Democratizing the Old Dominion*, 14, 16.

71. John Hampton Chamberlayne to George William Bagby, Dec. 18, 1860, GWB Papers.

72. Stephen Davenport Yancy to George William Bagby, Jan. 27, 1861, ibid.

73. George W. Bagby to John Esten Cooke, Jan. 29, 1861, ibid.

74. William C. Davis, *Rhett: The Turbulent Life and Times of a Fire-Eater* (Columbia: University of South Carolina Press, 2001), 391.

75. *Charleston Mercury*, Nov. 30, 1861.

76. Ibid., Dec. 6, 1862.

77. Robert Barnwell Rhett to George W. Bagby, Jan. 31, 1861, GWB Papers.

78. Robert Barnwell Rhett to George W. Bagby, Apr. 2, 1861, ibid.

79. Robert Barnwell Rhett to George W. Bagby, Nov. 25, 1861, ibid.

80. Robert Barnwell Rhett to George W. Bagby, Apr. 9, 1862, ibid.

81. *Charleston Mercury*, Oct. 28, 30, Dec. 11, 1862; *Mobile Register*, Jan. 10, 1863, Jan. 6, 1864.

82. W. G. Clark to George William Bagby, Feb. 15, 1864, and W. W. Cary to Col. Joseph Forsyth, Feb. 13, 1864, GWB Papers.

83. Bagby, *Old Virginia Gentleman*, xxii.

84. Lucy Parke Chamberlayne to George William Bagby, Oct. 8, 1862, GWB Papers. See also Bagby, *Old Virginia Gentleman*, xxii.

85. George W. Bagby to Lucy Parke Chamberlayne Bagby, May 20, 1865, GWB Papers.

86. George W. Bagby to Lucy Parke Chamberlayne Bagby, May 21, 1865, ibid.

87. George W. Bagby to Lucy Parke Chamberlayne Bagby, May 26, 1865, ibid.

88. George W. Bagby to Lucy Parke Chamberlayne Bagby, July 25, Dec. 23, 1865, ibid.

Courting Nationalism:
The Wartime Letters of Bobbie Mitchell and Nettie Fondren

LESLEY J. GORDON

CONFEDERATE NATIONALISM WAS MORE THAN AN ABSTRACT concept expounded by southern leaders in public forums. Its expression—devotion to the slave nation, belief in the superiority of the South over the North, faith in the Confederate military, confidence that independence would be achieved—could be evident in white southerner's private correspondence. Building on perceptions of southern superiority that had evolved during the antebellum period, Confederate nationalism championed the slave nation over northern society in every possible way. Young whites from the slaveholding class, coming of age on the eve of war and raised to believe in the South's cultural superiority and slavery's morality, easily adopted the rhetoric of Confederate nationalism. And their allegiance was not merely for show; it was this generation of southerners who filled the ranks of the army and, at least initially, willingly sacrificed all for the idea of a separate and independent South.[1]

This essay explores the personal correspondence between two elite young Georgians from July 1861 to August 1864, paying close attention to ways in which a clear concept of Confederate nationalism manifested itself within their relationship. Amaretta "Nettie" Fondren and Robert "Bobbie" Mitchell were only teenagers when the war began, but they found themselves deeply self-conscious about the vast historical drama in which they were participants. The letters, over one hundred of which survive today, serve as a sort of extended conversation about not only their intimate devotion to one another but also their thoughts, fears, and expectations for their new nation.[2]

Victorian love letters such as those exchanged between Bobbie and Nettie offer an important window into their inner selves. Although their words may sound formulaic, overly sentimental, and perhaps even insincere to the modern ear, they are in fact quite insightful. Letters were a crucial part of Victorian courtship. Pen and paper allowed men and women to be more intimate than they could ever behave in public. Moreover such missives could express what one historian calls the Victorian ideal of a "romantic self."[3] Another scholar has described the love letter as "one of the most private and therefore most sacred, romantic spaces": a space that allowed men and women to bridge the gap between separate spheres.[4] Thus, through the private written words of this young couple, we can better understand the realities, complexities, and even illusions of individual southerners' allegiance to the Confederacy. Their very definitions of man and woman, husband and wife, became closely tied to their identity and behavior as loyal Confederates.[5]

Bobbie Mitchell and Nettie Fondren were both products of Georgia's slaveholding planter class. Their families resided in Thomas County, located in the far southwestern corner of the state, just a few miles north of the Florida border. Cotton, corn, sugar cane, and rice fields stretched across the rich farmlands of the county. Nettie's father, John, had been born in South Carolina but moved to Dublin, Georgia, and eventually Thomas County to farm. By 1850 he and his wife, Nancy, were raising a growing family and plantation.[6] Bobbie had grown up with six siblings on his father's sprawling sugar plantation a few miles outside of Thomasville, the county seat. His parents, Col. Richard Mitchell and Sophronia Dickey, were wealthier and more established than the Fondrens, claiming to be some of the first white settlers in the county.[7]

When the war began in April 1861, Bobbie was a college student at Mercer University in Macon, and sixteen-year-old Nettie was his hometown sweetheart. War fever swept Thomas County, as it did much of the South. Nettie no doubt busied herself with patriotic activities such as sewing flags and uniforms and knitting socks.[8] Bobbie apparently bided his time until July, when he would turn eighteen and be old enough to join the army. Twelve days after celebrating his birthday, he enlisted in the 29th Georgia Infantry.[9] The Confederate nation was only a few months old, but already Bobbie felt a powerful allegiance to it. "Duty called," he wrote Nettie the day after he enlisted, "and I felt willing to obey and ever will I when my country is endangered [to] sacrifice my life in its cause. . . . I am proud to know and feel that my services are called upon in such a glorious cause." He was disappointed that his term was "only for twelve months" but added, "if my country needs my service longer I will freely resign myself to fate."[10]

Despite Bobbie's readiness to sacrifice his life for his new nation, the 29th Georgia would not see any real combat for two full years. Assigned to coastal positions in Georgia and the Carolinas, Bobbie's regiment was away from the center stage of war until July 1863.[11] Thus his initial military experience did not include the suffering and horrors of large-scale battle; instead he and his comrades fought monotony and boredom. Sickness and demoralization were greater enemies than Yankee bullets. In the early summer of 1862, Bobbie's own health was failing, and he was feeble enough in July to obtain a furlough and go home to recover. By September he was back with his unit and feeling much better.[12] But the inactivity continued. "It looks like we are doomed," he wrote Nettie on the nineteenth, "never to witness a grand fight."[13]

Bobbie was discovering soldier life to be tiring. Far from the front, he found himself doing "nothing exciting or encouraging."[14] The army seemed "cruel and despotic in its nature," and he grew annoyed with the antics of his fellow soldiers, whom he deemed "rough and unrefined." There was drinking and brawls and two attempts at suicide.[15] He tried to justify his lot as just another part of doing his duty, believing that battle would "redeem" the unit's character.[16]

At least twice Bobbie's unit was close enough to hear the sound of battle, though unable to participate. In early November 1861 the Union amassed a naval fleet to attack Port Royal Sound, South Carolina. The outgunned Confederates fled, surrendering one of the greatest natural harbors in the South. Sergeant Mitchell and his regiment could only listen to the reverberations of the fray from their post sixteen miles distant on Sapelo Island. "How bad did it make me feel," Bobbie wrote Nettie, "to remain here and listen to the booming of the cannon and not knowing but what every shot was sending death to some noble Georgian's heart." He added, "How my blood boiled to be there."[17] The following spring, Federals captured Fort Pulaski, protecting Savannah from the sea. Bobbie, stationed at nearby Mackay's Point, had no part in the fight, nor did he initially know how fellow Confederates were faring. "It is really provoking," he complained on the day of the battle, "to be so near the scene of action and an eyewitness to the engagement, and then not being able to find out how the victory was going."[18]

Through those early months of frustration and inactivity, Bobbie especially savored mail from Nettie. The letters not only invigorated and encouraged him but also helped while the time away. He could repeatedly express his love for her and his increasing devotion to the Confederacy. At one point Nettie instructed him to destroy her missives, and he obliged, at least initially. But he found that he had "nothing [else] to engage my idle moments with," attesting that they "afforded me pleasure just to glance at them and see your handwriting on the envelope."[19]

Bobbie and Nettie corresponded regularly, mixing news from home and playful banter with repeated declarations of their faith in the Confederate war effort. They both dreaded the prospect of a long war, yet they reassured one another that in the not too distant future, victory and peace would come. They associated their own happiness with the South's success. In fact it seemed that they were unable to imagine the future in any other way. Victory and peace meant an end to their anxiety and separation. "We will then begin a new life," Bobbie happily predicted, "with the proud assurance of being the greatest nation on earth."[20] The couple also began to consider marriage, and Bobbie vowed that his desire to see his lover gave him courage: "I've got the will to kill any set of men that will be the cause of my staying away from my sweetheart this long without a chance to see her."[21] For his part Bobbie urged Nettie to stay hopeful and bear their separation bravely.[22] He praised Nettie for her "patriotism and industry" and scolded her if he sensed any sign of despondency.[23] "You say," Bobbie wrote in late October 1861, "that the future seems that it will be a dark and dreary one to you." "O[h]!" he urged her, "dispel such thoughts and hope for better things."[24]

Still there were moments, especially during those first two years of war, when the young Georgians despaired. After the fall of Fort Donelson in Tennessee in February 1862, for example, Bobbie was in shock. "Surely something must be wrong," he wrote incredulously. "Surrendering fifteen thousand troops in one battle is outrageous."[25] Weeks later, after the fall of Fort Pulaski, Island No. 10, and the city of New Orleans, he felt as if "this world was nothing but a dark vale of tears, trials and tribulations."[26] He realized that the war would continue much longer than anyone had anticipated. "Suppose this war should last fifty years," Bobbie mused that April, "won't we have a hard time of it?"[27]

The loss of Nettie's older brother David to illness in March 1862, followed by the death of her sister Minnie the very next month, sent the young woman into an emotional tailspin. David served with Bobbie in Company E, 29th Georgia, and Minnie was but a child. Nettie's depression was so deep that at one point she told Bobbie she had no desire to live. "Never say you want to die," he chided her. "It is wrong, you should not give way to such feelings."[28] Bobbie regretted that he could not come home to comfort his beloved. "Nothing could prevent me," he wrote upon hearing the news of Minnie's death, "from being with you in the present trial and affliction if it was possible for me to get there. I know I feel as much for you all here as I could there, but being absent gives me [a] great deal of painful anxiety."[29]

Yet during that early part of the war, the couple's fidelity to the Confederate nation rarely fluctuated. Even when others, friends, family, or comrades, expressed doubts, Nettie and Bobbie's letters spoke of a promise and hope. Just a few weeks after Bobbie's gloomy assessment of Fort Donelson, he reassured Nettie, "All will be well."[30] "I am confident," he stated on March 30, "that God will crown our efforts with success. It is a noble and righteous cause, one which every son of liberty is deeply interested in."[31] Two weeks later he affirmed: "I am confident that victory will crown our efforts. The cause is too sacred and noble to be aided by the ruler of nations."[32] Indeed the two fervently believed, as did other staunch Confederates, that God was on the side of the South. They perceived military defeats or victories as divinely sanctioned and comforted each other with prayer. Religious references permeate their correspondence with constant reminders of God's omnipotence.[33]

With more discouraging news from the front, the couple's expressions of faith in God and the Confederate cause grew more strident. Bobbie believed the string of western defeats might prolong the war but not doom the Confederacy. When the Confederate Congress passed the first draft law in the spring of 1862, many members of the 29th were upset. But Bobbie, who gained commission as a second lieutenant in March, was not sure "whether it was good policy or not." "So far as I'm concerned," he concluded stoically, "it makes no difference. I expected to be in the war anyhow as long as it lasted. . . . We are soldiers now for the war."[34] A year later, learning that the Union too was adopting a draft law, Bobbie refused to consider that the increased manpower would have any effect on the war's outcome: "Never have I doubted one time the result [of this] war."[35] Nettie too occasionally admitted that "our national horizon is dark and threatening." Still she contended there was "no time to mourn over it all." "Onward! Onward! should be our motto," she proclaimed, "until the vile invader is driven from our sunny South, and the standard of Liberty is unfurled to the balmy breeze of our own beloved land."[36] She urged Bobbie: "All will yet be well. This suffering cannot always last and I think our prospects are daily brightening."[37]

Confederate women played a significant role in bolstering national morale, and Nettie, though only a teenager, was deeply aware of this. "Yes, Bobbie," she assured him, "I know it is my duty to cheer you in these hours of peril, and rest assured I do try to do so."[38] Bobbie was equally mindful of her role. When a newspaper article in February 1863 blamed southern women for causing desertion, he asked Nettie if she had seen it. "It was not done with the idea of depreciating woman's worth or the untold service she has done our bleeding country," he explained, "but to call their attention to the fact of writing letters of encouragement to the loved ones who were so much missed at home."[39]

Nettie, like many women during the war, also believed that it was her duty to keep Bobbie from "all the temptations" of army life.[40] Indeed the lures of sin seemed as dangerous as enemy bullets. She scolded her lover for reading novels and drinking wine, though he tried to assure her that he was behaving well since he enlisted.[41] Nettie had few doubts about the South's chances for victory; it was the fate of her beau that concerned her more. Sometimes in the same letter, her emotions oscillated between optimism and fear, wondering if she would ever see Bobbie again.[42] She tried to imagine what it must be like on the field of battle. "When I think of the carnage of a dreadful battle," she wrote on June 4, 1862, "my heart turns sick and every nerve seems weakened." She pictured soldiers "lying on the cold, wet ground with no cover, save the dark canopy of Heaven to shield them from suffering."[43] She worried too about illness, especially after the sudden death of her brother to disease. In September 1862 she advised Bobbie to come home quickly if he were ill. Then, catching herself, she added: "But I am talking as if you could come whenever you felt disposed. I do hope, though, if you are not well you will succeed in getting a furlough."[44] All Nettie really could do was pray that God would protect her soldier from both "sin and death."[45]

Bobbie too tried to prepare himself, at least mentally, for bloody combat. "I have strong hopes, and I believe sufficient courage," he wrote Nettie on April 12, 1862, "to meet the enemy on the field of battle."[46] He realized many of his comrades would fall and he might be one of them. He predicted that his company would perform bravely and "die like men although we are boys." "I had rather," he reflected further, "the O.S.I. were all killed upon the field of battle than to send a bad name back home to those, whom we would love to die for, if necessary."[47] He himself preferred to die in Virginia: "I don't know why it is unless it is that its name is associated with so many well and hard fought battle[s], both in this and the Revolutionary War."[48] Occasionally naive bravado seeped into his words: "I feel tonight like I could whip fifty Yankees."[49] But mainly Bobbie's reflections centered on his belief that he owed his life to the southern nation and that his fate was in God's hands. He reassured Nettie: "If I should happen to get killed in battle, console yourself with the idea that I was performing a sacred duty which I owed my country."[50]

As Bobbie and Nettie contemplated the prospect of battle and death, they often denounced the enemy. True to their race and class, and the fact that their families were successful large slaveholders residing deep in the Black Belt, they took for granted that slavery was right and any threat to it was unacceptable. No doubt taught at an early age to believe the worst stereotypes of the North, the war only strengthened their negative perceptions. They repeatedly denounced Yankees as greedy aggressors. Months before he was anywhere near Union soldiers, Bobbie already viewed them as "cowardly invaders," fanatical "poor fools," "vile," and "madmen" who were only "actuated by the deceitful promise of acquiring wealth and fortune."[51] As the weeks of inactivity rolled by, his name calling took on a sharper tone. In January 1863 he found his "hatred" for the enemy "growing stronger and stronger." "A Yankee," Bobbie explained to Nettie, "is surely the most despicable being on earth. Anyhow they are our greatest enemy. Enemy to mankind, liberty and freedom."[52] One month later, after apparently reading newspaper accounts of Yankees committing civilian atrocities, he demanded revenge: "Every day my hatred become[s] stronger and stronger for them. A Yankee is surely the most despicable being on earth."[53]

Despite their youth and the newness of the southern nation, the two Georgians' strong affection toward the Confederacy is striking. They often referred broadly to fellow Confederates as "chivalrous," "heroic," and "noble" in their pursuit of a "glorious cause for liberty," "independence," and freedom.[54] Interestingly, though, the young couple sometimes disparaged individual Confederates and specific regions, towns, or other southern states. Bobbie's disapproval of fellow soldiers in the 29th has already been mentioned. He also dismissed most male inhabitants of Savannah as "low and cowardly," predicting that they would "hoist the white flag and join hands with the enemy."[55] Bobbie had a decidedly low opinion of North Carolina and Florida, both of which he deemed poor, and Mississippi, where he judged most residents "half civilized" and even wealthy inhabitants unwilling to "give a soldier a meal of victuals to save his life."[56] In addition several Confederate officers earned his ire, including Generals Braxton Bragg and Alexander R. Lawton and the 29th's Capt. William S.

Rockwell and Col. William J. Young.[57] For Bobbie and Nettie the cause of Confederate liberty was perfect, but some of its proponents less so.

The couple's firm acceptance of slavery meant that their correspondence largely took the institution's existence for granted. Neither Bobbie nor Nettie specifically named slavery as part of the "cause," but they did make several references to slaves and overseers simply as part of everyday life.[58] Bobbie went to war with one of his slaves, Anthony, who could apparently read and write, as evidenced by a letter he wrote to "Aunt Jane" informing her, "I would like to come home but I can't leave Mas Robert for fear he may get wounded and there would be nobody to help him."[59]

The year 1863 marked a turning point in the lives of both Bobbie and Nettie. Nettie left home in February to attend Lucy Cobb Institute in Athens. It is not clear if it was her parents' decision to send their teenage daughter to the prestigious female boarding school, but Nettie herself described her desire to "keep up with my studies," something she was apparently unable to do in Thomasville once the war began. She had already delayed attending Lucy Cobb the year prior due to the deaths in her family. But her mother encouraged her to go, and Nettie seemed relieved to be resuming school again.[60] Opened in January 1859, Lucy Cobb Institute provided elite young women formal instruction on how to behave like southern ladies. The education offered there was not so much to inspire intellectual curiosity as to promulgate the South's hegemonic cultural values. Still there was instruction in Latin, French, rhetoric, and music.[61] Bobbie was not initially pleased with Nettie's decision. He wanted her home in Thomasville, and perhaps he worried that she would become too preoccupied to write him so often.[62] Busy with schoolwork, Nettie did have less time for letter writing, and she felt more cut off from the war in general. But she enjoyed her studies as well as socializing with her classmates, and with time Bobbie expressed support for her attending school.[63]

In early May Bobbie too found his life changing. Gen. P. G. T. Beauregard, commanding the Department of South Carolina, Georgia, and Florida, ordered the 29th Georgia to board trains for Jackson, Mississippi, where Union troops were converging to cut rail lines to Vicksburg.[64] Sent to reinforce Confederate forces at Jackson, the regiment arrived by mid-month and eagerly anticipated battle. The move from Georgia had cheered the troops, and Bobbie described his regiment as being "in fine spirits" and ready to fight.[65]

But as the days turned to weeks and the 29th Georgia marched to various positions around the Mississippi capital, the men grew restless. The weather was hot and the countryside barren and harsh. There was too much dust and not enough fresh water. Soldiers collapsed and some died from heat exhaustion and sunstroke.[66]

Union general U. S. Grant had commenced his siege of Vicksburg. Bobbie was concerned but hopeful: "We are all as yet confident," he wrote Nettie on June 8, "that she [Vicksburg] will be able to hold out against the many powerful assaults of the enemy—God grant that she may for Vicksburg is the key to the West and once lost will never be taken again."[67] He even admitted that Grant's men were hard-worn veterans who "fight like heroes," but he admired Gen. Joseph E. Johnston and expressed no qualms about his own readiness for combat.[68] Acutely aware of Vicksburg's strategic importance, Bobbie explained to Nettie that its preservation "is worth more to the Confederacy than a hundred thousand men. In fact we will not know how to appreciate its value until its loss is experience[d]."[69]

Bobbie's words were prophetic. On July 4, 1863, Vicksburg fell, and its loss to the Union proved a debilitating one for the South. Johnston, who had increased his numbers near Jackson, now faced the advance of William T. Sherman. It was during this fighting around Jackson after the fall of Vicksburg that the 29th finally experienced its baptism of fire. Unfortunately, none of Bobbie's letters survives from early July until early August 1863, so it is not known how the young lieutenant reacted to his first real engagement. The 29th Georgia participated in the fight on July 10 and, in the words of one member, "suffered some."[70] Lieutenant Mitchell, though, apparently did not sustain any injuries.

The next surviving letter from Bobbie to Nettie is dated August 4, 1863. Writing from brigade headquarters near Morton, Mississippi, Bobbie informed Nettie of his efforts to obtain a furlough. He was frustrated by the persistent idleness of his unit, convinced that Johnston should march to reinforce Braxton Bragg in Tennessee or Robert E. Lee in Virginia. If a "hard blow [were] struck in Va or Tenn," he worried, "we will not accomplish another victory this year, but will meet with reverses in every engagement owing to the simple fact that our forces are too badly scattered."[71]

Meanwhile Nettie had returned home to Thomasville in early July, where she discovered an odd mixture of mourning and gaiety. War's uncertainty rushed weddings; its carnage caused hasty burials. The young people of the town seemed caught up in dancing and frivolity.[72] For her part Nettie was happy to be among family and friends, but she waited nervously for letters from the front. She eagerly scanned newspaper accounts for any bit of news about the 29th Georgia.[73]

In August 1863 Bobbie too came home, having obtained a two-week furlough. No doubt he and Nettie enjoyed their time together. There probably was serious discussion of marriage and talk of their future together. By early September Bobbie had returned to his regiment, and the letters between the couple resumed.

The young lieutenant found the difference between his brief visit home and his life in the army dramatic: "You have no idea what a great contrast between the two quiet pleasant weeks I spent in old Thomas to the uproar and confusion that is now troubling my brain."[74] Bobbie was back in the thick of things as the 29th Georgia, now part of Bragg's army, readied for battle. "You must be hopeful as ever," he wrote, adding, "I was proud to see you are not like many others ready to despair on account of a few reverses. May all our women nobly do their duty in this contest. [A] great deal depends [on] their conduct."[75]

Nettie *was* concerned. Her faith in the Confederate cause, at least as expressed in her letters, was stronger than ever. But she sensed that people, notably the women of Thomasville, were faltering. Worried about the coming of winter, she failed to see the kind of activity common early in the war, when women eagerly sewed clothes to send to troops in the field. "Without exaggeration," she wrote ominously on September 23, "I do not believe I have seen a single piece of work on hand for the soldiers in more than six months and yet the Winter is coming steadily on like some powerful foe which I fear will take us unaware and the consequences of the surprise will be suffering and death." She sensed more: "A lethargy deep and fearful seems to have settled like some Evil Spirit over the land, and the consequences of which, will, I fear be deeply felt ere the coming of another year."[76]

Just days before Nettie penned those words, the 29th Georgia participated in the battle of Chickamauga. This two-day engagement in northwestern Georgia was a tactical Confederate victory but gained the South little strategically. Casualties were high, and the 29th Georgia, in the words of one sergeant, "suffered immensely—being in the thickest of the fight on both days."[77] Bobbie himself wrote his family on September 20: "We were overpowered and cut to pieces." His older brother William, who was the regiment's lieutenant colonel, received a severe shoulder wound, and Bobbie worried that he might not live. "I didn't receive a scratch myself fortunately," Bobbie mused. "Don't see how I escaped."[78] He wrote Nettie too of his brother's wound: "This hurts me worse than anything else could. I had rather me [be] wounded myself than see him hurt."[79]

It took time for Bobbie's message to reach Nettie, and in the meantime, unaware of where he was, she did not write him either. Finally on October 5 she mailed him a letter, concerned that he "needed encouragement and sympathy." She had not forgotten the role she had to play in bolstering her soldier. Having learned of William's injury, she tried to imagine what it must have been like for Bobbie: "I know your feeling sad heart must have been sorely tried when the stern call of duty forced you from him [William] after he lay a sufferer on the bloody battlefield, amid scenes of carnage and confusion." Nettie stressed to Bobbie her admiration for his bravery and self-sacrifice. "I know," she wrote, "you with the other noble men who shared with you the trials of that dreadful battle where the effusion of blood was sickening to the stoutest heart, have behaved nobly and carried with immortal honors your heads."[80]

On September 26 Bobbie composed a long missive to Nettie reflecting on his regiment's losses at Chickamauga. This massive engagement had been nothing like the fighting in Mississippi in July, and although he wanted to tell Nettie everything about the experience, he found that words failed him: "When I turn my eyes upon the most shattered and bleeding regiment which I have stood with so long and loved as an old friend, my heart is so stricken with sorrow that it prevents me from writing on anything else." His brother's wounding still upset him, and he mourned the deaths of several comrades. Bobbie consoled himself with the thought that the slain behaved "gallantly and nobly, dying as southern soldiers should." He recounted with pride that William had handed him his pistol and that he fired "four shots at the scoundrels." He only hoped that he had "succeeded in avenging his blood." Bobbie's Confederate nationalism remained unyielding. Although the army faced a difficult task of ridding the region of enemy troops, he continued to believe that, with God's help, victory was assured.[81]

Nettie was distressed to learn of Chickamauga, but she again did her best to be encouraging. She was utterly convinced that the 29th Georgia performed courageously and felt obligated, as one of the "weak, perhaps timid ones, at home," to thank Bobbie and his fellow Georgians for their self-sacrifice and sense of duty.[82]

The 29th Georgia, bloodied and bruised at Chickamauga, next participated in the siege of Chattanooga. Bragg, having defeated William S. Rosecrans's Army of the Cumberland, pushed the Federals out of Georgia and back into eastern Tennessee. When Rosecrans refused to budge from Chattanooga, Bragg surrounded the town and cut off nearly all communication and supply lines. By late October a member of the 29th Georgia described the regiment on the outskirts of Chattanooga "doing very heavy picket duty or building fortifications."[83] The weather was cold and wet, and illness continued to plague the troops. Bobbie himself battled a "scorching fever" and was anxious to obtain another furlough.[84] It was disheartening again to be inactive and the conditions so foul: "Under the present circumstances there is no doubt but the feeling of the Troops are considerably depressed," Bobbie explained, "but when the weather fairs off and the sun comes out again and Gen. Bragg makes some offensive move, the same cheerfulness and merriment will be manifested, and all things will probably work for the best again."[85] But it was not to be. By the end of November, the Federals, with the arrival of U. S. Grant and fresh reinforcements, broke the lines at Chattanooga and entirely routed Bragg's army.

Bobbie informed Nettie of the Confederates' desperate retreat from Tennessee into northwest Georgia, expressing shock and dismay at the troubling turn of events. "The whole thing seems like a dream to me," he wrote to her on December 3, "and [has] come upon us like a thunder clap." He said little about the hasty withdrawal except that his regiment "suffered more in that length of time than we ever have before." The march was exceedingly difficult through "rain, mud and ice with but little to eat." Bragg resigned his command in humiliation. Nonetheless Bobbie's support for the Confederacy was unmoved: "I am still hopeful as ever and will ever strive to prove faithful to my country."[86]

The bleak military news and the advent of winter tried Nettie's patience too. She imagined the "bitter frosts and chilling winds" her lover faced in the mountains of Tennessee and Georgia, and at times her worry was so overwhelming that she felt she would physically collapse from the stress. She clung to her religious faith as an anchor: "At this critical period in our national affairs where dark lowering clouds have thickened over our loved 'Sunny South,' apparently threatening her immediate and utter destruction, what condition would we be if that 'beacon star of life' had deserted us?" She mused, "We, you and I, Bobbie, can bear testimony of the might, strength, sweet mystery and joyous effects of hope, therefore how useless 'tis for me to *expatiate* on the subject." She continued to pray that Bobbie would return home to her unharmed.[87]

Bobbie did obtain another furlough in January 1864, but this time the couple decided to take advantage of their short time together and marry. Although Bobbie and Nettie had discussed marriage before, it is not clear what prompted them to wed so hastily. Perhaps the turn of military events the past several months convinced them to tie the knot as soon as possible. Their letters attest to their continuing faith in the Confederacy and their faith in God. But their correspondence also reveals a growing uneasiness about Bobbie's fate and fears that he might not survive the war.

On January 21, 1864, Nettie Fondren and Bobbie Mitchell married in Thomasville, Georgia. The newlyweds enjoyed their brief time together before Bobbie had to return to the front. They could only hope that the war would soon end, peace would follow, and they could begin their life together.

Bobbie returned to the army a contented married man and found the troops in the best condition he had ever seen them. Food was plentiful and winter camp provided a respite from hard campaigning. He was equally sanguine about Joe Johnston, who had assumed command of the army in late December 1863. The Yankees, Bobbie contended, were "rather afraid to meet Gen'l Johnston, knowing his superior ability as a commanding officer."[88] While the Federals turned their attention on Knoxville, Johnston planned a new Tennessee offensive. He reinforced his numbers and waited for warmer, drier weather. But by the end of March, the inactivity continued and so too did the winter weather. Soldiers drilled and staged sham melees in the snow.[89] Morale remained high, though the men were tiring of the tedium. Bobbie, pining to see his wife again, applied for another furlough: "Oh! For the speedy arrival of our meeting again. But for this war my darling we would be so happy, not a single care to mare [*sic*] our prospects for the future." He quickly added: "In speaking thus Nettie, I would not lead you to believe that I am despondent or dissatisfied with my lot. We have already been very fortunate in spending so long a time together."[90]

Meanwhile Grant ordered Sherman to dispel Johnston's army and advance into Georgia. On May 7, 1864, Sherman commenced operations. Just a few days earlier, Lieutenant Mitchell's confidence seemed to have reached an all-time high: "I wish you could know the feeling and see the proud tread of this army," he wrote his wife from Dalton on May 3. "Surely nothing on record has ever equaled it."[91] Three weeks later he proudly declared: "This army cannot be defeated. A braver nobler band was never arranged on the American continent."[92]

Sherman pressed and Johnston retreated, albeit skillfully, toward Atlanta, an important railroad and supply center. The armies clashed, but until the action at Kennesaw Mountain on June 27, where Sherman uncharacteristically assaulted the Confederates' strongly fortified position, direct encounters were limited. Bobbie's letters described the difficult marching and countermarching through rain and mud, attesting "this is one of the most complicated campaigns, Nettie that I have ever known." He maintained that once the cowardly and villainous Yankees were defeated, independence would quickly follow. "It is true," he acknowledged, "we have given up a large and fertile portion of our soil to the hated enemy, but when victory does come, I firmly believe that it will more than repay us for the loss of Northern GA."[93]

There are just a handful of extant letters from the summer of 1864, mostly written by Bobbie; those few underscore the couple's unyielding faith in the Confederacy. Bobbie showed no sign of doubt even as Sherman moved toward Atlanta and Johnston's retrograde continued. Witnessing more destruction and death, he was sure that he and his men "could not die in a better cause."[94] From the heights at Kennesaw Mountain, he watched with satisfaction as the enemy tried in vain to smash their position.[95] Near the Chattahoochee River he again regretted the loss of territory but predicted a final struggle that would annihilate the enemy. Bobbie refused to be concerned should Atlanta fall, contending: "We are able to carry on this war fifty years and I know they cannot whip us."[96] He could not understand why the people of Thomasville were fretting: "The enemy does not hold as much of our territory as they did two years ago. The Trans Miss[issippi] is almost entirely free from the invader again. We have two powerful Armies and great leaders in VA and GA fully able to cope with the foe and I believe able to ultimately achieve our Independence. Besides all this [a] great deal is being done in the North in our favor. Discord and contention is springing up that threatens to ruin Lincoln's government if persisted in."[97]

Of course much of what Bobbie claimed was not entirely correct. And Jefferson Davis did not trust Johnston as the young Georgian did. The president, angry at Johnston's withdrawal toward Atlanta, replaced him on July 17 with the aggressive John Bell Hood, who immediately confronted Sherman on the outskirts of the city. A series of sorties quickly followed, and the 29th Georgia suffered considerable losses. In Thomasville, meanwhile, Federal cavalry raids threatened the area, and the town itself became crowded with wounded. The mood was fearful and sullen. Nettie wrote her husband, "I had no idea one year ago that the war would be felt so sensibly in this part of Geo[rgia]."[98] "Do not despond at all," Bobbie assured her on August 1. "All will be well. These cavalry raids don't amount to much."[99]

Seven days after he penned these encouraging words, Bobbie received a serious wound near Jonesboro, Georgia. The injury was bad enough to gain him the furlough he had sought so earnestly for months. He returned home to recuperate and apparently rejoined the army, though it is not clear when. No other letters survive to record his final months of the war. Did Bobbie or Nettie express any loss of faith in the Confederacy? It is impossible to know. Bobbie surrendered as part of Maj. Gen. Sam Jones's force at Tallahassee, Florida, on May 10, 1865. Obtaining a parole, he returned to Thomasville soon after.[100]

In the years following the war, Bobbie and Nettie Mitchell devoted their energies to a growing family and Bobbie's law career. He became solicitor general, a state senator, and a superior court judge, active in the Democratic Party's defiant struggle to regain control of the state from the effects of Reconstruction. His strong commitment to the Confederacy became an equally strong commitment to Georgia's postwar Redemption and the South's Lost Cause. A postwar newspaper clipping credited him with doing "heroic service in redeeming Georgia from the second invasion known as 'Reconstruction'" and praising him as "one of the old guard, never departing from the faith."[101] In 1890 he gave a stirring speech before fellow Confederate veterans, celebrating their heroism and vowing never to forget their memory.[102] When Bobbie Mitchell died in 1926, a Savannah newspaper praised him for fighting "for his party and his people in the days that tried men's souls."[103]

Nettie died two years after her husband, but one can only guess that she remained equally committed to their Confederate past. Her obituary cited her dedication to family and church, hailing her as a woman who typified "the fine old traits of Southern hospitality and kindness."[104]

The question arises, why were these two young Georgians such devout Confederates? Why did they so rarely falter from their convictions? What kept them so hopeful, despite sickness, separation, death, and enemy invasion? It appears from their extended correspondence that their nationalism was closely tied to their deep devotion to each other. When one despaired, the other was quick to offer consolation and support. Young and romantic when the conflict began, they could only think optimistically of a future in which the Confederacy would be independent and they would be together. Their close affiliation with the new nation also seemed to become stronger as the war continued rather than really weakening at all.

Thus for these two young people, Confederate nationalism was immediate and personal. They perceived the southern nation to be real, justified, and worthy of their loyalty. As members of the slaveholding elite, they perceived the conflict as a fateful struggle between good and evil. While the war waged, neither Bobbie nor Nettie could imagine a world where the North prevailed. In the end of course, the Confederacy did fail. But their commitment to each other, tried and tested by war, did not.

NOTES

1. Emory M. Thomas defines and probes the concept of Confederate nationalism in both *The Confederacy as a Revolutionary Experience* (1971; repr., Columbia: University of South Carolina Press, 1991) and *The Confederate Nation: 1861–1865* (New York: Harper & Row, 1979). See also William Blair, *Virginia's Private War: Feeding Body and Soul in the Confederacy, 1861–1865* (New York: Oxford University Press, 1998), 153 n. 2.

2. Most of these letters are from Bobbie Mitchell to Nettie Fondren (hereinafter cited as RGM and AF respectively), apparently due to the fact that at one point early in the war Nettie requested that Bobbie destroy her letters to him. Nonetheless he did save some of her correspondence. See RGM to AF, Nov. 11, 1861, Robert Goodwin Mitchell Papers, Hargrett Rare Books & Manuscript Library, University of Georgia Libraries, Athens. The author wishes to thank Eric Millin, Barb Wittman, Steve Nash, Keith Bohannon, Jim Ogden, Steve Noble, and John Inscoe for their generous help in gathering research for this article. Peter Carmichael also provided a careful critique of an initial draft of the essay.

3. Karen Lystra, *Searching the Heart: Women, Men, and Romantic Love in Nineteenth Century America* (New York: Oxford University Press, 1989), 20.

4. Stephen W. Berry, *All That Makes a Man: Love and Ambition in the Civil War South* (New York: Oxford University Press, 2003), 89.

5. Other Civil War historians have routinely examined soldiers' letters to their wives and sweethearts, often taking the words out of context to support arguments about soldier motivation or home-front morale. But rarely do military or even political scholars consider such intimate exchanges between a married couple in their overall relationship or even in the context of Victorian courtship. Gender and women's historians have done a better job of this. Stephen Berry does recognize the importance of personal relationships and correspondence in his new book cited above. See also Steven M. Stowe, *Intimacy and Power in the Old South: Ritual in the Lives of the Planters* (Baltimore: Johns Hopkins University Press, 1987), 2; and Lesley J. Gordon, *General George E. Pickett in Life and Legend* (Chapel Hill: University of North Carolina Press, 1998), 100–101. Works dealing with southern marriage and the Civil War include Carol K. Bleser and Frederick M. Heath, "The Impact of the Civil War on a Southern Marriage: Clement and Virginia Tunstall Clay of Alabama," *Civil War History* (Sept. 1984): 197–220; and Joan Cashin, "'Since the War Broke Out': The Marriage of Kate and William McClure," in *Divided Houses: Gender and the Civil War*, ed. Catherine Clinton and Nina Silber (New York: Oxford University Press, 1992), 200–212. See also Catherine Clinton, ed., *Southern Families at War: Loyalty and Conflict in the Civil War* (New York: Oxford University Press, 2000); and Carol K. Bleser and Lesley J. Gordon, eds., *Intimate Strategies of the Civil War: Military Commanders and Their Wives* (New York: Oxford University Press, 2001). Examples of published couples' wartime letters include Nina Silber and Mary Beth Sievens, eds., *Yankee Correspondence: Civil War Letters between New England Soldiers and the Home Front* (Charlottesville: University of Virginia Press, 1996); M. Jane Johannson, ed., *Widows by the Thousand: The Civil War Letters of Theophilus and Harriet Perry, 1862–1864* (Fayetteville: University of Arkansas Press, 2000); and John Rozier, ed., *The Granite Farm Letters: The Civil War Correspondence of Edgeworth and Sallie Bird* (Athens: University of Georgia Press, 1988).

6. The Seventh U.S. Census, 1850, Thomas County, Ga., lists John G. Fondren, age thirty-nine, with real estate valued at $3,000. In 1850 the Fondrens had five children. Nettie was born April 3 or 10, 1845, in Dublin, Ga. This same census lists a "Nancy" Fondren, age thirty-four, but Nettie's obituary names her mother as Susie Thompson. See Mitchell Family Scrapbook, Mitchell Papers.

7. Bobbie's grandfather, Thomas Goodwin Mitchell, also fought in a Virginia regiment during the Revolutionary War. See Folks Huxford, *Pioneers of Wiregrass Georgia: A Biographical Account of Some of the Early Settlers of that Portion of Wiregrass Georgia Embraced in the Original Counties of Irwin, Appling, Wayne, Camden, and Glynn,* 6 vols. (Adel, Ga.: Patten, 1951), 1:184–85. The Seventh U.S. Census, 1850, Thomas County, Ga., lists Richard Mitchell, age fifty-nine, and his wife, Sophronia, forty-two, with eight children and real estate worth $10,274. Robert was born July 15, 1843, in Thomas County.

8. Nettie later complained of the lack of female patriotic activity. AF to RGM, Sept. 23, 1863, Mitchell Papers.

9. Bobbie joined Company E, 29th Georgia, on July 27 in Savannah and was soon made fifth sergeant. In March 1862 he was appointed second lieutenant and in December became acting aide-de-camp to Col. C. C. Wilson. Late in 1864 Bobbie became first lieutenant and adjutant. This appointment officially dated from September 16, 1864. Robert G. Mitchell, Compiled Military Service Record, RG 109, National Archives, Washington, D.C. (hereinafter cited as CSR, NA).

10. RGM to AF, July 28, 1861, Mitchell Papers. Bobbie's older brother William was captain and later colonel in the same unit. William D. Mitchell, CSR, NA.

11. The 29th Georgia was initially part of the Second Brigade, District of Georgia, in the Department of South Carolina and Georgia, commanded by Maj. Gen. John C. Pemberton. U.S. War Department, *War of the Rebellion: A Compilation of the Official Records of the Union and Confederate Armies,* 128 vols. (Washington, D.C.: Government Printing Office, 1880–1901), ser. 1, 14:487 (hereinafter cited as *OR;* all references to ser. 1). Occasionally selected companies of the 29th were detached to different locations, including Florida.

12. It is not known what was ailing Bobbie, though Nettie referred to him as suffering from fever and chills. AF to RGM, Nov. 21, 1862, Mitchell Papers. Mitchell's service records also list him as "Absent and Sick" in October 1862, but it is not clear if he returned to Thomasville. Robert G. Mitchell, CSR, NA.

13. RGM to AF, Sept. 19, 1862, Mitchell Papers.

14. RGM to AF, Dec. 9, 1861, ibid.

15. RGM to AF, Dec. 9, 31, 1861, ibid. One of these suicide attempts was successful. RGM to AF, Aug. 7, 1861, ibid. Bobbie also accused his colonel of being "shamefully drunk." RGM to AF, Nov. 11, 1861, ibid. For an account of fighting among the men, see RGM to AF, Jan. 1, 4, 1862, ibid.

16. RGM to AF, Dec. 9, 1861, Feb. 8, 1862, ibid. For more on his frustration and even disgust at his unit's long inactivity, see RGM to AF, Nov. 26, Dec. 11, 1862, ibid.

17. RGM to AF, Nov. 11, 1861, ibid. Another member of Bobbie's regiment also complained of the sickness, inactivity, and depravity. See John K. Mahon, ed., "Peter Dekle's Letters," *Civil War History* 4 (1958): 14–15. Private Dekle also wrote his wife that their camp was "no place for a nice women [*sic*] to be at." Ibid., 14.

18. RGM to AF, Apr. 11, 1862, Mitchell Papers. In January 1863 the 29th Georgia traveled to Wilmington, North Carolina, only to return to Georgia a few weeks later just as green as they left.

19. RGM to AF, Nov. 19, 1861, ibid. Apparently Nettie either changed her mind or Bobbie ignored her request because the majority of her letters survive from the spring of 1862 until the summer of 1864.

20. RGM to AF, Sept. 13, 1862, ibid.

21. RGM to AF, Dec. 28, 1861, ibid.

22. For example, see RGM to AF, July 28, 1861, ibid.

23. RGM to AF, Aug. 30, 1861, ibid.

24. RGM to AF, Oct. 24, 1861, ibid.

25. RGM to AF, Feb. 19, 1862, ibid.

26. RGM to AF, May 16, 1862, ibid.

27. RGM to AF, Apr. 22, 1862, ibid.

28. RGM to AF, May 7, 1862, ibid. David E. Fondren was a second sergeant in the 29th Georgia. He died of pneumonia at Mackay's Point on March 16, 1862. David E. Fondren, CSR, NA.

29. RGM to AF, Apr. 15, 1862, Mitchell Papers.

30. RGM to AF, Mar. 5, 1862, ibid.

31. RGM to AF, Mar. 30, 1862, ibid.

32. RGM to AF, Apr. 17, 1862, ibid.

33. For example, see RGM to AF, June 17, 1862 (first letter), and AF to RGM, Nov. 14, 1862, Mitchell Papers. In contrast Private Dekle of the 29th Georgia wrote his wife: "You and our child is all that I care for now. As for the Confedercy that is gone up. There is no use in fighting any more for that." See Mahon, "Peter Dekle's Letters," 22. See also RGM to AF, Apr. 19, 1862, Mitchell Papers.

34. RGM to AF, Apr. 19, 1862.

35. RGM to AF, Mar. 7, 1863, Mitchell Papers.

36. AF to RGM, May 14, 1862, ibid.

37. RGM to AF, Sept. 7, 1862, ibid. Another common example is her writing of banishing "gloomy thoughts to trouble your mind, but will *at all times* keep them far away, and let nothing but joy and peace reign in your heart." RGM to AF, Mar. 10, 1863, ibid. (emphasis in original).

38. RGM to AF, May 24, 1862, ibid.

39. RGM to AF, Feb. 26, 1863, ibid. Bobbie repeated similar sentiments on March 20, 1864, when he reaffirmed how much he appreciated her "cheerful letters," again blaming Confederate desertion on the "doleful and despondent letters received from home." Historian Drew Faust has argued that in fact women were so important to Confederate morale that perhaps their pleas for their men to come home contributed to the South's defeat. See Faust, *Mothers of Invention: Women of the Slaveholding South in the American Civil War* (Chapel Hill: University of North Carolina Press, 1996).

40. AF to RGM, Apr. 2, 1862, Mitchell Papers.

41. See AF to RGM, May 18, 1862, AF to RGM, Mar. 23, 1863, and RGM to AF, Apr. 5, 1862, ibid.

42. For example, see AF to RGM, Apr. 7, 1863, ibid.

43. AF to RGM, June 4, 1862, ibid. See also AF to RGM, Mar. 23, 1863, ibid.

44. AF to RGM, Sept. 12, 1862, ibid.

45. AF to RGM, Nov. 14, 1862, ibid.

46. RGM to AF, Apr. 12, 1862, ibid.

47. RGM to AF, Apr. 19, 1862, ibid. "O.L.I." refers to the Ochlochnee Light Infantry, another name for Company E, 29th Georgia.

48. RGM to AF, May 16, 1862, ibid.

49. RGM to AF, Apr. 12, 1862, ibid.

50. RGM to AF, Mar. 30, 1863, ibid.

51. RGM to AF, Nov. 2, 1861, n.d., July 2, 1862, Mar. 30, 1863, ibid. Nettie also referred to the enemy as "cowardly" and "heartless" in AF to RGM, Jan. 18, 1863, ibid.

52. RGM to AF, Jan. 28, 1863, ibid.

53. RGM to AF, Feb. 28, 1863, ibid.

54. See RGM to AF, Mar. 30, Apr. 22, and July 2, 1862, ibid.

55. RGM to AF, Jan. 29, 1862, ibid. Mitchell judged the people of Charleston as "more patriotic than those of Savannah." RGM to AF, Dec. 20, 1862, ibid. It is not clear why he viewed Savannah residents so negatively, but in one letter Mitchell claimed that there "are many there too who claim Foreign protection [and] made their fortunes here and still are not willing to fight for their adopted country." RGM to AF, Feb. 28, 1863, ibid.

56. For his views on North Carolina, see RGM to AF, Jan. 14, Feb. 9, 1863, ibid. In the January letter Bobbie did admit, albeit grudgingly, that North Carolina "troops at times have done splendid fighting." He called Mississippians "half civilized" and "too mean to feed a sick soldier that has left home, family and friends." RGM to AF, June 8, 15, 1863, ibid.

57. RGM to AF, Jan. 29, 1862, ibid. Mitchell labeled Bragg a "Humbug." RGM to AF, Jan. 6, 1863, ibid. He called Young "a man of a small mind very prejudiced and selfish with it." RGM to AF, Feb. 21, 1863, ibid. But he judged Robert E. Lee to be "shrewd and warlike looking." RGM to AF, Jan. 31, 1862, ibid.

58. See, for example, RGM to AF, Mar. 17, 1864, ibid., where Bobbie wrote Nettie of a doctor needing a "negro boy in the service with him." For Nettie referring to an overseer talking with her mother, see AF to RGM, Nov. 14, 1862, ibid.

59. Anthony Mitchell to "Aunt Jane," July 14, 1864, ibid. It is unclear who "Aunt Jane" was, but she may have been another slave, which of course would make this letter highly unusual and insightful.

60. AF to RGM, Feb. [?], 1863, ibid.

61. Nettie informed Bobbie, "I am studying music, French, Latin and Rhetoric—don't know yet whether I will take up any thing else or not." AF to RGM, Mar. 1, 1863, ibid. Also see William McCash, *Thomas R. R. Cobb: The Making of a Southern Nationalist.* (Macon, Ga.: Mercer University Press, 1983), 105.

62. Nettie had apparently discussed attending school as early as August 1861, when Bobbie told her, "If you do [go to school,] for gracious sake don't go as far as Tenn—as I feel like you are clear out of hearing." RGM to AF, Aug. 7, 1861, Mitchell Papers.

63. For Bobbie's change of heart, see RGM to AF, Feb. 21, 1863, ibid. See also AF to RGM, Mar. 8, 1863, ibid.

64. *OR,* 24(3):883–84.

65. RGM to AF, May 12, 1863, Mitchell Papers. See also Bell I. Wiley, ed., *The Confederate Letters of John W. Hagan* (Athens: University of Georgia Press, 1954), 17–18.

66. RGM to AF, June 15, 27, 1863, Mitchell Papers. John Hagan corroborated Mitchell's descriptions of conditions in Mississippi. Wiley, *Letters of John W. Hagan,* 19.

67. RGM to AF, June 8, 1863, Mitchell Papers.

68. Ibid. See also RGM to AF, July 1, 1863, ibid.

69. RGM to AF, June 15, 1863, ibid.

70. Wiley, *Letters of John W. Hagan,* 3, 22.

71. RGM to AF, Aug. 4, 1863, Mitchell Papers.

72. AF to RGM, July 3, 6, 1863, ibid. Mary Chesnut also noted this seemingly inappropriate socializing during the war. C. Vann Woodward, *Mary Chesnut's Civil War* (New Haven, Conn.: Yale University Press, 1981), 486–87. See also Faust, *Mothers of Invention,* 244–45.

73. AF to RGM, July 6, 1863, Mitchell Papers.

74. RGM to AF, Sept. 11, 1863, ibid.

75. Ibid.

76. AF to RGM, Sept. 23, 1863, ibid.

77. W. H. Reynolds to Mrs. W. J. [Anna M.] Dickey, Sept. 22, 1863, Dickey Family Papers (microfilm), Georgia State Archives, Atlanta. Sgt. William H. Reynolds, Company B, 29th Georgia, estimated that the unit went into battle with about 200 men but lost 130. Mitchell estimated that the loss was around 125. RGM to AF, Sept. 21, 1863, Mitchell Papers. The *Savannah Morning News* of September 29, 1863, calculated 24 killed, 97 wounded, and 8 missing for a total of 129 casualties.

78. RGM to "Brother," Sept. 20, 1863, Mitchell Papers.

79. RGM to AF, Sept. 21, 1863, ibid.

80. AF to RGM, Oct. 5, 1863, ibid. She may have learned of William's wounding through newspaper accounts. See, for example, the *Savannah Morning News,* Sept. 29, 1863.

81. RGM to AF, Sept. 26, 1863, Mitchell Papers.

82. AF to RGM, Oct. 7, 1863, ibid.

83. See Reynolds to Mrs. Dickey, Oct. 29, 1863, Dickey Family Papers. Reynolds described the 29th as "greatly reduced by sickness, there are only four men in my company present for duty."

84. RGM to AF, Oct. 7, 1863, Mitchell Papers. Bobbie wrote this letter from Lake City, Florida, so apparently he temporarily left the lines in Tennessee. See also RGM to AF, Nov. 5, 1863, ibid.

85. RGM to AF, Nov. 5, 1863.

86. RGM to AF, Dec. 3, 1863, Mitchell Papers.

87. AF to RGM, Dec. 7, 1863, ibid.

88. RGM to AF, Feb. 29, 1864, ibid.

89. See RGM to AF, Mar. 28, 30, 1864, ibid.

90. RGM to AF, Mar. 2, 1864, ibid.

91. RGM to AF, May 3, 1864, ibid.

92. RGM to AF, May 22, 1864, ibid.

93. RGM to AF, June 6, 1864, ibid.

94. RGM to AF, June 14, 1864, ibid.

95. RGM to AF, July 2, 1864, ibid.

96. RGM to AF, July 13, 1864, ibid. See also RGM to AF, July 11, 1864, ibid.

97. RGM to AF, July 2, 1864.

98. AF to RGM, Aug. 4, 1864, Mitchell Papers.

99. RGM to AF, Aug. 1, 1864, ibid. This letter predates Nettie's, but it seems that she had informed him of the raids in prior letters.

100. In December 1864 Bobbie was made first lieutenant and adjutant, which took effect on September 16. Robert G. Mitchell, CSR, NA. A postwar newspaper clipping claims that he was wounded on August 9, 1864, and "was entirely incapacitated for duty during the remainder of the war, and had to use crutches for six months after the war." "Judge Robert G. Mitchell," undated newspaper clipping, Mitchell Papers.

101. "Judge Robert G. Mitchell," undated newspaper clipping, Mitchell Papers.

102. "A Graceful Tribute," undated newspaper clipping, ibid.

103. "The Late Robert G. Mitchell," undated newspaper clipping, ibid.

104. The Mitchells had nine children, all of whom outlived their mother. Nettie died on January 20, 1929. Her obituary is in the Mitchell Family Scrapbook, ibid.

"And for the Widow and Orphan": Confederate Widows, Poverty, and Public Assistance

JENNIFER LYNN GROSS

MARY ANN MOSELEY AND BENJAMIN BAIRD WERE MARRIED IN January 1862. Their wedding took place less than a year after Benjamin enlisted in Company G, 21st Virginia Infantry—perhaps theirs was a marriage that was influenced by the heady romanticism that inspired many a southern union in the early days of the war. Mary Ann undoubtedly recognized, at least in the abstract, that the conflict could claim her new husband. She most likely did not *expect* to lose him, however, and she could not have foreseen his death occurring within the same year they married. Although Benjamin saw little action during his service, he died soon after he joined the Confederate ranks, a victim of disease like so many other Civil War soldiers.

Widowed at only twenty-four, Mary Ann had few options for survival open to her. After learning of Benjamin's death, she tried to make it on her own and continued living in the house she and her husband had "shared." Sometime before 1880, however, Mary Ann moved in with her widowed mother, Lucy Moseley. The two widows struggled together until Lucy's death several years later. In the 1880s, during the flush of reform that engulfed the United States and stimulated federal intervention on behalf of some of the "worthy" poor, southern states initiated efforts to provide assistance to their "worthy" poor, whom they emphatically defined as Confederate veterans and their widows. In 1888 Mary Ann Baird applied for and received a Confederate pension from the state of Virginia. The paltry thirty-dollar-per-year pension undoubtedly provided some economic comfort, and it must have given her some solace after having her provider and protector taken from her almost thirty years earlier. She collected her annuity until she died in 1914.[1]

While it lasted, the Civil War laid waste to the South's economic and social landscape and claimed the lives of at least 260,000 white men, among them Benjamin Baird. The wartime deaths of so many men created a new class of southern women—women like Mary Ann Baird—left without traditional male protectors and providers. Although it is virtually impossible to determine just how many southern women were widowed by the Civil War, it is likely that there were tens of thousands of them, often with fatherless children (defined by the state as "orphans").[2] These manless women, no longer part of traditional households, had to become the heads of and providers for their families, confronting new social, legal, and financial responsibilities as they struggled to survive in a patriarchal society in which women were expected to be helpmates for husbands, not heads of families.

Family wealth amassed before the husband's death certainly contributed to the economic support of many Confederate widows during the war and in the years afterward. Yet many of the wives of yeoman and even wealthy Confederates who died experienced economic instability. Mary Ann Baird's situation paints a revealing picture of Confederate widowhood. The 1860 census identifies her future husband as a farmer and the owner of three hundred dollars of real estate. She is listed as a resident in the household of her widowed mother—a farmer with one thousand dollars in real estate. Before the war, then, both Mary Ann and Benjamin would have been classified as part of the yeoman class.[3] Despite that prewar status and ownership of land, the 1870 census reveals that Mary Ann Baird had "no property" and before 1880 was forced to move back in with her mother. After her mother's death, Mary Ann moved into the home of two relatives of her deceased husband, both tenant farmers. Several years before her own death, she again moved, this time to live with a nephew, J. E. King. Such residence with family members by such women as they became older was not unique to Confederate widows. But Mary Ann's descent from the ranks of the yeomen landholders to the landless poor was more familiar than not to many Confederate widows and can be explained by two primary factors: the physical ramifications of the war on the South and the region's existing social and legal structures.

The sheer physical and economic devastation of the war itself, along with a dearth of opportunities for gainful employment and unfair inheritance laws and practices, often resulted in desperate situations for Confederate widows.

That they experienced their widowhood amid the war made their economic plight that much more severe. As a resident of Brunswick County, Virginia, Mary Ann Baird did not suffer directly from the devastation caused by battles, but she, like others throughout the South, felt keenly the ravages of inflation, property devaluation, impressment, and confiscation by both armies.[4] Additionally employment opportunities for women in the nineteenth century were fairly limited. Even during the war—a time that witnessed an "expansion" of work opportunities for women because of the absence of so many men from the home front—most in the South could not expect a great increase in their employment options.[5]

The existing legal system regarding estates and inheritance also added to the economic deprivation of Confederate widows. If a woman's husband died without leaving a will (which most did), southern estate laws limited her access to and control over her family's possessions.[6] Unlike the married women's property laws that had begun to emerge in some northern states during the 1840s, southern statutes until about 1890 stipulated that a widow's dower constituted only a one-third "life interest" in any real estate and one-third of any personal property that the husband had owned during the marriage. Because most Confederate widows had been married to yeomen or lower-class men, one-third of a husband's property could not adequately support them.[7]

Even if one did inherit all of her husband's property under the terms of his will, there was no guarantee that she would be able to keep it; she was still beholden to the legal processes of estate settlement and to the current property-valuation rates, which were extremely low during and after the war. Estate laws throughout the South dictated that before a will could be probated, all property in the husband's name—generally the entirety of the family's possessions—had to be inventoried and appraised.[8] Once that was accomplished, any or all of it had to be sold in order to pay the deceased's debts before any inheritances could be disbursed.[9] Consequently, whether their spouses died intestate or testate, most Confederate widows found themselves with significantly less property than they had enjoyed as wives before the war.[10]

Under these problematic circumstances, survival was all some women could hope for as they struggled to provide for their families on their own. Before the war remarriage was the usual answer to the question of a widow's survival. And for a few during the war, finding a new spouse allowed them to reestablish themselves as wives, provided for and protected by husbands. Yet remarriage in the postwar South was not always possible.[11] Indeed most Confederate widows were unable to remarry because there were simply not enough eligible single white men left in the South after the war.

Unable or unwilling to remarry, most struggled to support themselves. Certainly a few Confederate widows thrived as independent women and perhaps relished that role, yet these fortunate few were hardly typical. Mary Ann Baird's situation was more familiar to the majority of Confederate widows, who found themselves in need of economic assistance. The sources for such aid in the South varied over time.[12]

Initially those women in need had to depend wholly upon traditional sources for economic assistance. Like Baird they relied upon the charity and generosity of family, friends, and neighbors.[13] They also could appeal to their local or county governments for aid. In both the North and the South, welfare tradition held that assistance to the impoverished come strictly from local or private sources.

Colonial Americans, including southerners, had largely based their ideas about public assistance to the poor on a set of assumptions derived from English practices that mandated local support for the indigent. Accordingly each colony had divided their populace among local governing bodies that were individually responsible for the maintenance of the poor in their communities. In the southern colonies Anglican vestrymen had distributed assistance among needy residents from funds that were collected voluntarily from within their communities. By the late seventeenth century, however, most southern colonies had recognized that their people could not always be relied upon to give voluntarily. They therefore enacted some type of poor law to collect taxes from within each community. Despite the colonywide application of these poor laws, the funds collected locally provided only for the poor in that same community. The enactment of such laws did not change southerners' beliefs that the local populace was responsible for the poor in its midst.[14]

After the Revolution the demise of popular trust in the Anglican Church ended any reliance on vestrymen to provide for the poor. Instead southern states appointed "overseers of the poor" for each district or county.[15] As such the funding and distribution of aid to individuals still came from local sources.

The refusal of Americans and southerners specifically to create a nationally funded welfare system during this era was part and parcel of their fear of strong government embodied in the recent revolution. Yet their reticence to change their ideas about responsibility for the poor is more complicated. Generally speaking, the Revolutionary ideology that promoted individual liberty and opportunity, for whites at least, led to a social stigmatization of dependency, especially in the South, where slaves provided a readily apparent model of what dependency meant. Pensions for Revolutionary War veterans and their widows provide compelling evidence of this assumption. U.S. military pensions offered immediately after the Revolution were limited to soldiers who had been wounded, with "lifetime service pensions" at half pay for officers. A poor man who served his country and survived the war unscathed was not entitled to a pension. Only in 1818 did Congress extend benefits more generally to war veterans provided they could prove dire financial need—a condition whose likelihood increased as the soldier population aged. Unrestricted pensions for Revolutionary veterans did not emerge until 1832.

The widows of Revolutionary soldiers or other veterans had to wait until 1836 to begin collecting pensions, indicating the traditional American belief that if such women required assistance, they would receive it from private or local sources.[16] Other than these military pensions, state-generated provisions for the poor were generally ignored during this period; when it was acknowledged, allowance was only given to the disabled or insane—in other words those who in society's eyes were unable to work—and it was generally miserly.

Throughout most of the early national period, southern communities distributed their aid to the poor primarily in the form of outdoor relief—funds distributed by the overseers of the poor. There were a few state-run institutions that provided indoor relief, but these were reserved for the very old, the very young, and the disabled or insane.[17] Consistent with their objection to state-funded welfare, southern legislators' willingness to build and maintain institutions for indoor relief generally depended upon private sources of nontax revenue.[18] While widows might certainly have been among those few antebellum southerners who received either indoor or outdoor aid, they were not considered as a separate class of the "deserving poor" the way the insane or the infirm were.[19]

Over the course of the Civil War, southerners' understanding of welfare and the "deserving poor" changed. The war inspired a shift from a reliance on local resources to a reliance on the state in the form of the Confederate government and individual state governments. Both state and national governments allocated special monies in their budgets to assist the poor, especially soldiers and widows. At war's end, however, the southern poor found themselves once again reliant solely on local and private sources for assistance until the evolution of state-funded Confederate pensions in the late 1880s.

The temporary status of this welfare policy reflected not only the economic and physical realities of the South as a region during and after the conflict but also a change in southerners' perceptions about what was an acceptable role for the state in their lives as well as who belonged in the category of the "worthy poor." As Emory Thomas acknowledges in *The Confederate Nation,* one of the preeminent tenets of southern political thought that led to secession was that of states' rights. Of course this ideology served primarily to protect the institution of slavery from an ever-increasing northern and Republican majority in the federal government. Nevertheless it indicates a key component of southerners' understanding of the larger world around them. Since before the Revolution, southerners had relied on their local governments as the origin of day-to-day governance in their lives.[20] These sources, however, were unable to handle the sheer volume of destruction and suffering caused by the Civil War, forcing state governments and eventually the national administration to act on their citizens' behalf.

That many of those in need were the families of Confederate soldiers added an extra stimulus to expand responsibility for and sources of financial assistance. The shift from a reliance for economic assistance on local sources to state institutions and finally the national government reflected an acknowledgment that the "Confederate poor" were indeed worthy and deserving of public assistance. It was also an acknowledgment of the increasingly loud and active vocalization of pain and suffering on the part of soldiers' wives and widows who believed they were sacrificing too much for the cause.[21]

The transition from a reliance on local sources to a reliance on the state can also be seen as recognition by southern policymakers that a loose confederacy of independent states could not wage and win a war. Thus it was a reflection of the increasing centralization of the power of the Confederate government. As Thomas argues, the need for the South to become a nation rather than a loosely connected group of states forced it to become more Confederate than southern, taking on both roles and responsibilities heretofore considered inappropriate. Relief for the poor, especially soldiers and widows, was one such responsibility.[22] Correspondingly the shift back to local resources after the war was based both on the reality that the Confederacy was gone and that state governments did not have the ability—or, during Reconstruction, the inclination—to meet the needs of their poor. But it was also an implicit acknowledgment that the southern experiment with nationalism had failed.

During the four-year conflict, Confederate widows in need found that they could rely upon a broader spectrum of sources for economic assistance, sources that had developed as an outgrowth of the war itself. At its outbreak in 1861, deeply embedded notions that benevolence was a local concern shaped the immediate response of southerners to the poor and needy in their midst, including soldiers' wives and widows. Ladies throughout the South formed soldiers' aid societies, whose immediate goal was to provide supplies for the valiant fighting men from their locales.

Not long into the conflict, however, it became apparent that soldiers were not the only ones in need of assistance; their families were also suffering. In response to this realization, many aid societies broadened the scope of their activities to include the wives or widows of their local servicemen.[23] Additionally, long-established organizations, including churches and social clubs, often collected money and food for indigent soldiers' families within their communities while some southern businessmen offered services such as grinding corn or transportation at discounted rates to dependents in an effort to do their part for the cause. Most of these efforts remained locally focused, however, and cooperation among relief groups never materialized in the South the way it did in the North in the form of the Christian Commission and the Sanitary Commission.[24]

Local county or municipal governments also provided aid to soldiers' wives and widows as part of their traditional efforts to aid the poor in their communities. At first most local authorities relied upon existing structures and practices for the care of the poor to deal with needs of the servicemen's families or provided assistance in the form of free water and discounted prices on fuel and foodstuffs.[25] Soon after the first casualties, however, local officials realized that the need was greater than their typical resources and began appropriating extra funds specifically to relieve the suffering of soldiers' families. From the war's outset Brunswick County (Virginia) commissioners, for example, voted appropriations "for the benefit of the wives and children and families of the soldiers that have volunteered who are in indigent circumstances."[26] Such increases in funding for aid certainly helped, but they were not always limited to the families of soldiers; often local aid was available to anyone in poverty, which consequently reduced the amounts for soldiers' families. In Richmond, Virginia, for example, the municipal government, reacting to the infamous "bread riots" that erupted in 1863, appropriated seventy thousand dollars to meet the city's welfare needs. Although servicemen's wives and widows most certainly received some of this aid, the capital was full of other needy citizens as the bread riots revealed.[27]

Despite local governments' expanded efforts, it soon became clear to state officials as well as the general population that traditional sources of aid were simply inadequate to meet the needs of both the poor and the widows and wives of soldiers. Before the first year of the war was over, many southern state governments had joined the ranks of "aid providers." In a region in which local control reigned supreme, such "big government" action was somewhat unprecedented, but it quickly became acceptable and indeed expected, at least for the duration of the conflict.[28]

Rather than continue to rely primarily upon local efforts, southerners willingly turned to state governments to aid the poor, and legislators throughout the South rose to the occasion. Actions by the Virginia, North Carolina, and Georgia legislatures provide informative examples. Virginia's General Assembly passed the Act for Relief of Indigent Soldiers and Sailors on October 31, 1863—just seven months after the bread riots. This law offered benefits to "the widows and minor children" of "soldiers or sailors who had died in service" as well as to indigent families of soldiers or sailors still serving. Aid in the form of money or in-kind services would be distributed through the county governments to qualified individuals within their borders. Disabled or honorably discharged soldiers or their widows had to apply for aid at county offices. The law authorized local officials to impress goods or supplies within their jurisdictions according to the needs of their communities. The reliance on county institutions to distribute such aid was both the most efficacious method as well as the most socially acceptable.[29]

In 1864 the Virginia General Assembly amended the previous law and appropriated "one million dollars for the care of the families of soldiers and sailors who resided in counties controlled by the Federal Army."[30] Under this act legislators stipulated that dependents who had been driven from their homes by the Union army into other counties were eligible for aid in their new counties of residence. By ending established-residency requirements for aid, the law effectively exerted the power of the state government over county authorities by establishing a statewide definition of who was included in the "deserving poor" population. In addition to the 1863 and 1864 laws addressing the distribution of monetary aid, two other measures in 1864 provided for the doling out of cotton, cotton cards, and salt to needy citizens. Although unprecedented, the ease with which such legislation became law indicates that Virginia lawmakers and citizens saw such state-sponsored assistance as legitimate under the exigencies of war.[31]

In North Carolina, legislators passed the first law to aid widows and other members of soldiers' families in February 1862. Although this first law only allowed for bounties due and any arrears of pay to go to the widows and families of soldiers after their death, a year later the General Assembly appropriated one million dollars for the assistance of the families of individual soldiers.[32] As it was in Virginia, this aid was distributed through the county governments. At the end of 1863, the legislature set aside another one million dollars in aid to soldiers' families.[33] Like Virginia's state officials, the increasing generosity of North Carolina lawmakers was probably influenced by the displays of unrest among their citizenry; both Salisbury and High Point were, like Richmond, the site of bread riots earlier in the year. On December 23, 1864, they increased the appropriation to three million dollars after Gov. Zebulon Vance, undoubtedly influenced by the constant stream of letters he received from women requesting assistance, reminded legislators, "It is admitted to be our imperative duty to provide for these persons [soldiers' families]."[34] Vance's impassioned plea reveals his recognition that the responsibility for aiding the poor had passed from the hands of local officials to the General Assembly.[35]

Other North Carolina politicians also called upon the citizens' sense of duty to justify state aid for the poor. J. M. Leach, in an 1863 bid for the Confederate congressional seat from the Seventh District of North Carolina, avowed, "I am in favor of increasing the pay of the soldiers, and think that adequate provision should be made by law, permanently to provide them with clothing at low rates and also to supply the families of the needy at home and keep them from suffering and want, and I have been active in my own county in endeavoring to effect this."[36] In total the state government appropriated over six million dollars as well as tons of foodstuffs and supplies for the purpose of aiding soldiers' families.[37] North Carolinians clearly saw state aid as not only justified but also as a sacred duty.

Georgia also took steps to provide financial assistance to the families of its soldiers during the war. Although the majority of state expenditures during 1861 went toward creating and outfitting military units, the national government increasingly took on such costs, leaving Georgia free to dedicate its monies to the support of its civilians. As expected most of this aid initially originated in the individual counties, but as Gov. Joseph Brown admonished legislators, "The problem required a state solution rather than a local one." Georgians "from every part of the State, fight for the protection of the liberties of the whole people, and the wealth of the whole State. Let our soldiers know that their loved ones at home are provided for." He continued, "Many of Georgia's volunteers were almost destitute of property, and their families should be supplied, if need be, at the public expense, with such of the necessaries of life as their labor will not afford them, cost the State what it may."[38]

In November 1861 Georgia began a program of home-front assistance by providing for the distribution of salt, cotton cards, and corn free of charge to soldiers' families and at low cost to other indigents. To facilitate this largesse the state offered financial incentives to encourage private manufacturing and importing. When such efforts failed to yield sufficient returns, the government established its own factories and import trade to pick up the slack. Moreover, when a serious grain shortage threatened Georgia in the summer of 1862, officials responded by limiting cotton production to three acres per hand and threatening the confiscation of unauthorized stills, for grain that was distilled into alcohol could not be turned into bread.[39] In addition to these "real" forms of assistance, beginning in 1863 the legislature appropriated money for direct distribution "to assist families of soldiers in the service, children and wives of deceased soldiers, and disabled veterans." In 1863 Georgia lawmakers set aside $2.5 million, while 1864 and 1865 saw such appropriations increased to $6 million and $8 million respectively.[40] As was the case in Virginia and North Carolina, the funds went to the counties for distribution according to the number of beneficiaries reported.

Throughout the war years, Georgia, like other Confederate states, struggled to find the means to provide aid to soldiers' families. To pay for such programs, state taxes on income, cotton, and property rose for elite citizens, while the families of yeoman soldiers paid at reduced rates.[41] As Governor Brown surmised, "By the adoption of this plan, all who purchase are taxed something for the assistance of the soldiers' families and widows."[42] That wealthy citizens, who provided most of the leadership, did not object to the tax increase indicates their understanding that the state should take responsibility for those citizens who were less fortunate, provided they were serving the cause.

Even the extra efforts made by state governments proved insufficient to meet the needs of the growing numbers of indigents. Accordingly assistance to the poor evolved to include an unprecedented source of aid—the national government. In March 1862 the Confederate Congress appropriated five million dollars for "the relief of the Families of Soldiers in the Service of the Confederate States . . . in needy circumstances."[43] These funds were distributed among the states at the request of the governors in proportion to the number of troops they furnished. Within each the state government disbursed the money to its counties in like manner. Although this funding was not designated solely for soldiers' widows, legislators surely considered widows as among those "in needy circumstances." In January 1864 Congress acted again on behalf of the Confederacy's needy, passing a bill entitled "An Act to provide additional compensation for the soldiers of the army of the Confederate States, and for the families of those who die in the service." Section 1 of this act ordered that every noncommissioned officer or private who was honorably discharged from the military receive a Confederate bond worth the amount of the soldier's pay while in service, drawing 8 percent interest. Section 2 specified that "the wife and children, or widowed mother, of any private or non-commissioned officer who shall die in service shall be entitled to a bond of like character and conditions, bearing date on the day of the death of the father, husband, or son."[44] This was the first Confederate law to recognize the specific hardships the war caused for soldiers' wives and widows. Unfortunately for the recipients, Confederate bonds became worthless with Lee's surrender at Appomattox.

Why did Confederate officials, who ostensibly were advocates of the same states' rights ideology that had driven secession, so willing begin and continue a national welfare program? Undoubtedly the bread riots that occurred in Richmond, Virginia; Atlanta, Macon, Columbus, and Augusta, Georgia; and Salisbury and High Point, North Carolina, during the spring of 1863 influenced Congress's 1864 largesse as much as they had those of each of the three state governments. Additionally, as the war progressed, Confederate officials could not fail to notice increasing rates of desertion among soldiers with families at home. This combined with a constant torrent of letters from families requesting some sort of assistance in lieu of the return of their soldier–loved ones convinced politicians that desertion was largely an expression of the men's concerns for their wives and children. Accordingly they attempted to alleviate this drain on the ranks by enacting relief measures on the home front.

The citizens' willingness to turn to Confederate rather than state or local officials indicates a shift in southerners' beliefs that the national government should be responsible for their welfare amid their suffering. But this expanding sense of the Confederacy's responsibility for the poor was not born solely out of the necessity caused by the greater scale of need that existed during the war. Rather, southerners demanded that the government provide for the poor because so many of them were the destitute wives and widows of soldiers.

When the war ended in Confederate defeat, southerners once again had to revise their expectations and assumptions about assistance to the poor. Although the end of fighting may have softened some of the economic deprivation suffered throughout the South, it also brought an end to the Confederacy's wartime aid. Additionally assistance from the southern state governments also ended when they came under U.S. military administration during Reconstruction. While some needy individuals could find brief assistance from the federal government through the Bureau of Refugees, Freedmen, and Abandoned Lands, many found themselves reliant primarily upon traditional sources. Until the 1880s countless widows like Mary Ann Baird were limited to going it alone and barely eking out a living or acquiring the limited economic assistance that could be had from family, friends, charitable organizations, and their county or municipal governments.

More than fifteen years after the South's experiment with nationalism, Baird and others like her could turn once more to the state for assistance. In the 1880s, with the national move toward reform and its use of the federal government to fix the ills of society, southern states became willing to open their pockets to the Confederate poor once more. At the same time that the federal government began offering pensions to any Union veteran who had served during the Civil War, regardless of whether or not he had been wounded, southern state legislatures created their own Confederate pension systems.[45] These were not just an effort to "catch up" with the pro-Union efforts or simply a recognition by southern citizens and legislators that men and women were still suffering from sacrifices they had made for the Confederacy during the war. As Theda Skocpol argues, "Civil War benefits [Confederate or Federal] . . . cannot be set aside as mere unavoidable concomitants of the human damage inflicted by the original military conflict, for the extension of Civil War benefits came after claims directly due to wartime casualties had peaked and were in decline."[46] Rather, the move to assist Confederate veterans and their widows was motivated by citizens' willingness to insist on such efforts. Southerners' turn to the state was a reflection of a shift in their expectations of government, in which they were not unlike other Americans. But where others understood the state to mean the federal government, southerners preferred to see that authority exclusively in their state governments, at least where aid to the Confederate poor was concerned.

Southerners' flirtation with the idea of federal pensions to Confederate veterans and their widows is revealing in this respect. The issue arose during the late 1890s, several years after most southern states had begun their pension programs. Although the idea of federally funded pensions for ex-Confederates was largely supported by the northern populace and their politicians, the South ultimately rejected the idea and the definition of the "state" that it implied. In many respects the debate over federal pensions broke down between the upper and lower classes. Southern legislators and many outspoken leaders of the United Confederate Veterans' camps—the more affluent contingent—led the charge against the pensions.[47] Some, like the Ben T. Duval Camp in Fort Smith, Arkansas, even published official resolutions damning the effort. In an 1899 resolution, the camp leadership asserted: "We are not in sympathy with any movement or contemplated movement to the end that surviving ex-Confederate soldiers be pensioned by the (General) Government of the United States, and that our representatives and senators in congress be so advised and requested to oppose any proposition or measure which may be introduced, tending to that end."[48] The Pickett-Buchanan Camp of Norfolk, Virginia, went so far as to declare, "A Federal pension is worse than Confederate poverty."[49]

Many poor veterans, who could have used the extra money, disagreed with such bravado, and a few brave southern politicians embraced and promoted the idea of federal Confederate pensions on their behalf. In a letter to Congress, B. P. Maddox, himself a former Confederate soldier, encapsulated the class division over the issue: "Towering monuments to our dead generals, and flowers on our graves meet, in the South, a more ready response than the needs of our living. . . . They say for us, without our consent, that we would 'feel insulted if offered a Government pension.' Why should we be more afraid of Federal money than they who receive it for service in the Federal Congress or Senate, or in a thousand other offices distributed all over the South? And why should the old soldier be thought an ingrate because he would like a few of those comforts that were his (besides 'board and clothes') before he made sacrifice of everything, even of health, for a cause he once thought was the Public Good?"[50] Despite such convincing logic, opinions like Maddox's were largely drowned out by the cacophony of those who rejected federal pensions out of hand. Opponents demanded that any assistance rendered to poor Confederate veterans or their families come from the southern states rather than the U.S. government. Their rejection of federal pensions, despite the reality that such entitlements would have been much more lucrative and helpful to those in need, indicates a continued hostility and wariness on the part of elite southerners toward the federal government, which they felt had "tormented" southerners during Reconstruction. Additionally the rejection of federal pensions by former Confederates reveals the power of the emerging myth of the Lost Cause. Whether or not the myth became a central feature of white Protestant religious practice in the South, as Charles Reagan Wilson has asserted, it was powerful enough to make payment to Confederate soldiers by their former enemy intolerable.[51]

Sen. William Bate of Tennessee demonstrated the perceived link between loyalty to the cause and the refusal of federal pensions. He argued before the Senate regarding "most" Confederate veterans: "They are a brave, noble, patriotic, self-sacrificing set of men. They are not alms-begging nor pension-seeking men. They are proud, poor, and patriotic, and ask no pensions of the Government. Neither have they any apology to make. . . . I have never apologized, and never expect to, for my course as a Confederate soldier. I believed I was right, and I believe it now. . . . I think the Confederate soldier feels that he has had to pay a great deal, and a great deal too much, for Federal pensions. He does not approve of it."[52] Finally the refusal to accept federal pensions was part and parcel of the southern leadership's reclamation of the states' rights ideology of the prewar period with a continued rejection of a centralization of government power, be it the Confederate government during the war or the U.S. government during the 1890s.[53]

Although many southerners, white and black, had received aid from the U.S. government through both the army and the Freedmen's Bureau before the end of Reconstruction in the 1870s, southerners largely rejected the ideological underpinnings of that aid. Their legislators during the 1880s were willing to use state resources to provide welfare to veterans and widows largely because they considered such aid a payment for services rendered to the state; those services had not been rendered to the federal government and therefore should not be paid for by them. Destitute Confederate widows, the logic specified, were poor not because their husbands had been "lay abouts" but because they had sacrificed their lives for the Confederate cause. Accordingly it was the responsibility of the South, exercised through the states, to reward them for their or their husbands' service. When in 1894 the federal government offered to take over the payment of Confederate pensions, the reaction from many, especially southern politicians, was an emphatic "No." To turn to the national authorities for such assistance in their minds would not only cheapen the principles that justified southern aid to former Confederates but also violate the ideology of states' rights that they were championing once again.

Despite assistance, the war devastated many southern families, especially those who sent husbands, sons, and fathers to the battlefield never to return. Both during the war and afterward, state governments found it necessary to attend to such needs through formal policy and public-relief programs. The scale, and to some extent the ideology, of such efforts were relatively unprecedented in the South and tapped already overtaxed resources. Yet proportionally, southern state-sponsored relief programs exceeded such efforts in the North during the war. Southerners justified this spending within the definition of duty. Men who went to war fulfilled their manly duty to protect their homes and their state from northern invaders. It was the duty of those who remained at home to provide for their families in their absence, whether that absence was temporary or permanent. In the end the war brought about what one historian has called "the most extensive welfare system ever in the South," setting a precedent for similar efforts, at least at the state level, at the turn of the century.[54]

Both during and after the war, southerners considered those who had sacrificed for "the cause" especially deserving of public aid because of that sacrifice. Using special measures rather than standard poor-relief laws, legislators set veterans and their families apart as worthy recipients of governmental assistance rather than paupers dependent upon the largesse of individuals and charitable organizations. Moreover veterans who had survived the war unscathed physically felt "a strong desire" to help the families of those comrades who did not return as well as "those fellow comrades who had been disabled." Indeed many former soldiers were deeply moved by the needs of other veterans and the families who had been deprived of their providers and protectors.[55]

Certainly not all widows shared the experiences of Mary Ann Baird, but many could probably relate to her plight. The assistance available to Confederate widows during the war and afterward varied over time. Baird's story reveals the development of southerners' understanding of aid to the poor between 1861 and the century's end and just whose responsibility it should be. Despite their numerous struggles, widows survived in the postwar South. For those women who never recovered from the economic devastation of losing their husbands, financial assistance from both private and public sources could mean the difference between life and death. At the close of her wartime diary, Cornelia Peake McDonald, a Virginia widow, poignantly states, "And here ends my account of my trials; and though they were not at an end entirely, I was able in various ways to take care of my family."[56] No doubt for many Confederate widows, such was the case.

NOTES

1. U.S. Bureau of the Census, Brunswick County, Va., Eighth Census, 1860; Ninth Census, 1870; Tenth Census, 1880; Twelfth Census, 1900; Thirteenth Census, 1910; and Fourteenth Census, 1920, Library of Virginia, Richmond (hereinafter cited as LV); Brunswick County Land Taxes, 1859–1900, Brunswick County Library, Lawrenceville, Va.; the Brunswick County Personal Property Taxes, 1860–1900, ibid.; Confederate Pension Records, 1888, 1900, 1902, 1909–13, LV.

2. No complete count of women widowed by the war has ever been conducted, but from William Glasson's research of Confederate pensions in 1906 and Jeffrey Morrison's study of Virginia pensioners in 1905, we can surmise that there were at least 29,084 widows collecting pensions in the southern states in 1905 and 1906. Glasson, "The South's Care for her Confederate Veterans," *Review of Reviews* (July 1907): 40–47; Morrison, "'Increasing the Pensions of These Worthy Heroes': Virginia's Confederate Pensions, 1888–1927" (M.A. thesis, University of Richmond, 1996), 41. See also Jennifer Lynn Gross, "'Good Angels': Confederate Widowhood and the Reassurance of Southern Patriarchy in the Postbellum South" (Ph.D. diss., University of Georgia, 2001), 3–5. One can reasonably assume, however, that the actual number of widows was much higher than 29,084. First, these are the figures for 1906. They exclude widows who died before 1906, of which there were likely many, as forty years had passed since the end of the war. Second, though certainly not all of the 260,000 white southern men that died were married before or during the war, it seems likely that more than a mere 9 percent would have been. Finally, there were maximum property allowances to receive a pension, so pension counts only included widows in the lower economic classes of society. James M. McPherson, *Battle Cry of Freedom: The Era of the Civil War* (New York: Oxford University Press, 1988), 854. That 260,000 southern men died in the Civil War is generally accepted as fact, however, some scholars assert that the number should actually be higher since rates of death off the battlefield are often miscounted.

3. Although there were very wealthy as well as very poor southerners before the war, most whites in agricultural areas were, like the Moseleys and the Bairds, members of the yeoman class. Accepted practice divides the South's population as approximately 20 percent poor white, 67 percent yeoman, and 13 percent planter. See Frank L. Owsley, *Plain Folk of the Old South* (Baton Rouge: Louisiana State University Press, 1949); Stephanie McCurry, *Masters of Small Worlds: Yeoman Households, Gender Relations, and the Political Culture of the Antebellum South Carolina Low Country* (New York: Oxford University Press, 1995); and Gavin Wright, *The Political Economy of the Cotton South: Households, Markets, and Wealth in the Nineteenth Century* (New York: W. W. Norton, 1978).

4. In addition to a landscape and economy crippled by the war itself, the end of slavery beginning in 1863 meant that all money invested in human property disappeared. While less than a quarter of the southern population owned slaves, many of those owned five or less, indicating that their loss was a significant amount of their total property. In a case study of Confederate widows in Brunswick County, Virginia, one-fifth of the households owned at least one slave; only two owned more than five. See Jennifer L. Gross, "'You All Must Do the Best You Can': The Civil War Widows of Brunswick County, Virginia, 1860–1920" (M.A. thesis, University of Richmond, 1995). The economic and physical devastation of the war has been well documented by many historians

over the years. See, among others, Ralph Adreano, ed., *The Economic Impact of the American Civil War* (Cambridge, Mass.: Schenkman, 1962).

5. Drew Gilpin Faust, *Mothers of Invention: Women of the Slaveholding South in the American Civil War* (New York: Vintage Books, 1996).

6. Will writing was still relatively rare during this period except among men with large amounts of property.

7. For a brief discussion of women and estate laws, see Gross, "'Good Angels,'" 84–90. For a more in-depth discussion of women and estate laws, see Suzanne Lebsock, *The Free Women of Petersburg: Status and Culture in a Southern Town, 1784–1860* (New York: W. W. Norton, 1984), chap. 3; Marlene Stein Wortman, ed., *Women in American Law* (New York: Holmes and Meier, 1985), 14, 17; Carole Shammas et al., *Inheritance in America from Colonial Times to the Present* (New Brunswick, N.J.: Rutgers University Press, 1987), 37, 64–65, 248; Joan Hoff, *Law, Gender, and Injustice: A Legal History of U.S. Women* (New York: New York University Press, 1991), 89–189; and Linda Speth, "More Than Her 'Thirds': Wives and Widows in Colonial Virginia," *Women and History* 4 (1982): 8. See the sources in note 3 for information on the southern population.

8. Although some fathers established separate estates for their daughters when they married, this was generally a rare occurrence and was usually only practiced among elites. For a discussion of this practice, see Lebsock, *Free Women of Petersburg;* Wortman, *Women in American Law;* Shammas et al., *Inheritance in America;* Hoff, *Law, Gender, and Injustice;* and Speth, "More Than Her 'Thirds.'"

9. For many widows their husbands' debt, along with the state of the economy, meant that it was more advantageous to renounce their husbands' wills, refusing their inheritance in favor of their dower third. For a more in-depth discussion of will renunciation, see Lois Green Carr, "Inheritance in the Colonial Chesapeake," in *Women in the Age of the American Revolution: Perspectives on the American Revolution,* ed. Ronald Hoffman and Peter J. Albert (Charlottesville: University Press of Virginia, 1989), 170–71, 196; Gloria L. Main, "Widows in Rural Massachusetts on the Eve of the Revolution," in ibid.; Lebsock, *Free Women of Petersburg;* Carole Shammas, "Early American Women and Control over Capital," in Hoffman and Albert, *Women in the Age of the American Revolution;* and Joan R. Gunderson and Gwen V. Gampel, "Married Women's Legal Status in Eighteenth-Century New York and Virginia," *William and Mary Quarterly* 39 (Jan. 1982): 114–34.

10. In Brunswick County more than one-third of the widows whose husbands had owned property had less property five years after the war's end. See Gross, "'Do the Best You Can.'"

11. More than two-thirds of the seventy widows in Brunswick County did not remarry. See ibid.

12. For more in-depth information about the plight of southern widows during and after the war, see Gross "'Good Angels'"; and Robert Kenzer, "The Uncertainty of Life: A Profile of Virginia's Civil War Widows," in *The War Was You and Me: Civilians in the American Civil War,* ed. Joan E. Cashin (Princeton, N.J.: Princeton University Press, 2002).

13. In addition to receiving gifts of money and supplies, many widows relied on family members for a larger commitment of assistance in the form of cohabitation, either for a short time or permanently. Of Brunswick County widows, more than one-third of them resided in other people's households at one time or another after losing their husbands. Brunswick Co., Va., Ninth U.S.

Census, 1870; Tenth U.S. Census, 1880; Twelfth U.S. Census, 1900; Thirteenth U.S. Census, 1910; and Fourteenth U.S. Census, 1920, LV.

14. Summary of colonial poor relief from Elna Green, ed., "Introduction," *Before the New Deal: Social Welfare in the South, 1830–1930* (Athens: University of Georgia Press, 1999), vii–xxvi. Virginia Bernhard has argued that because poor relief in the South was funded by public taxes, the majority of which were provided by the gentry, southerners saw provision for the poor by the more fortunate as part and parcel of noblesse oblige. This notion, that poor relief was the responsibility of the community and its leaders in particular, contributed to the development of a southern social-welfare ideology that differed from that of the rest of the American colonies. Virginia Bernhard, "Poverty and the Social Order in Seventeenth-Century Virginia," *Virginia Magazine of History and Biography* 85 (Apr. 1977): 153–55.

15. Green, *Before the New Deal,* xi.

16. Theda Skocpol, *Protecting Soldiers and Mothers: The Political Origins of Social Policy in the United States* (Cambridge, Mass.: Harvard University Press, 1992), 105.

17. According to Michael Katz, during the first decades of the nineteenth century, many rural counties in the South abandoned previously built almshouses in favor of outdoor relief. Katz, *In the Shadow of the Poorhouse: A Social History of Welfare in America* (New York: Basic Books, 1986), 14. For an overview of early welfare beliefs and policy, see the introduction in Skocpol, *Protecting Soldiers and Mothers,* 1–66.

18. Peter Wallenstein, *From Slave South to New South: Public Policy in Georgia in the Nineteenth Century* (Chapel Hill: University of North Carolina Press, 1987), 29.

19. Although some antebellum southerners participated in the "evangelical religiosity" that swept the nation during the early 1800s inspiring benevolence on the part of suffering members of society, there were limits to such efforts in the South, engendered by the link between benevolence and more-radical reform movements, including the abolition movement. Green, *Before the New Deal,* xii–xiv.

20. The conflicts between royal governors and southern colonial assemblies throughout the eighteenth century—the Pistol Fee Controversy in Virginia in the mid-1750s, the "Regulator" movements in North and South Carolina during the 1760s, and the Gadsden Election Controversy in South Carolina in the 1760s—reveal the jealousy with which southerners had historically guarded the power of their local governments. For a cogent synopsis of the development of this emphasis and reliance on local and state power rather than colonial or national governments from the pre-Revolutionary period through the 1860s, see John Boles, *The South through Time: A History of an American Region,* vol. 1, 2nd ed. (Upper Saddle River, N.J.: Prentice-Hall, 1999), 89–184, 260–306; and William J. Cooper Jr. and Thomas E. Terrill, *The American South: A History,* vol. 1, 3rd ed. (New York: McGraw-Hill, 2002), 54–58, 72–74, 122–72.

21. One need only consult the papers of Jefferson Davis, Confederate senators and representatives, and southern governors and state legislators to find multitudes of letters from constituents, very often wives, widows, and mothers, requesting governmental financial assistance while their husbands were employed in the war effort.

22. Emory M. Thomas, *The Confederate Nation: 1861–1865* (New York: Harper & Row, 1979).

23. There are numerous scholarly studies that describe the creation of these aid societies and their work in the South among the needy. Some of the best include Faust, *Mothers of Invention;* Jean Friedman, *The Enclosed Garden: Women and Community in the Evangelical South* (Chapel Hill: University of North Carolina Press, 1985); Anne Firor Scott, *The Southern Lady: From Pedestal to Politics* (Charlottesville: University Press of Virginia, 1970); and LeeAnn Whites, *The Civil War as a Crisis in Gender: Augusta, Georgia, 1860–1890* (Athens: University of Georgia Press, 1995).

24. Robert H. Bremer, "The Impact of the Civil War on Philanthropy and Social Welfare," *Civil War History* 12 (Dec. 1966): 298–300.

25. For an examination of Richmond's efforts to aid its poor, see Emory M. Thomas, "To Feed the Citizens: Welfare in Wartime Richmond, 1861–1865," *Virginia Cavalcade* 22 (Summer 1972): 22–29.

26. Order Book 38, 1851–65, Brunswick County, LV.

27. Thomas, "To Feed the Citizens," 28–29.

28. The Confederacy enacted its first provision for aid to soldiers' families and widows in March 1862. Confederate Congress, House Bill No. 2, Mar. 19, 1862, Virginia Historical Society, Richmond (hereinafter cited as VHS). Virginia began providing assistance to soldiers' families and widows in 1863. *Acts of the General Assembly of the State of Virginia, Passed at a Called Session, 1863* (Richmond, Va., 1863), chap. 31, pp. 21–23. Whether or not Mary Ann Baird received aid from one or all three of these sources is unknown—records that list those individuals or families who received such aid no longer exist—but it is likely that she was among them based on her financial situation.

29. William F. Zornow, "Aid for the Indigent Families of the Soldiers of Virginia, 1861–1865," *Virginia Magazine of History and Biography* 68 (Oct. 1958): 456.

30. Ibid., 457.

31. Thomas, "To Feed the Citizens," 22–29. For a discussion of wartime aid in Virginia, see Gay Neale, *Brunswick County, Virginia, 1720–1975* (Lawrenceville, Va.: Brunswick County Bicentennial Committee, 1975), 158–89; Zornow, "Aid for the Indigent Families," 454–58; and Mark E. Rodgers, *Tracing the Civil War Veteran Pensions System in the State of Virginia: Entitlement or Privilege* (Lewiston, N.Y.: Edwin Mellen Press, 1999), 1–13.

32. Chapter 26, *Public Laws of the State of North Carolina Passed by the General Assembly at its Session 1862–1863* (Raleigh, N.C.: W. W. Holden, 1863).

33. Chapter 34, *Public Laws of the State of North Carolina Passed by the General Assembly at its Session 1863* (Raleigh, N.C.: W. W. Holden, 1864).

34. Chapter 33, *Public Laws of the State of North Carolina Passed by the General Assembly at its Session 1863–1864* (Raleigh, N.C.: W. W. Holden, 1865); "Governor's Message," Legislative Documents, 1864–65, No. 1, cited in Clyde Olin Fisher, "A Brief History of Confederate Pensions and Soldier Relief in North Carolina" (M.A. thesis, Columbia University, 1918), 9.

35. Vance received letters throughout his governorship from women requesting aid or exemptions. See Letters, 1861–65, Zebulon Vance Papers, 1861–65, North Carolina State Archives, Raleigh.

36. Letterbook 4, p. 485, Vance Personal Papers, ibid. The information in this paragraph came from Fisher, "Confederate Pensions"; and Fisher, "The Relief of Soldiers' Families in North Caro-

lina during the Civil War," *South Atlantic Quarterly* 16 (Jan.–Oct. 1917): 60–72. It is important to note that despite the impressive figure of $6 million, this money was paid in Confederate specie, so it was highly inflated.

37. Fisher, "Relief of Soldiers' Families," 68.

38. Wallenstein, *From Slave South to New South,* 116.

39. Ibid., 104.

40. Ibid., 102.

41. Ibid., 99–128.

42. Ibid., 103.

43. Confederate Congress, House Bill No. 2, Mar. 19, 1862.

44. Confederate Congress, House Bill No. 376, Jan. 8, 1864, VHS.

45. For complete coverage of Union pensions, see Skocpol, *Protecting Soldiers and Mothers,* 65–151.

46. Ibid., 7. Between 1880 and 1910, the U.S. government spent more on aid to its veterans and their dependents than all other major categories of spending aside from payments on the national debt. By 1910 more than 500,000 American men aged sixty-five or older and some 300,000 widows, orphans, and other dependents received federal benefits for their or their providers' Civil War service in the Union army. Ibid., 65.

47. R. B. Rosenburg, *Living Monuments: Confederate Soldiers' Home in the New South* (Chapel Hill: University of North Carolina Press, 1993).

48. Ben T. Duval Camp, United Confederate Veterans, "Resolution," Feb. 28, 1899, Samuel Lewis Collection, VHS.

49. Pickett-Buchanan Camp, United Confederate Veterans, "Pensioning of the Confederate Soldier by the United States" (Jan.–Dec. 1898), 314, Southern Historical Collection, University of North Carolina, Chapel Hill.

50. B. P. Maddox, "An Appeal of the South's Old Soldier to Congress for a Pension by the Government" (Richmond, Va.: 1916), VHS.

51. Charles Reagan Wilson, *Baptized in Blood: The Religion of the Lost Cause, 1865–1920* (Athens: University of Georgia Press, 1980).

52. "Remarks of Honorable Wm. B. Bate, of Tennessee, on the Resolution of Senator Butler of North Carolina, to Pension Ex-Confederate Soldiers, in the Senate of the United States, Jan. 26, 1899," VHS. Later in his remarks Bate asserted, "I think there is no considerable number of ex-Confederate soldiers anywhere in our Southland who have either sought or will seek pensions of the Government."

53. Emory Thomas argues that during the war, southerners in varying degrees were willing to give up various tenets of the "status quo" for which the South had seceded, including even slavery, which is epitomized by the Duncan-Kenner mission and the proposal to arm the slaves. He concludes, however, that by 1865 they were not willing to sacrifice the "primacy of people and place." Consequently, when Jefferson Davis ordered Lee, Johnston, and the rest of the Confederate men at arms to continue the fight through partisan warfare, the overwhelming majority of southerners, including the military leadership, rejected the command. That set in motion a reclamation of many of the ideological tenets that prompted secession, including the sanctity of states' rights ideology,

that lives on for many southerners in the myth of the Lost Cause and has continued in modern politics since. Thomas, *Confederate Nation,* 305–6.

54. Rodgers, *Pensions System in the State of Virginia,* 3.

55. Ibid., 4.

56. Cornelia Peake MacDonald, *A Diary with Reminiscences of the War and Refugee Life in the Shenandoah Valley, 1860–1865,* annotated by Hunter MacDonald (Nashville, Tenn.: Cullom and Ghertner, 1935), 245.

"Talking Heroines": Elite Mountain Women as Chroniclers of Stoneman's Raid, April 1865

JOHN C. INSCOE

BY THE FALL OF 1865, CORNELIA PHILLIPS SPENCER WAS ALREADY at work on a book that would be published the following year, *The Last Ninety Days of the War in North Carolina.* The Chapel Hill widow took on this task at the suggestion of David Lowery Swain, former governor of the state and longtime president of the University of North Carolina. She originally conceived—and contracted—her narrative as a series of articles in *The Watchman,* a new journal established by a UNC professor at war's end to promote sectional reconciliation and published in New York. The "unexpected favor" with which the series was received by readers led her to expand her narrative and reissue it in book form, as the author explained in a brief preface.[1]

While she acknowledged in her opening pages that it would be long before the "history of the late war can be soberly and impartially written," Spencer also recognized that future historians would need to have evidence from private sources in order to do so, noting that "history has no more invaluable and irrefragable witnesses for the truth than are to be found in the journals, memoranda, and private correspondence of the prominent and influential men who either acted in, or were compelled to remain quiet observers of the events of their day."[2]

In this statement Spencer reveals both class and gender biases common to her era and long afterward as to who made history and whose perspectives were worthwhile in capturing and preserving it—"prominent and influential men." She was diligent in her attempts to obtain from such sources their own memories, correspondence, and other records in order to construct her account of the conflict's waning days in her home state. Her own prominence in the university town—a professor's daughter and close friend and confidante of Swain—gave her entrée to a number of such connections who provided her with considerable materials, including former governors Zebulon B. Vance and William A. Graham and state supreme court justice Thomas Ruffin. Not surprisingly Spencer did not seem to have actively sought such input from women around the state, though their voices occasionally made their way into her narrative.

A major part of Spencer's book—three full chapters—chronicles Stoneman's raid through western North Carolina in April 1865, a mission one later historian described as "a knife thrust into the virtually undefended back of the South."[3] As with the rest of her book, the female perspective on that traumatic culmination of the war in the southern highlands appears only fleetingly. Yet what renders this raid so striking to historians since, or should, are the unusual number and fullness of written accounts by women who lived along Stoneman's route and endured encounters of various sorts with his troops. Like an outspoken woman in Winchester, Virginia, who verbally challenged disruptive Union troops and was called by an admiring neighbor "one of the talking heroines," a number of these Appalachian women in North Carolina also confronted the enemy at their doorsteps and demonstrated real courage and resolve in doing so.[4] But the trait shared by all of them was their impulse to record their experiences in vivid and often heartfelt terms.

Several of these accounts take the form of extended diary or journal entries; some are long, descriptive letters written in the moment or just afterward; and others are memoirs, which may or may not have been meant for publication, composed well after the fact. Of those preserved and accessible to us today, these narratives, taken together, provide fresh insights into the ways in which the elite women of the Carolina highlands experienced this incursion that so threatened their homes and their families and how they chose to convey their observations, feelings, and actions in written form.[5] In "talking" with pen to paper about what they had endured, these women provide us not only with alternative perspectives on the war's latter days than those provided by the "prominent and influential" men on whom Cornelia Spencer depended for her book, but they also reveal much about class and racial tensions, for which Stoneman's raid proved a catalyst, and about the considerable void that separated the region's elite from their less fortunate neighbors and fellow highlanders.[6]

The women who left such vivid written records of their encounters with Stoneman were (with one exception) natives of western North Carolina and fully part of the local elites that dominated the county seats or their rural environs. Their families had been among the first to settle in these towns and fertile valleys. While not plantation mistresses, they probably shared more in common with such women of the lowland South than they did with most women in their own region, those situated on more isolated highland homesteads in more remote parts of the mountains and far more vulnerable to the fierce guerrilla warfare and bushwhacker harassment that had plagued the outlying areas for much of the war's duration.

Most of those "talking heroines" were part of slaveholding families who owned between four and forty-two slaves in 1860.[7] Their husbands and/or fathers held extensive farmlands but were just as likely to be lawyers, merchants, or engaged in other business or professional endeavors. While these women endured some of the tribulations of the wartime home front—the absence of husbands and other men in Confederate service as well as shortages of various foodstuffs and household goods—they had been relatively insulated from the violence and abuse of enemy armies or domestic mobs. Perhaps because they remained out of harm's way until the war's final month, these women remained committed to the Confederate cause and portrayed themselves as true southerners in their narratives.

In hindsight it seems rather remarkable that most of these women remained so oblivious to such attacks and other upheavals. Katherine Polk Gale commented on the French Broad Valley of Buncombe County soon after moving there from her family's Mississippi plantation in 1862. "Peace & plenty ruled everywhere," she noted. "The country was so shut in from the world, it seemed almost impossible for the desolations of war to reach the happy homes along the route." Much of her account of the war years in Asheville dwells on the hospitality she enjoyed and the friendships she made among "the many charming, cultivated people" there. "Though we knew in Asheville, the war was going on relentlessly," she wrote, "there was nothing in our surroundings to suggest it, as we were so far removed from everything connected with it."[8]

A number of these women, situated as they were in county seats or in the broad valleys along the eastern slopes of the Blue Ridge, expressed similar degrees of complacency in terms of their own comfort and safety for much of the war's duration. Most were part of close kinship or neighborhood networks that provided both social interaction with other women of their own class and a mutual support system that allowed them to weather the burdens imposed by the war, both materially and emotionally. Emma L. Rankin in McDowell County spoke for many of her peers when she wrote: "Up to the winter of '64–'65 our experience of the trials of the war was confined to the anxiety about friends in the army, and the privations which were lightly esteemed and cheerfully borne, hoping always for a joyful end. True we were far from blockade goods, but what cared we. . . . We had thought it highly improbable that a blue-coat would ever be seen in our secluded region."[9] As late as February 1865, Ella Harper, Rankin's sister-in-law in Lenoir, acknowledged to her husband their good fortune in being "exempt from the severe forms of trial incident to this dreadful war."[10]

Such impressions could hardly have differed more from those of those far less privileged and far more vulnerable women elsewhere in the region. As Katherine Gale was enjoying a pleasant social life in Asheville, women in adjacent Madison County were being whipped and hanged by their fingers by Union troops seeking information about their husbands' whereabouts. The guerrilla warfare that wracked the more remote parts of both the Blue Ridge and the Smoky Mountains made many women both active agents and likely targets of the ruthless violence and deliberate cruelties it spawned.[11] For other poor women, crop failure, the disruption of access to market goods, and the destruction or theft of livestock, foodstuffs, or other property vital to their welfare meant that starvation posed the greatest challenge they faced during the war years. Much of that desperation comes through in the letters of such women, often barely literate, to Gov. Zebulon Vance, himself a native of the region and thus assumed by many in the mountains to be a sympathetic resource for alleviating their problems.[12]

There is little evidence that elite women felt much sympathy for the suffering of their more beleaguered neighbors. Class distinctions were never far from the surface in their commentary on those from whom they so distanced themselves. Mary Bell of Franklin, North Carolina, for instance, expressed her disdain for less fortunate men and women who faced a Union raid in the northwestern part of her own county. "It was the most ridiculous thing I ever heard of," she wrote to her husband, Alfred. "I think evry man in Macon Co., except those that were too old to get away skidadled." She was no more sympathetic toward the frightened women left behind as she described the two or three days in which they had had to endure the prospect of "fine times during yankee holadays." In a somewhat scornful tone, she detailed a variety of mishaps other women encountered in their efforts to hide their valuables and livestock and to safeguard their homes, much of which comes across as little more than slapstick in her irreverent retelling of various incidents.[13]

In Wilkes County, Lizzie Lenoir, a member of one of that area's oldest and most prominent families, conveyed nothing but contempt for women who raided granaries in nearby Jonesville in January 1865. This was the last of a number of such "bread riots" instigated by groups of women throughout the Confederacy, driven to mob action by food shortages and their frustration at local officials to respond in any equitable way. Like most others, this effort failed, much to Lenoir's satisfaction. Somewhat bemusedly she informed her aunt of a "band of *women,* armed with axes," who converged in wagons on a granary and demanded its ground corn. "There was only one man in the place," she wrote, "and he (Leonidas like) stood in the door of the house and bid defiance to the crowd. You know women generally want to carry their point, and it was with great difficulty that our hero could withstand them. They were happily thrown into confusion by an old drunk man coming up with a huge *brush* in his hand, striking their horses with it, causing them to run away with their wagons, and some of *them* in it." She concluded smugly, "They didn't get any of the corn."[14]

Neither of these women showed any sympathy, much less empathy, for the desperate plight of the wives and mothers driven to such drastic measures. Only with Stoneman's raid three months later did the region's female elite face the same sort of trauma themselves. Their complacency came to an abrupt end thanks to a New York general and the six thousand cavalrymen he led in wreaking havoc on their towns, villages, and valleys in April 1865. Maj. Gen. George Stoneman, a West Point graduate, headed up the District of East Tennessee early in 1865 when U. S. Grant ordered him to lead a cavalry raid into the interior of South Carolina, "visiting a portion of the state which will not be reached by Sherman's forces," including Columbia. His orders were to destroy railroads and other military resources, then to move to Salisbury, North Carolina, the site of a major Confederate prison, on his way back to East Tennessee and liberate its Union prisoners. Grant also saw Stoneman's mission as a diversionary tactic, drawing away from Sherman's path at least some of the Confederate forces that would otherwise challenge his march northward.[15]

A series of delays meant that Sherman had already taken Columbia and had moved on into North Carolina by the time Stoneman was ready to move. His mission was thus scaled back to a raid on the Salisbury prison, with the destruction of property and military resources a secondary goal as his troops moved through the North Carolina mountains, thus preventing either Robert E. Lee's army in Virginia or Joseph E. Johnston's around Raleigh from making a westward retreat through North Carolina.

On March 28 Stoneman crossed the state line into North Carolina with his six thousand horsemen, nearly all the available cavalry then in East Tennessee. While most of these troops consisted of units from Pennsylvania, Michigan, Ohio, and Kentucky, there were a sizeable number of "home Yankees" along as well, many of them Carolina highlanders recruited into Union service. They first attacked and ransacked the small town of Boone, among the only group of residents the approaching raiders caught fully by surprise. From there they moved east out of the mountains and through foothill communities until they reached their ultimate destination, Salisbury, on April 12 and destroyed vast supply depots, public buildings, cotton mills, tanneries, a foundry, and the prison, though Confederate authorities had moved its few remaining occupants to Charlotte a month before. From Salisbury Stoneman's forces split: two brigades under Brig. Gen. Alvan C. Gillem headed directly west again, attacking similar targets in several towns as they moved toward Asheville, like Salisbury a community that Union forces targeted because of its role as a center of Confederate activity. Col. William Palmer led a third brigade south toward Lincolnton and Charlotte before turning west toward Asheville. Stoneman himself, having achieved the primary goal with Salisbury's destruction, returned to Tennessee, taking with him nearly one thousand prisoners, mostly home guardsmen and Confederate veterans who had returned home either injured or ill.

The destruction of Boone set a pattern of disruption and property damage that the Union cavalrymen continued to inflict on other towns along their route—though with significant variations. The degree of damage done depended in part on how local citizens responded to the raiders. Thus Winston and Salem, then two separate towns, escaped harm when the mayor and a contingent of leading citizens greeted the invading force on the outskirts of each town waving white handkerchiefs. At the other extreme Morganton citizens sought to ambush Stonemen's men as they moved west from Salisbury and paid a heavy price for their resistance. In reaction to such local aggression, the most intense home defense they had faced on this mission, the Federal troops were allowed to engage in wholesale plundering of the nearly deserted town and harassment of the few remaining residents—mainly women—on a scale not yet authorized. Likewise Asheville, simply by its well-recognized role as the region's center of Confederate authority, faced the final and most brutal attack by Stoneman's men. The unexpectedness of an incursion on this scale caught many, if not most, residents there off guard. Part of their shock came from the fact that this attack came two days after an armistice had been reached by General Gillem and the Confederate commander, James G. Martin, on April 26.

One of the more striking aspects of the encounters between these Union forces and the elite women whose homes and property they threatened was the willingness of many to play the role of "talking heroines," that is, to personally confront either Stoneman himself or another of his officers either as supplicants or in defiance. Emma Rankin of Lenoir, who tutored Col. Logan Carson's children at his Pleasant Gardens farm in nearby McDowell County, was quick to challenge "an impudent lieutenant" who asked her where the horses had been hidden. When he refused to believe her reply that the slaves had hidden them, noting that he was from Kentucky and knew as much about blacks as she did, "I told him that if he was a Kentuckian he ought to be ashamed of being in that band of marauders." After more of his insolence, Rankin wrote, he left in search of the horses, assuring her that they would find the horses: "Yankees never fail in search."[16]

Rankin, like others, also reported kindnesses from individual soldiers. When a Union cavalryman strayed from his passing company and galloped up to the door and asked to see Miss Rankin, she said, "If his Satanic majesty had called for me, I could scarcely have been more astonished." He told her that he had guarded her father's house in Lenoir from the vandals that often followed in their wake and was delivering to her a letter from her father, as he had promised to do. He assured her that "Lenoir was not injured by us at all," though she claimed she knew that they had "eaten up the meager supplies which the village afforded, if nothing more."[17]

The detail with which these women recounted such exchanges suggests that they took real satisfaction in their own boldness in confronting the enemy invaders. In Lenoir, one of the towns taken early by Stoneman's raiders, General Gillem confronted Callie Hagler and "impertinently" said to her: "I know you are a rebel from the way you move—Ain't you a Rebel?" She replied by asking him if he had ever heard the story of the tailor's wife and the scissors. When he said he had, she said, "Then I am a rebel as high as I can reach," and wrote that her answer seemed to amuse him. Yet on another occasion soon afterward, Gillem was not so amused. Hagler recalled, "While denouncing the cruelties of the Confederates to their prisoners, he became very angry at [me] for venturing to suggest that the Federal authorities might have saved them all the alleged suffering by exchanging and taking them North where provisions were plenty."[18]

That such women could actually debate such issues with the enemy raiding their towns and homes suggests a certain affinity, based on mutual class consciousness, between Union officers and local elites, who each sensed were their socioeconomic equals. Many of these women recognized and appreciated the distinction between well-bred Union officers and the more uncouth soldiers under their command. Mary Taylor Brown, who lived on the outskirts of Asheville, defended her socializing with General Gillem and other Union officers. "When I come in contact with a *gentleman,*" she wrote, "I respect him as a gentleman, no matter if he does not agree in sentiment with me. I think some of the people of Asheville make themselves appear very ridiculous in their scornful manners toward the Federals."[19]

Such respect was often mutual. Colonel Palmer, one of Stoneman's commanders, confirmed his own sensitivity to such bonds. He later wrote of the leading citizens of Wilkes County's Happy Valley community that he respected their leadership and the extent to which their neighbors looked up to them. He singled out one man for particular praise, describing him as "one of the finest specimens of a country gentlemen that I have ever met . . . although he was a rebel, [he] belonged to the Free-Masonry of Gentlemen, and before I knew it I found myself regretting every bushel of corn that we fed, and sympathizing for every one of his fence rails that we were compelled to burn. . . . He was a man of fine feelings, had always been generous and kind to his poor neighbors, who were chiefly loyal, and was spoken of in the highest terms." Palmer concluded, "We frequently meet such gentlemen in our marches, and always make it a point to leave them as far as possible unmolested so that they may remain to teach nobility by example to the communities in which they live."[20]

Those residents fortunate enough to have been the beneficiaries of this partiality toward "country-gentlemen" of course were relieved to be spared, and some seemed a little smug in taking credit for the exemptions they were well aware had not been enjoyed by many in the region. After seeing that her town escaped any severe repercussions from yet another visit from the invading Yankees, Laura Norwood declared, "I was proud of the way Lenoir acted—all stuck together and the Yankees said they liked us better than any people they had met." Lest that observation imply any undue consorting with the enemy, Norwood added with equal pride that they claimed "it was the d——est little rebel town they ever saw."[21]

But such appreciation for southern noblesse oblige and class hierarchy did not extend to the rank and file of Stoneman's troops, and it certainly did not save all of the western Carolina elite from pillaging and harassment. Nor were all officers as sympathetic as others. "Much depended on the personal character and disposition of the commanding officer of these detachments," Cornelia Spencer observed. "If he happened to be a gentleman, the people were spared as much as possible; if he were simply a brute dressed in a little brief authority, every needless injury was inflicted, accompanied with true underbred insolence and malice."[22] The term "underbred" suggests the extent to which class distinctions underlie these judgments, just as insolent and malicious behavior marked men as common and unschooled in the deference they should have shown their social superiors, even if they were southerners.

Gillem and his men were among those most resented for their ruthless disregard for women in particular. Callie Hagler paid dearly for confronting him (as mentioned earlier). She had "naturally supposed that his presence would protect her person and property" and that of her daughter and her niece, who lived nearby. But according to a local informant, "On the contrary, his proximity seemed to give license to great pillage and outrage, for they suffered more than any one else in the village." The home of Hagler's daughter was "pillaged from top to bottom" as soldiers broke open barrels of sorghum and poured it over a large supply of wheat and over the floors of the house. They destroyed furniture and crockery, and "what was not broken was defiled in a manner so disgusting as to be unfit for use." When Hagler went to Gillem and asked him to control his men, he turned his back on her, stating simply, "Well, there are bad men in all crowds."[23]

Verena Chapman, the wife of a Presbyterian minister in Hendersonville, had an equally negative experience with Gillem's contingent. Writing a year later to Cornelia Spencer, her anger at the treatment inflicted on her and others in the area was still palpable. Much of it was due to the fact that they were victimized after the armistice with Martin had been signed: "Not supposing for a moment that even these faithless, dishonourable, Constitution-breaking vandals would be utterly regardless of the law of nations," she vented, "as to proceed in the face of a known truce to overrun and destroy the region through which they were passing." Nothing in their treatment toward highland residents had changed as a result of this truce. "All the way from Rutherfordton," Chapman claimed, "they had swept the country of negroes, horses, and carriages, clothing, and supplies of every kind." (The very items she listed suggest that it was not the poor whose violation she resented.) Not only did such theft continue as they moved from Hendersonville to Asheville, but when "some delicate high-bred ladies followed them to their encampment to endeavour to regain their horses and carriages, they were treated by the yankee officers with great indignity and disrespect."[24]

This effrontery earned them her long-sustained contempt. As late as May 1866, Chapman continued to defy the efforts of her reverend husband to moderate her resentment and see some redeeming features in the reunited nation brought about by the war's end. "Please tell me," she implored Spencer, "if it wouldn't be just as sinful to 'pray' for *these* 'enemies' as for the Devil?" Over the past year, she confided, she had never dared to pray the passage of the Lord's Prayer that reads, "Forgive me my trespasses as I forgive those who trespass against me." "I know that I am wicked—and those wretches have made me so," she concluded, "but I cannot be a hypocrite."[25]

Even during the war itself, few other mountain women expressed bitterness this intense over the Yankee invaders, even when they were victims of their vandalism. In fact for many such treatment by Stoneman's troops proved less troublesome, and certainly less frightening, than the actions of the so-called rear guard, those roving bands of bushwhackers, deserters, and other local malcontents whose aggressions were unleashed by the Union troops' presence. In the wake of Stoneman's march, such groups were emboldened to take action of their own. As soon as the Federals left Lenoir, Joseph Norwood described his relief at how little damage the troops had inflicted on the town but wrote of a still-gnawing worry: "We have been under constant apprehension about tory—or robber raids, and I have been serving on guard at town every third night. . . . We are in danger constantly." Indeed local raiders did attack the vulnerable town, ransacking houses and threatening the women who were forced to watch the plunder. According to one account, "the ladies were firm in resisting their demands and they left without doing much mischief."[26]

In Morganton, where the Federal troops, then under Gillem's command, were allowed to engage in their most wholesale plundering yet, it was women from the nearby South Mountains who moved down to the Burke County seat to add to the chaos. According to a local source, they "swarmed our streets proclaiming their 'jubilee' and rejoicing that the Yankees had arrived . . . thus these dishonest traitorous hordes, of our own beautiful mountain clime, conspired and leagued with the Yankees, urging them on in the work of plunder, and wholesale theft which was carried on during Monday, Tuesday, and a part of Wednesday."[27]

Among the most vividly described of such attacks was that inflicted on Robert C. Pearson's home in the western part of Burke County. Pearson, a prominent banker and railroad official, was not home at the time, but a member of his household left an account that clearly reveals her class and cultural biases. In language far more derogatory than any used to describe Stoneman's men, she called the vandals, both men and women, "lazy and disloyal elements that inhabit our 'South Mountains' around the town of Morganton, that class of people . . . an ignorant, illiterate, uncultivated set, untrue in every respect, false to their God and traitors to their country." She went on to describe their actions: "When the 'rear guard,' the nine robbers, entered the house to plunder and pilfer, their women followed in, to reap their share of the spoils . . . the mountain women were laden with everything they could carry, such as clothing, bedding, even dishes, and such." With contemptuous amusement she described the reaction of an "old hag" when the mob discovered a wine cellar of sorts and distributed bottles of champagne among themselves. The sound of the cork popping from the first bottle they opened led to a panic. The old woman fled, declaring that "it was pizen, put there to kill them for nobody had ever seen liquor pop that way."[28]

In light of these flagrant attacks by the poor in their midst, elite women often assumed the Yankee invaders to be the lesser threat and even asked those officers with whom they sensed some rapport for protection from either further abuse by those under their command or from the even more unruly native rabble. Ella Harper noted in her diary on April 15: "At sunset the Yanks rushed in on us. We obtained a guard about our house after they came in, and fared better than some others."[29]

At Pleasant Gardens, Emma Rankin called on a "young lieutenant . . . who looked more like a gentleman than any of them I had seen . . . and asked him if he could not stay and guard us while a negro regiment that was just coming in sight was passing. He politely acceded to my request, and orderd a big black negro in an officer's uniform, who was just going into the back door, back to the lines." She concluded that story, declaring: "Oh! How horrid those negroes looked in that blue uniform; and how the air was filled with oaths! But that was characteristic of their white comrades also." Lieutenant Davis warned her that "stragglers who followed the raid, and belonged to no command, were the worst, and . . . we would probably be more annoyed than we had been before." He regretted that he could stay no longer to protect her and the Carsons but told her to tell these stragglers that he, the officer of the day, had just left, and thus "threaten them with him." They were indeed soon beset by "a half dozen men dashing up the creek, whooping and yelling and cursing, and as drunk as they could be," who tormented the family for several hours and demanded all the jewelry and watches in the house before eventually moving on.[30]

The most dramatic instance of the class-based differences between the threat posed by local rowdies and Yankee invaders was recorded by Mary Taylor Brown in an extraordinary letter she wrote to her stepson in Australia. Brown, who lived with her husband, W. Vance Brown, on the road between Hendersonville and Asheville, vividly recounted her terror when faced with the local marauders unleashed by the approach of Stoneman's raiders on Sunday night, April 23: "Squads of armed ruffians were coming in and plundering and cursing all night long while I was the only one to encounter them in the house and Pa was the only one to contend with them at the stables, barn, corn crib and smoke house, where they robbed us of every thing but a little hay and few pieces of bacon. . . . My soul stood trembling within me lest some demon would lay violent hands upon my person and I might be deprived the use of the firearm I had concealed to use in self defense. . . . But, thank God my prayers were heard and I escaped untouched, tho' a thousand curses were hurled into my face and I was called a thousand times 'a damned lying rebel.'"[31]

If the trauma Mary Brown endured on Sunday night was not untypical of what many western North Carolina women faced at the time, the events of the following day certainly were. It was on that Monday, and at a site not far from the Brown farm, that General Gillem met James G. Martin, his Confederate counterpart based in Asheville and a West Point classmate, and reached a truce. Vance Brown invited Gillem and several of his staff to stay with them, which resulted in an extraordinary scene of sectional reconciliation. "Little indeed was the sum of all we had to offer for the repasts of our invited guests," Mary Brown wrote, "but the best our little we gave as unto friends, tho' there were all our foes." Following dinner, "the officers and men enjoyed their pipes and laughed and talked in gay good humor, feeling quite at home among such friendly rebels. . . . Maria [her stepdaughter] played and sang some of her Rebel airs and the gentlemen sang some of their Union songs. Genl. Gillem had his band come up and play some beautiful old Union pieces." In a rather understated assessment of the evening, Brown concluded, "Monday night quite a different scene was presented from the one on Sunday."[32]

That gathering must have seemed to those involved a very intimate expression of the war's end. But it was not to be. Mississippi refugee Katherine Polk Gale, who lived in Asheville, picked up where Mary Brown's narrative ended to describe an even more curious turn of events over the next few days. On

Tuesday, April 25, Gillem's troops marched through Asheville in an orderly and nonthreatening manner, and local residents breathed a sigh of relief, having heard of how differently they moved through other towns along their route. On Wednesday morning, Gale recalled, "We all felt very secure" as the troops continued to move on westward toward Tennessee, "having strictly regarded the rights of property." But she quickly added, "That was in the morning of an ever memorable day."[33]

Late that afternoon the Union forces took Asheville residents completely by surprise when they turned back on the city in an undisciplined spree of looting and ransacking. Gale was on a quiet walk with friends, during which they were "discussing the affairs of the day & congratulating ourselves on its peaceful termination," when suddenly they heard galloping horses and clanking sabers. They "turned to see the meaning of it all; a troop of Yankee Cavalry in hot pursuit of three women. Pistols were fired in quick succession." Thus began two harrowing days during which Gale and other women were chased through the streets, harassed by various groups of "ruffians," had their houses searched and looted, and in many cases witnessed their men (in Gale's case, her uncle) arrested and carried away by "these wretches."[34] Not even Fayetteville, destroyed by Sherman's troops two months earlier, "suffered more severely by pillage," according to Cornelia Spencer in her narrative. "The Tenth and Eleventh Michigan regiments certainly won for themselves in Asheville a reputation that should damn them to everlasting fame."[35]

Another Asheville resident, Sarah Bailey Cain, left a harrowing account of a gang of "villainous looking men" who rushed into her parents' home, ransacked it, beat her father and then fired shots at him when he attempted to resist their thefts, and carried her brother, a Confederate officer, away under arrest, along with all their jewelry and much bacon. ("Watches," she wrote, "seemed to be their favorite loot," and she related several instances of physical force against acquaintances, both women and men, in order to get them.) On Friday, April 28, as the prisoners, over thirty local men and officers, including General Martin, were to be led off to Tennessee, Cain went with her father, a prominent judge, to the town's center to bid farewell to her brother, one of the prisoners. "We passed through an immense crowd of a few citizens, a great many privates, and insolent negroes in U.S. uniforms," she wrote. "One of these negroes called out to my father, 'How do you like this, old man?'" As a result of that incident alone, she stated, "I have loathed the uniform ever since." In moving quickly to find her brother, Cain walked under a U.S. flag that the troops had suspended from the Eagle Hotel out over the street. She was later reprimanded by other women who had walked around the square to avoid passing under what they still viewed as an enemy's emblem.[36]

The ransacking of Asheville marked the end of Stoneman's raid. That it concluded on such an unexpectedly hostile and destructive note, particularly given that news of the war's end elsewhere had already reached the region, cast a pall over many residents and compelled the area's elite women to describe it so emotionally on paper. The fullest accounts we have of the highs and lows of those turbulent few days all come from women who witnessed or experienced them firsthand. For some, like Verena Chapman and Sarah Bailey Cain, their bitterness was still very much in evidence well after the war's end. For others such resentment waned more quickly, though not without similar expressions of defiance.

As dreaded as the incursion of Union troops was, for some of the more affluent women whose homes they violated, there was another enemy more dreaded—those living around them. That reality suggests the complexities of the region's divided loyalties and the extent to which class identity shaped both the security and insecurities of the elite in western North Carolina and its sustained commitment toward the Confederacy in its waning days. In this part of Appalachia, such divisions were not as clearly determined by class—wealthy Confederates and poor Unionists—as the stories here may indicate. Yet they do depict the additional tensions and pressures that both class and gender brought to bear on home-front hardships in the southern highlands and on the war's legacy for the region.

That written legacy in itself suggests another distinction that pervades much of this historical record—that, as elsewhere, it was largely provided by the region's literate elite. But why did females in particular feel so compelled to tell their stories? Whether recorded in journals, letters, or memoirs, these were for the most part lengthy narratives in which these women recorded not only the many incidents of their own experiences and those of their neighbors and other acquaintances but also their feelings at the time and afterward. Some were matter of fact and rather objective in tone; others remained far more impassioned by their resentment of the Union invaders and made their emotional responses integral in shaping their memories into narrative form.

Most of the women cited here were already writing regularly—in letters, diaries, or journals—about their wartime experiences. So it was not Stoneman's raid alone that inspired them to put pen to paper. Yet the raid was, for most of these women, indeed for most residents of western North Carolina, the most traumatic and memorable event in a war that until its final month had kept major armies and military incursion at bay. Had they not been in the path of Stoneman and his cavalry, their wartime experience and how they interpreted it afterward would have been far different, and perhaps far less pronounced.

While some did so more consciously than others, these women used their narratives—particularly in describing this traumatic episode at war's end—to articulate for themselves and for others their own roles and those of other women and to rationalize their efforts, their sacrifices, and the ultimate failure of the cause and the nation for which both were made.[37] Only a few weeks after the conflict's traumatic conclusion in Buncombe County, Mary Taylor Brown wrote: "I will boldly say, I am a Southern woman! and have battled for her rights. . . . To defend the South, love prompted me to action and an undying confidence that she was right carried me onward through fire and blood." Yet, she concluded, "Now that in God's providence slavery is abolished and the state again brought into union and under the same government, I cordially respond from my heart, All is well!"[38]

By the same token Katherine Polk Gale philosophized not only about the meaning of the war's end for herself and other women but also on the role they would play in coping with defeat. "The consciousness of having tried to preserve home & fireside, therefore having done that which they conceived to be right, sustained the sorrow-stricken hearts throughout the whole Southland," she wrote. "The women will again do their part in bearing bravely whatever the future has in store for them and will prove themselves to be worthy mothers, wives & daughters of the brave soldiers who have so manfully borne the horrors of the four years war."[39] Like the subjects of Sarah Gardner's recent book on southern women as chroniclers of the war, Gale, Brown, and other mountain women "participated directly and influentially in a conscious effort to fashion a distinctly Southern story of the war."[40]

The luxury of privilege allowed these women to see and to commemorate themselves and their peers in such ennobling terms. These "talking heroines" considered themselves vital to the defense of their households and region and took great pride afterward in having performed their roles well. As much as any other factor, that self-satisfaction in how they handled themselves probably drove their impulse to write at such length about their experiences. It probably never occurred to them that poorer mountain women—that "ignorant, illiterate, uncultivated set" for whom they had shown such disdain—might have interpreted the conflict, its effect, and their roles in it in very different terms.

NOTES

1. Cornelia Phillips Spencer, *The Last Ninety Days of the War in North Carolina* (New York: Watchman, 1866), preface. For the circumstances surrounding the book's authorship and publication, see Phillips Russell, *The Woman Who Rang the Bell: The Story of Cornelia Phillips Spencer* (Chapel Hill: University of North Carolina Press, 1949), chap. 9; and Sarah E. Gardner, *Blood and Irony: Southern White Women's Narratives of the Civil War, 1861–1937* (Chapel Hill: University of North Carolina Press, 2004), 49–52.

2. Spencer, *Last Ninety Days,* 14–15.

3. Ina W. Van Noppen, *Stoneman's Last Raid* (Raleigh: N.C. State Archives, 1961), 112. This is the fullest scholarly account of the raid in recent times. It appeared first as a series of articles in the *North Carolina Historical Review* (4 issues, 1961) and subsequently, like Spencer's narrative, in book form.

4. Quoted in Drew Gilpin Faust, *Mothers of Invention: Women of the Slaveholding South in the American Civil War* (Chapel Hill: University of North Carolina Press, 1996), 200.

5. It is probably coincidental that the fullest account of Stoneman's raid besides Spencer's narrative is also by a woman, Ina W. Van Noppen (see note 3).

6. There are a variety of other themes in addition to class that the writings of these women could also support, but on which I do not focus in this essay. They all discuss the loss of their slaves with various degrees of anger, disdain, and relief. Several of them note the violation of domestic space and the invasion of privacy by Stoneman's men, a theme Lisa Tendrich Frank has found central in her study of southern women's reactions to Sherman's troops. Frank, "'I Am a Southern Woman': Patriotic Femininity in the Invaded South, 1864–1865" (paper delivered at SHA meeting, Baltimore, Nov. 2002). One could also use these writings to examine the psychological means by which these women rationalized Confederate defeat—as Jean V. Berlin has done in "Did Confederate Women Lose the War?" in *The Collapse of the Confederacy,* ed. Mark Grimsley and Brooks D. Simpson (Lincoln: University of Nebraska Press, 2002)—or to explore the gender ideologies of both southern women and Union troops as reflected in their encounters—as Jacqueline Glass Campbell does in *When Sherman Marched North from the Sea: Resistance on the Confederate Home Front* (Chapel Hill: University of North Carolina Press, 2003).

7. For a list of major slaveowners and their holdings in the region in 1860, see John C. Inscoe, *Mountain Masters: Slavery and the Sectional Crisis in Western North Carolina* (Knoxville: University of Tennessee Press, 1989), app. 1 (265–66).

8. Katherine Polk Gale, "Recollections of Life in the Southern Confederacy, 1861–1865" (typescript), pp. 14, 17, Leonidas Polk Papers, Southern Historical Collection, University of North Carolina, Chapel Hill (hereinafter cited as SHC).

9. E. L. Rankin, "Stoneman's Raid," 1885 in *In Memorium: Emma Lydia Rankin* (privately published, 1908), 18–19, 20, North Carolina Collection, University of North Carolina, Chapel Hill.

10. Ella Harper to George W. F. Harper, Feb. 2, 1865, George W. F. Harper Papers, SHC, quoted in David H. McGee, "'Home and Friends': Kinship, Community, and Elite Women in Caldwell County, North Carolina, during the Civil War," *North Carolina Historical Review* 74 (Oct. 1997):

386. McGee's article focuses on the mutual support system these women provided each other over the course of the war.

11. Phillip Shaw Paludan, *Victims: A True Story of the Civil War* (Knoxville: University of Tennessee Press, 1981), 96; James O. Hall, "The Shelton Laurel Massacre: Murder in the North Carolina Mountains," *Blue & Gray* (Feb. 1991): 23; John C. Inscoe and Gordon B. McKinney, *The Heart of Confederate Appalachia: The Civil War in Western North Carolina* (Chapel Hill: University of North Carolina Press, 2000), 194–95. For other violence and cruelty committed against women in the region, see Margaret Walker Freel, *Unto the Hills* (Andrews, N.C.: privately printed, 1976), 129–61 (on such incidents in Cherokee County, N.C.); William R. Trotter, *Bushwhackers: The Mountains,* vol. 2 of *The Civil War in North Carolina* (Greensboro, N.C.: Signal Research, 1988), 188–200; and Keith Bohannon, "'They Had Determined to Root Us Out': Dual Memoirs by a Unionist Couple in Blue Ridge Georgia," in *Enemies of the Country: New Perspectives on Unionists in the Civil War South,* ed. John C. Inscoe and Robert C. Kenzer (Athens: University of Georgia Press, 2001), 97–120.

12. The best account of these women, drawn largely from their letters to Governor Vance, is Gordon B. McKinney, "Women's Role in Civil War Western North Carolina," *North Carolina Historical Review* 69 (Jan. 1992): 37–56. See also Inscoe and McKinney, *Heart of Confederate Appalachia,* chap. 8; and Inscoe, "Mountain Women, Mountain War," *Appalachian Journal* 31 (Spring/Summer 2004): 343–48 (part of a roundtable discussion of the historical realities of the film *Cold Mountain*).

13. Mary to Alfred Bell, Feb. 19, 1864, in Alfred W. Bell Papers, Special Collections, Duke University Library, Durham, N.C. For a full account of Mary Bell's wartime experience, see John C. Inscoe, "Coping in Confederate Appalachia: Portrait of a Mountain Woman and Her Community at War," *North Carolina Historical Review* 69 (Oct. 1992): 388–413.

14. Lizzie Lenoir to Sarah J. ["Sade"] Lenoir, Jan. 22, 1865, Lenoir Family Papers, SHC. On other such raids, see Inscoe and McKinney, *Heart of Confederate Appalachia,* 197–98; Paul D. Escott, "The Moral Economy of the Crowd in Confederate North Carolina," *Maryland Historian* 13 (Summer 1982): 1–17; and Teresa Crisp Williams and David Williams, "'The Women Rising': Cotton, Class, and Confederate Georgia's Rioting Women," *Georgia Historical Quarterly* 86 (Spring 2002): 49–83.

15. Van Noppen, *Stoneman's Last Raid,* 4–5. For briefer accounts of the raid, see Inscoe and McKinney, *Heart of Confederate Appalachia,* 243–58; and Trotter, *Bushwhackers,* pt. 5. It is curious how little attention is paid to Stoneman's raid in broader histories of the war. It rates no mention at all, for instance, in three recent treatments of the war's end: Grimsley and Simpson, *Collapse of the Confederacy;* Jay Winik, *April 1865: The Month That Saved America* (New York: HarperCollins, 2001); or William C. Davis, *An Honorable Defeat: The Last Days of the Confederate Government* (New York: Harcourt, 2001).

16. Rankin, "Stoneman's Raid," 26–27.

17. Ibid., 29.

18. Robert L. Beall to Cornelia Phillips Spencer, Aug. [?], 1866, Cornelia Phillips Spencer Papers, SHC.

19. Mary Taylor Brown to John Evans Brown, June 20, 1865, W. Vance Brown Papers, SHC.

20. Quoted in Thomas Felix Hickerson, ed., *Echoes of Happy Valley: Letters and Diaries, Family Life in the South, Civil War History* (Durham, N.C., privately printed, 1962), 105. These class-based

responses by southern women to Union troops are analyzed in Faust, *Mothers of Invention,* chap. 9; and Stephen V. Ash, *When the Yankees Came: Conflict and Chaos in the Occupied South, 1861–1865* (Chapel Hill: University of North Carolina Press, 1995), 19–20, 42–44. On the reaction of Union troops to southern women, see Reid Mitchell, *The Vacant Chair: The Northern Soldier Leaves Home* (New York: Oxford University Press, 1993), chap. 6 (entitled "She Devils").

21. Laura Norwood to Walter Gwyn, Apr. 25, 1865, James Gwyn Papers, SHC.

22. Spencer, *Last Ninety Days,* 196.

23. Beall to Spencer, Aug. [?], 1866.

24. Verena Chapman to Cornelia Phillips Spencer, May 8, 1866, Spencer Papers, SHC.

25. Ibid. Of this letter Spencer informed Zebulon Vance: "Mrs. Chapman sent me a 16-page letter! She is certainly a smart woman & very *womanish* (High praise, I know!)" Cornelia Phillips Spencer to Zebulon B. Vance, Aug. 24, 1866, Spencer Papers.

26. Joseph C. Norwood to Walter W. Lenoir, Apr. 2, 1865, in Hickerson, *Echoes of Happy Valley,* 104; Ella Harper Diary, Apr. 17, 1865, George W. F. Harper Papers, SHC; Beall to Spencer, Aug. [?], 1866.

27. Robert L. Beall, "Notes on Stoneman's Raid in Burke County and the Town of Morganton," 1866, Spencer Papers.

28. Ibid.

29. Ella Harper Diary, Apr. 15, 1865.

30. Rankin, "Stoneman's Raid," 29–31.

31. Mary Taylor Brown to John Evans Brown, June 20, 1865, W. Vance Brown Papers, SHC.

32. Ibid.

33. Gale, "Life in the Southern Confederacy," 50.

34. Ibid., 52. Historians offer various explanations for this sudden reversal of policy by the Union forces, all of which rest in part on the fact that Gillem gave up command to others and proceeded to Nashville, where the first postwar session of the Tennessee legislature was convening. See Spencer, *Last Ninety Days,* 232; Van Noppen, *Stoneman's Last Raid,* 89–90; John G. Barrett, *The Civil War in North Carolina* (Chapel Hill: University of North Carolina Press, 1963), 363–65; and Inscoe and McKinney, *Heart of Confederate Appalachia,* 255–57.

35. Spencer, *Last Ninety Days,* 231–32.

36. Sarah Jane Bailey Cain, "The Last Days of the War in Asheville, N.C." (typescript), pp. 35–36, John Lancaster Bailey Papers, SHC.

37. For recent studies of southern women writing about the war and its aftermath, see Gardner, *Blood and Irony,* esp. chaps. 1–2; and Jane Turner Censer, *The Reconstruction of White Southern Womanhood, 1865–1895* (Baton Rouge: Louisiana State University Press, 2003), chaps. 6–7.

38. Mary Taylor Brown to John Evans Brown, June 20, 1865, W. Vance Brown Papers, SHC.

39. Gale, "Life in the Southern Confederacy," 57.

40. Gardner, *Blood and Irony,* 5.

RACE

The Costliness of Discrimination: Medical Care for Black Troops in the Civil War

JOSEPH T. GLATTHAAR

DURING THE CIVIL WAR, BLACK SOLDIERS ENDURED DISCRIMINATION in a variety of forms. They served in segregated units and almost always under white officers. Enlistment bounties and pay were unequal for black troops throughout much of the war, and they had severely limited opportunity for promotion or appointment as commissioned officers. Men in the U.S. Colored Troops (USCT) endured harassment and violence from "friend" and foe alike because of their skin color. Although they all donned the same Union blue, at times the Federal government issued them inferior equipment and deficient food rations. And high-ranking officers called upon black men in the USCT to perform subordinate and sometimes degrading duties in place of whites.

Although scholars have discussed and documented these racial abuses thoroughly, they have devoted scant attention to the most costly aspect of discrimination in the Union army, its medical care. Throughout the war black soldiers suffered from a shortage of qualified physicians and staff, endured abusive treatment at the hands of harshly racist surgeons, lost untold lives due to separate and woefully unequal hospital facilities, and served a disproportionate amount of duty in the most unhealthy environments. All this resulted in a mortality rate due to illness two and a half times greater than for white soldiers.[1]

Approximately 179,000 blacks served in the Union army. According to official records, there were over 600,000 cases of illness and over 10,000 wounds among black troops. Nearly 37,000 black soldiers, or one of every five, died during the war, and of those almost 30,000 died from disease alone.

The burden for this enormous workload fell to a couple of hundred white and a few black physicians.[2]

Once the War Department began organizing black units in earnest, it had problems securing competent medical officers. The war placed unusual demands on the services of physicians, particularly those with medical-school training who were physically fit for field duty. White volunteer units already had gobbled up many of these men to serve as surgeons and assistant surgeons, and among those who were left, few found the prospects of duty with black soldiers pleasing.

The surgeon general of the army realized that he could not compel whites to join the USCT, nor could he lower standards for applicants. What he could do, though, was make the examination more accessible to those who wanted to take it. He ordered the formation of permanent boards for the examination of USCT medical-officer candidates in the six largest cities and authorized temporary boards in various other locations "as the exigencies of the service demand." Officially there was to be no softening of the requirements. "Qualifications of Medical Officers of Colored Troops," the surgeon general ordered, "should be equal to the standard required for those serving with other Troops."[3]

These efforts alone proved wholly unsatisfactory, for boards could not provide enough surgeons and assistant surgeons to keep pace with the rapid expansion of black units. Meanwhile departmental commanders protested the critical shortage of medical personnel in the USCT. In reply, all Maj. Charles W. Foster, the head of the Bureau of Colored Troops, could write was "there are no candidates available for appointment" and "great difficulty is experienced in obtaining medical officers."[4]

One seemingly logical place to turn was to black physicians. The small number of qualified black doctors in the United States certainly had an interest in serving in the USCT. The problem was that prejudiced whites had a powerful desire to keep them out of the service. Government officials feared the reaction of white soldiers who went before black physicians, especially during the chaos of battle, when surgeons treated men brought before them regardless of unit. They also worried about the implications of having blacks as field-grade officers, which was the rank surgeons received. By the war's end the army could only entice eight black physicians to serve.[5]

While the War Department made limited progress procuring surgeons for the USCT, commanding officers needed someone to care for their sick and injured troops. Usually they assigned anyone with medical training, no matter how slight. In most cases former hospital stewards assumed the role of acting assistant surgeon. But a large percentage of these men did not receive their appointments as stewards based on their medical or pharmaceutical knowledge. Most were merely recuperating patients who had demonstrated intelligence and could handle light duties. Men like Lt. Herman W. Dickinson, a former sergeant in the 23rd Michigan Infantry who had served temporarily as an orderly, began his duty in the USCT as acting assistant surgeon in a regimental hospital, a terrible ordeal for Dickinson and his patients. In the Department of the Gulf, officers appointed "Hospital Stewards of low order of qualifications" to posts as surgeons and assistant surgeons so often that complaints of the "inhumanity of subjecting the colored soldiers to medical treatment and surgical operations by such men" flooded department commander Maj. Gen. Nathaniel P. Banks's office. Even more influential were officers from white volunteer units who complained "upon the ground that in the exigencies of battle any officer might be subjected to the necessity of surgical treatment by this class of officers."

On the verge of a huge scandal, Banks and a few other officers took action. A prominent Massachusetts politician before the war, Banks used his extensive contacts to arrange a deal with some of the best medical schools in New York and New England to obtain their finest students for black units in his department. The adjutant general of the army, Lorenzo Thomas, formed a similar pact. He first sent a medical officer to New England to induce physicians to appear before the medical board for commissions in the USCT, and he later arranged an early graduation program with selected medical schools for students who agreed to enter the USCT immediately upon successful completion of the college's oral examination and thesis.[6]

The head of black recruitment in Tennessee, Col. Reuben Delevan Mussey, embraced a different solution. Mussey believed that anyone with formal medical training would be an improvement over the people he had caring for black soldiers. As an inducement to lure physicians into the USCT, he agreed to appoint anyone who "can procure a diploma from some recognized medical school." The implicit inducement was that the prospective surgeon would not have to appear before the medical board unless he exhibited such gross incompetence as to warrant the examination.[7]

Officers who were responsible for securing physicians for black units also expanded their recruitment efforts within the military service. They searched the army for physicians who signed a one-year agreement to work for the military, known as contract surgeons, and medical cadets, who were medical trainees employed by the War and Navy Departments, more akin to the modern medical corpsmen, for appointment in the USCT. Both of these groups were attractive because they had an understanding of military structure and experience in the types of injuries and illnesses they were most likely to encounter in the USCT.[8]

Despite these efforts most units were understaffed with medical officers, a problem that illnesses among physicians exacerbated. Working with the sick every day, especially in black commands, which frequently served in the unhealthiest environments, surgeons and assistant surgeons were particularly susceptible to illness and disease. Sgt. James Thompson of the 6th U.S. Colored Infantry found he had to reverse roles with the regimental surgeon. When he had been sick, the doctor cared for him; with no other medical personnel in the regiment, he took care of the ailing surgeon after his own recovery. In the 2nd U.S. Colored Infantry, a Virginia regiment performing occupation duties in Florida, illnesses wreaked havoc on the command. In a two-week period, sickness that took the lives of eight officers so debilitated the surgeon that he had to go north to recuperate and forced an assistant surgeon to accept a discharge for physical unfitness. That left one assistant surgeon to care for the entire regiment, which authorities had scattered over a huge area for garrison duty. In a division of black regiments in Virginia, so many physicians were ill simultaneously that each regiment had only a single medical officer present except one, which had none and relied on a second lieutenant who knew a little about medicine. The 65th U.S. Colored Infantry, a Missouri regiment with an awful health record, struggled to maintain a medical staff at partial strength throughout the war. Its first surgeon received a discharge for a hernia, and his successor suffered from fever for four months. The first assistant surgeon came down with a fatal case of diarrhea on his fifth day with the unit, and a contract surgeon assigned to temporary duty endured bouts of dysentery and epilepsy. A second assistant surgeon died of "inflammation of the brain," while his replacement suffered from gastritis and then was murdered. Only one retained any reasonable health. Nor did the existing military policy work toward alleviating these problems. The 67th U.S. Colored Infantry, another regiment raised in Missouri, got caught in a vicious cycle in part through army regulations. Because of the tremendous losses due to disease, the 67th U.S. Colored Infantry was not permitted to fill an assistant surgeon vacancy, which could help check the terrible death rate that deprived it of the services of good medical officers and other military personnel.[9]

A skilled medical staff, such as hospital stewards and nurses, would have helped ease the burden considerably, but like physicians, they too were in short supply. In regiments composed of free blacks, there were enough literate men that doctors could train soldiers to perform these jobs, even if no one had any previous medical or pharmaceutical experience. When freedmen comprised the black units, though, it was often difficult to find men whose reading and writing skills had developed well enough to handle such duties, and those who had the necessary level of literacy opted for stripes as noncommissioned officers rather than labor in hospitals. White soldiers, particularly in the Virginia theater, were fortunate enough to receive effective care from white women who volunteered as nurses. These angels of mercy helped maintain the cleanliness of patients and alleviate the suffering in sundry ways. The color barrier, however, dissuaded nearly all of those nurses from caring for black troops. Thus surgeons, like one in the 88th U.S. Colored Infantry from Tennessee, had to "work like a—colored person; in old times called a Slave," so explained a fellow surgeon in the USCT, for his comrade had a hospital filled with patients and "no help—nor even a Hosp. Steward."[10]

Although there were complaints that a surgeon "did not evince much knowledge of his duties," as the inspector general of the army charged, or that some were "murderers," as an enlisted man insisted, most surgeons and assistant surgeons in the USCT were as knowledgeable and skillful as their peers in white volunteer regiments. The vast majority had received training in medical schools and had passed an examination to weed out the worst practitioners.

Much more detrimental was the racial attitudes that these doctors possessed, which one white surgeon delicately alluded to when he wrote, "Very few surgeons will do precisely the same for blacks as they would for whites." In fact a number of medical officers were utterly brutal in their treatment of black soldiers. According to the inspector general, a surgeon in Arkansas lost all interest in caring for black soldiers. He let the hospital buildings fall into disrepair, failed to remove a dead body from the hospital for over forty-eight hours, and neglected the health and comfort of his patients in general. A surgeon in the 30th U.S. Colored Infantry refused to treat a wounded soldier, and instead someone had to get a surgeon from another regiment to care for the man. The doctor's excuse was that it was late, cold, and rainy, and he was eating his supper. Even worse was a surgeon in the 5th U.S. Colored Infantry stationed in Virginia who declined to attend a black soldier whose foot was partially severed by a shell because he was conducting sick call. His commanding officer promptly levied charges against the physician. In the general court-martial, the doctor argued in his defense that "a man with a part of his foot cut off by a piece of shell was not suffering much pain." The division commander, enraged by the affair, responded with biting sarcasm: "While the Brig. Genl. Comdg. regrets extremely that a medical officer in this Division should be found so ignorant of his profession as to set up such a defense, he much prefers it to be so than to think any officer could be so grossly inhuman as to leave a wounded man to suffer."[11]

Some white physicians apparently lost all compassion for black troops in need of care. A soldier complained that a surgeon had bucked and gagged a black man for feigning illness. That afternoon the doctor sent the victim to the hospital, where he died the next day. On another occasion a surgeon kicked a sick soldier for leaving his tent to relieve himself; that night the soldier died. One surgeon was so unfeeling that he cursed a dying man who was moaning in pain, yelling "god damn him if he was going to die and dont [make] So much fuss about it."[12]

The most incomprehensible case of racial insensitivity, though, was the butchery of the body of a deceased black soldier from the 23rd U.S. Colored Infantry who collapsed unexpectedly. Although no one suffered physically from the physician's behavior, his shameless treatment of the corpse, under the ruse of a postmortem examination, revealed a shocking level of disrespect for a former slave who was serving his country in time of crisis. The surgeon removed several major organs—the heart, liver, a kidney, small intestines, and the spleen—without securing the proper arteries and veins, and he also unintentionally sliced the jugular vein. Thus blood poured all over the floor. He then severed the head from the body and affixed a bottle with an old blanket wrapped around it in its place. The autopsy began late at night, and feeling tired, the doctor put the organs and head in a sack and placed them under a bench. The body and mess remained in the regimental dispensary where he conducted the autopsy and where enlisted men entered regularly. Later that night, fearful "that something might happen [to] the head and other viscera, animals such as dogs being in the camp, and no person remaining with the body," he returned to the dispensary and brought the sack to his tent. Unable to sleep and excited by what he had found, the surgeon "proceeded at once to remove the scalp" in preparation of the removal of the brain. By this time the regimental commander learned of the "autopsy" and had heard rumors that were racing through the camp that the doctor had offered an enlisted man one dollar to spend the night with the body. He immediately ordered the surgeon to return the head, now slashed horribly, to the body.

The regimental commander insisted on levying charges against the surgeon, arguing vigorously to the corps commander "that such actions as these known to enlisted men being permitted to pass unnoticed will demoralize troops and destroy all confidence and discipline is beyond doubt: especially among men of Such Supersticious cast of mind as these Colored Men." The corps medical director concurred, admitting "a proper post mortem would have been interesting and of importance to the profession, as showing the nature and course of disease; but it should have been made at a *proper* time, a *proper* place, and in a professional *manner.*" He then concluded, "This case was not a Post Mortem examination, or a dissection; it was a mutilation of the body not justifiable." A court dismissed the surgeon from the service, but through his political contacts, Pres. Andrew Johnson reinstated him, only to be cashiered a second time for refusing to appear before a medical board.[13]

Because so many whites believed the racial stereotype of lazy blacks, medical and line officers were far too quick to accuse blacks of malingering. Like white soldiers, some blacks did feign illness, such as a private in the 65th U.S. Colored Infantry who escaped duty for six months by claiming to have a severe case of hemorrhoids and putting a turkey heart up his rectum to confuse the physicians. Yet most troops had legitimate reasons for lining up at sick call, and surgeons and other officers too frequently mistreated genuinely ill soldiers, merely assuming that the ailments were fictitious and that the best way to discourage frivolous complaints was to threaten or abuse the troops.[14]

What made this experience even sadder was that for all the insults, mistreatment, and abuse they endured, black soldiers actually received the best care with their regiments. There of course were limitations on the number of physicians who treated troops as well as the extent of the facilities, but the doctors were for the most part competent, and with the entire command stationed nearby, soldiers had direct channels to superior officers for their complaints, and regimental commanders could oversee the hospital organization and rectify problems as they developed. While some physicians were callous in their conduct toward sick or injured black troops, regimental surgeons served in the same command as the troops they treated, and most of them were truly devoted to the art of healing and sensitive to the miseries of the men.

Unfortunately surgeons in the USCT were by no means the only physicians who cared for black soldiers. Due to the limited staff on the regimental level, when soldiers became very ill or suffered serious wounds or injuries, medical officers were supposed to send the patients to more advanced facilities.

The problem was that most black commands performed occupation duties and seldom constituted even brigades until late in the war so that there were few division hospitals for blacks. Most often the institutions for severe cases were post or general hospitals, which were outside the direct chain of command for the USCT and typically had separate and grossly unequal facilities for blacks and whites. Physicians who worked at these facilities were not part of the USCT, demonstrated little concern for the plight of black soldiers, and, as a result of their neglect, caused unnecessary pain, suffering, and even death for their black patients.

Time after time, post or general hospitals for black troops were understaffed and extremely unsanitary, and their mortality rates were dramatically higher than in adjacent or nearby facilities for whites. At Fort Smith, Arkansas, an inspector found that in the black hospital "there were evidences of habitual neglect of proper police regulations. The kitchens, out buildings and grounds were filthy in the extreme, and the medical officer in charge did not manifest much efficiency in the discharge of his duties." Out of 343 patients, 92 died, a far worse rate than for the white hospital. At Pine Bluff, Arkansas, where there were also separate and unequal facilities, an inspector made a side-by-side comparison that clearly indicated the inferiority of the black hospital: "The police of the wards in the hospital for white soldiers was fair but the police of the negro hospital was filthy in the extreme." Hospital linen was "tolerably clean in the white hospital but not so in the negro ward." One of the worst hospitals for black troops was in Helena, Arkansas, which "was the dirtiest place inside and the filthiest place out side it has fallen to my lot to inspect," wrote a colonel. "The sick men are dirty their beds filthy and uncomfortable. The police about the hospital, kitchens & c disgraceful. Not a thing about the whole establishment could I find to mention in favorable terms."

On the eastern side of the Mississippi River, there was little improvement. After six months in service, the black hospital in Vicksburg had treated 646 patients, 197 of whom had died, or 30.5 percent, while the white hospital had 415 deaths out of 2,963 cases, or 14 percent. The black facility, so noted the inspector, had a good location, but "neither the General police or the beds were in as good order as in the other hospitals [white]. The sinks were old, and in bad police." At the nearby black smallpox, or "pest" hospital, as contagious-disease hospitals were called, the tents were "old and badly pitched, no floors and no drainage." Again the mortality rate was over 30 percent.

In New Orleans by far the worst medical facility was the Corps d'Afrique

Hospital. According to the inspector, "The police of the hospital and grounds was bad, the floors and bedding were dirty, and there seemed to be a lack of system and discipline." One day earlier the same inspector had examined Sedgwick General Hospital in the city and considered it a "model hospital" in "most perfect condition." Of course it housed white soldiers only.[15]

Back east, black commands were more frequently part of an organized military structure and thus had brigade or division hospitals. This generally ensured them superior medical care to the pest and post hospitals out west. Nevertheless they had their share of problems. One officer lamented that "our treatment in hospitals [is] worse than a criminals in penetentiary." In fact complaints among the troops were so rampant that the regimental commander of the 1st U.S. Colored Cavalry, a unit raised in Virginia, sent a medical officer to investigate the conditions of a smallpox hospital, then notified brigade headquarters that "the colored soldiers in the Small Pox Hospital are neglected, that the rooms they occupy are unventilated and unclean."[16]

Perhaps the worst assemblage of hospital facilities for black soldiers existed in Nashville. Before blacks had entered the service, Nashville hospitals already had a reputation as notoriously bad, and when officials had to establish facilities for black troops, they were inferior, even for these substandard institutions. Capt. Josiah V. Meigs, commander of Battery A, 2nd U.S. Colored Light Artillery, a unit that consisted of local ex-slaves, protested in vain. He claimed the pest house that cared for some of his men was "completely disorganized, men lay in the filth of their disease without change of clothing from the time of entry until they deserted or died." His warning passed unheeded. As a result authorities made no improvements, and in the aftermath of the battle of Nashville in December 1864, the system for black soldiers all but collapsed. Within one week Colonel Mussey complained that hospital accommodations for the USCT were "very insufficient." Several weeks later, after Adjutant General Thomas received a complaint from a captain about the treatment of sick and wounded in his company, he inspected a black hospital. The sight appalled him. Haunted by incompetent physicians and a severe shortage of skilled nurses, men were wearing the same clothing they had donned in the battle a month earlier, bloodstains and all. One amputee complained of lice bites; another had no shirt because ten days earlier he had to discard it because of filth. "Had these been white soldiers," penned the outraged adjutant general to the officer in charge, "think you this would have been their condition? No!" Yet in February Mussey continued to uncover inadequacies, including a shortage of two hundred beds.[17]

In all likelihood, once word of these dreadful conditions reached the troops, some soldiers may have unwittingly exacerbated problems by refusing to report illnesses early for fear of going to such wretched places. When their regimental surgeons learned of the illness and sent them to hospitals, it was too late to treat the patients properly, which in turn drove up mortality rates.

That, however, in no way detracts from the disgraceful condition of these separate and unequal facilities, nor its effect on the lives of sick black soldiers. Civil War physicians sometimes cured patients and other times unintentionally made matters worse, but at least assignment to hospitals placed sick white soldiers in a sanitary environment, which was conducive to recovery. But hospitalized blacks reaped no such benefit. Their facilities were filthy and represented gross neglect on the part of white physicians and staff.

Under such circumstances many surgeons in the USCT sensibly preferred to keep soldiers on hand at their regimental hospitals, even serious or critical patients, except for men with contagious diseases. Although this augmented their workload considerably, at least they were able to retain control of medical treatment for soldiers in their regiments, while the sick or injured troops benefited by remaining among friendly and familiar faces. Despite inadequate facilities and the excess burden on surgeons, regimental hospitals in the USCT in the most unhealthy environments were certainly no worse than most general or post hospitals that cared for black soldiers, regardless of location.[18]

The shortage of qualified medical staff, racist attitudes among physicians, and separate and unequal facilities all took a terrible toll on the black ranks, but the type and location of duty made their situation even worse. Because most whites doubted that blacks had the character to sustain themselves in combat, high-ranking officers usually assigned black troops to garrison and fatigue duty, frequently in the unhealthiest areas. As weeks and months passed in garrison, camp sanitary problems invariably compounded, and the ensuing illnesses inflicted fearful losses.

Diarrhea and dysentery, a most common affliction in the Civil War, was often caused by unclean water, contamination from human waste, and bad food. Diarrhea, dysentery, and food poisoning were all the result of organisms that entered the body orally. Acute diarrhea, in addition to cramps and discomfort, could lead to dehydration. Dysentery, known also as the "bloody flux" from internal hemorrhaging (blood in stools, thus "bloody flux"), caused severe diarrhea, bleeding, dehydration, and possibly peritonitis. Food poisoning often resulted in severe cramps, vomiting, and diarrhea. All could prove fatal, and troops who performed garrison duty were particularly susceptible to these illnesses. Even when commanders enforced rigid sanitary standards, prolonged service in the same location increased the chance of human waste contaminating the water supply, which often caused widespread diarrhea or dysentery. Although the frequency of these illnesses was only 35 percent more than among white troops, the severity was greater in the USCT as evidenced by a higher mortality rate, nearly 250 percent more, from diarrhea and dysentery.[19]

Another scourge among black troops due to improper sanitary conditions and generally unhealthy environments was typhoid fever. A form of salmonellae poisoning spread through contaminated water, food, and feces, it caused prolonged high fevers. Some evidence indicates that many blacks are more resistant to typhoid fever than whites, but during the Civil War it was proportionately more prevalent among the USCT and also more deadly, taking the lives of well over two thousand black soldiers.[20]

Whites had long recognized that African Americans were more resistant to certain tropical diseases than whites. For that reason high-ranking officers assigned the USCT to the unhealthiest semitropical areas, especially the swampy regions of Louisiana, the Mississippi Valley, South Carolina, and Florida. Yet none of those officers anticipated that malaria would have such a disastrous effect on the ranks of the USCT. At the time physicians did not know that the swarms of mosquitoes infesting these areas were the carriers of malaria. Although these pests were almost always bothersome to soldiers, they were more a source of sarcastic humor than a health concern. At Fort Jackson, Louisiana, a black sergeant penned, "We are attacked on the right and left flank by millions upon millions of mosquitoes, which, by night, charge upon us, front and rear, and cause us to beat a hasty retreat to our nets for protection from their daggers, which they plunge with a will." In South Carolina a company commander in the 1st South Carolina (Colored) Infantry, later called the 33rd U.S. Colored Infantry, filed a protest too: "The nits gnats and sandflies together with mosquitoes and house flies are simply terrific especially when there is no breeze to blow them away. I tried to write up my company books and found it almost impossible even if I scratched and slapped until my fingers and skin were alike sore." As a last resort he bought a box of cigars and had enlisted men come into his tent, light the cigars, and puff the smoke at him, which he found to be a reasonably effective repellant.[21]

Under these unrelenting mosquito assaults, black soldiers suffered almost five times the rate of fatality from malaria that white volunteers did and nearly double the frequency of infection. Apparently the lack of resistance among some blacks and the prolonged exposure to severe strains of the disease resulted in the high death rate.[22]

The leading killer among black troops, pneumonia, was also in part a result of discriminatory treatment. Although some physicians and scholars have discovered a greater frequency of respiratory illnesses among blacks, that in no way accounts for the staggering difference between the races in the Union army. Out of some 16,000 cases, pneumonia struck down 5,233 USCT soldiers, a much higher disease rate and a mortality rate almost five times greater than among white volunteers. Early in 1863 a surgeon in the USCT noticed the excessively high rate of pleurisy and pneumonia as compared to white regiments, but he could not pinpoint the reason. His best hypothesis was that the men's religious meetings had something to do with it. A much more likely reason was that excessive fatigue duty wore clothing rapidly, and officers had problems keeping their troops clad properly and fed well. While white volunteers spent most of their time in winter quarters, blacks still had to labor regardless of the season, and in the cold months, exposed to the elements and improperly clothed, they contracted pneumonia more readily.[23]

Another respiratory ailment, tuberculosis, afflicted black soldiers in much heavier proportions than whites. The disease rate among blacks was nearly triple that for whites, and the death rate was well over three times higher. Like diarrhea, dysentery, and typhoid fever, other great killers of black troops, this was mainly due to the unsanitary conditions of camps and hospitals, which promoted the rapid spread of tuberculosis.[24]

Without doubt one of the most inexcusable illnesses that took a terrible toll on the USCT was smallpox. Even though whites had known of a vaccine for nearly two hundred years, almost 4 percent of all black soldiers came down with smallpox, and more than 13 in every 1,000 who caught the ailment died from it. By comparison with white troops, the rate of illness was 764 percent greater among black troops, and the rate of death was 692 percent higher. Clearly Federal authorities failed to adopt a systematic immunization process, and black soldiers suffered terribly as a result.[25]

The frequency of death from scurvy was probably the grossest instance of negligence, though this time it was not the doctors' fault but that of the commissary department. By the time of the war, physicians mistakenly attributed to all fruits and vegetables the power to check scurvy rather than just selected potables with vitamin C. Yet efforts to diversify the diet and include fresh fruits and vegetables had helped considerably, and by late 1862 the surgeon general boasted, "Scurvy has been almost entirely prevented" within the army. There were some cases of the condition as well as other undiagnosed illnesses due to deficient diets. According to physicians, though, these were more the fault of individual soldiers who failed to consume their rations in full or of bad foraging during campaigns than anything else.[26]

During the last few months of the war in Virginia, black soldiers began to show signs of scurvy and other dietary ailments. One surgeon complained that his troops had not received vegetables in five months, and "Scorbutic Diathesis [scurvy] prevails strongly"; another levied a protest about scurvy in his regiment to the XXV Army Corps medical director, but "My *representations were disdainfully spurned, and no attention paid to me or them.*" After Lee's army surrendered, the War Department sent the black XXV Corps to Texas for occupation duty and as a show of force to the French, who had seized control of Mexico, and there scurvy reached epidemic proportions. En route via ships, cases of scurvy became more and more frequent, and within one week of their arrival at Brazos Santiago, the situation was critical. After seven days a post hospital with beds for eighty troops had five hundred patients, and these were only the worst cases. Medical officials sent hundreds of men to New Orleans for care, yet there was no checking the problem. One surgeon wrote that soldiers became dejected and physically listless, and they lost interest in providing themselves with good shelter and caring for themselves generally. The gums of some swelled so badly from scurvy that they completely hid their molars, bicuspids, and canine teeth. During the summer of 1865, the medical inspector in Texas estimated that 60 percent of the XXV Corps had scurvy. Physicians and their staffs worked frantically, but to little avail. A surgeon insisted that many troops were "actually begging to be left with their comrades to die in the regt. rather than be sent to the place where neither sufficient attendants, nor food can be obtained." Another distributed all the canned tomatoes and pickles he had on hand and wrote his father despondently: "We have no fresh vegetables, except a few from the 'sanitary arm,' all antiscorbutic medicines exhausted—and discouragement *everywhere.* Men are taken down one day—& the next are in unmarked graves." To aid his men a surgeon even traveled into Mexico to purchase barrels of onions and tomatoes, but Mexican authorities would not permit such a large quantity of vegetables and fruit to pass over the border. By mid-August fresh vegetables and fruits began to pour into Texas, and within two weeks a surgeon announced ecstatically to his father that the sick list had declined 40 percent as a result of recoveries. Nevertheless angered medical officers insisted that the entire affair was inexcusable and hoped that military authorities would punish commanding officers for such "wilful neglect or culpable ignorance" in their failure to provide for the men, but prosecutions were not forthcoming. Such negligence resulted in an increased death rate from scurvy, per 1,000 men, of 1,447 percent more for black soldiers, and a 736 percent greater rate of illness generally among men in the USCT.[27]

The total cost to the USCT in lives lost and bodies damaged due to wounds, injuries, and disease is difficult to determine precisely. Government records show that nearly 37,000 black soldiers died during the Civil War, more than the United States lost in all its other colonial and nineteenth-century wars combined. Barely 4 percent were killed in battle, and almost 30,000 died of disease alone. Within specific commands the number of deaths was at times shocking. A black heavy artillery regiment lost over 800 men, and one infantry regiment, in service less than a year, had 524 deaths, nearly 50 percent of its strength. "The mortality in our Regt. beats anything I ever saw," wrote a lieutenant stationed in Louisiana, whose regiment also suffered disastrously. "They frequently drop dead in the streets, and in two or three instances have been found laying dead in the weeds some distance from camp." He had just ordered his men to build one dozen more coffins and pondered in disillusionment, "How long do you suppose they will last the old Dr.?"[28]

It is unlikely that blacks brought these illnesses with them into military service. Dr. Todd Savitt, arguably the most knowledgeable scholar on medical care and illness among slaves, discovered a high death rate among bondsmen from pneumonia, tuberculosis, diarrhea and dysentery, and diseases of the nervous system. Savitt also found that rheumatism and other nonfatal disabilities afflicted many slaves. Yet according to official army policy, enlistees had to undergo two medical examinations, one by an initial examining physician and another by the regimental surgeon. The government then held physicians financially responsible for all expenses incurred, including bounty and pay, if the soldier's commander found a recruit unfit for duty. Certainly that did not preclude unhealthy men from enlisting and serving, or even those with mild disabilities, injuries, and even deformities, but the penalty was serious enough to discourage doctors from accepting men with pneumonia, tuberculosis, dysentery, severe diarrhea, and a host of contagious diseases. Some prospective black soldiers may have entered military service with rheumatism and other less serious problems, but these in no way altered the death rate.[29]

No doubt the rural backgrounds of most black soldiers contributed to the high disease rate during the war. Living in low population density limited their prewar exposure to illness. When they contracted germs and viruses in wartime, they simply could not fight them off. Of the 179,000 blacks who served in the Union army, approximately 150,000 came from slave states, where only 10 percent of all slaves lived in urban areas. Yet that alone does not explain the staggering illness and death rates among men in the USCT. Most northerners lived in rural areas, yet blacks died at a rate two and a half times greater.[30]

Along with physicians in and out of the USCT, military authorities share culpability for the inordinately high mortality rate. Not only did they assign black commands to garrison and fatigue duty in the most unhealthy environments, but they also made little effort to rectify the problem of inferior medical care. Ample information on medical treatment for men in the USCT was available through complaints by their white officers and numerous inspection reports.

Several factors, however, seem to have contributed to this inaction. Many department commanders held black troops in low regard and devoted scant attention to their well being. Other times inspectors could find no reason for the high mortality rate of black troops, or when they did, they usually ascribed it to the inadequate condition of blacks prior to military service. "The regiment was raised without proper medical examination," noted Lt. Col. W. H. Thurston on the inspection report of black troops stationed at Morganzia, Louisiana, "and the men had contracted diseases before entering the service, and are now quite worthless. Many have old rheumatism, vericose, crippled feet, & c." Such endorsements as this never dealt with the issue of mortality, though.[31]

A final and very important reason was that complaints and reports seldom reached authorities in Washington, who could or tried to rectify the difficulties. In the Civil War the army had no general staff to coordinate affairs among different bureaus and between the bureaus and the troops. As a result several of the most damaging inspection reports never received an endorsement, indicating that no one had read them. Others had endorsements like "contents noted," but no one took action. Rare indeed was the inspection report in which Surgeon General J. M. Barnes commented, "Extracts furnished for information and action of Medical Director Smith, Dept. of Arkansas," but even then the surgeon general failed to follow up to ensure that medical care had improved. Three months later an inspector in the Department of Arkansas found that little had changed for sick black soldiers.[32]

Based on medical knowledge at the time of the war, thousands of black servicemen most certainly would have fallen from disease. Physicians were able to treat only a handful of illnesses, and as the war came to a close, Joseph Lister was just publishing his startling discoveries on germs in far off Scotland. In addition, blacks, like whites, came predominantly from rural areas. While they possessed certain genetic resistance to particular illnesses and diseases, their relative isolation limited their exposure to other diseases and inhibited their ability to build up acquired immunities. Thus rural blacks and whites were particularly susceptible to specific maladies that spread through army camps.

Yet this does little to diminish the role of discrimination in the deaths of the almost 30,000 black troops from illness. A shortage of qualified medical personnel, racism among physicians, separate and unequal hospital facilities, and garrison and fatigue duty in the most unhealthy environments all played a heavy hand in a mortality rate that was more than double that of white soldiers.

NOTES

1. *The Medical and Surgical History of the War of the Rebellion,* 3 vols. in 6 pts. (Washington, D.C.: Government Printing Office, 1870–88), 1(1):641, 712 (hereinafter cited as *MOR*). Fatalities by disease in the USCT were 165.71 per 1,000, and in general volunteers it was 68.2 per 1,000, based on figures in Frederick H. Dyer, *A Compendium of the War of the Rebellion,* vol. 1 (1908; New York: Thomas Yoseloff, 1959), 12, 18.

2. Dyer, *Compendium,* 12, 18; "Final Report of the Provost Marshal General," Mar. 17, 1866, U.S. War Department, *War of the Rebellion: A Compilation of the Official Records of the Union and Confederate Armies,* 128 vols. (Washington, D.C.: Government Printing Office, 1880–1901), ser. 3, 5:667–69 (hereinafter cited as *OR;* all references to ser. 3); *MOR,* 1(1):712. Battlefield mortality was 16.11 per 1,000 in the USCT and 35.10 per 1,000 among white volunteers. Information in the *Medical and Surgical History,* it seems, is not complete. It lists 128,937 whites who died of disease, when in fact 169,287 died, just over 76 percent complete. By comparison the volume includes 27,499 black soldiers as having died from disease, when in fact 29,658 actually died. This is nearly 93 percent accurate. In order to compensate for the discrepancy, I have assumed that the number of cases and fatalities taken by specific illnesses for black soldiers were underreported by 7 percent, and those for white soldiers by 24 percent. While this method does not provide precise figures, no method can, and it more accurately reflects the true number of cases and fatalities. The method, moreover, reduces the statistical discrepancies between black and white soldiers, which works against my arguments. Still my statistical evidence is so overwhelming, in my opinion, that I am willing to make the adjustment for what I believe to be greater accuracy. The ratio of almost two and one-

half to one is calculated from the actual number of fatalities due to disease and the actual number of men who served. The raw data comes from the *Medical and Surgical History.* Thanks to Dr. Karl Eschbach, a sociologist and statistics expert, who reviewed my approach and found it more accurate than simply employing the raw data.

3. Annual Report of Joseph K. Barnes, Surgeon General, Oct. 20, 1864, *OR,* 4:792; C. H. Crane to Surg. Adam N. McLaren, Oct. 16, 1863, Edgar L. Draper File, Personal Papers, Medical Officers and Physicians, Prior to 1912, Records of the Adjutant General's Office, RG 94, National Archives, Washington, D.C. (hereinafter cited as NA)

4. C. W. Foster to Maj. Gen. J. G. Foster, Dec. 20, 1864, Letters Regarding Recruiting, Division of Colored Troops, RG 94. Also see R. D. Mussey to Major Foster, Mar. 13, 1864, Letters Sent by the Commissioner, Dept. of the Cumberland, Records of the U.S. Army Continental Commands, 1821–1920, pt. 1, RG 393, NA.

5. The eight were Drs. Anderson R. Abbott, Alexander T. Augusta, William B. Ellis, William Powell, John De Grasse, Charles Burleigh Purvis, John Rapier, and Alpheus Tucker.

6. N. P. Banks to Maj. C. T. Christenden, July 18, 1864, The Negro in the Military Service of the United States, 1607–1889, ser. 2694–95, RG 94. Also see Pension File of Herman W. Dickinson, RG 15, NA; H. H. Hood to wife, Jan. 20, 1863, Humphrey H. Hood Papers, Illinois State Historical Library, Springfield; [Col. Risdon] to Brig. Gen. L. Thomas, May 11, 1864, Risdon Papers, Western Reserve Historical Society, Cleveland, Ohio (hereinafter cited as WRHS).

7. Mussey to Mr. Edwin H. Cooper, Jan. 20, 1865, Letters Sent by the Commissioner, Dept. of the Cumberland, RG 393.

8. Also see Thomas to Stanton, Sept. 19, Nov. 7, 1864, *OR,* 4:733, 922; Rufis Ollogin to Friend Moulton, Mar. 1, 1865, Palmer Collection, WRHS; J. K. Bandery to Maj. G. L. Stearns, Dec. 9, 1863, Proceedings of Boards of Examination for Commissions in the USCT, Dept. of the Cumberland, 1863–64, RG 393; Memorandum, May 19, 1863, William Bidlack File, Personal Papers, Medical Officers and Physicians, Prior to 1912, RG 94; J. O. Moore to Lizzie, July 10, [1864], James O. Moore Papers, Duke University, Durham, N.C.; C. G. G. Merrill Papers, Yale University, New Haven, Conn., esp. C. G. G. Merrill to father, Jan. 22, 1864; George W. Adams, *Doctors in Blue: The Medical History of the Union Army in the Civil War* (New York: Henry Schuman, 1952), 175.

9. Paul E. Steiner, *Medical History of a Civil War Regiment: Disease in the Sixty-Fifth United States Colored Infantry* (Clayton, Mo: Institute of Civil War Studies, 1977), 52–53. Also see Sgt. James Thompson to "Sir," Oct. 2, 1863, Marcus A. Stults Folder, Civil War Miscellaneous Collection, U.S. Army Military History Institute, Carlisle Barracks, Pa. (hereinafter cited as MHI); Col. B. R. Townsend to Maj. C. W. Foster, Aug. 22, 1864, Letters Sent, 2nd USCI, RG 94; Charles G. G. Merrill to father, July 23, 1864, Merrill Papers; H. H. Hood to wife, June 18, 1865, Hood Papers; Thomas Montgomery to mother, Nov. 27, 1864, Thomas Montgomery Papers, Minnesota Historical Society, Minneapolis.

10. H. H. Hood to wife, July 18, 1863, Sept. 6, 1865, Hood Papers. Also see J. B. Roberts to mother, Jan. 24, 1865, Roberts Family in Civil War Miscellany, Library of Congress, Washington, D.C.; Dr. Seth Rogers to ?, Jan. 18, 1863, MOLLUS Collection, MHI; R. D. Mussey to Col. C. R. Thompson, May 14, 1864, Letters Sent by the Commissioner, Dept. of the Cumberland, RG 393.

11. Dr. Seth Rogers to ?, Apr. 4, 1863, MOLLUS Collection; W. W. McDowell, Dr. at Small Pox Hospital at Natchez, to Surg. George S. Kemble, May 3, 1864, File of Elias W. Gray, Personal Papers, Medical Officers and Physicians, Prior to 1912, RG 94; Trial of Surg. Lyman Allen, with endorsement by Brig. Gen. C. J. Paine, LL 3199, Proceedings of General Courts-Martial, RG 153, NA. Also see W. W. McDowell to Adj. Genl. Thomas, May 7, 1864, Court of Inquiry, May 24, 1864; E. W. Gray to Gen. Thomas, May 7, 1864, File of Elias W. Gray; and Trial of Surg. E. Jackson, MM 1664, Proceedings of General Courts-Martial, RG 153.

12. ? to Sir, Aug. 20, 1864, in *Freedom: A Documentary History of Emancipation, 1861–1864,* ed. Ira Berlin et al. (Cambridge: Cambridge University Press, 1982–93), ser. 1, 2:640–41.

13. George J. Potts to Adjutant General, Mar. 22, 1865, Lt. Col. M. L. Dempcy to E. W. Smith, Mar. 22, 1865, and Report of Wm. A. Conover, Medical Director, 25th AC, Mar. 25, 1865, Trial of Dr. George J. Potts, MM 3067, Proceedings of General Courts-Martial, RG 153. Also see Edward W. Bacon to Kate, Sept. 24, 1865, Edward W. Bacon Papers, American Antiquarian Society, Worcester, Mass.

14. T. D. Freeman to William, Mar. 26, 1864, Brown Family Papers, American Antiquarian Society; B. W. to Mr. Editor, July 8, 1864, *Christian Recorder,* July 30, 1864; D.I.I. to Mr. Editor, Aug. 6, 1864, ibid., Aug. 6, 1864. Also see Steiner, *Medical History of a Civil War Regiment,* 84; Trial of Pvt. Robert Morse, MM 3226, and Trial of Pvt. Weston Gray, LL 2284, Proceedings of General Courts-Martial, RG 153. An officer in one of these units had similar sentiments. Albert Rogall Diary, July 6, 26, 1864, Albert Rogall Papers, Ohio Historical Society, Columbus.

15. Inspection of Medical Dept. for Dept. of Arkansas by Col. R. B. Marcy, Aug. 15, 1864; Inspection Report of Medical Dept., Dept. of the Mississippi by Col. R. B. Marcy, Mar. 1865; and Inspection Report of Dept. of Arkansas, Jan. 13, 1865, by Col. R. B. Sackett, Letters Received, Office of Inspector General, Inspection Report of the Medical Dept. of the Mississippi by Col. R. B. Marcy, June 7, 1865, Inspection Reports, 1865, RG 159, NA. Also see Wm. M. Chambers et al., Report on the Conditions of U.S. (Small Pox) Hospital No. 11, Oct. 1, 1864, Letters Received Relating to Recruiting, RG 94; and Inspection Report of Troops at District of Vicksburg, Aug. 20, 1864, by Capt. S. Bostwick, Inspection Reports, Mississippi, RG 159.

16. Rogall Diary, Aug. 24, 1864, Rogall Papers; Col. Jeptha Garrard to Maj. Davis, Mar. 1, 1864, Letters Sent, 1st USCC, RG 94.

17. Capt. Josiah V. Meigs to Adjutant General, July 25, 1864, Letter Book, Battery A, 2nd USCLA, RG 94; R. D. Mussey to Capt. C. P. Brown, Dec. 21, 1864, Letters Sent by the Commissioner, Dept. of the Cumberland, RG 393; Adjutant General to Col. R. C. Wood, Jan. 16, 1865, in Berlin et al., *Freedom,* ser. 1, 2:645. Also see Ch. G. G. Merrill to sister, Apr. 11, 1863, Merrill Papers; and Mussey to Capt. Rusling, Feb. 7, 1865, Letters Sent by the Commissioner, Dept. of the Cumberland, RG 393.

18. See Circular No. 4, HQ, Mil. Div. of West Miss., Sept. 10, 1864, Surgeon's Morning Reports, Hospital Records and Letters, 4th USCC, RG 94; Testimony of Surg. James Thompson, Trial of Surg. James Thompson, MM 2636, Proceedings of General Courts-Martial, RG 153; Inspection Report of Troops at Morganzia, Louisiana, Oct. 9, 1864, by Maj. Geo. Baldy, Inspection Reports, Louisiana, Inspection Report of the Medical Dept. of the Dept. of Mississippi by Col. R. B. Marcy, Mar. 1865, Inspection Reports, 1865, RG 159. Only two hospitals for black soldiers won

the praise of inspectors. One was at Natchez and the other at Fort Smith. See Inspection Report of the Medical Dept. of the Dept. of Mississippi by Col. R. B. Marcy, Mar. 30, 1865, Inspection Reports, 1865; and Inspection Report of the Dept. of Arkansas, Jan. 13, 1865, by Col. R. B. Sackett, Letters Received, Office of Inspector General, RG 159.

19. Among black troops there were 860.11 per 1,000 cases of diarrhea and dysentery, and 37.79 per 1,000 died of the ailment. Among white troops there were 635.45 cases and 15.15 deaths as a result. Since these statistics represent 92.3 percent of all black soldiers and 76.2 percent of all white soldiers who died of disease, projections for all deaths, assuming they occurred proportionately from the same ailments, would give 40.56 per 1,000 black soldiers and 18.76 per 1,000 white soldiers. See *MOR,* 1(1):641, 711; and Todd L. Savitt, *Medicine and Slavery: The Diseases and Health Care of Blacks in Antebellum Virginia* (Urbana: University of Illinois Press, 1978), 62–63.

20. See *MOR,* 1(1):636–41, 710–12, 1(3):79–80. Among black soldiers 20.01 per 1,000 died and 64.94 per 1,000 suffered from typhoid fever. With white soldiers, 12.47 per 1,000 died and 50.20 per 1,000 caught the illness. Since these statistics represent 92.3 percent of all black soldiers and 76.2 percent of all white soldiers who died of disease, projections for all deaths, assuming they occurred proportionately from the same ailments, would give 21.47 per 1,000 black soldiers and 15.44 per 1,000 white soldiers. Savitt, *Medicine and Slavery,* 61–62.

21. Leonard G. Phenix to Mr. Editor, Feb. 21, 1865, *Christian Recorder,* Mar. 25, 1865; Sam to Mary, July 6, 1864, Quincy, Wendell, Holmes, and Upham Families, Massachusetts Historical Society, Boston; H. H. Hood to wife, May 22, 1865, Hood Papers; James Rogers to ?, Apr. 18, 1863, James Rogers Papers, Sophia Smith Collection, Smith College, Northampton, Mass.

22. See *MOR,* 1(1):636–41, 710–12, 1(3):79–80; John [Wilder] to Eben, May 28, Aug. 21, 1864, Loomis-Wilder Family Papers, Yale University; Surg. E. M. Pease to Lt. Rhodes, Jan. 9, 1865, Letters Received, USCT, Dept. of Virginia and North Carolina, RG 393. Since these statistics represent 92.3 percent of all black soldiers and 76.2 percent of all white soldiers who died of disease, projections for all deaths, assuming they occurred proportionately from the same ailments, would give 11.70 per 1,000 black soldiers and 2.75 per 1,000 white soldiers.

23. See *MOR,* 1(1):636–41, 710–12; Dr. Seth Rogers to ?, Jan. 10, 1863, MOLLUS Collection; T. W. Higginson Diary, Jan. 14, [1863], in *Letters and Journals of Thomas Wentworth Higginson, 1846–1906,* ed. Mary Thatcher Higginson (Boston: Houghton Mifflin, 1921), 55; Thomas Wentworth Higginson, *Army Life in a Black Regiment* (Boston: Beacon, 1962), 55. Evidence indicates that blacks do have a higher incidence of pulmonary problems than whites. Dr. Todd L. Savitt comes to a similar conclusion on pneumonia and slaves. *Medicine and Slavery,* 37. Among black troops 29.24 per 1,000 died and 90.14 per 1,000 caught the illness. Among white troops 5.91 per 1,000 died from pneumonia and 24.53 caught it. Since these statistics represent 92.3 percent of all black soldiers and 76.2 percent of all white soldiers who died of disease, projections for all deaths, assuming they occurred proportionately from the same ailments, would give 31.37 per 1,000 black soldiers and 7.32 per 1,000 white soldiers.

24. See *MOR,* 1(1):636–41, 710–12. The rates for blacks were 7.22 per 1,000 for death and 21.45 per 1,000 for cases. Among white troops the number of deaths was 2.16 per 1,000 and 7.83 per 1,000 for cases. Since these statistics represent 92.3 percent of all black soldiers and 76.2 percent of all

white soldiers who died of disease, projections for all deaths, assuming they occurred proportionately from the same ailments, would give 7.75 per 1,000 black soldiers and 2.67 per 1,000 white soldiers. A recent study of tuberculosis among blacks and whites in nursing homes and prisons in Arkansas finds a greater susceptibility among blacks. See William W. Stead et al., "Racial Differences in Susceptibility to Infection by Mycobacterium Tuberculosis," *New England Journal of Medicine* 322, no. 7 (Feb. 15, 1990): 422–27. Other physicians have challenged the thesis. See correspondence regarding the Stead article and his response in *New England Journal of Medicine* 322, no. 23 (June 7, 1990): 1670–73.

25. See *MOR,* 1(1):636–41, 710–12. For black troops 13.08 per 1,000 died from and 37.52 per 1,000 caught smallpox. Among white troops 1.7 per 1,000 died and 27.16 per 1,000 caught it. Since these statistics represent 92.3 percent of all black soldiers and 76.2 percent of all white soldiers who died of disease, projections for all deaths, assuming they occurred proportionately from the same ailments, would give 14.03 per 1,000 black soldiers and 2.34 per 1,000 white soldiers.

26. Annual Report of William A. Hammond, Surg. Gen., Nov. 10, 1862, *OR,* 2:750. Also see Adams, *Doctors in Blue,* 212–13; and *MOR,* 1(1):636–41, 710–12, 1(3):694.

27. Dr. Francis Minot Weld Diary, May 24, 1865, in *Diaries and Letters of Francis Minot Weld,* ed. Susan Swan Weld Blake (Boston: Stetson, 1925), 203; Surg. Potts to Surgeon E. P. Mooney, Aug. 5, 1865, and Monthly Report of July 1865 of Surg. George Potts, Trial of Surg. George Potts, MM 3069, Proceedings of General Courts-Martial, RG 153; Charles to father, Aug. 13, 29, 1865, Merrill Papers. Also see S. Hemenway, "Observations on Scurvy and Its Causes among U.S. Colored Troops of the 25th Army Corps, during the Spring and Summer of 1865," *Chicago Medical Examiner* 7 (Oct. 1866): 582–85; Lorenzo Gould Diary, Sept. 9, 1865, Civil War Miscellaneous Collection, MHI; Monthly Report for June 1865 and Monthly Report for July 1865 by Dr. Henry Grange, 7th USCI Regimental Hospital Records, RG 94; Surg. Potts to Adj. Gen., July 12, 1865, and Potts to Maj. Gen. Jas. K. Barnes, July 20, 1865, Trial of Surg. George Potts, MM 3069, Proceedings of General Courts-Martial, RG 153; and *MOR,* 1(3):694–96. For black soldiers 2.17 per 1,000 died from scurvy and 90.61 per 1,000 suffered from it. Among white troops 0.15 per 1,000 died from it and 12.31 per 1,000 felt its effects. Since these statistics represent 92.3 percent of all black soldiers and 76.2 percent of all white soldiers who died of disease, projections for all deaths, assuming they occurred proportionately from the same ailments, would give 2.33 per 1,000 black soldiers and 0.19 per 1,000 white soldiers.

28. [Duren Kelley] to Emma, July 24, 1864, in *The War Letters of Duren F. Kelley,* ed. Richard S. Offenberg and Robert Rue Parsonage (New York: Pageant, 1967), 111. Also see Steiner, *Medical History of a Civil War Regiment,* xvii, 45; [Daniel Ullman] to Lt. Col. C. T. Christensen, Oct. 29, 1864, in Berlin et al., *Freedom,* ser.1, 2:513–14; T. Montgomery to father, Sept. 16, 1864, Montgomery Papers; William H. Chenery, *The Fourteenth Regiment Rhode Island Heavy Artillery (Colored)* (Providence: Snow & Farnham, 1898), 105; Dyer, *Compendium,* 12, 18; and Final Report of the Provost Marshal General, Mar. 17, 1866, *OR,* 5:667–69. Casualties by disease in the USCT were 165.71 per 1,000, and in general volunteers it was 59.22 per 1,000. Battlefield mortality was 16.11 per 1,000 in the USCT and 35.10 per 1,000 among white volunteers.

29. See Savitt, *Medicine and Slavery;* Joseph T. Glatthaar, *Forged in Battle: The Civil War Alliance*

of Black Soldiers and White Officers (New York: Free Press, 1990), 76; Circular, HQ, U.S. Colored Cavalry, Aug. 8, 1864, Instructions and Reports Sent, Organization of USCC, Dept. of Kentucky, RG 393. Dr. Edward M. Coffman confirmed that this was the standard army practice.

30. Perhaps Confederate soldiers would be a better standard to judge the influence of rural backgrounds on wartime deaths by disease. To a large extent these white and black soldiers came from the same general vicinity and should have shared prewar exposure to the same illnesses. But once again a comparison of the death rate of black soldiers with Confederate troops, who lived in equal proportions in country areas, supports the contention that the rural argument does not retain its merit. Although black soldiers and Confederates died of disease in roughly the same percentages, Rebel soldiers contended with poor diets, a lack of clothing, and severe shortages of medical supplies. The combination of these elements unquestionably played a major role in the high death rate due to disease. Union armies did not suffer from the same deficiencies.

31. Endsmt. by Lt. Col. W. H. Thurston, Nov. 1, 1864, to IR of USCT commanded by Brig. Gen. D. Ullmann at Morganzia, La. by Maj. Geo. Baldy, Oct. 9, 1864, box 8, Inspection Reports, 1864, Louisiana, Letters Received, Inspector General's Office, 1863–76, RG 159.

32. Endsmt. of Col. Jas. A. Hardie, Sept. 29, 1865, to IR of Medical Dept. of the Dept. of Mississippi by Col. R. B. Marcy, May 1865, box 9, Letters Received, Inspector General's Office, 1863–76, RG 159; Endsmt. of Surg. Gen. Barnes, Oct. 6, 1864, to IR of Medical Dept. of Arkansas by Col. R. B. Marcy, Aug. 15, 1864, box 4, ibid. Also see Inspection Reports of Medical Dept. for the Dept. of Arkansas by Col. R. B. Marcy, Aug. 15, 1864, box 8, Letters Received, Inspector General's Office, 1863–76, RG 159; Inspection Reports of Dept. of Arkansas by Col. D. B. Sackett, Jan. 13, 1865, box 10, ibid.; and Inspection Reports of Troops at District of Vicksburg by Capt. S. Bostwick, Aug. 20, 1864, box 10, Inspection Reports, 1864, LA-MS, RG 159.

The Atlanta Campaign and the African American Experience in Civil War Georgia

CLARENCE L. MOHR

DURING THE PAST GENERATION KNOWLEDGE OF BLACK LIFE before and after emancipation has grown exponentially. One result has been a reconceptualization of the Civil War as not simply a military struggle with civilian consequences but as a key transitional episode in the story of American race relations—a final chapter in the tragedy of bondage and an opening scene in the drama of freedom. For students of black history, the Atlanta campaign partakes of the dualism inherent in the larger war experience.

Although blacks were conspicuous by their absence in the early weeks of the Atlanta campaign, Maj. Gen. William T. Sherman's invasion had a profound effect on Georgia slavery. Coming relatively late in the war, Sherman's thrust southward from Tennessee supplied external pressure that accelerated the ongoing collapse of the slave system's internal mechanisms of stability and control. In northwestern Georgia during May and June 1864, just as along the coast some two years earlier, Yankee invaders prompted slaveowners to flee in panic with their human property.[1] Approaching armies brought near chaos to already unstable conditions in Atlanta by creating emergency demands for black labor to build fortifications, to work in weapons factories and hospitals, or to provide direct logistical support for the Confederate and Union armies. At the same time, Sherman's advance created a steadily growing area of free territory in northwest Georgia, where hundreds of blacks experienced their first taste of life beyond the reach of southern whites. The liberty available behind Yankee lines was precarious to be sure, tainted by the antiblack prejudice of Sherman and his men, and often short lived once Confederates regained control of invaded areas. But it was freedom nonetheless, and it added to the repudiation of the old regime that had begun with massive black flight to the Sea Islands after the appearance of Union warships off Georgia's coast early in 1862.

The slave system that Sherman's troops encountered in 1864 had been transformed and significantly weakened by the combined effect of refugee life, urban and industrial expansion, white military conscription, and the hiring or impressment of slaves for military labor. All of these processes, operating more or less simultaneously, helped erode structures of traditional authority in plantation society by disrupting black family life and diluting the paternalistic content of master-slave relations. Indeed, in their push toward Atlanta, Sherman's soldiers triggered what was often the second phase of a process of forced removal that had begun in 1862–63, when northwest Georgia became a major destination for slaves withdrawn by their owners from exposed areas of the Georgia coast.[2] Although precise estimates are impossible, it is clear that many hundreds—and probably several thousand—refugee slaves spent lengthy periods in the counties north and west of Atlanta, where they were employed in subsistence agriculture; coal, iron, and niter mining; in war industries such as Mark A. Cooper's Etowah Iron Works near Cartersville; and as employees in the extensive hospital system established for the Confederate Army of Tennessee. Partial records show that during 1863, Medical Director Samuel H. Stout employed some 384 slaves in nineteen of the twenty-nine hospitals located between Catoosa Springs and Atlanta, along the line of the Western and Atlantic Railroad. Slaves represented nearly half of all hospital workers and some 80 percent of the hired employees. All of these facilities and their black workers would be moved repeatedly in 1864—first to Atlanta, then to Macon, Columbus, and on into Alabama and Mississippi.[3]

Extractive industries absorbed a considerable number of refugee slaves. Niter, or saltpeter, a basic component of gunpowder, was mined in natural limestone caves throughout north Georgia, and by mid-1862 some sixty-six slaves were at work digging four hundred pounds of niter per day from caves in Bartow County alone. But their efforts ceased with Sherman's approach in 1864. The war also provided a major stimulus to Georgia's fledgling iron industry, which assumed new importance after major iron-producing regions of Tennessee and the border states fell into Union hands. Before the Atlanta campaign interrupted mining and smelting operations, at least three of the state's six antebellum iron makers had reactivated or expanded blast furnaces in Bartow County, and four new companies had begun operations in Dade County or adjacent areas.

Typical of the new ventures in its scale of operations was the Empire State Coal and Iron Mining Company, which purchased extensive holdings in the Wills Valley section of Dade County and sought to hire three hundred slaves in January 1863 to amass stockpiles of iron ore, limestone, charcoal, and other materials necessary for blast furnace operations. In August 1863 the firm's slaves were hastily evacuated to Macon when Union forces entered north Georgia prior to the battle of Chickamauga. A similar fate awaited slaves hired in January 1864 by the Bartow Iron Works on the condition that they would be sent southward if Yankee troops approached. By late February 1864 Union scouts reported that "most all the planters in Floyd, Polk, and Paulding Counties . . . have moved their stock, negroes, and valuables south."[4] Most did so, but not all. Near Cartersville, for example, a group of slaves belonging to an Alabaman were virtually abandoned when the owner's son, a Confederate soldier, appeared briefly to advise them that northern troops would soon reach the area. "I could give no advice other than to tell them to take care of themselves the best they could," the young Rebel later recalled.[5]

Many black refugees left north Georgia farms to face a life of considerable hardship in southwestern areas of the state, which had long since exhausted their capacity to absorb displaced planters. The experiences of slaves owned by Edward Harden, a small planter in Whitfield County, illustrate the abrupt manner in which many bondsmen were thrust into a new environment. Before abandoning his north Georgia home in the fall of 1863, Harden sold some slaves, including a valuable man known as "Big Henry," who was parted from his wife, Laura, and their child, "Little Henry." Upon arriving near the town of Cuthbert in Randolph County, Harden took steps to relieve himself of the financial burden that a large force of unemployed blacks would have entailed, making clear as he did so that paternalistic obligations took second place to securing an optimal return on his investment in human capital. "I have hired Ed at the depot here for $250 a year to be fed and clothed," he reported. "Mary with the Professor at the Baptist College . . . at $30 per month and clothes—Cloe is hired to a clever gentleman at the same [rate] all payable monthly. I have not yet hired out Joel. Laura will have to do our cooking and washing; she and little Henry are all that we intend to keep at home except Cloe's two children."[6]

In terms of physical welfare, Harden's slaves may have faired reasonably well. But many others made the southward trek away from Sherman's advance only to face conditions of extreme privation. Writing to Georgia governor Joseph E. Brown in October 1864, a refugee from Cobb County described the

Valdosta region as being thronged with black and white refugees facing serious food shortages. Confederate policy was partly to blame. Desperate to feed what remained of the Army of Tennessee, Confederate impressing officers and tax-in-kind agents seized food from local farmers that might otherwise have been sold locally. But the government refused to aid displaced civilians by hiring refugee slaves to gather provisions in return for a portion of the food collected.[7] Harden employed blunt language to describe a similar situation in Randolph County. "We are nearly starving here," he reported in the summer of 1864, adding, "Everybody is bonded to furnish the Gov[ernmen]t all their supplies. God only knows what is to become of us all."[8]

In modern wars the displacement of civilians has come to be taken more or less for granted as a temporary phenomenon requiring the attention of relief agencies operating across national borders. What Georgians of the 1860s referred to as "refugeeing" involved change of a more fundamental nature. For slaves as well as masters, flight from the Yankees introduced a new element of uncertainty into black-white relations. If paternalism was the first casualty of refugee life, geographic isolation and the cyclical rhythm of plantation routine also fell victim to exigencies of forced removal. Just as important, refugeeing struck a heavy blow at the myth of southern white invincibility. The belief that whites were in control of life as actual or potential wielders of ultimate power—that they were in the most basic sense "masters"—had been a key factor in preserving the equilibrium of day-to-day life under slavery. Throughout the war, however, every hostile incursion by Union forces produced scenes of pandemonium among Georgia slaveowners. Bondsmen who participated in panicked evacuations or who witnessed the spectacle from the sidelines could hardly continue to look upon masters as omnipotent authority figures.

The personal authority of masters came under especially heavy stress in Atlanta, where crowded living conditions; explosive wartime population growth, with its resulting anonymity for newcomers; third party supervision of slaves by police or employers; the presence of an active Unionist fifth column; and by mid-1864 the incessant boom of Yankee cannons all combined to render black loyalties fluid and uncertain. During the course of the war, Atlanta's population probably exceeded 20,000, more than twice the figure for 1860, and the 2,523 slaves and 11 free blacks enumerated by the city tax collector in November 1863 almost certainly understated the actual size of the black population.[9] During the two years preceding Sherman's arrival, the city had become known as a major refugee center and the state's most congested metropolis, with arrangements for self-hire and unsupervised living by slaves accepted as a fact of life.

Atlanta's twenty-man police force provided only sporadic oversight of black residents, and the city's Confederate garrison offered more obstruction than assistance to local authorities, who were often at odds with the post's quarrelsome commander, Maj. George W. Lee.[10] The degree to which the pass system and other traditional mechanisms of urban-slave policing had faltered under wartime pressure became evident in March 1863, when the Atlanta City Council instructed the mayor to give public notice that "passes to slaves from the military authorities alone is [*sic*] not sufficient to escape such slaves being arrested by the city policemen after nine o'clock at night." In August 1863 the council drafted a new ordinance providing that "all negroes (unless they be body servants) who come into our city to stay over night or any length of time and [are] not on special business shall be kept in some negro yard or house, and not permitted to go at large through the city."[11]

Some of the best firsthand testimony about black life in wartime Atlanta comes from the pen of Cyrena Stone, a Vermont native who moved to the city in 1854 and remained there throughout the war, concealing her pro-North sympathies and rendering covert aid to the Union cause. Her diary records the ebb and flow of wartime emotions among whites and blacks and attests to the fact that while control mechanisms grew weaker during the war, slaves remained under intense surveillance. During and immediately after the secession crisis, many white Atlantans succumbed to panic over reports of slave revolts. "[T]he fear was universal, that there would be 'risings' and 'insurrections' without number," Stone recalled. In time the panic subsided only to flare up again in the wake of the Emancipation Proclamation of January 1863. Stone believed that blacks as a race were naturally submissive. But she also recognized that organized resistance to white authority would be an exceedingly difficult matter. In January 1864 she reported, "If negroes are found out after nine o'clock in the evening, even with passes from their owners, they are carried off to the 'Caliboose.'" City authorities also tried to suppress slaves' "social pleasuring—and long before their church was taken for a hospital, no meetings were held without a force of policemen being present."[12]

Stone was convinced that virtually all Atlanta slaves knew of the Emancipation Proclamation and understood its meaning. Certainly by early 1864 talk of freedom was in the air, not only among slaves but also in the badly outnumbered Army of Tennessee. Still reeling from the sixteen thousand southern casualties suffered a few months earlier at Chickamauga, in January 1864 a group of respected Confederate officers met near Dalton, Georgia, where Maj. Gen. Patrick R. Cleburne unveiled a detailed proposal for the immediate enlistment and training of "a large reserve of the most courageous of our slaves" who, together with all other bondsmen remaining faithful to the South, would be guaranteed freedom at the end of the war. Despite initial attempts to suppress the document, Cleburne's proposal marked the beginning of a public debate that would later be called the "fullest and freest discussion of slavery in which the South as a whole ever engaged."[13]

Atlanta blacks took an active interest in the Confederate slavery debate. Cyrena Stone reported that the prospect of being armed to repel a Yankee invasion "amuses them [the slaves] exceedingly." She cited the example of a black "waiting man" who declared "Missus, they better keep them guns out of our folks hands—cause they dun'no *which way we going to shoot!*" As the Union army approached the city, some slaves expressed concern that they would be removed out of freedom's reach. When the owner of a hired slave appeared unexpectedly one morning at the Stone residence, Dan, the slave in question, told Cyrena, "I just expect he has come to take me away, because the Yankees are so near." The master eventually left, though only after shaking hands with his bondsman and expressing the hope that they would meet again when the war was over. Afterward Dan entered the Stone house "half laughing, and half crying. 'He didn't take me off with him did he!'" Dan declared, adding, "I felt mighty bad to part for good with Mas' George, for him & me was raised together." Thoughtful Atlanta whites agreed that black loyalties were conditional at best. A local southern woman concluded that only "a grand faith in their final freedom" had given slaves the patience "to wait and see what this war would do for them." Mrs. Stone agreed, noting that efforts at strict policing of black Atlantans could easily backfire, "for there is no surer way to convince them that the whole thing [slavery] is wrong, and a consciousness of power is thus forced upon them—should they choose to use it."[14]

Although the war ended without meaningful efforts to raise black battalions for the southern combat service, many of the slaves in wartime Atlanta were employed by the army or by civilians engaged in war production. Military hospitals for the Army of Tennessee were concentrated in the city until June 1864, and as the Atlanta campaign progressed, hired slaves replaced civilians and soldiers initially detailed to perform routine hospital labor. Detailed statistics from two facilities illustrate patterns that prevailed at other medical units across the city. At both the Receiving and Distributing Hospital and the larger Fairgrounds Hospital No. 1, black employment rose steadily throughout the first half of 1864. A 90 percent increase in black employment at the former raised the proportion of slave attendants from 26 percent to 60 percent, while a 57 percent increase at the latter resulted in a workforce that was 73 percent black. As early as the summer and fall of 1863, some 177 slaves were employed in seven Atlanta hospitals, a figure that undoubtedly tripled or quadrupled as the number of hospitals and the proportion of black workers increased during 1864.[15] Whatever their precise numbers, the vast majority of Atlanta's black hospital attendants labored at one of three basic occupations: cooking, laundry work, or nursing. The first two tasks fell to slaves from the outset, and by 1864 blacks had replaced most of the soldiers previously detailed as hospital nurses. Laundry workers were almost exclusively black women, while cooks might be male or female. Nursing, which involved physically strenuous chores such as cleaning wards, shaking out bed ticks, and lifting patients, was an overwhelmingly male occupation. Some Georgia hospitals designated adult black nurses "wardboys" and apparently gave them more menial tasks than those assigned to white nurses. (A further blurring of occupational lines was apparent at Tunnel Hill Hospital, where the chief surgeon felt "obliged to require nurses to perform laundry duty—that is, negro women who aid in cleaning the wards are also required to wash.")[16]

By the time of the Atlanta campaign, the city had assumed a dual importance as a symbol of Confederate resistance and as a center of military transportation and supply. Determined to hold the city at all costs, Confederate authorities began work in mid-1863 on an elaborate system of defenses, the outer lines of which stretched some seven miles by year's end. Thousands of plantation slaves hired or impressed from nearby counties with the aid of local sheriffs continued to labor on the fortifications through the spring of 1864, living in temporary barracks and being fed and clothed at government expense. The blacks' daily regimen of clearing hillsides of brush and trees, digging trenches, constructing redoubts, and moving a vast tonnage of red-clay soil for earthworks of all descriptions resulted in an imposing system of defenses that was compared to those erected at the besieged city of Sebastopol during the Crimean War a decade earlier.[17]

By transferring plantation slaves directly into nonagricultural jobs, fortification labor placed additional stress on the stability of rural bondage. The typical bondsman who worked on Atlanta's military defenses was not an urban or industrial slave, but rather an unskilled adult male field hand impressed from an interior agricultural district. Quite often his stint as a military laborer involved separation from family members and exposure to living conditions that were unappealing even by the standards of slavery. Like refugeeing, fortification work meant an end to the plantation's cultural insularity and physical isolation. When assembled by the hundreds or thousands to help fortify strategic points like Atlanta, black military laborers mingled with slaves and free blacks from all parts of Georgia, exchanging information and forming firsthand impressions about the meaning and progress of the war.

Confederate labor policies ensured that the ramifications of such experiences would extend well beyond the slaves immediately involved. In contrast to other types of nonagricultural employment, fortification building was nearly always a short-term temporary assignment for blacks. Within a few weeks or months, a given project was usually finished or else fresh squads of slaves were brought in to continue the work. In the ongoing labor exchange dictated by impressment schedules, black workers became the living links connecting front-line areas with remote plantations. The frequent labor drafts imposed on central and southwestern Georgia left few plantations untouched and kept many slave compounds in regular contact with the outside world. Masters generally considered the repeated coming and going of black military laborers to be an unsettling process even when it posed no direct challenge to white authority. In the minds of many planters, eagerness to regain possession of valuable slave property was tempered by a brooding suspicion that impressed bondsmen would return to "demoralize" blacks who had remained at home.[18]

Whatever its effect on slavery's peacetime structure, the mobilization of black labor continued throughout the Atlanta campaign. Facing a Federal force twice the size of his own army, Gen. Joseph E. Johnston sought black workers to replace white soldiers detailed as company cooks, pioneers, and laborers for engineer battalions. In April 1864 local slaves were employed to strengthen the defenses of Rome, where many would soon return as recruits to the Federal army.[19] As Johnston's outnumbered forces crossed the Etowah River and fell back toward Kennesaw Mountain, black labor was indispensable for the rapid preparation of defensive lines into which hard-pressed Confederates could retreat. Although white soldiers became expert at open-field entrenchment in close proximity to the Yankee foe, more elaborate earthworks and fortifications required advance preparation by engineer units using slave workers.

In the absence of detailed records, one must settle for individual glimpses of a process that was repeated many times during the Army of Tennessee's long retreat. On June 22, 1864, a reconnaissance officer from the 136th New York Infantry reported that Confederates were working feverishly to close a gap in their defenses near Kennesaw. Most of the labor was supplied by "a large gang of negroes at work with axes and spades." Union scouts "heard the order, 'This way with your axes,' 'This way with your spades,' and the entrenching party were singing *en masse* at times."[20] One of the more detailed accounts of black contributions to Confederate defenses during the Atlanta campaign was provided long after the war by Brig. Gen. Francis A. Shoup, Johnston's chief of artillery in the Army of Tennessee and a principal engineering officer during the long retreat from Dalton to Atlanta. In mid-June 1864, recognizing the likelihood that both Marietta and Kennesaw Mountain would soon be abandoned to the enemy, Shoup received permission to fortify the west bank of the Chattahoochee River with a line of log redoubts standing twelve feet high with walls of a similar thickness, largely impregnable to direct attack, and each capable of being defended by a company of eighty men. Stretching some four miles along the Chattahoochee above and below the railroad bridge to Atlanta, the "Shoupades," as they were soon called, were intended to allow Johnston to concentrate his entire army in the hope of gaining a momentary advantage over some portion of Sherman's larger force. Placed eighty yards apart and connected by a ten-foot-high log stockade, the redoubts were protected by crossfire from small arms and heavy cannon and furnished with "[h]and grenades, fire balls, [and] all sorts of contrivances for repelling assault."[21]

The Chattahoochee defenses, plus additional entrenchments farther downriver, were completed within two weeks by a force of approximately one thousand slaves. Special agents traveled down all major railroad lines impressing slaves from local planters and sending them to Atlanta in gangs with tools and provisions. As Shoup later recalled: "This sort of work was well understood by the negroes accustomed to build[ing] log cabins, so that the construction went on with great rapidity. Timber was plentiful and immediately at hand. The line sprung into existence as if by magic." Much to the general's dismay, however, the works were abandoned without a fight on July 9, when Johnston moved his army to the east bank of the river. In the course of the retreat, the slave force was allowed to disperse, and subsequent efforts to strengthen Atlanta's defenses were abandoned when Shoup was unable to secure authority from either the Confederacy or from Governor Brown to impress additional black workers.[22] The next major draft of slave labor was made in August 1864, when Johnson's successor, Gen. John Bell Hood, dispatched quartermaster officers into counties along all major railroad lines in central and southwestern Georgia. The men were under orders to obtain two thousand slave teamsters for immediate service with the army. Reluctant masters were advised to furnish bondsmen promptly if they wished to avoid the impressment, "which the officers are authorized to make, and will make if necessary."[23]

Blacks also served as pioneers in Sherman's armies, though some dispute exists concerning the actual number of ex-slaves involved. In his memoirs Sherman describes the rifle-trench parapets constructed by both armies in the field and states categorically, "I endeavored to spare the soldiers this hard labor by authorizing each division commander to organize out of the freedmen who escaped to us a pioneer corps of two hundred men who were fed out of the regular army supplies, and I promised them ten dollars a month under an existing act of Congress. These pioneer detachments became very useful to us . . . for they could work at night while our men slept." In reality the situation was never so simple or clear cut. From the time he took charge in Memphis in 1862, Sherman had employed thousands of escaped slaves on various labor projects, housing and feeding them from army rations and, initially, paying them one pound of chewing tobacco per month in lieu of wages.[24]

During the Atlanta campaign, as historian Philip Shiman has noted, arrangements for pioneer labor varied widely, with organization into companies, brigades, or battalions being employed at various times by the Army of the Cumberland, the Army of the Tennessee, and the Army of the Ohio. Existing records suggest that some four thousand to five thousand men served as engineers and pioneers during the push toward Atlanta; around a thousand or more were black. The presence of black pioneers, including perhaps some who had recently helped fortify Confederate lines, was confirmed by no less an authority than General Shoup, who reported on August 23, 1864 that "the enemy have employed a strong force of negroes to fortify Kennesaw Mountain and strengthen the works around Marietta." Barely two months earlier Union observers could have applied identical language to Shoup's efforts.[25]

Writing from the immediate vicinity of Kennesaw Mountain on June 26, Sherman advised Adj. Gen. Lorenzo Thomas that "we find gangs of negro laborers well organized on the Mississippi [now working] at Nashville and along the railroads most useful, and I have used them with great success as pioneer companies attached to divisions." These comments, which were made within the context of Sherman's ongoing struggle to prevent or delay the enlistment of ex-slaves as Union soldiers, might easily obscure the true nature of the general's racial attitudes. A reluctant liberator at best, Sherman was determined that the forces under his command would remain all white, and he believed that "black troops should, for some years be used with caution and with due regard for the prejudice of the races." His position had been a matter of controversy since June 3, when Sherman had issued Special Field Order No. 16, forbidding recruiting officers to enlist blacks who were employed by the army in any capacity.[26]

In private correspondence Sherman made no effort to conceal his contempt for blacks or to disguise the racialist dogma behind his opposition to using them as soldiers. Phrases such as "niggers and vagabonds," "niggers and bought recruits," and "niggers and the refuse of the south," fill his letters to his wife, Ellen, and to various personal friends. Dismissing blacks as the "kind of trash that will merely fill our hospitals and keep well to the rear," Sherman deplored the supposed fact that white soldiers would become laborers "whilst the nigger parades and reclines in some remote & soft place."[27] To a considerable extent his racial attitudes resembled those of the men under his command—battle-hardened western troops who despised abolitionists as much as aristocratic planters and who viewed black people through a lens heavily tinted by color prejudice and group stereotype.

Something of the tone and texture of race prejudice among Sherman's troops is revealed by a letter from Charles R. Pratt, a black soldier assigned to duty with the 11th Regiment, Ohio Volunteer Infantry. Writing from the vicinity of Atlanta on August 3, Pratt held out no hope for a policy of multiracialism in the western theater. "I am a colored man, " he explained, "and my position as a private in a white regiment is very unpleasant. My feelings are constantly outraged by the conduct of those who have no respect for my race." He sought and subsequently obtained a transfer to the all-black 55th Massachusetts Colored Infantry. When Union forces entered Marietta in July, a Federal soldier "cursed the 'damned nigger' and said he would like to kill the whole race." On another occasion northern troops declared that "they hated the negro race, and [that] they would as quickly shoot a negro as a dog." One Yankee veteran expressed a willingness that "the war should continue for 7 years longer if only to kill the negroes off." Racist attitudes among Sherman's troops increased the likelihood that both slaves and free blacks would be treated unjustly. In Marietta enlisted men deprived an elderly female house servant of "all her provisions and clothing, even her needles and thread, leaving her nothing but the clothing she had on."[28]

And yet despite numerous acts of cruelty and callousness toward ex-slaves committed by northern soldiers, personal contact led some Yankees to reflect, at least momentarily, upon the larger meaning of a war that allowed black people to affirm their freedom and their humanity in public for the first time. Thomas Hart Benton McCain of the 86th Indiana Volunteer Infantry recorded one such episode while encamped near Calhoun in Gordon County on May 17, 1864. "But few slaves are to be seen along our march," McCain noted. "Came across one or two today. One old slave I was particularly amused at. He was standing by the roadside shouting at the top of his voice, thanking God that the Yankees had at last come and that he was now a free man." Upon further consideration McCain's initial amusement gave way to a more serious and sober reaction. "The scene was indeed affecting as the tears trickled down his cheeks while he implored the blessing of God upon the Yankees," the Indiana soldier concluded.[29]

Similar moments of epiphany took place in late July and early August as Sherman dispatched cavalry units on daring raids to cut Atlanta's rail links with the outside world. The raids took northern horsemen east and south of Atlanta into the "finest and best country" they had seen in Georgia, a rich agricultural heartland of "fine plantations, [and] large mansions, everything indicating wealth and prosperity."[30] Here the state's agricultural economy was intact, and encounters with slaves occurred frequently. East of Atlanta near Lawrenceville, a Michigan trooper in Brig. Gen. Kenner D. Garrard's command commented on the reaction of his comrades to the dozens of runaway slaves—all "intelligent looking people"—who appeared after the soldiers had halted for the night. There were few if any abolitionists in the Union ranks, and the Michigan writer was especially struck by the reactions of those in his brigade "who had been most against the freedom of the slave." Garrard stated: "The impulse to help the helpless was too much for Yanks, and [in] spite of principles they divided their rations [with the black fugitives,] and it seemed as though they could not do enough to make them comfortable. If a person wants to become fixed against slavery, he wants to go on a raid into slave lands. These same negroes tell us they had been made to believe that the Yanks killed all the niggers. But they preferred death by Yanks than longer to live with their cruel masters, in slavery. Is not that enough of an argument against slavery, when the slave prefers to go where he has been made to believe he will meet certain death, [rather than] to longer remain in bondage?"[31]

Even as Garrard's men were discovering slavery's human face, bands of mounted black fugitives were beginning to follow Maj. Gen. George Stoneman's cavalry, determined to accompany the blue-clad soldiers and "fight 'de white trash.'" As Stoneman turned north after abandoning efforts to liberate Unions prisoners at Macon and Andersonville, some five thousand slaves followed in his wake. "You could see them . . . , their eyes shining in a most wonderful manner," wrote Lt. Richard E. Huffman of the 1st Kentucky Cavalry (U.S.).[32]

A short time later Stoneman clashed with Rebel forces at Sunshine Church and was forced to surrender more than four hundred of his men. Hundreds of other Yankee horsemen fled into the unfamiliar Georgia countryside, where labor impressment and the emergency mobilization of state militia forces had stripped local plantations of nearly all male adults, black and white. Desperate to avoid capture by Confederate forces or local home guard units, the northern horsemen relied upon courageous slave women to point the way back toward Atlanta. The roles of captive and deliverer were temporarily reversed as black women accompanied the cavalrymen of the 8th Michigan on foot for some distance as they made their way across middle Georgia without maps on a moonless night. Capt. James Wells described a typical incident:

> At a rugged crossing in a deep forest where all were compelled to dismount and lead, two young colored women with red turbaned handkerchiefs around their heads and carrying torches (our guides for a long distance) stood on the banks of the stream and lighted the command across. The varying and uncertain glare of the burning pine knots cast weird shadows into the waters below, and over men and horses as they plunged down the banks; while the forest, lighted up but a few yards overhead and beyond, soon shaded off into impenetrable darkness. There was just enough light to reveal the desperate earnestness depicted on the faces of these slave girls (with flashing eyes darker than the night itself) who had entered upon this task that might prove death or torture to them.[33]

Such a passage, for all its seeming melodrama, leaves little doubt that face-to-face contact with black Georgians prompted at least some of Sherman's soldiers to look past racial stereotypes and recognize the war's larger moral meaning.

In the end ex-slaves were destined to join Federal forces despite Sherman's opposition. All told, more than 3,500 black Georgians served in the Union army and navy before hostilities ended in 1865.[34] Slaves from coastal counties accounted for most of the recruits, but bondsmen from the interior also joined the ranks in growing numbers during the last eighteen months of the war. Enlistments began in Tennessee among the handful of Georgia fugitives who reached Chattanooga in time to be mustered into the newly created 44th U.S. Colored Infantry (USCI) early in 1864.[35] For several months, however, the number of black soldiers obtained in northern Georgia remained small. Prior to the Atlanta campaign, miles of rugged terrain together with a large Confederate army and an alert populace of white civilians stood between bondsmen and free territory. Under the circumstances few blacks struck out for Yankee lines, and fewer still arrived at their intended destination.

Slaves who decided to make a bid for liberty recognized the futility of fleeing in conspicuous and slow-moving family groups. When collective escape efforts occurred, the participants were most likely to be young, robust men who could travel rapidly and withstand severe physical hardship. In March 1864 a Floyd County woman recorded the details of a fairly typical runaway episode involving five slaves owned by two different masters: "On last saturday night 3 of Mr. Frankses negroes went off, each one of them taking a mule with him. they are supposed to have started to the Yankees. Tom is the only one . . . left at home. . . . 2 of Richard Gainses [slaves]—Will & Finn are also gone. they left on saturday night too, takeing a horse a piece; they are all supposed to have gone togather. Gaines [slaves] succeeded in getting 4 pieces of meat from his smokehouse to take with them."[36] The owners pursued their human property diligently, and by April 3 two of the fugitives had been incarcerated at Dalton, suffering from the effects of prolonged exposure and severe frostbite. One of the prisoners subsequently died from the ordeal, while the search for the remaining escapees continued.

Unlike their coastal counterparts, upcountry runaways needed food, horses, and a calculated willingness to gamble against long odds if they hoped to make good on early escape plans. During the spring and summer of 1864, however, the picture changed markedly as Union forces took control of most counties north and west of Atlanta. Throughout the occupied regions chattel bondage officially ceased to exist, but the speed and finality of emancipation varied. Liberty sometimes came swiftly and forced blacks to make fundamental choices about the future with minimum deliberation. After southern troops withdrew from Rome, Georgia, in mid-May, for example, Federal occupation forces allowed all civilians a period of free movement into or out of Union lines. Departing slaveowners were forbidden to interfere while their bondsmen decided what course to pursue. Many blacks chose to stay behind Union lines, but to the Yankees' surprise, and occasional disgust, not all African Americans made the same choice. One slave who elected to accompany his master was "cursed for a fool, and then told to go away, but never to look to them [the Federals] again for help or succor."[37]

In reality the alternatives presented to black Georgians at the moment of northern conquest were often more complex than outsiders realized. A bondsman's hatred of slavery might be strong, but the prospect of forfeiting material possessions on a distant plantation or of losing touch indefinitely with family members still in Confederate territory represented a form of silent coercion that Federal soldiers were powerless to prevent. Equally troubling to newly liberated blacks was the widespread uncertainty over what fate awaited them at the hands of white northerners. On the latter point the Union army's labor policies were hardly reassuring. Blacks who became nominal employees in Sherman's pioneer companies or in other military support capacities were apt to notice little immediate difference between slavery and free labor. The experiences of four black women who worked as laundresses in field hospitals attached to the Army of the Cumberland tell a tale of blatant official indifference to fraud and exploitation. The women—Anna and Laura Irwin, Rhoda Wills, and Milly Humphries—"commenced work at Rasacca Geo. in the month of April 1864." As recounted by one of their number:

> [We] remained there about two months—then went to Big Shanty. Stopped there four days—went to Cartersville [and] stayed there four days—then went to Marietta [and] stayed there about three weeks—then went to Vining station [and] stayed there about two months. then went to Atlanta & stayed there about two months. then came to Chattanooga Tenn. All the time under the charge of surgeon Woodruff. When we came to Chattanooga we were turned over to surgeon E. L. Bissell. then went to Huntsville AL. left there on Christmas day 1864, then went to Bulls Gap Tenn [and] remained there one month. then went to Nashvill where we remained until we were mustered out—was to recieve $5.00 pr week. . . . Stewart Johnson & John Hardenberg took the money and made away.[38]

Numerous witnesses testified to the callous nature of Sherman's policies concerning black labor, but no one was more forthright than the general himself. In a widely published letter dated July 30, 1864, Sherman criticized Congress for authorizing the enlistment of black troops. "I prefer some negroes as pioneers, teamsters, cooks, and servants, others gradually to experiment in the art of the soldier," he explained. In private his language was less measured. "I care not a straw for the nigger," he declared on August 10. "Let us capture negroes, of course, and use them to the best advantage," though not in roles that would raise the specter of racial equality. "I like niggers well enough as niggers, but when fools & idiots try & make niggers better than ourselves I have an opinion," he wrote a short time later.[39]

On the latter point the actions of Sherman's men spoke even louder than their leader's words. During the Federal occupation of Atlanta, Sherman implemented a Confederate-style pass system in which all blacks employed as officers' servants were required to carry papers indicating age, height, complexion, and color of hair and eyes. Whenever away from the quarters of their "master or employer," black servants were further required to "have a pass issued and approved by the Corps Provost Marshal." On October 3 Atlanta's post commander was ordered to "seize every negro that may be found in this city without proper authority . . . and put them to work on the fortifications."[40] A few days later another officer complained that there were "a great number of negroes about Atlanta and following the Army who are of no service to the Government." He urged provost marshals to show "proper vigilance" in their efforts to "rid the Army of these 'lazy loungers' and put them to work." Nearly four months earlier Adjutant General Thomas put the matter succinctly when he predicted that black workers secured during the Atlanta campaign would be kept "at hard labor—in many instances greater than they were subjected to by their former owners."[41]

Throughout the Atlanta campaign Sherman excluded African American troops from his own army and effectively stymied most efforts by recruiters operating in his rear to enlist ex-slaves for service in units that would be credited to the quotas of various northern states.[42] Eventually, however, the enrollment of black soldiers began in occupied areas of northwestern Georgia under authority granted to Col. Ruben D. Mussey, the Nashville-based commissioner for the organization of U.S. Colored Troops in the Department of the Cumberland.[43] Most activity took place between July and September 1864, when the 44th USCI was stationed in Rome for recruiting purposes. Using methods perfected the previous year in Tennessee, the regiment sent racially mixed scouting parties into the countryside on a regular basis, offering protection and assistance to any residents who wished to enter Union lines. A local woman described one such evacuation in the Texas Valley section of Floyd County in early September. From her vantage point as a loyal southerner, the departure scene appeared little short of scandalous: "They had a train of 17 wagons & an escort of between 150–200—I don't know what to call them, though part of them was black and others white, but to say the least of them I guess they have black hearts."[44]

By late summer the 44th USCI contained some eight hundred enlisted men, approximately three-fourths of whom were doing garrison duty in Dalton on the morning of October 13 when advance units of the forty-thousand-man Army of Tennessee converged unexpectedly upon the little village, cutting off all avenues of retreat. Initial skirmishing between black troops and Rebels left several Confederates dead and their comrades "over anxious to move upon the 'niggers.'" Impatient to resume his northward advance, Gen. John Bell Hood demanded that the black garrison surrender immediately or face annihilation. Hood vowed to take no prisoners if the Federal defenses were carried by assault and later added that he "could not restrain his men and would not if he could."[45]

Although the black soldiers displayed the "greatest anxiety to fight," their white commander, Col. Lewis Johnson, surrendered to Hood around 4:00 p.m. and was released two days later after securing paroles for himself and the 150 or so other white troops attached to the garrison. A considerably harsher fate awaited the regiment's 600 African American enlisted men, many of whom were native Georgians only a few months out of slavery.[46] All were immediately stripped of their shoes and ordered to begin destroying a nearby section of the Western and Atlantic Railroad. At least six black prisoners were shot for refusing to obey commands or failing to keep pace with the line of march. Near the hamlet of Villanow on October 14, an unspecified number of freedmen were "returned to their former masters," but most of the ex-slaves remained in military custody and were sent to work on fortification projects in Alabama and Mississippi. Several hundred of them escaped en route, but many others ended the war as prisoners in Columbus and Griffin, Georgia, where they were released in May 1865 in a "sick, broken down, naked, and starved" condition. Fearful of reprisals from embittered Confederates, the black veterans concealed their connection with the Union cause.[47]

In retrospect the fate of the 44th USCI seems emblematic of the on-again, off-again nature of Yankee attitudes toward black equality. Occasionally during the Atlanta campaign, General Sherman paid lip service to the need to protect black families, but then, as later, his actions belied his rhetoric. During five months of Union occupation, Rome became a rendezvous for African American refugees of all ages and sexes, including the spouses and children of many black soldiers. In June 1864 about three hundred Georgia freedpeople were transported from Rome to Pulaski, Tennessee. The evacuees consisted mainly of women and children, half of whom were estimated to be under twelve years of age. But such sanctuary as Rome provided was tenuous at best. A few months later, as Sherman prepared to leave Atlanta on his celebrated March to the Sea, black women, children, and elderly men became excess baggage to be abandoned as military circumstances dictated. In at least one instance, ex-slaves who tried to follow the Union forces on foot from Rome to Kingston succumbed to fatigue and exhaustion and eventually returned to their former owners.[48]

In Rome and northwestern Georgia, no less than in central and south Georgia during the latter phase of Sherman's march, blacks who had looked to the Union army for protection often faced bitter disillusionment. Postwar testimony suggests that official indifference, racial prejudice, and military necessity often combined to produce a pattern of stark economic predation when Union troops encountered blacks with personal property. During the early and mid-1870s, at least seventeen black residents of Atlanta and northwestern Georgia (the actual total is probably larger) filed claims seeking compensation for property seized by Sherman's men. Most of the claimants were ex-slaves, and nearly all the property was lost during the occupation of Atlanta and the subsequent redeployment triggered by Hood's desperate northward thrust into Tennessee. Papers filed with the Southern Claims Commission tell a fascinating story of a robust "secondary economy" in which free-black artisans plied skilled trades and bondsmen were permitted to cultivate land, acquire livestock, or engage in small-scale commerce in order to improve their meager standard of living or save money toward purchasing freedom for themselves or their relatives.

Such considerations, so central to the lives of individual African Americans in antebellum Georgia, counted for nothing with Sherman's foragers, who went about their work with a systematic zeal. Lewis Richardson, a slave whose master had "relinquished all control" in July 1864, cultivated fifty acres of land near Dalton, making a crop on shares. In November the Yankees took his entire production of corn, fodder, and potatoes. Albert Berrien, a Floyd County slave, was allowed by his master to cultivate a small farm near Rome during the spring of 1864. When Sherman's forces passed through in September, he lost crops and livestock, a wagon, provisions, and even his wooden fence rails. Allen Witcher, another Floyd County slave, had hired his time before the war and purchased seven hogs, which the Yankees seized in November. A similar fate awaited Chattooga County slave John McConnell, who had been allowed to cultivate a few acres of corn and buy hogs and heifers with the proceeds. In September he lost the corn and livestock to Sherman's foragers, who also took a horse the slave had purchased the previous year for one hundred dollars.[49]

Blacks in urban areas were if anything more vulnerable to Federal looting than were rural residents. Monemia Johnson was a free black woman in Marietta who "kept an eating saloon and store." Her husband, a free black barber, shaved Confederate officers and passed intelligence to the Union side. His loyalty was of no avail in the face of soldiers bent on plunder. When northern forces left Marietta in November 1864, they destroyed the railroad tracks and burned much of the town. In the ensuing confusion Federal soldiers came to Johnson's store and demanded all that she had. An army wagon was needed to carry off the bacon, sugar, tobacco, rice, and other commodities thus seized.[50] A still more wanton act of pillage took place in Atlanta, where the fate of Polly Beedles, a free black woman married to Henry Beedles, a slave owned by the Georgia Railroad Bank, has been recorded in fascinating detail. Historian Thomas G. Dyer's careful reconstruction of the couple's story merits quoting at length:

> Polly hired out for twelve dollars a month, and Henry worked on his own until midnight most nights. The two saved nearly everything they made and were able to buy a lot in Atlanta and build a house and stable on it. The couple took great pride in their achievement and put aside money to buy Henry from the Bank. . . . Soon after the Yankee occupation, the blue wagons of the Federals appeared at the Beedles' house near the fairgrounds. About 150 men were in the group of soldiers that confiscated the house and provisions. They methodically pulled down the plank fence around the property, and they tore down the house and the stable. Polly Beedles was at a neighbor's house when the wagons arrived; Henry was downtown. She ran toward their home and pleaded with the soldiers to stop. Henry soon arrived, and they both tried to halt the destruction. "Old man," the Union officer said to Beedles, "we must have your house and fence. My boys and myself have no tents and we must [have your] house to build some tents." Uncle Sam would pay the couple for their loss the officer promised. Beedles begged him to stop but the Yankee refused. "They took down all my house, my dwelling, stable, well house, fence and posts. They did not leave a stick of anything on the place."[51]

Presumably few black Georgians expected egalitarian treatment from whites on either side of the sectional conflict, and most seemed willing to ignore or endure even egregious exploitation if freedom hung in the balance. The campaign for Atlanta left little doubt that slavery's days were numbered in Georgia, but just as important, it made clear that African Americans were ready and able to become the agents of their own deliverance when the opportunity arose. No one, black or white, doubted in the summer of 1864 that the Civil War was "about slavery." It remained to be seen if white Americans would conclude that the peace that followed should be about freedom.

NOTES

1. On coastal evacuations and escapes, see Clarence L. Mohr, "Before Sherman: Georgia Blacks and the Union War Effort, 1861–1864," *Journal of Southern History* 45 (Aug. 1979): 331–52.

2. Mary Elizabeth Massey, *Refugee Life in the Confederacy* (Baton Rouge: Louisiana State University Press, 1964), 85; Wade Banister Gassman, "Rome and Floyd County, Georgia, in the Civil War" (M.A. thesis, Emory University, 1966), 56–57.

3. Clarence L. Mohr, *On the Threshold of Freedom: Masters and Slaves in Civil War Georgia* (Athens: University of Georgia Press, 1986), 128–35, esp. table 10.

4. Ibid., 151–52, 155–56; Grenville M. Dodge to John A. Rawlins, Feb. 26, 1864, *The War of the Rebellion: A Compilation of the Official Records of the Union and the Confederate Armies,* 128 volumes (Washington, D.C.: Government Printing Office, 1880–1901), ser. 1, 32(2):476 (hereinafter cited as *OR*).

5. Lee Kennett, *Marching through Georgia: The Story of Soldiers and Civilians during Sherman's Campaign* (New York: HarperCollins, 1995), 85.

6. Edward R. Harden to his mother, Aug. 9, Dec. 26, 1863, Edward R. Harden Papers, Duke University, Durham, N.C.

7. Arch Smith to Joseph E. Brown, Oct. 17, 1864, Telamon Cuyler Collection, Hargrett Rare Book and Manuscript Library, University of Georgia Libraries, Athens.

8. Harden to his mother, July 6, Sept. 26, 1864, Harden Papers.

9. Minutes of the Atlanta City Council, Nov. 6, 1863, Atlanta Historical Society.

10. James Michael Russell, *Atlanta, 1847–1890: City Building in the Old South and the New* (Baton Rouge: Louisiana State University Press, 1988), 109.

11. Minutes of the Atlanta City Council, Mar. 6, Aug. 28, 1863, Atlanta Historical Society.

12. Thomas G. Dyer, *Secret Yankees: The Union Circle in Confederate Atlanta* (Baltimore: Johns Hopkins University Press, 1999), 159–60.

13. Robert F. Durden, *The Gray and the Black: The Confederate Debate on Emancipation* (Baton Rouge: Louisiana State University Press, 1972), vii, 61.

14. Dyer, *Secret Yankees,* 160, 167.

15. Mohr, *Threshold of Freedom,* 130–31, table 10.

16. Dr. B. W. Wimble to Dr. S. H. Stout, Mar. 21, 1863, Samuel H. Stout Papers, Southern Historical Collection, University of North Carolina, Chapel Hill (hereinafter cited as SHC).

17. Ralph B. Singer Jr., "Confederate Atlanta" (Ph.D. diss., University of Georgia, 1973), 208–12, 244; Kennett, *Marching through Georgia,* 117.

18. Mohr, *Threshold of Freedom,* 161–62; *Macon Daily Telegraph,* Aug. 16, 1862; Howell Cobb to George W. Randolph, Aug. 5, 1862, *OR,* ser. 4, 2:34–35; James Tinsley to Joseph E. Brown, Aug. 8, 1862, Telamon Cuyler Collection. In protesting slave impressments Georgia planters employed all of the arguments summarized in Bell I. Wiley, *Southern Negroes, 1861–1865* (New Haven, Conn.: Yale University Press, 1938), 123–25; and Harrison A. Trexler, "The Opposition of Planters to the Impressment of Slaves as Laborers by the Confederacy," *Mississippi Valley Historical Review* 27 (Sept. 1940): 211–24.

19. Joseph E. Johnston to Commanding Officer, C.S. Army, Rome, Ga., Apr. 24, 1864, *OR,* ser.1, 37(3):861. Slaves hired from local planters had been employed intermittently on Rome's defenses since the summer of 1863. See Gilbert Smith, "A History Experience at Fort Norton/Jackson: The Fortifications of Rome," www.romegeorgia.com/fortnortonjackson.html.

20. Lt. Col. L. B. Faulkner to Captain Speed, June 22, 1864, *OR,* ser. 1, 38(4):564.

21. F. A. Shoup, "Dalton Campaign—Works at Chattahoochee River—Interesting History," *Confederate Veteran* 3 (Sept. 1895): 262–65.

22. Ibid.

23. *Macon Daily Telegraph,* July 28, Aug. 11, 12, 1864; *Columbus Daily Sun,* July 28, Aug. 14, 1864.

24. W. T. Sherman, *Memoirs of General William T. Sherman,* 2 vols., 2nd ed. (New York: D. Appleton, 1931), 2:55; Michael Fellman, *Citizen Sherman* (New York: Random House, 1995), 150.

25. Philip Shiman, "Sherman's Pioneers in the Atlanta Campaign," *The Campaign for Atlanta and Sherman's March to the Sea,* ed. Theodore P. Savas and David A. Woodbury, 2 vols. in 1 (Campbell, Calif.: Savas Woodbury, 1994), 251–66; Journal of Brig. Gen. Francis A. Shoup, C.S. Army, July 25–Sept. 7, 1864, *OR,* ser. 1, 38(3):692 (Aug. 23, 1864). The estimate of black pioneers is my own and not that of Shiman.

26. William T. Sherman to Lorenzo Thomas, June 26, 1864, *OR,* ser. 3, 4:454; Special Field Order No. 16, June 3, 1864, ibid., 434.

27. Fellman, *Citizen Sherman,* 160.

28. Charles R. Pratt to Thomas, Aug. 3, 1864, Colored Troops Division, ser. 360, Letters Received, P-276 (1864), Records of the Adjutant General's Office, RG 94, National Archives, Washington, D.C. (hereinafter cited as NA); William King Diary, July 5, 24, 27, 1864, SHC.

29. Richard K. Rue and Geraldine M. Rue, eds., *In Song and Sorrow: The Daily Journal of Thomas Hart Benton McCain, 86th Indiana Volunteer Infantry* (Carmel, Ind.: Guild, 1998), 155.

30. David Evans, *Sherman's Horsemen: Union Cavalry Operations in the Atlanta Campaign* (Bloomington: Indiana University Press, 1996), 177.

31. *Wolverine Citizen* (Clint, Mich.), Aug. 13, 1864, as quoted in Evans, *Sherman's Horsemen,* 189.

32. Evans, *Sherman's Horsemen,* 293, 325.

33. James M. Wells, *"With Touch of Elbow," or Death before Dishonor: A Thrilling Narrative of Adventure on Land and Sea* (Philadelphia: John C. Winston, 1909), 216–17, as quoted in Evans, *Sherman's Horsemen,* 342.

34. *OR,* ser. 1, 5:138.

35. Bobby Lee Lovett, "The Negro in Tennessee, 1861–1865: A Socio-Military History of the Civil War Era" (Ph.D. diss., University of Arkansas, 1978), 301–3.

36. Margaret Espey to Joseph S. Espey, Mar. 21, 1864, Joseph Espey Papers, SHC.

37. *Macon Daily Telegraph,* May 27, 1864.

38. "Statement of Anna Irwin, Washerwoman in Genl Field Hospital [Chattanooga, Tenn., Feb. 27, 1866]," in *Freedom: A Documentary History of Emancipation, 1861–1867,* ed. Ira Berlin et al. (Cambridge: Cambridge University Press, 1982–93), ser. 1, 2:466–67. The same document is reprinted in Ira Berlin et al., eds., *Free at Last: A Documentary History of Slavery, Freedom, and the Civil War* (New York: New Press, 1992), 230.

39. Sherman to John A. Spooner, July 30, 1864, *Sherman's Civil War: Selected Correspondence of William T. Sherman, 1860–1865,* ed. Brooks D. Simpson and Jean V. Berlin (Chapel Hill: University of North Carolina Press, 1999), 678; Sherman to Daniel Martin, Aug. 10, 1864, ibid., 688; Sherman to General [Henry W.] Halleck, Sept. 4, 1864, ibid., 699; Sherman to William M. McPherson Esq. [ca. Sept. 15–30, 1864], ibid., 727.

40. Circular Order of J. B. Parkhurst to All Provost Marshals in the Army of the Cumberland, Oct. 5, 1864, ser. 6480, Letters and Reports Received and Orders Issue and Received, 20th AC, 1st Division, 2nd Brigade, Records of the U.S. Army Continental Commands, 1821–1920, pt. 2, RG 393, NA; H. W. Perkins to Col. William Cogswell, Oct. 3, 1864, ser. 6472, Letters Sent, vol. 1, 20th AC, ibid. I wish to thank Leslie Rowland of the University of Maryland and the Freedmen in Southern Society Project for bringing this material to my attention.

41. W. P. Whitney to William C. Rockwell, Oct. 7, 1864, 20th Army Corps, ser. 6480, Letters and Reports Received and Orders Issued and Received, 20th AC, 1st Division, 2nd Brigade, RG 393; Thomas to Edwin M. Stanton, June 15, 1864, *OR,* ser. 3, 4:434.

42. Special Field Order No. 16, June 3, 1864, *OR,* ser. 3, 4:434; Sherman to Thomas, June 26, 1864, ibid., 455.

43. C. W. Foster to Ruben D. Mussey, May 31, 1864, ibid., 416. For a summary of recruiting activities for the 44th USCI in northern Georgia, Alabama, and western Tennessee, see Mussey to Foster, Oct. 10, 1864, ibid., 762–74.

44. Margaret Espey to Joseph S. Espey, Sept. 6, 1864, Joseph Espey Papers, SHC.

45. Lewis Johnson to Mussey, Oct. 17, 1864, *OR,* ser. 1, 39(1):717–21.

46. Mohr, *Threshold of Freedom,* 90, table 5.

47. *OR,* ser. 1, 39(1):720; Johnson to William D. Whipple, Oct. 17, 1864, ibid., 721–22; Application for Removal of Charge of Desertion, Case of Hubbard Pryor, Dec. 4, 1889, box 22, Record and Pension Division, D90, RG 94. For additional background on the Dalton affair, see Noah Andre Trudeau, *Like Men of War: Black Troops in the Civil War, 1862–1865* (Boston: Little Brown, 1998), 278–79.

48. Gassman, "Rome and Floyd County," 118–20 n. 43; Margaret Espey to Joseph S. Espey, Sept. 6, 1864, Espey Papers.

49. Testimony of Lewis Richardson, George Richardson, and Others, Apr. 15, 1874, Claim of Lewis Richardson, Dalton, Whitfield County, Ga., box 171, Approved Claims, ser. 732, Records of the Third Auditor of the General Accounting Office, Southern Claims Commission, RG 217, NA; Testimony of Albert Berrien and Others, Mar. 1, 1878, Claim of Albert Berrien, Rome, Floyd County, Ga., box 146, ibid.; Testimony of Allen and Amy Witcher and Others, Mar. 5, 1878, Claim of Allen Witcher, Cave Spring, Floyd County, Ga., box 148, ibid.; Testimony of John McConnell

and Others, June 10, 1873, Claim of John McConnell, Chattooga County, Ga., box 137, ibid. I am deeply indebted to Leslie Rowland of the University of Maryland for sharing with me indexed summaries of the Southern Claims Commission material prepared by the staff of the Freeedmen and Southern Society Project.

50. Testimony of Monemia Johnson and Others, Nov. 6, 1872, Claim of Monemia Johnson, Marietta, Cobb County, Georgia, box 142, ibid.

51. Dyer, *Secret Yankees,* 198.

Half Slave, Half Free:
Unionist Robert Webster in Confederate Atlanta

THOMAS G. DYER

IT MUST HAVE TAKEN ENORMOUS COURAGE FOR THE TWELVE-year-old "coloured boy" to walk up the marble steps into the U.S. Capitol in 1832. And it would have required resourcefulness and resolve on his part to find the Senate chamber. Once there, with some luck, he encountered Isaac Bassett, a page who owed his position to a senator from Massachusetts, Daniel Webster. The youth informed Bassett that he had come to see Senator Webster. "He told me," Bassett reported, "that Daniel Webster was his *father*." Thereafter, Bassett went on, the youth often "came up to the Senate Chamber to see Senator Webster."[1]

Thirty-four years later, scarcely a year after the conclusion of the Civil War, an official of the American Missionary Association posted in Atlanta commented to a northern correspondent about prospects for beginning schools for freedpeople in the Georgia city. The official, Frederick Ayer, had become acquainted with Benjamin C. Yancey, a Georgian and a former slaveowner who was showing interest in the education of freedpeople. The official noted that when Yancey visited Atlanta, he frequently stayed overnight with one of his former slaves, "Robert Yancy, alias Robert Webster," who lived across the street from Ayer. In an almost offhanded way, Ayer also mentioned that Robert Webster was "the reputed son of Dan'l Webster."[2]

These two incidents, one in 1832, the other in 1866, raise questions about the paternity of Robert Webster, a mulatto slave who came to prominence in Civil War Atlanta. The issue, while intriguing, cannot be finally resolved here, but it does help us understand Webster, whose story illuminates the spaces between slavery and freedom that only a few African Americans occupied in antebellum and Civil War Atlanta.

A paucity of source materials makes it generally difficult to reconstruct the lives of individual African Americans who lived in the early and middle nineteenth century. Such materials as do exist are often scattered, fragmentary, and insufficient for a detailed portrait. Thus very large gaps exist in our knowledge of Webster, but we have enough sources to sketch a partial view of the difficult path between slavery and freedom that he followed during the antebellum period and a somewhat fuller picture of him during the Civil War. During the conflict Webster became part of a resilient group of Atlantans who retained their loyalties to the Union and resisted the Confederacy. From the scattered record left by and about Robert Webster, we can also offer some tentative conclusions concerning his paternity.

Slaves sometimes took the surnames of their owners, and thus Webster was known at various times as Bob Gadsby, Bob Yancey, and possibly Bob Cunningham. Most frequently, no doubt, he was called simply "Bob," given the disposition of slaveholding society not to confer the dignity of last names on slaves. Throughout this chapter he is referred to as Robert Webster. That is the name that he chose for himself once he became free to do so.

Webster told a newspaper reporter in 1879 that he was born on August 20, 1820, in Gadsby's National Hotel, one of the large hostelries in Washington, D.C. His mother, he said, was Charlotte Goo[d]brick, "a mulatto of rare beauty" and a slave who was purchased by the owner of the National, John Gadsby, from a man who lived in Fredericksburg, Virginia. Charlotte, it was said, had been the offspring of "one of the old aristocrats of Virginia." How long Gadsby owned her before Robert was born cannot be ascertained.[3]

Throughout childhood and into young adulthood, Robert Webster was probably known as Bob Gadsby. As a boy he seems to have moved freely about Washington, as indicated by his multiple visits to the Capitol. What his childhood was like can only be speculated upon, but he probably worked in the hotel or in his owner's home. Gadsby, also a slave trader, owned several slaves, thirty-nine of whom staffed the National. Still others lived and worked in Decatur House, Gadsby's elegant home in Washington. Webster's master was not universally admired. The French minister to the United States described Gadsby as "an old wretch who has made a fortune in the slave trade, which does not prevent Washington society from rushing to his house." Webster could have learned his trades (barbering and cooking) in the hotel, or possibly at Decatur House, while Gadsby owned him.[4]

When Webster was about twenty, he became the property and manservant of William Gadsby, son of the hotel owner, and a "rash, hot headed Southerner" with a fondness for drinking and gambling. Apparently the elder Gadsby gave the slave to his son for his personal use. Once while gambling in Richmond, William Gadsby was losing heavily in a high-stakes card game, and in an incident that reveals the utter depravity of slavery and slaveowners, he wagered Webster against another gambler's bet of fifteen hundred dollars in gold. Gadsby lost. And so of course did young Webster, who had become a literal pawn in the white men's game of chance. Ripped from his moorings in Washington, the young slave thus became the property of a Richmond gambler who needed cash more than a manservant. He soon sold Webster to a man in South Carolina.[5]

Webster's new owner was named John Cunningham. That is nearly all that is known about him except that he owned Webster from about 1840 until 1846, when he sold him, ironically enough, because he had grown tired of his slave's fondness for gambling. We also know that Cunningham was the uncle of this fourth owner, Benjamin Cudworth Yancey, a prominent Georgia and Alabama plantation owner and politician who had became acquainted with Webster. Many years after he purchased Webster, Yancey claimed that Robert himself requested the purchase and that the deal also included the purchase of a female slave who was Webster's wife. Yancey said that as a condition of the dual purchase he had extracted a promise from Webster that he would give up "card playing." Otherwise he had nothing but praise for Webster, who was, Yancey declared, "truthful, sober, affectionate, [and] honest." Moreover he was "a very intelligent and accomplished House servant; a fair cook, meat & pastry: a fine maker of Preserves & Pickles—a good barber."[6]

The wealthy Yancey, who owned several plantations in Georgia and Alabama, lived at locations in both states and in South Carolina before moving to Atlanta in 1856. Webster was probably the slave of highest standing in the household, if Yancey's reference that Webster had "training up under him several young favorite negroes" indicates his status. In time the household included more slaves than Yancey thought necessary, so shortly after moving to Atlanta, he agreed to permit Webster "to rent a shop & go to public barbering—& trading." Thus Robert Webster "bought his time," that is, he leased himself from his owner so that he could strike out on his own and attempt to survive as a quasi-free black man living in a slave society. Yancey helped Webster start his business by cosigning for the rent of a shop but charged him an annual fee of $150 for the privilege of "hiring his time," a healthy 10 percent return for Yancey if Webster, who was a valuable asset to the slaveowner, was worth $1,500.[7]

Webster immediately prospered. Hardworking and shrewd, he had managed to accumulate a few hundred dollars before he embarked on his barbering and trading business. In addition to operating the barbershop, Webster bought and sold produce, including fruit, fish, and chickens. He also began to make risky loans to white gamblers, accepting gold, jewelry, and diamonds as security. By the late 1850s he operated two barbershops, employed nine barbers, had amassed several thousand dollars, and was ready to buy a home. He became well known in Atlanta for his business acumen and particularly for his astuteness as a trader. According to G. C. Rogers, an Atlanta businessman, Webster had money, gold, and gold watches "always about him" and was "about one of the biggest traders we had here." Rogers believed that Webster prospered mainly by lending money and getting good collateral, such as diamonds and gold, which he would keep when borrowers defaulted.

Webster's personal life did not seem to flow as smoothly as his businesses. He apparently had domestic difficulties and separated from his wife. During 1858 and 1859 Yancey was out of the country serving as U.S. minister to the Argentine Confederation in Buenos Aires. When his master returned to the United States in 1859, Webster told him about the separation and said that he wanted to marry another woman, also a slave. He asked Yancey to purchase the woman, which his owner did with $1,500 that Webster provided.[8]

This period of business success coincided with the intensification of the great sectional crisis and the coming of civil war. A complex set of political and economic pressures would have been exerted upon any free black, or as in Webster's case a semi-free black, during that time. We have no evidence concerning how he navigated the hazards of the secession crisis and the accompanying agitation for southern independence without arousing the attention or ire of partisans in Atlanta. We do know, however, that fairly soon after the beginning of the war, Webster had quietly allied himself with an active group of Unionists who continued to live in the city after Fort Sumter.[9]

Many Unionists lived in pre–Civil War Atlanta, if by "Unionists" we mean those persons who placed a high value on the Union of states and who opposed secession. During 1860 and 1861 that number dramatically diminished, so much so that by the summer of 1861, after Fort Sumter and First Manassas, perhaps no more than a hundred families in the city could fairly be described as strict or unconditional Unionists. In a city of about eight thousand persons, this was a small but significant minority made more so because many of its key members were among the influential and the wealthy with strong, long-established ties to the community.[10]

Unionists came in a variety of shapes and sizes. After the war those men who survived were fond of recalling the perdurable works of a few dozen "Union men," and thus they defined Unionism along gender lines, though in their recollections they sometimes recognized the parts played by women and blacks, like Robert Webster, who engaged in some of the most dangerous resistance work. Webster was fully accepted by the white male Unionists as one of their own and was an active risk taker whose loyalties to the cause of the United States became almost legendary among his compatriots.[11]

The wartime activities of Atlanta Unionists ranged from passive resistance to espionage and became evident as men and women, black and white, began a steady, nearly silent program of aid to the thousands of Federal prisoners brought to the city. Unionists often used stealth and subterfuge to assist the prisoners held in the jails and the hospitals. Webster had entree to the jails because of his trade and perhaps because local Confederate officials might have thought a black man incapable of giving material assistance to the prisoners. He would arrive with his barbering tools and bundles of towels and would freely pass in and out of the barracks, where he was permitted to shave the prisoners. Webster may have initially gained entry into the stockade in the company of William Lewis, a slave who served in the Confederate army as a barber and drummer.[12]

Webster used his access not only to assist Union prisoners but also to turn a profit by illegally dealing in the currency black market, an extremely dangerous activity. He would get much-desired greenbacks (U.S. currency) from prisoners and then sell them to other Atlanta Unionists. He used the Confederate money he received from the Unionists to buy various items, including tobacco and other commodities that retained their value. One Unionist recalled that he had purchased U.S. cash from Webster for as many as three hundred Confederate dollars to one greenback. Another man, who worked for the Confederate provost marshal, testified after the war that he knew that Webster had bought greenbacks, "though it was a dangerous thing for a man to do."[13]

Later in the war Webster took even greater risks. In his visits to the jails, he came to know many of the prisoners, including a "Colonel Cliff," an East Tennesseean. "Colonel Cliff" was actually William D. Clift, a Unionist whose imprisonment in Atlanta resulted from unusual circumstances. Seventy years old, Clift had been a prominent leader in the anti-secessionist movement in Tennessee and a leader in the Greenville Convention of 1861, which tried to carve a separate, loyal state out of East Tennessee. As the Confederates ascended to power, he led much of the opposition in the Chattanooga area. When a series of local conflicts broke out between Union and Confederate sympathizers in the area, it became known as "Clift's war." On a mission to Knoxville in 1863, he was arrested by a Confederate officer and handed over to Rebel authorities, who shipped the aging man to the military prison in Atlanta. The arresting officer was Clift's own son, a captain in the Confederate cavalry.[14]

In prison Clift asked Webster to help him escape. After the war Webster recounted their conversation:

> "Bob, I want to get out of this place," Clift said.
> Webster demurred. "Captain, you know I can do nothing for you."
> "Yes, you can," Clift insisted.
> "Now you want to get me into a scrape and then tell Wash Lee [Col. George W. Lee, Confederate provost marshal] about it, and he will hang me."
> "I will die before," Clift replied. "This fellow out here will pull me over the fences if you will bring me a line."

Webster provided the rope and apparently rejected the twenty dollars in greenbacks the Union colonel offered him in gratitude. He never knew who in Atlanta agreed to help Clift, but there were several East Tennesseeans among the Unionists, and they were probable candidates. Clift succeeded in escaping and ultimately made his way back to the relative safety of the East Tennessee mountains.[15] Confederate authorities did indeed arrest Webster, probably based more on suspicions than hard evidence since he was questioned but held only a short time. Or possibly Webster bribed his way out of jail, a common enough occurrence in Civil War Atlanta and not an impossible feat for a well-off black man to accomplish.[16]

Webster disappears from the historical record for a time, then reappears as the city moved closer toward the climactic moment of its encounter with the forces of Union general William T. Sherman. Already underway by January 1864, Sherman's descent into Georgia focused on control of the city of Atlanta, which was increasingly seen as critical to Pres. Abraham Lincoln's reelection and the outcome of the war. The gargantuan struggle for the city climaxed with the battle of Atlanta on July 22, 1864. We have brief glimpses of Webster during the fighting, glimpses that come from the diary of Cyrena Bailey Stone, a Unionist who lived in the city from 1854 until late 1864 and who knew Webster not only through his contact with the Unionist circle (though this is uncertain) but also because Webster's home was on Houston Street, not far from where Stone lived. As the battle drew nearer, it appears that Webster and his wife became temporary members of Stone's household. A few nights before, the Websters had been visited by Confederate soldiers who suddenly burst into their home, "pretending to search for runaway Negroes," and while holding guns against the couple's throats had stolen all of their valuables: "silk dresses—jewellry watches & spoons were carried off." The two took refuge in Stone's barn and were being protected by a "kind officer" who was also staying there. Sometime during or soon after the conclusion of the battle, Webster left the Stone residence and went back to his own home to find it still standing, one of the few houses in that part of Atlanta that survived the fighting.[17]

A few days after the battle, Webster undertook a mission of mercy that earned him the lasting admiration of the white Unionists of Atlanta. On July 25 or 26 one of those Unionists, James Dunning, a prominent citizen, was passing through the city park when he discovered a group of wounded Union soldiers who had been deposited there during the battle and had gone untreated for nearly three days. Their exact number is unknown; certainly there were several dozen, perhaps more. What Dunning saw was wrenching. The soldiers were in unimaginable conditions due to heat and filth, racked by pain and tortured by putrid, maggot-infested wounds. They seemed to have been without food and water since the battle. Their "sufferings," Dunning said, "were intolerable."[18]

He soon encountered Webster and another Unionist as well as some other persons. Webster's assistance to the soldiers was particularly valuable, Dunning recalled. Not only did he dress their wounds, but he also recruited other black men to aid in the task and to take the soldiers to one of the hospitals in the city. Webster's job required fortitude. Dunning had always been the most critical of the Atlanta Unionists in judging who should be counted as members of the underground community. He had no doubts about Webster and conferred upon him what Dunning would have considered the highest honor: "Mr. Robert Webster was one of the 35 or 36 loyal men of the city during the war."[19]

Other Unionists agreed. Webster stayed with the prisoners all afternoon and all night until he was able to arrange for them to be taken to the Roy

Hospital, where they would receive treatment. "Webster took charge of the whole matter himself," John Silvey said, "hired other colored people to help him and paid for their services. . . . His conduct was noticed by the Union men here, and met with their hearty approbation and cooperation." A leader of the Unionist group, William Markham, concurred. Webster was "heart and soul a Union man," who had constantly nursed wounded Union soldiers since the battle of Chickamauga. He was, Markham said, "entitled to great credit for his conduct." Yet another observer, a slave, noted that until Webster began his relief effort, "white and black people" had been afraid to attend to the wounded soldiers, fearing "to go in among them" because of the high level of agitation among the Confederates still in the city. The slave also claimed that Webster somehow managed to take two Union prisoners to his own house, where they hid in his attic throughout the remainder of the siege.[20]

For the white men who came to the square, the risk of retribution from Confederates was outweighed by their devotion to the Union. For the blacks, the prospect of early liberation and deliverance from a slave society would be enough. A cynic might object that these men were hedging their bets that huge numbers of Union troops would soon be in the city and that they would then be hailed for the aid given the wounded. This argument loses its force, however, when one recalls that all of the men had, for the better part of three years, run considerable risks to advance the Unionist cause. Interpreted in that light, the scenes in the city park after the battle were but a logical extension of the wartime experiences of the Unionists, black and white.

Webster comes to light again after the six-week siege of the city, which extended from the conclusion of the battle until the surrender of Atlanta on September 2, 1864. As Confederate forces fled, the mayor, James M. Calhoun, decided to meet the Yankees before they actually entered the city. Calhoun gathered a number of citizens to accompany him out of the city to find a Union commander, perhaps hoping to locate Sherman himself, though the general was nearly twenty miles away near Jonesboro. So well known and so often rehearsed are the details of the ride of Calhoun and the citizens to meet the Yankees that Civil War experts have never paused to inquire into the membership of this party. Such an inquiry might seem to be an excursion into historical minutiae except that Mayor Calhoun chose carefully in assembling the members of his surrender committee, which included a healthy number of Unionists. Among them was a black man, Robert Webster, who rode along with the white citizens to present the city of Atlanta to General Sherman.[21]

After years of living under constant pressure and peril, Unionists such as Webster and the other members of the band had been severely affected by the coming of the Federal armies. Union shells destroyed Unionist as well as Confederate houses. Union soldiers burned Unionist businesses. And the Federal army confiscated loyalist property, including commodities such as cotton and tobacco as well as corn beef, horses, and virtually anything else of importance to the war effort. To be sure, many of the transfers of property were voluntary, though some of what the Unionists provided was taken under conditions of compulsion or near compulsion. Still receipts were issued and promises of compensation made when Unionists surrendered their property to the officers of Sherman's army.

Federal troops made no distinctions between black and white citizens, Unionists or Confederates, when confiscating needed materials and supplies. Several black Atlanta Unionists lost nearly everything they owned. One couple, Polly and Henry Beedles, watched while soldiers dismantled their home to use the lumber in constructing wooden "tents" in which the occupiers lived. Black Unionists like Webster, who had waited for deliverance by the Federals, were completely dismayed when their property was taken. Webster claimed the loss of large amounts of tobacco (far more valuable than currency in the inflated southern economy) and the confiscation of livestock. "My Lord," he was reported to have said, "I thought they had come here to protect us but they have taken everything I have got."[22]

The Union armies left Atlanta in mid-November 1864. Before going Sherman granted permission for a few residents to remain in the city while the vast majority of the population evacuated, choosing to go north or south. Probably Webster was one of those who received permission to remain. John S. Wise, who in later years was the Fulton County jailer, recalled that he returned to Atlanta shortly after Sherman's departure and that Webster was there. He also remembered how the black Unionist provided food to him and to some of his friends. Webster told Wise that Sherman's army had "ruined him." Another source, however, reported that Webster still seemed to have some of his wealth. "Bob was better off than any of us," G. C. Rogers, another businessman, reported. "[He] had money & had more money than his old master."[23]

To be sure, Robert Webster did have more money that Benjamin Yancey. His former master recalled that after the war he was destitute and had nothing left on his plantation except four horses. "I wrote to Bob," he reported, "& asked him if he could loan me $150.00 & in answer to this he sent me by

Express $100 in gold & $100 in silver & sent me word that I could get more if I wanted it." Although the sum was not large, Yancey was evidently without cash and relied upon his former slave to see him through those difficult times.[24]

In the tumultuous postwar era, the recently freed Webster began to take an active interest in local and state politics. E. T. Hunnicutt, who had been the deputy Confederate provost marshal, recalled that Webster became politically active after the war and that he and other blacks had "run off" another black man who sought to make a "Democratic speech." Tunis Campbell, the black abolitionist and carpetbagger who served in the Georgia Constitutional Convention of 1867 and later in the state senate, met Webster at about that time. He and the other black members of the convention had experienced great difficulty in finding a place to stay in Atlanta—likely no hotel would have them—but neither did they have funds to pay for lodging. Webster took them in and kept them in his own home. According to Campbell, when the black members of the convention finally received small payments for subsistence, Webster "told them to get them selves clothes suitable to their position first, and he would wait until they received more money."[25]

Webster's postwar political activities brought him mention in the city's newspapers on at least one occasion. In 1868, after the city had succeeded in becoming the state capital, the *Atlanta Daily New Era* reported on "A Soiree" hosted by that "clever friend of the public, Robert Webster, more familiarly known as 'Bob Yancey.'" Webster, whom the newspaper characterized as "one of the most enterprising and public spirited of his race," was congratulated on "having the interest of the city at heart." While the newspaper referred to him by both names (Yancey and Webster), it is clear that he had referred to himself as Robert Webster for at least two years.[26]

Like many other Unionists, Webster used his political connections in an effort to win compensation from the U.S. government for the property that he had lost to Sherman's armies. He first sought aid from Congress and made a direct plea, with the support of many of Georgia's black legislators, to Charles Sumner, the longtime senator from Massachusetts. This effort did not succeed, but Webster renewed his claim after Congress established the Southern Claims Commission in 1871. The commission became the principal vehicle for the adjudication of claims against the federal government. Essentially claimants had to be able to prove that they had been loyal to the United States throughout the war, navigating a rigorous process intended to establish loyalty, and they had to be able to document that their property had indeed been confiscated for the Union war effort.[27]

Robert Webster easily persuaded the commissioners of his loyalty. The testimony of other members of the Unionist group was simply overwhelming in its praise of Webster for his ministrations to Yankee prisoners throughout the war, especially during the battle of Atlanta's bloody aftermath. He filed a sizable claim—slightly more than ten thousand dollars—nearly all of it for tobacco he said was taken from him during the occupation. The commission heard extensive testimony in the case but rejected his claim primarily because the prominent mulatto barber-businessman could not produce any documentation from the Union armies that they had confiscated his tobacco. Moreover the commissioners accused Webster of attempting to produce false testimony to support his claim.

This charge largely rested on the allegation that Webster had taken large amounts of tobacco from the ransacked store of John Silvey, also a member of the Unionist group, on the morning after the Confederate evacuation of Atlanta, later claiming it as his own and seeking compensation for it from the government. Despite testimony from several key Unionists (including Silvey) rejecting the allegation that extensive looting had actually occurred and testimony from Silvey himself that his store had not been pillaged, commissioners relied upon the statements of several ex-slaves that Webster had participated in the looting and thus acquired his tobacco. In the end, however, the board rejected the claim because Webster could produce no receipt from the U.S. Army for the tobacco, despite Silvey's testimony that he had accompanied Webster to get a receipt that he later claimed to have lost. More than thirty years after the rejection of the claim, Webster's heirs sought to reopen the matter before the U.S. Court of Claims, but they had no more success persuading the judges in 1908 than Webster had with the commissioners in the 1870s.[28]

This assiduous pursuit of compensation from the government probably reflected Webster's own declining economic fortunes. Although the evidence is not conclusive, probably no black man in Atlanta had as much wealth as he had during the prewar and wartime periods. After the war, however, his wealth seemed to decline steadily, possibly in part because he had developed a drinking problem that plagued him for years thereafter. By the early 1870s he was clearly in economic trouble. Benjamin Yancey pointed to the drinking as one cause but also noted that after the war Webster's "trading" had gone badly. Throughout the 1870s his relative standing among other black men of property clearly declined, and by 1880 he had fallen into such economic distress that he wrote plaintively to Yancey asking for a small loan to get started in barbering again. Webster blamed alcohol for many of his problems, both professional and personal. "My Old master and friend," he wrote, "pleas give me a start in this World once more." No record exists to indicate whether Yancey complied, but given the closeness that existed between the two men and Webster's record of helping Yancey, it is hard to imagine that he did not assist.[29]

We have only a few bits of evidence concerning how Webster viewed his own racial identity. We cannot say how Atlanta's antebellum black population may have regarded him, but there was a tiny free black population and a few other slaves who bought their time as Webster did. After the war some degree of tension apparently existed between him and freed slaves. E. T. Hunnicutt recounted a conversation between Webster and a black man in which the two exchanged racial epithets. The man allegedly referred to Webster as a "Yaller Dog" or a "Yaller Hound," probably references to his being mulatto. In turn, it was said, Webster claimed to be white and asserted that the other man was just "a Negro." On another occasion, when some black Atlantans (including his own son) attempted to gain access to segregated businesses including bars, barbershops, and billiard parlors under the protection of the Civil Rights Act of 1875, Webster felt that his own business was threatened. In a letter to one of the local newspapers, he used strong racial invective: "I keep a barber-shop for white men—have shaved no negroes, and even under the civil rights bill no negro can have his face scraped or his wool oiled in my shop." "I am a colored man," he concluded, "but still, I am a white man in principle, and I want my colored friends to know that, in their places, I am their friend, and that out of their places, I am not their friend."[30]

Robert Webster disappears from the historical record in 1880. It seems likely that he died in that year, but no record has yet been found. He did not appear in the U.S. census of Georgia for 1880 or in publications in that and subsequent years listing the residents of Atlanta. His life had followed a highly uncommon path that defies easy analysis or categorization but was one that illustrates the variety of experiences a slave could know in antebellum America and indicates the resourcefulness and adaptability of African Americans during the prewar and postwar periods of the nineteenth century.

Born into slavery in Washington, D.C., Webster was at various times the property of at least five different white men. His early life exposed him to urban slavery in the capital city, where he probably worked as a slave in one of its busiest and most prominent hotels. As a young man he clearly believed that he was the son of a great American statesman, and he reached out to him apparently without success. If he did manage to establish any relationship with Daniel Webster, it is hard to see any benefits. Clearly illiterate as a young man, he obviously had no formal education or even any informal tutoring. When he was scarcely out of his teens, Webster suffered the degradation and shock of becoming a human wager in a card game played by his master and other white gamblers. Almost immediately thereafter he was sold into Deep South slavery, which would have been a terribly frightening prospect for a slave accustomed to the urban environment of Washington. Sold for yet a third time to a master whom he would come to regard as a friend, he persuaded that master to let him try to survive economically in a white man's world by "buying his time." In this half-slave, half-free status, Webster achieved notable success as a shrewd businessman and trader who accumulated a significant amount of wealth during the 1850s and 1860s. In Confederate Atlanta he became a member of the Unionist group and had the high regard of the city's loyal population, who admired him for the great personal risks he took in aiding Union captives in the city. After the war he became a citizen and was, for a time at least, politically active and well regarded by the emerging black political elite. At the same time, however, he watched his economic fortunes decline, probably because of deep personal problems (perhaps partially alcohol related). Webster's status may have also subtly changed as more and more freedmen entered his economic world, providing competition and complications for the mulatto businessman who had been accustomed to occupying a special place in the economic life of the city prior to emancipation. In the end, ironically, Webster was far more successful economically as a slave who "bought his time" than he was as a free man.[31]

The "coloured boy" who claimed to be the son of one America's most powerful white politicians could never have anticipated the complexity and cruelty of the adult world that he was entering. Half slave and half free, neither black nor white, Robert Webster lived in a world of harsh ambiguity where clear identity, racial or otherwise, was difficult to achieve.

A Note on the Patrimony of Robert Webster

For decades Daniel Webster was the subject of rumors in Marshfield, Massachusetts, where he lived, that he had fathered children by his cook, Monica Carty, a female slave whom he bought in Virginia sometime in the 1820s and later freed. Rumors of Webster's sexual adventurism had extensive circulation beyond Marshfield in large part because Jane Swisshelm, an abolitionist journalist, wrote of the senator's reputation as a hard drinker and a womanizer in a widely copied article published in the *Pittsburgh Saturday Visiter* in 1850. She alleged that he kept mistresses, "generally, if not always, colored women—some of them big black wenches as ugly and vulgar as himself." Historians have commented upon Webster's reputation for "sexual promiscuity," but there is no concrete evidence that he fathered children out of wedlock. Nevertheless the rumors endured and, as recently as the 1970s, have occasionally resurfaced in Marshfield; Irving Bartlett, a biographer of Webster, heard them at that time from a local man who cited a boyhood conversation with Webster's ninety-year-old coachman as his source.[32]

Swisshelm, who also wrote for Horace Greeley's *New York Tribune,* added yet another layer to the story in her memoirs when she repeated accounts that circulated in Washington about "a family of eight mulattoes bearing the image and superscription of the great New England statesman, who paid the rent and grocery bills of their mother as regularly as he did those of his wife." The sources for Swisshelm's stories about Webster are by no means clear, but while she worked in Washington, she lived with a friend, novelist E. D. E. N. Southworth, whose stepfather, Joshua Henshaw, had served as the senator's secretary. Robert Remini, the most recent biographer of Daniel Webster, reports that Swisshelm and her stories have "generally been discredited" but also notes that numerous "other sources corroborate his reputation for moral delinquency." Bartlett agrees and notes that late-nineteenth-century historians who were sympathetic to Webster largely accepted the stories of his alleged sexual adventures.[33]

Most of the evidence concerning Robert Webster's possible connection to Daniel Webster comes from an undated note written by Isaac Bassett and from two undated newspaper clippings in the Isaac Bassett Papers, housed in the Office of Senate Curator in the U.S. Senate.[34] For approximately fifty years Bassett was an employee of the Senate, serving in several positions, including doorkeeper. He first joined the Senate staff as a twelve-year-old page in 1831, garnering his appointment through the influence of Daniel Webster.

Many years later, exactly when cannot be determined, Bassett recorded in a note his recollections of the 1832 appearance of the young "coloured boy" who claimed to be the son of Senator Webster. A particularly important part of this evidence asserts that the child came to the Senate more than once. Bassett, an uncommonly bad speller, recalls that the boy "freekently came up to the Senate Chamber to see Senator Webster." The wording implies that the boy saw the senator more than once, but the language is ambiguous. Either Robert Webster came to the Senate and sought unsuccessfully and frequently to see Daniel Webster or he succeeded in speaking with the senator on a frequent basis. It is not clear which occurred. In his recollection Bassett refers to the youth as Bob Gadsby and records that his mother's name was "Mrs. Goodbright" (a name bearing considerable similarity to Goodbrick) and that she lived in "Gadsby['s] hotel."[35]

The first undated newspaper clipping offers the only extant evidence that Robert Webster actually claimed to be the son of Daniel Webster. Sometime in the post–Civil War era, probably in 1879, a reporter for the *Chicago Times* interviewed Webster in Atlanta and concluded that indeed he was the son of the great senator. The reporter based his conclusion on his conversations with Webster himself ("a man of more than ordinary intelligence") and the corroborating statements of "several prominent citizens," including "members of his former master's family, who are still living," probably a reference to relatives of Benjamin Yancey. The reporter's account provides the evidentiary basis for several of the stories concerning Webster's early life, identifying his mother as Charlotte "Goo[d]brick," linking the two of them to John Gadsby and his hotel, and providing the particulars concerning Webster's being lost in a poker game to the gambler who sold him south.[36]

The reporter also saw in Robert Webster a "striking" physical resemblance to Daniel Webster. "His broad forehead and widely separated eyes are noticed as circumstantial proof as soon as you hear the story of his birth," he noted. In oblique language common to the nineteenth-century American press, the writer left no doubt that Robert was the product of a sexual union between Charlotte Goodbrick and Daniel Webster. The two had met, he said, while the senator resided at Gadsby's National Hotel. "The matter was kept quiet at the time," the reporter concluded, "although the truth was suspected by several of Mr. Webster's friends." He also wrote that Robert Webster had told him that his mother "talked freely to him of his origin, and told him many anecdotes of the private life of Mr. Webster to whom she was passionately devoted." According to this account, Senator Webster purchased Charlotte and "took her to Boston and gave her perfect freedom, though she continued to be a housemaid in his home." But no corroborating evidence has surfaced that Daniel Webster "boarded" at the National Hotel, though it is possible that he (like many politicians, including Henry Clay) lived or stayed there. The newspaper account is also the source for Robert Webster's birth date, August 20, 1820. Could the senator have been in Washington, possibly staying at the National Hotel, during the timeframe in which Robert Webster was probably conceived? Senator Webster's correspondence indicates that he was in Massachusetts for most of the period between mid-November 1819 and February 1820, but he left for Washington on about January 27, 1820, and apparently arrived there before February 1, approximately seven and a half months before Robert's birth.[37]

Ongoing work in manuscript censuses and city directories has not yet produced evidence of a Charlotte Goodbrick (or Goobrick), Charlotte Goodbright, or other variations (Goodrich, Goodrick) who can be linked to this subject. Some obvious similarities exist between the newspaper account about Charlotte Goodbrick and the Marshfield, Massachusetts, rumors concerning Webster's alleged relationship with his cook, Monica Carty. The Marshfield rumors allege that Webster bought Carty in Washington and took her north as his cook, just as the reporter for the *Chicago Times* claimed Webster had purchased Goodbrick in Washington and taken her to Boston, where she served him as a housemaid. In both cases Webster is said to have freed each slave. The similarities suggest that there may have been some conflation of stories. And there is yet another complicating factor. Webster had an intense personal relationship with Sarah Goodridge, a Boston miniaturist. The similarity of her surname to the others may also suggest a conflation of stories.[38]

A key passage in the *Chicago Times* article, perhaps fatal to Robert Webster's claim, pertains to a supposed wartime encounter in Atlanta between Webster and "Captain" Daniel Fletcher Webster (usually referred to as Fletcher Webster), a Union officer and the son of Senator Webster. The passage recounts how Captain Webster was with Sherman's army during the Atlanta campaign and that when he passed through the city, "he heard the story of Bob's nativity, and accidentally found him . . . [,] bestowed various attentions on him," and gave him a picture of Daniel Webster, which Robert still owned. Fletcher Webster, the article goes on, "was killed in a battle near Atlanta."[39]

The second undated clipping found in the Bassett Collection is a very brief letter to the editor of another newspaper (identified only as the *Post*) taking issue with the veracity of the Fletcher Webster incident and implicitly the entire story. The unidentified writer correctly points out that *Colonel* Fletcher Webster of the 12th Massachusetts Volunteers could not possibly have visited Robert Webster in Atlanta because he was killed at the second battle of Bull Run in 1862, not "in a battle near Atlanta" in 1864.[40]

Yet Fletcher Webster had a son named Daniel Fletcher Webster Jr., who also served in the Union army as an enlisted man, not as an officer. Although he was a member of one of America's most prominent families, very little information exists concerning the younger Webster, and this compounds the difficulty of the research problem. He was born in 1840. In 1860 he lived in Boston, listed "cordage" as his business, and styled himself "Daniel Webster, Jr." He died of tuberculosis in 1865. Those bits of information and the fact that he served in the Union army constitute the sum of the knowledge that we have about him.[41]

Could Daniel Fletcher Webster Jr. have encountered Robert Webster in Atlanta? The answer is probably not. The younger Webster was apparently a member of the 3rd Regiment, Massachusetts Volunteers, Heavy Artillery, which did not serve in the Atlanta campaign. Until other military records have been more thoroughly examined, however, the possibility that Robert Webster encountered Daniel Fletcher Webster Jr. in Atlanta cannot be completely excluded.[42]

Swisshelm's accounts, the rumors in Marshfield, the national gossip about Daniel Webster, the unflattering estimate that some of his peers put on his moral character, and the *Chicago Times* accounts collectively support the idea that Daniel Webster might have engaged in a sexual relationship with a slave and thereby sired Robert Webster, but the evidence is quite flimsy. Reputable scholars (Bartlett and Remini) minimize the likelihood that the Swisshelm accounts have any credibility. The Marshfield rumors, the national gossip, and the low estimates of the senator's moral character are also weak evidence. The case is further undermined by the impossibility of an Atlanta meeting between Robert Webster and Daniel Fletcher Webster in 1864. Thus Robert Webster's physical resemblance to the senator (according to the writer for the *Chicago Times*), the recollection of Bassett concerning the appearance of the "coloured boy" at the Senate, and Daniel Webster's presence in Washington seven and a half months before Robert's birth are the only pieces of independent evidence that suggest possible links between the two men.

Clearly not enough evidence exists to conclude even tentatively that Daniel Webster sired Robert Webster. It remains theoretically possible that he did so and possibly true that Robert Webster's mother spoke to her son openly and affectionately about the senator, as Robert reportedly claimed.

If Webster's story of his parentage is untrue, then why would he have concocted it? He does not appear to have had anything to gain financially from identifying himself with Daniel Webster unless he thought that the connection might somehow benefit him in his quest for compensation by Congress for property lost during the Civil War. Neither does it appear that he would have had anything to gain in Atlanta from establishing a link to Senator Webster before, during, or after the war. If Robert Webster did make up the story, he did so at a very young age. In this connection the validity of the statement by Bassett recalling visits to the Senate by "Bob Gadsby" is critical. It is the evidence that independently links the twelve-year-old Bob Gadsby with the adult Robert Webster and the two of them to Daniel Webster. Bassett clearly wrote his recollection years after the fact, but whether his memory had been jogged or influenced by a newspaper account concerning either Webster is impossible to ascertain. In any event Bassett would have had no reason to fabricate his notation, and thus the story of the twelve-year-old's visits to the Senate chamber rings true.

In the end the most intriguing possibility is that Robert Webster actually believed that Daniel Webster was his father based upon what his mother reportedly told him, and thus he did not concoct the story, only embellished it. If he or his mother did create the story, their actions would not have differed significantly from other nineteenth-century Americans who longed to link themselves to famous ancestors. Historian David Herbert Donald has commented upon this phenomenon in connection with Abraham Lincoln's view of his antecedents on his mother's side. He observes that the future president, "like other gifted young men" of the nineteenth century, "wondered how he could be the offspring of his ordinary and limited parents." "Lincoln," Donald goes on, "imagined a noble Virginia ancestor" who would have been the father of his illegitimate mother. Thus Lincoln could claim to be the grandson of a "well-bred Virginia planter."

In addition to the linkage to Daniel Webster, a part of Robert Webster's story supposed that his grandfather was "one of the old aristocrats of Virginia." If he (or his mother) constructed the account of his parentage out of whole cloth, they could have acted from motives similar to those of Lincoln and others who invented such "family romances" (to use Sigmund Freud's term) for psychological gratification and in order to construct socially elevating myths about their own origins. But just as likely, they may have acted from an understandable impulse of slaves to establish their parentage. Or perhaps they simply told the truth. We will probably never know if they did.[43]

NOTES

1. Isaac Bassett Papers, Office of Senate Curator, U.S. Senate, Washington, D.C. For the location of this and other items in the Bassett Papers, I draw upon Robert V. Remini, *Daniel Webster the Man and His Times* (New York: W. W. Norton, 1997), 307. Remini also reports the 1832 incident

in the Capitol. I thank Scott M. Strong, Office of the Senate Curator, for providing copies of pertinent documents from the Bassett Papers.

2. F[rederick] Ayer to Rev. Sam Hunt, June 2, 1866, Papers of the American Missionary Association (microfilm), American Missionary Archives, Amistad Research Center, New Orleans; James Michael Russell, *Atlanta, 1847–1890: City Building in the Old South and the New* (Baton Rouge: Louisiana State University Press, 1988), 47.

3. "Bob Yancey's Claim," n.d., *Chicago Times,* in Bassett Papers. Robert Remini refers to Charlotte *Goodbrick,* while the source in the Bassett Papers refers to Charlotte *Goobrick.* After searching numerous genealogical and historical sources, I am inclined to agree that the name is more likely Goodbrick than Goobrick, though it may well have been Goodrich or Goodrick. For clarity she is referred to throughout this chapter as Charlotte Goodbrick.

4. Undated statement by Isaac Bassett, Bassett Papers; "Determining the Facts: Readings 4, Decatur House Lives On," in "Decatur House: Home of the Rich and Powerful," Teaching with Historic Places: Washington, D.C. History, www.cr.nps.gov/nr/twhp/wwwlps/lessons/19decatur/19facts4.htm. For additional instances of Robert Webster referred to as Bob Gadsby, see Anne Werley Smallman, "Furnishing/Interpretive Plan for Service Win of the Decatur House, an NTHP Property, Washington, D.C.," www.gwu.edu/~mstd/anne.html; and "John Gadsby, 1836–1844," in "Decatur House Residents," Stephen Decatur House Museum, www.decaturhouse.org/museum/biographies.htm.

5. "Bob Yancey's Claim," Bassett Papers. John Gadsby died in 1844. His will lists the slaves that he owned at the time of his death together with their names and ages. No slave of Robert Webster's age is noted in the inventory. Thus Webster had clearly been sold before the elder Gadsby's death. "Will of John Gadsby, of City of Washington, D.C. (dtd. Mar. 11, 1844, probated May 28, 1844; bk. 5, pp. 352–358: O.S. 2479; box 16)," from "Obituary and Death Notices—Surnames [G]," Historic Congressional Cemetery, www.congressionalcemetery.org/PDF/Obits/G/Obits_Gadsby.pdf.

6. John Cunningham to Benjamin C. Yancey, July 12, 1850, Benjamin Cudworth Yancey Papers (microfilm), Southern Historical Collection, University of North Carolina, Chapel Hill, reel 2; Ben C. Yancey to Reuben Arnold, May 16, 1872, *Webster v. United States,* case file 13502, Court of Claims, RG 123, Federal Records Center, Suitland, Md.; Deposition of B. C. Yancey, Sept. 27, 1875, ibid.

7. For a biographical sketch of Yancey, see the introduction to the Yancey Papers, reel 1. Also see "Part III of the Survey of the B. C. Yancey Papers: Papers, 1870–1931. General Description," ibid., reel 7; Thomas McAdory Owen, *History of Alabama and Dictionary of Alabama Biography,* 4 vols. (Chicago: S. J. Clarke, 1921), 4:1819–20; and Yancey to Arnold, May 16, 1872, in *Webster* v. *U.S.*

8. Deposition of Robert Webster, May 31, 1872, *Webster v. U.S.;* Yancey to Arnold, May 16, 1872, ibid.; Deposition of B. C. Rogers, Oct. 21, 1875, ibid.

9. Thomas G. Dyer, *Secret Yankees: The Union Circle in Confederate Atlanta* (Baltimore: Johns Hopkins University Press, 1999).

10. Ibid., 3, 5–6.

11. Ibid., 5–6.

12. Deposition of Robert Webster, May 31, 1872; Deposition of William Lewis, July 26, 1873, *Webster v. U.S.*

13. Deposition of Thomas Crussell, May 31, 1872, ibid.; Deposition of E. T. Hunnicutt, May 31, 1872, ibid.

14. Deposition of Robert Webster, May 31, 1872; Gilbert E. Govan and James Livingood, *The Chattanooga Country* (New York: E. P. Dutton, 1952), 180–89, 240–41; Robert P. Rowland, undergraduate paper, University of Miami, n.d., Clift Family Papers, Tennessee State Archives, Nashville.

15. Deposition of Robert Webster, May 31, 1872. The testimony regarding Clift comes from questions put by Webster to another witness, E. T. Hunnicutt, during Hunnicutt's testimony the same day.

16. William D. Clift to Col. J. Merritt, Dec. 6, 1863, Clift Family Papers; E[lizabeth] H. Clift to William D. Clift, Feb. 17, 1864, ibid.; Robert H. Ramfery [?] to Mrs. Elizabeth H. Clift, Sept. 24, 1864, ibid.

17. Dyer, *Secret Yankees,* 176, 184.

18. Wallace P. Reed, *History of Atlanta, Georgia* (Syracuse, N.Y.: D. Mason, 1889), 206; Deposition of James Dunning, Jan. 8, 1870, *Webster v. U.S;* Dyer, *Secret Yankees,* 184.

19. Deposition of James Dunning, Jan. 8, 1870; Dyer, *Secret Yankees,* 185.

20. Deposition of John Silvey, Sept. 28, 1875, *Webster v. U.S.;* Deposition of William Markham, Jan. 8, 1870, ibid.; Deposition of William Lewis, July 26, 1873; Dyer, *Secret Yankees,* 185.

21. James M. Calhoun to Reuben Arnold, Nov. 27, 1875, *Webster v. U.S.;* Dyer, *Secret Yankees,* 191.

22. Dyer, *Secret Yankees,* 198, 254–55; Deposition of Polly Beedles, July 5, 1873, Claim of Henry Beedles, Fulton County, Ga., Records of the Southern Claims Commission (Allowed Claims), RG 217, National Archives, Washington, D.C.; Deposition of Henry Beedles, July 5, 1873, ibid.; Deposition of Joseph A. Wood, n.d., *Webster v. U.S.*

23. Dyer, *Secret Yankees,* 202–12; Deposition of John S. Wise, Oct. 22, 1875, *Webster v. U.S.;* Deposition of B. C. Rogers, Oct. 21, 1875. By late 1864, when significant numbers of the Atlanta citizenry started to return to the city, Webster had reopened his "shaving emporium" on Decatur Street and was back in business. Franklin M. Garrett, *Atlanta and Environs: A Chronicle of its People and Events,* 2 vols. (Athens: University of Georgia Press, 1954), 1:661.

24. Deposition of B. C. Yancey, Sept. 27, 1875, *Webster v. U.S.*

25. Deposition of Eli T. Hunnicutt, Oct. 26, 1875, ibid.; Deposition of T. G. Campbell, Dec. 29, 1869, ibid.

26. *Atlanta Daily New Era,* Feb. 29, 1868.

27. T. G. Campbell et al. to Charles Sumner, Feb. 18, 1870, *Webster v. U.S.;* Frank Klingberg, *The Southern Claims Commission* (Berkeley: University of California Press, 1955); Dyer, *Secret Yankees,* 254–55.

28. Dyer, *Secret Yankees,* 254–55.

29. Jerry J. Thornbery, "The Development of Black Atlanta, 1865–1885" (Ph.D. diss., University of Maryland, 1977), 323, 325, 327, 328–30; Deposition of B. C. Yancey, Sept. 27, 1875; Robert Webster to Benjamin C. Yancey, Mar. 18, 1880, Yancey Papers, reel 11.

30. Deposition of Eli T. Hunnicutt, Oct. 26, 1875; *Atlanta News,* Mar. 7, 1875.

31. Webster appears in neither the Atlanta city directory for 1880 and subsequent volumes nor in the 1880 census.

32. Irving H. Bartlett, *Daniel Webster* (New York: W. W. Norton, 1978), 322 n. 30, 284; Remini,

Daniel Webster, 307, 308. Also see Jane Grey Swisshelm, *Half a Century* (1880; repr., New York: Source Book, 1970).

33. Swisshelm, *Half a Century,* 128; Remini, *Daniel Webster;* Bartlett, *Daniel Webster,* 201–2. The Swisshelm quotation is used by both Remini and Bartlett. For the connection between Jane Swisshelm and E. D. E. N. Southworth, see Swisshelm, *Half a Century,* 129–30. For the information concerning Southworth and Joshua Henshaw, see Susan Coultrap-McQuin, *Doing Literary Business: American Women Writers in the Nineteenth Century* (Chapel Hill: University of North Carolina Press, 1990), 53. Also see Donald A. Ritchie, *Press Gallery: Congress and the Washington Correspondents* (Cambridge, Mass.: Harvard University Press, 1991), 44–45. I am indebted to Sylvia Hoffert of the University of North Carolina for generous assistance regarding Swisshelm and Southworth.

34. Bassett Papers.

35. Ibid.

36. I base the date of the article on internal evidence that refers to Benjamin C. Yancey serving in the "present" Georgia legislature; the only year in which Yancey served was 1879. *Georgia House Journal Regular Session 1879* (Atlanta, 1879). The article in question is located in the Bassett Papers.

37. Bassett Papers.

38. Ibid.; Bartlett, *Daniel Webster,* 284. For a discussion of the relationship between Goodridge and Webster, see Remini, *Daniel Webster,* 306–9.

39. Bassett Papers.

40. Ibid.; Remini, *Daniel Webster,* 758n.

41. Charles M. Wiltse et al., eds., *The Papers of Daniel Webster,* 7 vols. (Hanover, N.H.: University Press of New England), 5:29; *Boston Directory for the Year Commencing July 1, 1861* (Boston: Adams, Sampson, 1861; Remini, *Daniel Webster,* 758n.

42. Massachusetts Adjutant General's Office, *Massachusetts, Soldiers, Sailors, and Marines in the Civil War,* 8 vols. (Norwood, Mass.: Norwood, 1931–35), 5:841.

43. David Herbert Donald, *Lincoln* (New York: Simon & Schuster, 1995), 20. For a discussion of Freud's theory of "family romances," see Ron Rosenbaum, *Explaining Hitler: The Search for the Origins of His Evil* (New York: HarperCollins, 1998), 8.

"What Price Must We Pay for Victory?": Views on Arming Slaves from Lynchburg, Virginia, to Galveston, Texas

PHILIP D. DILLARD

IN THE FALL OF 1864, THE BITTER WIND OF MILITARY DEFEAT whipped through the Confederacy and fanned an open and often heated debate concerning the introduction of slaves into the Confederate army. As long as the gray lines held firm, no one had to choose between slavery and independence, but stunning Union victories and thinning army ranks forced southerners to decide what they held most dear: Did the preservation of slavery remain the "cornerstone" of the Confederacy as it had been in 1861, or had other war aims become more important during the struggle? While calls for new soldiers echoed through government offices across the South, southerners considered how a nation built with slavery as its foundation might choose to end the institution in the name of self-preservation. As this debate raged from November 1864 to April 1865, citizens had to determine the importance of slavery and define the sacrifices they would make in the name of their Confederate nation.[1]

While leaders discussed the issue in Richmond, an equally important debate occurred among the people all across the Confederacy.[2] This essay compares the debate as it unfolded in Lynchburg, Virginia, and Galveston, Texas. Powerful Union armies in the Shenandoah Valley and in central Virginia provided a very real portrait of potential defeat and forced the citizens of Lynchburg to consider revolutionary measures to attain victory. In contrast the vast distances to the key battlefields and strong economic forces still at work in Texas caused the citizens of Galveston to see the war quite differently. After the failure of the Union campaign along the Red River in the spring of 1864, no enemy troops threatened Texan homes or the state's still stable slave economy. In many ways Texas provides a clear picture of southern views on slavery without any hint of desperation and places the revolutionary influence of warfare upon society in great relief.

Three key events propelled the slave-soldier debate in the South: Pres. Jefferson Davis's annual address to Congress in November 1864, the defeats at Nashville and Savannah in December, and the final efforts to gain congressional approval for black troops in February 1865. Although fifteen hundred miles apart, Lynchburg and Galveston shared several common features and therefore provide an exceptional picture of how the debate developed in these states. First, as the Union armies advanced, large numbers of refugees arrived in southwestern Virginia and in coastal Texas. Second, both cities possessed strong newspapers that served as platforms for the debate.[3] Third, each represented a distinct region of the Confederate nation. Nestled in southwestern Virginia, Lynchburg reflected the views of the Upper South directly touched by the war. Galveston, however, represented a distinct Trans-Mississippi outlook. While northern troops sat in New Orleans and occasionally threatened the coastline, Galveston experienced the war less intensely. In general the events that affected popular views in Lynchburg also resonated in Galveston. Despite some similarities in the two cities, the citizens of each framed the debate quite differently in response to their experience of the war.

President Davis opened the national debate on arming the slaves in his annual address to Congress on November 7, 1864. While proposing legislation on many subjects, Davis requested "the enrollment of 40,000 negroes to be employed as pioneer and engineer laborers." It would have drawn little comment if he had stopped there, but the president claimed that although a slave was property, he or she also bore an obligation to the state as a person. Arguing that while employed by the army the slave's role as a person took precedence over his status as property, Davis contended that the government must purchase the slaves so serving and free them at the end of their service. This new proposal far exceeded the previous practice of impressing slaves for limited periods and returning them to their masters. While not immediately advocating arming slaves, Davis speculated that such a measure might eventually be necessary: "Should the alternative ever be presented of subjugation or of the employment of the slave as a soldier, there seems no reason to doubt what should then be our decision." His proposal to free the slaves working for the army, along with his admission that conscripting them might eventually become necessary, began an unprecedented national debate on slavery.[4]

The president's message to Congress graced the pages of the *Lynchburg Virginian* in early November as the sound of Union general Philip Sheridan's cavalry echoed in the ears of the citizens of southwestern Virginia. The *Virginian* printed numerous accounts of barns burned, mills destroyed, and provisions lost. Such wanton destruction of property and the accompanying loss of life, the paper concluded, furnished "one of the foulest and blackest pages in human history." With Sheridan's raids as a backdrop, the *Virginian* presented a wide variety of views on how slaves should be used but favored pieces that accepted the need for some change. While differing with a column from the *Richmond Enquirer* that called for the immediate enlistment of 250,000 black troops, on October 20 the Lynchburg paper praised the services of black units in the southern revolution and suggested that the South had few viable options remaining: "We must, if this war continues, sacrifice the last able-bodied white man left and consent to have our negroes taken by force, . . . or we must defeat the enemy at his own game, and make the negro fight for us and against the hated foe." The most influential news item to appear in Lynchburg during this opening phase of the debate came from Richmond. In his message to the Virginia House of Delegates, Gov. William Smith boldly proclaimed that Virginians as well as southerners everywhere faced fearful choices: "Has the time arrived when this issue is . . . liberty and independence, or subjugation[?] . . . A man must be blind to current events; to the gigantic proportions of the war; . . . who does not see that the issue above referred to is presented now." Contending that necessity forced the South to use all means available, Smith affirmed, "Standing before God and my country, I do not hesitate to say that I would arm such portion of our able-bodied slave population as may be necessary and put them in the field, so as to have them ready for the spring campaign."[5]

From his editorial desk in Lynchburg, Charles Button eagerly joined the discussion regarding slave soldiers. In response to Davis's message, Button stated that he had always seen black soldiers as a logical "dernier resort" that would provide freedom to some "who should vindicate their title to it by deeds of valor." Conceding that the military situation might not yet demand the step, the Lynchburg editor argued that when the necessity was clearly established, slaves must be used: "We should be madmen not to avail ourselves of every means in our power to wage war against the unnatural foe who first seduced and then armed our domestics against us." On December 6 Button, noting Union general William T. Sherman's collection of able-bodied slaves in Georgia, suggested that southerners might prefer to choose the best slaves to enter the military rather than let the Union troops make the first selections: "Would we have them to earn their freedom in periling their lives to secure our liberties; or let them join the serried host of the enemy to assist in enslaving free white men?" Two weeks later he cited Lincoln's assertion that the North could not have continued the struggle without 200,000 black troops and questioned the intelligence of Confederate policies that sacrificed "our sons rather than our slaves."[6] The thundering hooves of Yankee horsemen no doubt added considerable emphasis to the news items and editorials appearing in Lynchburg.

Like many island residents, the *Galveston News* had moved inland to avoid Union threats and was publishing from offices in Houston when President Davis's message arrived. An editorial from Richmond first broached the topic of slave soldiers in the columns of the *News* on November 9 and supported the purchase, enlistment, and emancipation of 250,000 slaves. Two weeks later, on November 25, an editorial from the *Mobile News* hailed the potential moral effect of black men in gray and asserted that southerners and not northerners should choose how the slaves would participate in the war: "If our slaves are to take part in this unhappy conflict, certainly we have a choice as to the side they shall take."[7] During December, pieces from the *Richmond Whig, New York Herald,* and *Chicago Times* also appeared in Galveston, expressing differing views of the debate in the South.[8]

Willard Richardson, editor of the *Galveston News,* harshly rebuked the president for considering even limited emancipation: "If it be admitted that the negro can enjoy freedom, without injury to their own condition or to those around them, but that, having the physical power, we will compel their servitude, the declaration would be ignoble; for it would assert the maintenance of injustice by force." Driving home the point, he declared, "If they are capable of being safely entrusted with freedom, they ought to be emancipated without conditions." Lastly the Galveston editor proclaimed that any Confederate emancipation effort would be the ultimate usurpation of local power. In Richardson's view the consequences of Davis's speculations had the potential for profound consequences: "The proposition which has been broached at Richmond to arm and drill . . . three hundred thousand slaves, will be very apt to finish the 'institution' and the 'Confederacy' before the spring campaign is opened." Yet the idea that the failure to fill the gray ranks might "finish" both institutions appears not to have occurred to Richardson.[9]

Davis's address to Congress sparked considerable discussion in Lynchburg and Galveston. With Sheridan devastating the valley to their north, the citizens of Lynchburg focused on the war. Leaping forward from a discussion of noncombatant laborers, the local editor pushed forward a series of opinion pieces and news items designed to promote a thorough debate of slavery. Far from the lines at Petersburg and Sherman's path through Georgia, Galvestonians failed to grasp the depth of the manpower crisis. But with international trade booming along the Texas coast, consumer items, unknown in Lynchburg, graced the streets of Galveston and obscured the picture of impending crisis, causing few residents to call for modifying slavery.[10] Clearly the separation of the Trans-Mississippi from the rest of the Confederacy was reflected in the cool reception of Davis's proposals in Texas.

In the East Sherman's long, destructive march through Georgia ended with the capitulation of Savannah on December 21, sending despair racing across the South. Just five days earlier Union general George Thomas had destroyed the Army of Tennessee at Nashville, leaving the Confederacy without a creditable field force in the West. News of these two great defeats arrived in Virginia at approximately the same time, producing a most sobering Christmas week and complementing well the somber view of the war presented in Lynchburg. Reports of the twin misfortunes arrived in Texas during the first week of the new year, shaking some from their complacency. Yet without a large influx of refugees or wounded soldiers and with the continuing strength of the Texas cotton economy, the magnitude of the twin defeats east of the Mississippi did not become immediately apparent. Few Texans lost sight of the fact that steps taken to meet the manpower crisis would permanently change the social fabric of the South. After these December reverses, though, the debate over arming slaves entered a distinct second phase due to the military necessity to place a new army in the field.

The capture of the important salt works in Saltville, Virginia, just prior to Christmas added significantly to the sense of urgency produced by the failures at Savannah and Nashville. In the wake of these disasters, the *Virginian* sought to find a ray of hope on the horizon: "We are not as badly off as we were this time last year. The enemy has tried his best and he can never make such another exertion." Black soldiers provided one of the few active alternatives to waiting and hoping that Union forces could not match their 1864 campaign. On January 12, 1865, the *Virginian* printed an item from the London *Times* that suggested that southerners were too worried about how others would perceive the decision to arm slaves and too little about how well it would work. The London editor contended that black men in gray would be as loyal as the men of Baltimore in blue. Several days later the words of Kentucky Unionist George D. Prentice appeared in the Lynchburg paper and expressed the earnestness of the southern debate: "The Jeff Davis Government has conclusively resolved to free and arm the slaves—that two hundred thousand of them would soon be equipped and put into the field to fight us, under the stimulus of the promise of their own liberty and that of their wives and children, and of a proprietary interest in the soil." On February 4 the comments of Rep. John Atkins of Tennessee burned across the pages in Lynchburg: "Between subjugation and using our slaves in our defense every principle of nature and self-preservation requires the latter; therefore, we should at once put one hundred thousand slaves . . . in the field." In Congress many echoed Atkins's sentiments, but most stopped short of saying that the action must be taken immediately.[11]

The continuing setbacks found Charles Button at the *Lynchburg Virginian* struggling with the demon of despair as he declared his willingness to make any sacrifice to stave off defeat: "Give up slavery; everything but our freedom, to save ourselves from the domination of the beastly Yankee." Despite these brave words, on January 3 he refused to agree with several Richmond colleagues who recommended immediate abolition and acceptance of a colonial protectorate from a European power. The *Virginian*'s editor feared that widespread emancipation would harm the ex-slave as well as the South. "No matter how this struggle may eventuate," Button asserted, "slavery in some form or other, in effect, if not in name, will exist in these Southern States." Clearly he understood the call for black assistance as a necessary war measure rather than a statement of support for racial equality. Three days later he drove home the point by examining the financial demise of Haiti after the black masses won their freedom. While many considered him a radical on racial issues for his advocation of black troops, Button displayed significant racial prejudice even as he called for black assistance on the battlefield.[12]

With conditions remaining relatively tranquil, the magnitude of Nashville and Savannah did not become immediately apparent in Texas. Yet as the overall military situation deteriorated in January and February 1865, it became harder to ignore the argument of necessity, even in Texas. Upon confirmation of the fall of Savannah, the *Galveston News* contended that Sherman had gained little. Further reports from Tennessee caused some fear that John Bell Hood's defeat might lead to a movement toward Texas.[13]

In addition to wire-service reports of congressional action and editorials on the subject, the largest news item on black troops to appear in Galveston originated in Texas. On January 20 Judge John T. Mills addressed a letter to the *Galveston News* concerning the role of the slave in the war effort. Prefacing his remarks by noting his vote for secession and his longstanding ownership of slaves, Mills stated that there were only two roads to peace: submission and reunion or emancipation and continuing the struggle. Slavery, he averred, was not worth the cost that southerners were paying. "In fact," Mills proclaimed, "more of that [southern blood] has already been shed than every slave in the Confederacy is worth." Acknowledging that the idea of arming blacks required "meditation" and "reflection" on the part of slaveowners, he argued that the institution was doomed because "not only the Yankees, but the world, is against us on the slavery question." In his opinion the reverses of 1864 proved that the South could not win its independence alone: "The North will never recognize our independence until she is compelled by a greater power than we alone can bring to bear upon her." By freeing the slaves and offering themselves as a colony to England or France, the Confederate States, the judge believed, could thwart northern aims and secure the right of self-government. "The blood of our brave soldiers," Mills concluded, "will not have been shed in vain, should we gain our independence and lose our slaves."[14]

In the next two months, fifteen Texans responded to Mills by writing the *News* to counter his arguments. While many of these writers covered similar ground, two stand out. On February 19 Col. Clayton C. Gillespie, commander of the 26th Texas Cavalry, penned a lengthy reply that denied that any necessity existed to justify such a step. While approving of the military use of slaves as laborers, Gillespie asserted that the army was "not yet ready to fight for a free negro Confederacy or to allow one to exist on this Southern land." Indignant, the colonel proclaimed Mills's letter "the fruit of panic, the pitiful panic that is now upon the country, and of which every man who participated in it ought to be ashamed." In another vein a letter from Ashbel Smith appeared on February 22 and questioned the idea that emancipation would have any effect on foreign relations. Having negotiated recognition with Britain and France for the Republic of Texas, Smith ridiculed all who thought slavery was the reason Europe failed to recognize the Confederacy: "The poor simpletons, why, slavery in its moral aspects, has never delayed recognition for an hour, nor would its abandonment now hasten by one hour our recognition." Self-interest and not any moral ideal, he averred, guided the European powers. Both Smith and Gillespie had statewide reputations and forcefully rebutted Mills's contentions. Soldiers, planters, and old politicians all took turns jousting with the judge. Most predicted dire consequences if the South armed slaves, and all suggested that the time for even considering the question had not yet arrived.[15]

While many southerners remained skeptical about black troops, Nashville and Savannah served as catalysts in Lynchburg and Galveston. In Lynchburg, Charles Button struggled with the implications of his conviction that slaves must be armed. Union military activity ensured that Virginians could not forget the urgency of the issue. In contrast Texans along the Gulf Coast had difficulty identifying an immediate need to change the social system. The bold epistle of Judge Mills sparked a number of insightful responses, which all clearly demonstrated that the war had not affected Texas as it had Virginia. Slavery had not been disrupted by Union raids, cotton could still be sold profitably on the world market, and no Federal armies threatened the state. It seems that the response to the idea of slave soldiers was directly related to the proximity of the war.

On February 3, 1865, three Confederate commissioners rode slowly back from the failed peace conference at Hampton Roads and into the southern lines at Petersburg, ending all realistic hope for a negotiated settlement to the war. Since Lincoln offered no terms except submission and reunion, the unsuccessful peace initiative quieted many of Davis's critics and reenergized the efforts to fill the army's ranks. Black soldiers provided the only viable option. Without hope for foreign intervention or a negotiated peace, southerners had to choose between slavery and independence. The final phase of the debate began on February 9, with Secretary of State Judah P. Benjamin's speech in Richmond demanding passage of the bill to arm slaves. Employing an apt metaphor, Benjamin attempted to show the shortsightedness of his opponents: "It looks to me very much like a man rushing forth from his burning house, and begging his neighbors, for heaven's sake, not to throw water on the blazing roof, because it might spoil his furniture."[16] From this speech to final passage of the act to arm slaves on March 13, the debate raged ferociously as the Confederate people attempted to determine the sacrifices necessary to preserve the "southern way of life."

The failure of the Hampton Roads conference and Benjamin's speech added potent fuel to the debate raging in Lynchburg. Of greater popular interest, on February 25 the *Virginian* published a letter from the new general in chief strongly advocating arming the slaves. "I am," Robert E. Lee affirmed, "favorable to the use of our servants in the army. . . . I would hold out to them the certainty of freedom and a home, when they shall have rendered efficient service." The release of his letter addressed to Ethelbert Barksdale confirmed the views attributed to Lee earlier and made it easier for others to openly espouse black troops and emancipation. Two men running for election to the Virginia House of Delegates wrote letters to the *Virginian* trumpeting their support for the measure.[17]

The citizens of Roanoke, Campbell, and Bedford counties and the city of Lynchburg held public meetings to discuss the situation after the Hampton Roads conference. Each gathering noted the support of Lee for black troops and passed a resolution calling for the measure's immediate adoption. The wording of the resolutions adopted in Roanoke demonstrated well the sincerity of these men and women: "While there have been differences of opinion amongst us as to the necessity and policy of enlisting a portion of our slaves in the army . . . and whether with or without changing the social status of the slaves, yet holding our independence to be paramount . . . , we compromise all differences of opinion and urge . . . the immediate adoption of some plan to put as many slaves in the army as the Commander-in-Chief may deem necessary." Obviously the citizens of the Lynchburg area had struggled with the issue of arming, but particularly freeing, the slaves. While military necessity must have played a key role in the debate, the Union threat had not caused them to unthinkingly accept radical steps.[18]

As Confederate defeats mounted, communications between Texas and Richmond suffered. On March 3 a Confederate synopsis of Benjamin's speech arrived, but the *Galveston News* rejected the secretary's suggestions as vehemently as the *Virginian* had embraced them: "Mr. Benjamin presented some disagreeable truths as he said the necessity of using negro soldiers could not be avoided. He . . . said if the Virginia Assembly would recommend the measure, Lee would be reinforced by twenty thousand in twenty days." In the same issue of the *News,* the arguments of Henry Burnett of Kentucky, John Atkins of Tennessee, and James Orr of South Carolina rang out in detailed accounts of the House and Senate debates over arming slaves. While continuing to follow the debate in the Confederate Congress, the Galveston paper attempted to lead public opinion by choosing its news items carefully. For example, on March 10 the editors took excerpts from Vice President Alexander Stephens's speech in 1861 in which he declared slavery the cornerstone of the Confederacy. This selection allowed the *News* to argue that calm, rational men had long considered slavery the cause and purpose of the war.[19] As prominent leaders and respected journalists in Richmond endorsed the idea of black troops, the Galveston paper had difficulty locating news items that supported its resolute opposition to arming slaves.

After sitting on the sidelines for almost a month, on March 3 editor Richardson reported that he had received from thirty to forty letters in response to Judge Mills's advocacy of using black troops. Mills's letter had caused Galvestonians and Texans in general to address the idea of slave soldiers in detail. From these letters, Richardson deduced, "If we may judge public opinion by the sentiments of our correspondents, the people of Texas are not in favor of lowering themselves to the level of the negro." Richardson blasted the idea as the cry of the weak hearted and disaffected: "To say that we are ready to emancipate our slaves, would be to say, that we are ready to relinquish what we commenced fighting for. It would be an abandonment of principles, as well as a confession of weakness." Countering the arguments of his opponents, he reassured his readers that the self-interested states of Europe would more eagerly acknowledge a prosperous slave power than a nation without slaves or marketable crops. "We look upon emancipation as an impractical myth," Richardson concluded, "calculated to amuse some ingenious minds . . . , but one that will not receive a single practical recommendation."[20]

During this final phase of the debate, no correspondent of the *Galveston News* was able to match the fire and eloquence of Judge Mills. Yet five more responses to Mills's "emancipation" letter were included in the columns of the *News* in the immediate aftermath of the peace conference. On February 27 a private stationed in the Galveston defenses wrote and declared that the talk of arming slaves had begun to have ill effects: "The discussion is untimely and fraught with evil; it engenders panic when there is no danger." In addition "Pelican Private" challenged southerners to think of those who had gone before to steer their course: "Shall we sell slavery, the legacy of our fathers—a legacy halloed by the best blood of the Caucassian race—to purchase independence: Go to the red fields of Manassas, Sharpsburg and Shiloh . . . and tell their whitened bones that you are *so base, so low, so abject* that you are ready to abandon the cause for which they fell."[21] Similarly, on March 6 the *News* printed the minutes of a public meeting in Goliad in which the citizens scolded those who had broached the issue of emancipation, terming the debate as "premature, unwise and unnecessary." Only one correspondent entered the fray to recommend the adoption of black troops. On February 27 M. Estis argued that the conscription and fielding of three hundred thousand black Confederates would have a dramatic moral effect: "It will convince them [northerners] that we are in earnest, in solid earnest, and that we are ready and willing to make any and all sacrifices."[22]

Without the Union threat that was so apparent in Lynchburg, Texans could not see the wisdom of arming slaves.

On February 20 the Confederate House passed a bill authorizing the president to call on the states for a "quota of three hundred thousand troops . . . to be raised from such classes of the population, irrespective of color, in each State as the proper authorities thereof may determine." Although far less than Davis and Lee would have liked, they had won a narrow victory by a vote of forty to thirty-seven. After the measure failed in the Senate on February 25, the *Lynchburg Virginian* decried the negative votes of the two Virginia senators: "Messrs. Hunter and Caperton voted against the negro bill—against giving Gen. Lee more soldiers! These gentlemen will find ere long that they mis-represented Virginia upon the subject." While opponents of black troops trumpeted the bill's defeat, the friends of the measure regrouped.[23] In a series of resolutions adopted on March 4, the House of Delegates authorized the Confederate government to call upon Virginia for all of her free blacks and up to 25 percent of her slave population. Further, the legislators instructed the state's senators to change their votes: "Our senators are hereby instructed and our representatives requested to vote for the passage of a law to place at the disposal of the Confederate authorities as many of the male slaves . . . as he [Lee] shall deem best." Even before the Senate could again address the issue, on March 6 the House of Delegates passed a bill making it lawful for blacks in the army to bear arms and carry ammunition in all areas of Virginia. Unlike the state's national senators, Virginia legislators vigorously pursued the enrollment of black troops into the Confederate army. With every district in the state either overrun or under severe threat, these bold and desperate Virginians were seizing the only means of defense they had remaining.[24]

From his editorial desk Charles Button lamented the slow pace of congressional action: "We cannot but regret, and regret deeply, that the measure was not adopted months ago, so that the army might by this time be enjoying the benefit of the recruits." Congress's omission of the emancipation feature also troubled him: "It will devolve upon the patriotic slave-holders themselves to supply . . . an undoubted evidence of their freedom, conditioned upon their rendering faithful service." Looking over some old clippings, Button suggested that southern trepidation about placing black men in the ranks resembled that expressed in northern journals as the first black units entered the Union army.[25] A strong proponent of black soldiers, Button must have taken considerable pride in how Lynchburg and southwestern Virginia as a whole responded to the idea of making soldiers of slaves.

When word arrived in Texas on March 29 that Congress had passed legislation to allow black Confederate troops, Willard Richardson grudgingly accepted the fact: "We have always had serious objections to employing slaves as soldiers, but we are willing in this as in other matters of a military character to waive our objection in deference to the wisdom of Congress and the matured judgment of such men as President Davis and Gen. Lee." The Galveston editor drew considerable satisfaction from the lack of a promise of freedom: "We have had some fears that the employment of negroes in the army would be predicated . . . on their final emancipation. We are glad to see that our Congress has authorized no such change in the condition of the negro." Instead of freedom Richardson contended that "the greatest boon they [slave soldiers] can have for faithful service in our armies, will be their future protection from Yankee tyranny and deception, and the heartless neglect and cruelty with which they have been invariably treated." Many southerners hoped that the Union army's indifference to the difficulties facing refugee slaves would convince blacks that they had been better off living on the plantation. Slaves may have become a bit disillusioned with their liberators, but they had not become so discouraged that they remained on the plantations when Union troops offered the opportunity to leave. Although Texas was now playing host to many black and white refugees, the institution of slavery remained stable within the Lone Star State. Consequently many readers of the *Galveston News* clung to the illusion of black contentment. If the Confederacy were to arm black troops, this method—enlistment without emancipation—least bothered the citizens of Galveston.[26]

In Virginia Lee struggled to command his army while directing efforts to form black units in Virginia. Two days after the bill passed in Congress, he ordered J. W. Pegram and Thomas P. Turner to recruit the first unit. On March 17 the *Lynchburg Virginian* announced the plans underway: "Recruiting offices will be opened immediately all over the country and the slave-holders of Virginia, especially, will, we trust, respond promptly. Let Virginia in this emergency show . . . that no sacrifice is too great to make for the holy cause of freedom." The following day the paper printed an appeal from Pegram and Turner for masters to bring in their slaves to enlist. On March 23 and 24 the *Virginian* published the names of thirty slaveowners offering to free their bondsmen to give them to the cause. Subsequently the newspapers reported that five hundred black troops, recruited from slaves already working for the army, had paraded in Richmond: "The interest of the occasion was lessened by the failure to uniform and equip the negro soldiers. They were armed with muskets." With Lee abandoning the Confederate capital on April 2, few if any of these black soldiers ever made it into the trenches. Yet in the last issue of the *Richmond Whig,* on April 3, the editor praised the battalion created by Pegram and called on slaveowners for additional black troops.[27]

Based on the appeals in the Virginia papers, it appears that black recruits did not flock to see the enrolling officers and that the army was poorly prepared for those who did. Even so, after considerable soul searching, the citizens of Lynchburg had embraced the idea of black troops and did what they could to aid recruitment in the waning days of the Confederacy. The lists of owners' offering their slaves to the army demonstrated that a number of Virginians were ready to live up to their word. In the final crisis of the war, these citizens had come to believe that independence was far more important than the preservation of slavery. Black troops had come too late to aid the South militarily, but this fact does not discredit the importance of this fateful decision.[28]

Lynchburg and Galveston provide an interesting contrast in opinions across the South concerning the arming of slaves and illustrate well the dramatic effect of hard war on southern communities. The struggle may have begun as a conservative attempt to avoid change, but hard war revolutionized not only battlefield tactics but also the objectives of the war. Union threats and harsh sacrifices had made true Confederates out of many Virginians. Efforts to arm slaves in southwestern Virginia show that weary men and women who had seen destruction all about them were willing to make any and all sacrifices that might lead to victory. Citizens in this Virginia community went far beyond the idea of black teamsters and engineer laborers; they discussed the necessity of arming large numbers of black combat troops and debated the effect of these radical steps on southern society. Conversely the vast distances to the key battlefields coupled with strong economic forces still at work in Texas caused the citizens of Galveston to see the necessities of war quite differently. After the failure of the Union campaign along the Red River in the spring of 1864, no enemy troops threatened Texan homes or the state's slave economy. In many ways Texas provides a clear picture of antebellum views on slavery and when contrasted with Virginia illustrates well the effect of warfare upon society. In this final crisis of the Civil War, the selection of independence over slavery by those who had seen and felt the full effect of war provides an eloquent statement about the strength of Confederate nationalism.

NOTES

1. In *The Confederacy as a Revolutionary Experience* (Englewood Cliffs, N.J.: Prentice-Hall, 1971), Emory Thomas argues persuasively that slavery was the last in a long line of revolutionary sacrifices. He believes that the conservative revolution of 1861 had been transformed into a true revolution by the winter of 1864. William Blair reaches similar conclusions in *Virginia's Private War: Feeding Body and Soul in the Confederacy, 1861–1865* (New York: Oxford University Press, 1998). But he suggests that many of the revolutionary steps noted by Thomas were taken in order for the planter class to retain their political primacy. Blair does not see the issue of slavery as a key test of Confederate nationalism, as I argue here. In *Why the South Lost the Civil War* (Athens: University of Georgia Press, 1986), Richard Beringer and his coauthors focus exclusively upon the debate over war aims. They summarily dismiss the idea that independence could ever replace slavery as the South's primary war goal. Although "resentment, guilt, and disillusionment" may have played a part in the reappraisal of Confederate war aims, these authors too quickly deny the revolutionary power of warfare upon individuals and nations.

2. Although most historians have dismissed this revolutionary debate, Robert F. Durden addresses the issue in *The Gray and the Black: The Confederate Debate on Emancipation* (Baton Rouge: Louisiana State University Press, 1972). Durden presents a well-crafted, superbly organized survey of the documents concerning the Confederate debate about slave soldiers. Focusing primarily on the views expressed in Richmond, he argues strongly that most southerners lacked the "intelligence, imagination, and moral courage" necessary to emancipate the slaves (287). While presenting considerable support for this conclusion from the city's newspapers, Durden fails to follow consistently the debate beyond the capital and leaves the reader wondering about attitudes in the Deep South and the Trans-Mississippi concerning arming and emancipating the slaves. In *Southern Negroes: 1861–1865* (1938; reprint, Baton Rouge: Louisiana State University Press, 1974), Bell Wiley provides an excellent narrative detailing the course of the efforts to place slaves in the Confederate army. Unfortunately he fails to question how the acceptance of black regiments reflected changes in public war aims. The most complete examination of the debate in Georgia is Clarence Mohr, *On the Threshold of Freedom: Masters and Slaves in Civil War Georgia* (Athens: University of Georgia Press, 1986). Although recognizing the debate as a "search for Southern identity and a quest for national purpose," Mohr focuses upon the views of black Georgians and addresses the intriguing question of whether the slaves would have fought for the South. In contrast to many historians who have assumed that all slaves felt a sense of loyalty to the North, Mohr contends that black wartime "loyalty" to both sides was always conditional. Disillusionment with Union officers, family concerns, personal relationships with individual whites, and uncertainty over the war's outcome often combined to make individual decisions difficult. The black actors that Mohr describes are "loyal" enough to gain their owners' trust but ever ready to seize their freedom. Finally in *Black Confederates and Afro-Yankees in Civil War Virginia* (Charlottesville: University Press of Virginia, 1995), Ervin L. Jordan Jr. attempts to demonstrate the diversity of roles played by black Virginians. He does not explore the stakes in the Confederate debate of emancipation but rather examines the Afro-Virginians drawn to the southern cause. In short Jordan vastly oversells his case for black

Confederate patriotism. None of the realism of Mohr's "conditionally loyal" Georgians surfaces in Jordan's account.

3. In both states, newspapers provide the clearest reflection of the mood of the people as they struggled to define a new role for the slave. They reported developments that provoked and fueled the debate, attempted to lead public opinion with editorials, and served as sounding boards as they printed numerous letters to editors. Although a clear understanding of public sentiment is usually elusive, especially so during the nineteenth century, these newspapers provide overwhelming evidence that by the spring of 1865, many southerners strongly supported arming the slaves.

4. "The President's Message," *Galveston Tri-Weekly News,* Dec. 5, 1864.

5. "Employment of Negroes in Our Armies" and "Sheridan's Torch Everywhere Visible," Oct. 20, 1864; "The Raleigh Standard . . . ," Oct. 25, 1864; "The Battles of Cedar Creek," Oct. 27, 1864; "The Valley," Nov. 28, 1864; and "The Governor's Message," Dec. 12, 1864, all in the *Lynchburg Virginian.*

6. "Negro Soldiers," Nov. 11, 1864; "Sherman Is Laying . . . ," Dec. 6, 1864; and "Negro Recruits," Dec. 19, 1864, all by Charles Button in the *Lynchburg Virginian.*

7. "Opinion of the Press," Nov. 9, 1864; "A Richmond Correspondent Writes . . . ," "If the Yankees Determine . . . ," and "The President's Message, Synopsis," Nov. 25, 1864; and "President Davis' Proposal for Manumitting Slaves," Dec. 14, 1864, all in the *Galveston Tri-Weekly News.*

8. "News Items," Nov. 27, 1864; and "*The Chicago Times* . . ." and "Divide the South," Dec. 9, 1864, all in the *Galveston Tri-Weekly News.*

9. "Some Time Ago . . . ," Nov. 25, 1864; and "Mr. Davis' Recommendation of the Employment of Slaves in the Army," Dec. 12, 1864, both by Willard Richardson in the *Galveston Tri-Weekly News.*

10. Discussing plans for the holidays, editor John P. Osterhout of the *Bellville (Tex.) Countryman* marveled at the abundance of merchandise available in Gulf Coast Texas: "All sorts of good things can be had on the streets, for Christmas, at very reasonable rates; far more than we had anticipated." "For Several Days . . . ," *Bellville (Tex.) Countryman,* Dec. 20, 1864.

11. "Stoneman-Burbridge Raid," Dec. 30, 1864; "The Situation," Jan. 3, 1865; "Stoneman's Raid—A List of Munchausens," Jan. 6, 1865; "Arming the Negroes of the South," Jan. 12, 1865; "The Arming of Slaves," Jan. 16, 1865; and "Congressional," Jan. 28, Feb. 2, 4, 1865, all in the *Lynchburg Virginian.*

12. "It was considered a Roman virtue . . . ," Dec. 31, 1864; "A Republic to Let," Jan. 3, 1865; and "We have heretofore said . . . ," Jan. 6, 1865, all by Charles Button in the *Lynchburg Virginian.*

13. "The Dispatches of Friday . . ." and "He had heard . . . ," *Galveston Tri-Weekly News,* Jan. 8, 1865.

14. John T. Mills, "Judge Mills' Letter," Feb. 24, 1865, *Marshall Texas Republican.* The letter first appeared in the *Galveston News* on February 8, 1865. This issue of the *News* did not survive the war, but the letter was reprinted in several other papers across the state. John Mills was born in Ireland and raised in South Carolina. Coming to Texas in 1837, he used his legal skills for the Republic as a district judge. Although he failed in his bid for governor in 1849, Mills was well known and respected throughout the state. "John Mills," *New Handbook of Texas* (Austin: Texas State Historical Association, 1996), 4:750.

15. Clayton C. Gillespie, "The Confederate Motto—No Compromise," Feb. 19, 1865; and Ashbel Smith, "Col. Ashbel Smith on Slavery as It Affects Our Foreign Relations," Feb. 22, 1865, both in the *Galveston Tri-Weekly News.*

16. "Speech of Hon. J. P. Benjamin," *Lynchburg Virginian,* Feb. 13, 1865.

17. "Employment of Negroes Soldiers," Feb. 25, 1865; "To the Voters of Campbell and Lynchburg," Mar. 18, 1865; and "To the Voters of Campbell and Lynchburg," Mar. 21, 1865, all in the *Lynchburg Virginian.*

18. G.W.D., "Campbell County," Feb. 21, 1865; P. H. Huff, "At a meeting of the citizens of Roanoke County . . . ," Feb. 25, 1865; Jno. Speed, "War Meeting in Lynchburg," Mar. 2, 1865; G.W.D., "At a meeting of the citizens of Bedford County . . . ," Mar. 8, 1865; "The Right Spirit," Mar. 21, 1865; "The People of Roanoke . . . ," Mar. 23, 1865; and "The Right Spirit," Mar. 24, 1865, all in the *Lynchburg Virginian.* Meetings like these provide one of the clearest reflections of mass sentiment concerning the slave-soldier debate. Local officials chaired such gatherings, but common citizens participated in the discussions and were called upon to make monetary and other contributions to prove their resolve. Although he offered strong analysis in other contexts, William Blair dismisses the importance of a similar meeting in Augusta County, Virginia. Words are often hollow, but the meeting in Staunton collected over 7,000 pounds of meat, 135 barrels of flour, and $115,000 in Confederate securities. The provisions offered at a time of tremendous scarcity in the Valley were clear proof of continued commitment to the southern cause. While the sacrifices offered in Staunton may have set up a number of prominent leaders for postwar political success as Blair suggests, he failed to see the significance of these actions during the war. Blair, *Virginia's Private War,* 132.

19. "Telegraphic," Mar. 3, 1865; and "Vice President Stephens on Slavery," Mar. 10, 1865, both in the *Galveston Tri-Weekly News.*

20. Willard Richardson, "Lately we have had . . . ," *Galveston Tri-Weekly News,* Mar. 3, 1865.

21. "Pelican Private" and M. Estis, "Shreveport Correspondence," Feb. 27, 1865; and Lance Corporal, "(Duff's) 33D. Tex. Cav. Bee's Brigade," Mar. 15, 1865, all in the *Galveston Tri-Weekly News.*

22. Estis, "Shreveport Correspondence," Feb. 27, 1865; and "Public Meeting," Mar. 6, 1865, both in the *Galveston Tri-Weekly News.*

23. "Defeat of the Negro Bill" and "Our Virginia Senator . . . ," *Lynchburg Virginian,* Feb. 25, 1865.

24. U.S. War Department, *The War of the Rebellion: A Compilation of the Official Records of the Union and Confederate Armies,* 128 vols. (Washington, D.C.: Government Printing Office, 1880–1901), ser. 1, 51(2):1068, 46(3):1315 (hereinafter cited as *OR*).

25. "The important message . . . ," Feb. 20, 1865; "The Negro Bill," Mar. 8, 1865; and "In looking over . . . ," Mar. 16, 1865, all by Charles Button in the *Lynchburg Virginian.*

26. Willard Richardson, "The Negro Question," *Galveston Tri-Weekly News,* Mar. 29, 1865.

27. *OR,* ser. 4, 3:1093; "Gen. Lee is now accepting . . . ," Mar. 17, 1865; "Colored Troops," Mar. 18, 1865; and "Parade of Negro Troops in Richmond," Mar. 23, 1865, all in the *Lynchburg Virginian*; "The City: Drill of Colored Troops," *Richmond Whig,* Apr. 3, 1865.

28. "The Right Spirit," *Lynchburg Virginian,* Mar. 24, 1865; "Correspondence," *Richmond Whig,* Apr. 1, 1865. On the attitudes of Lynchburg residents, see Steven Elliott Tripp, *Yankee Town, Southern City: Race and Class Relations in Civil War Lynchburg* (New York: New York University Press, 1997).

MEMORY AND LEGACIES

"While the Participants Are Yet Alive": The Association of Medical Officers of the Army and Navy of the Confederacy

GLENNA R. SCHROEDER-LEIN

WHEN RICHMOND FELL TO THE FORCES OF ULYSSES S. GRANT ON April 2, 1865, considerable destruction ensued. Among the buildings incinerated were those housing the papers of the Confederate Surgeon General's Office. Years later a small group of doctors who had served as Confederate medical officers during the Civil War were distressed that they could have no counterpart to "a very large gathering of official records and anatomical samples, in a Government Museum in Washington City." They came to see *themselves* as potential primary sources who might meet "for the advancement of science, to rescue from oblivion all the important medical and surgical facts developed in the Confederate army and navy record." In other words their goal was to replace what had been lost. They did not want Yankee medical information to be the only source available.[1] For these doctors the Civil War was something of a "watershed"—either propelling them further in their medical career or itself serving as the high point of that career. Therefore they valued their Civil War experiences and wanted to make sure that these were preserved and remembered.

While several doctors later claimed a major role in instigating the first meeting of Confederate medical veterans, a gathering of Atlanta physicians on March 28, 1874, issued the actual call. Thirty-two former Confederate medical officers, mostly Georgians, responded and met in the Senate chambers at the state capitol on May 20–21. Their temporary chairman, Samuel H. Stout, former medical director of hospitals behind the lines for the Army of Tennessee, explained the purposes of the organization. The group established a number of committees, selected persons to prepare papers on specific medical topics for their 1875 meeting, and elected officers, some of whom were not in attendance. These included the new president, former Confederate surgeon general Samuel P. Moore of Virginia, who had sent a letter of support while regretting that he must be absent.[2]

At the time some of the surgeons blamed the smaller-than-expected attendance on a lack of advertising. This certainly contributed to the problem, for a group of medical veterans in Savannah reported that they had heard about the meeting too late to send a representative. But a substantial article discussing the call for the meeting appeared in the *Nashville Union and American* on April 8, 1874, six weeks before the event, yet no doctors came to the meeting from Tennessee. A more likely cause of mainly local attendance, though not mentioned by the doctors, was the dire economic situation in the South and in the nation as a whole in 1874. Much of the southern economic infrastructure had been destroyed during the war and was slow to recover. Stout, who resigned as secretary of the association for personal financial reasons before the 1875 meeting, was doubtless representative of many Confederate surgeons who had lost their wealth during the war and never really regained economic security. Travel too probably precluded others who suffered as a result of the panic of 1873, which began nationally in September with the collapse of Jay Cooke's banking enterprises and lasted for six years.[3]

These economic factors most likely affected the attendance at the 1875 meeting in Richmond, where just six of the thirty-four attendees came from outside Virginia. Only one doctor, Edwin D. Newton of Georgia, who had served with the Army of Northern Virginia on the staff of Gen. Robert E. Lee's medical director Lafayette Guild, attended both meetings. The veterans met in the hall of the House of Delegates on October 19–20. Because their gathering coincided with the annual meeting of the Medical Society of Virginia, which began on October 20, they probably had more physicians in attendance than they would have otherwise. Samuel P. Moore delivered his presidential address, which generally summarized the contributions of the Confederate medical service. Although several doctors had been assigned to prepare and present papers on various Civil War medical topics, none of them did.[4]

It appears that a conflict arose over the election of officers. Edwin D. Newton objected to selecting *new* officers because he understood that the group would have Moore as its permanent president and with Richmond as its permanent headquarters in association with the Southern Historical Society. Other physicians believed that presidential honors should be spread to other deserving members as well and that the annual meeting locations should rotate. This faction nominated "Stonewall" Jackson's former medical officer, Hunter H. McGuire, for the presidency. Newton then nominated Moore for reelection. The balloting resulted in a tie, with eleven votes for each candidate, broken when Moore voted for McGuire, resulting in the latter's election. But McGuire, due to his own poor health and other responsibilities, did nothing as president, and the organization lapsed into what Newton called "a state of innocuous desuetude [that is, harmlessly doing nothing]." Some members later blamed unspecified disagreements within the Virginia medical community for the collapse of the veteran's organization. Whatever the exact cause, the group remained inactive for almost two decades, despite an abortive attempt to restart it in 1890.[5]

In 1898 Charles H. Tebault, the surgeon general of the United Confederate Veterans (UCV), sent out a circular urging former Confederate surgeons to gather at the group's meeting in Atlanta. When about forty medical veterans, including Stout and Newton, met on July 20, the doctors organized the Association of Medical Officers of the Army and Navy of the Confederacy, wrote a constitution, and elected officers. They chose as president James B. Cowan of Tullahoma, Tennessee, formerly chief surgeon under Gen. Nathan Bedford Forrest.[6]

The constitution specified certain restrictive membership qualifications for the association. Only Confederate surgeons, assistant surgeons, acting assistant (or contract) surgeons, hospital stewards, and chaplains could join. In 1899 two categories of associate members were added: military veterans who had become doctors after the war, and doctors who were the sons and grandsons of Confederate veterans (usually called junior members). These associates could participate fully, though they were not permitted to hold office until the organization's later years.[7]

The association always met in conjunction with the UCV. Virtually all the members belonged to local UCV chapters, but the medical association was not itself a chapter. Although it tried several times to join the UCV in a more formal way, this proved to be impossible, mainly because the association's membership was restricted rather than open to all Confederate veterans.[8]

Although it occasionally met in Richmond or Charleston, the UCV's tendency (and therefore that of the medical association) was to meet in the "west" in such places as Louisville, Nashville, New Orleans, and Atlanta.[9] Membership statistics for the association, sketchy at best, also show a tendency toward postwar residence in the west. But the association urged all former Confederate medical officers to join, no matter what their present location or their former region of service. It published a list of members in March 1901 and an update in April 1902. These show 134 associate and junior members and 272 regular members, a total of 406. Of those whose service was specified, one had been a naval surgeon, one a chaplain, and four hospital stewards; twelve had served with the Army of Northern Virginia, eight with the Army of Tennessee, and two or three served in the Trans-Mississippi Department. More than fifty listed a regiment or hospital service but did not say where these were located. The majority were listed by current address only, therefore it is hard to give a breakdown of how many people served with each army.[10] Other information about the backgrounds of active speakers and meeting participants suggests that both the Army of Northern Virginia and the Army of Tennessee were well represented.

The membership of the organization continually changed as veterans died and new members were recruited. As late as 1915 three new members were added to the association, but no other membership lists or statistics were ever published. At the association's peak at the Dallas (1902) and New Orleans (1903) meetings, attendance reached around 150 but rapidly declined thereafter as the veterans aged and died. In 1904 only 37 attended the Nashville meeting, while only 12 members attended the 1913 meeting in Chattanooga. In 1910 Secretary A. A. Lyon estimated that 90 percent of the association's membership had attended only one meeting (most likely in their hometown).[11]

As stated in its constitution and frequently repeated over the years, "The objects of the Association are to cultivate social and fraternal relations by means of annual meetings, and to collect all matters of history, all facts and data pertaining to the medical services in the Confederate States Army and Navy during the late war as observed and recorded or remembered by the survivors. It is hoped by this means that the facts and data in connection with surgical operations, the medical and surgical treatment of the sick and wounded, the various measures and devices resorted to from time to time, rendered necessary by limited resources may be placed on record." They wanted to be sure that "the whole *truth* and nothing but the *TRUTH* may be perpetuated."[12]

The urgency of collecting information at once was brought home to association members in a forceful way by the death of their president, Preston B. Scott, on September 24, 1900. Scott, a Kentuckian, had served as, among other positions, medical director of hospitals for the Department of Alabama, Mississippi, and East Louisiana in 1864. The major organizer of the association's meeting at Louisville that year, Scott had been rewarded with the association presidency but succumbed to typhoid fever a couple of months later. His death provoked Samuel Stout, the only other surviving Confederate medical director of hospitals, to begin writing his series of *Southern Practitioner* articles on his experiences in the Army of Tennessee hospitals.[13]

The former Confederate surgeons had two main ways to fulfill their objectives. The first was of course the annual meeting, at which the doctors were urged to present papers or reminiscences and to participate in discussions on various topics. In the earliest gatherings programs were not planned ahead of time and later, when planned, were subject to change.[14]

A typical meeting opened with a prayer by a local minister (often a Confederate veteran), followed by local-arrangements information and welcoming addresses. The president of the association then delivered his address. In the early years the meetings lasted three to four days, during which time doctors presented various papers.[15] These might be a lengthy overview, as was Stout's "Address" in 1902 about medicine in the Army of Tennessee or John R. Gildersleeve's 1904 presidential address discussing Chimborazo Hospital in Richmond.[16] They could also be very short and specific, such as the reports on "remarkable" gunshot wounds to various parts of the anatomy. In several instances the subjects of these case studies were available for the doctors to examine.[17] Sometimes a report would stimulate discussions on topics such as smallpox vaccination, treatments for hospital gangrene or for "camp itch," whether anyone had treated a victim of a gunshot wound to the liver who survived, or the nature of "camp fever" (whether it was typhoid or not).[18] The perennial favorite was the use of chloroform instead of ether for anesthesia during operations and if anyone had witnessed the death of a soldier patient from its use. Even at the 1913 meeting, having nothing else to do, the members ruminated on this issue. The doctors always concluded that chloroform was almost universally used and hardly anyone had seen a death from it because it was administered carefully and usually outdoors.[19]

The participants frequently stressed the disadvantages under which they had worked during the Civil War, particularly the effects of the blockade and the Union declaration of medical supplies as "contraband of war." Several described southern innovations and the use of indigenous plants to replace quinine and other scarce imported medicines. Others found medicines and surgical instruments captured from the Federal army to be sufficient. As John S. Cain reported in his 1905 presidential address, "In consequence of the energy of our medical purveyors and the liberality of the enemy in yielding up their stores when surprised and forced to abandon them, kept us in a reasonable supply of all essentials."[20] Undoubtedly the doctors were proud of their work, and they stressed the superior quality of southern military physicians as compared to the druggist's clerks and other inferior sorts who allegedly made up the Union medical staff.[21]

Several quoted statistics to prove that because of the cruel Union policy of refusing to exchange prisoners of war, the South had more Federal soldiers in prisons and hospitals but had a lower death rate than that of southern prisoners of war in northern prisons. The doctors, no doubt reacting to the stigma of Andersonville, emphasized that they always gave their prisoners the same rations and hospital treatment as their own soldiers.[22] W. J. W. Kerr stressed the injustice of blaming the situation at Andersonville prison on its commander, Henry Wirz, while Samuel E. Lewis reported that in 1862 at Winchester, Virginia, Stonewall Jackson and his surgeon, Hunter McGuire, had anticipated later Red Cross guidelines for the treatment of captured surgeons.[23]

The purpose of sharing cases and experiences was not to advise anyone how medical treatments *should* presently be performed but how they *had* been performed. A number of doctors commented that Civil War treatments took place before the days of aseptic surgery and any understanding of germs, thus they were unable to perform some procedures that had become routine in the early 1900s. Given the treatments available at the time, it was remarkable that some of the patients actually got well. The point was to preserve a record of what Confederate doctors did in this premodern period, for as Surgeons Samuel E. Lewis and James M. Keller pointed out, neither *The Medical and Surgical History of the War of the Rebellion* (1870–88) nor the *Official Records* (1880–1901) contained anything about Confederate medical history.[24]

During later meetings the papers were fewer; sometimes there were none at all except for the presidential address. As time passed there tended also to be a diminution in the quality of material as well as quantity. When the veterans had less medical information to share, they focused more on the history of their organization. The majority of doctors who made presentations did so only once or twice. In some cases death intervened, but in others the participants had only one or two things they believed were relevant to report. As the roster of surviving and attending doctors shrank, the pleas of leaders for members to record their experiences grew more desperate. As Secretary A. A. Lyon put it in 1910, "It clearly appears that we who made this history constitute the only true source from which the facts involved can be brought to light and handed down to posterity." It was imperative for the members to publish their information immediately because, as Lyon said, "We are not *growing* old—we have grown old." Former secretary Deering J. Roberts had urged the veterans "to collect and place before the public as much as may be possible while the participants are yet alive."[25] A few of the most active and historically oriented of the doctors, such as Edwin D. Newton and Samuel E. Lewis, responded to these urgings with accounts of their own experiences, histories of the association itself, a reprint of the 1875 address by Samuel P. Moore, and other items. Even these men were not inexhaustible founts of information, for their later speeches and writings were mainly a reprise of earlier material.[26]

At the conclusion of the papers, or sometimes interspersed with them, were business meetings that included such matters as the association's relationship with the UCV, several vigorous disagreements over the design of a distinctive badge or button, attempts to amend the constitution, and in all years but 1914, the election of new officers. Although it was not always the case, the members tended to elect as their president someone from the host city who had been heavily involved in arrangements for their current convention.[27] Beginning in 1910 these meetings also included discussions of the future of the organization. Some suggested simply adjourning to meet in "the sweet bye and bye," a proposal always voted down by those who wanted the associate and junior members to take over and change the purpose from gathering information about Civil War medicine to erecting a statue in Richmond honoring Samuel P. Moore, a project the association had been discussing since 1909 (but was never accomplished).[28]

Eventually some of the doctors also wanted to have less medical discussion and more participation in other parts of the UCV meeting. In fact in New Orleans in 1903, there was somewhat of a rebellion. J. C. Abernathy said he wanted the medical association to meet only in the afternoons because "I want to get with the boys and holler a little, and cut up Jack." Thereafter the secretary made sure to include in the annual-meeting announcements that sessions would be arranged to allow the veterans to attend UCV activities.[29]

In the early years ladies' memorial associations and church groups provided luncheons for the veterans each day. In Louisville in 1900, for example, the doctors feasted on "lobster salad, chicken croquettes, sandwiches, pickles, olives, coffee, [and] claret punch" served by a group of young ladies. But after 1906 the veterans had to fend for themselves.[30]

Not only did members of the association try to fulfill their goal of gathering Confederate medical information by holding meetings, but they also sought to propagate by publication the information they had gathered. In 1900 Deering Roberts of Nashville offered to add sixteen pages to each monthly issue of his medical journal, the *Southern Practitioner,* for the publication of "Records, Recollections, and Reminiscences," an idea association members enthusiastically endorsed.[31] Not only did Roberts print the papers delivered at the meetings, but he also published some other works sent directly to him. The most important of these was the previously mentioned series of articles by Stout detailing his experiences with the Army of Tennessee hospitals, of which he was medical director for a time. Unfortunately he died in September 1903 after completing only twenty-two articles, probably about half of what he could have written based on where he was chronologically in his last installment.[32]

Roberts also printed minutes of the association meetings. In the early years (1900–1905) these were extremely detailed and might continue for several issues because a stenographer recorded the proceedings verbatim. Later, and often shorter, meetings were reported with considerably less detail, some in just a sketchy synopsis. For the first several years, Roberts printed biographies of the association officers, usually accompanied by a photograph. Yet after 1903 he simply printed obituaries of medical officers, both the prominent and the obscure.[33] Roberts and the association also proposed to edit and publish the fifteen hundred pounds of the Army of Tennessee hospital records held by the heirs of the late Samuel Stout. But a lack of funds prevented them from doing more than talking about the project.[34]

The association eventually faded away. Although a meeting was announced for Washington, D.C., in 1917, it is not clear whether the group actually convened. There was no printed report, though the *Southern Practitioner* carried two articles by women who had served as a medical purveyor's clerk and a nurse. This suggests that there *may* have been some meager gathering. Doubtless the death of the association's secretary, Samuel E. Lewis, on November 17, 1917, and the fact that the *Southern Practitioner* ceased publication in 1918 quenched any spark of life that may have remained in the association.[35]

An examination of Gaines Foster's study of Confederate veterans movements in his book *Ghosts of the Confederacy* suggests some ways in which the Association of Medical Officers differed from the regular UCV. The UCV began in 1889, and the medical association started its active period in 1898. Foster suggests a decline in unity and interest in the UCV after 1900, but both the rise and decline of the UCV were much slower than that of the medical association. The association peaked in 1902 and 1903 but disappeared in 1917, years before the UCV, which held its last meeting in 1951. Foster sees the timing of the establishment of the UCV and other commemorative associations as a response to late-nineteenth-century social tensions. Thus he thinks that the idea of preserving history as the veterans approached death was not any real motivation for the founding and development of the UCV. Perhaps that very lack of interest helped provoke the resuscitation of the medical association. As has been discussed, the desire to gather information about the Confederate medical service "while the participants are yet alive" was *the* major motivation for the association. As Foster points out, the majority of military veterans were still under fifty-five in 1890. But the majority of medical veterans were significantly older, having interrupted established careers to serve the Confederacy. While Foster writes that the UCV seemed to downplay the interpretation that the Confederates were defeated by overwhelming numbers and resources, the medical association stressed that very thing when they emphasized the tremendous resources of Union forces in contrast to their own substitutions.

It was evident from the dispute of 1903 and in later meeting minutes that medical association members still saw themselves as part of the larger UCV and wanted to participate. Attending the big reunion parade was every bit as important to them as Foster demonstrates that it was to veterans generally. Yet it seems clear that the medical association was formed to meet a need for preserving medical history, which the larger UCV could not address.[36]

To what extent then was the Association of Medical Officers able to accomplish its goal of preserving Confederate medical information? First, it raised a certain consciousness among its members of the importance of preserving historical material. Second, quite a number of doctors contributed information. Certainly the materials received were a very mixed bag. Some of the anecdotes and the later repetitious contributions are of very limited value, but often case reports provide a useful perspective on the state of medical knowledge during the Civil War. As with all memoirs, these accounts should be used with some caution. The articles on the Chimborazo and Winder Hospitals, for example, paint an incredibly glowing picture, unlike other accounts of the trials of wartime Richmond. Alex G. Lane, former head of Winder Hospital, described the organization, operation, and results of the hospital in important detail, but he did not mention a single problem or inadequacy nor indicate any decline in resources over time. Samuel Stout's series on the Army of Tennessee hospitals was the best and most extensive material collected, but because he used few of the primary records he had amassed, he could sometimes be inaccurate about dates. But even with these reservations, much of the material preserved by the association is valuable to historians.[37]

Members of both major Confederate armies—the Army of Northern Virginia and the Army of Tennessee—were active in the medical association and contributed information. Neither army group controlled the association nor did disputes flair up along geographical lines. Members of the medical service in other armies, such as that in Missouri, also participated. But the "Navy" part of the association's name seems to have been largely wishful thinking. Only one naval medical officer was ever listed in the roster, and he never made a comment at a meeting or wrote anything for the *Southern Practitioner.*

Finally, it is clear that many of the medical officers active in the association tried hard to gather Confederate medical information. But ultimately the reminiscences of a bunch of devoted old men, while helpful and better than nothing, could not fully make up for the loss of the large quantity of primary sources that burned in Richmond on April 2, 1865.

NOTES

1. *Nashville Union and American,* Apr. 8, 1874; Edwin D. Newton, "The Evolution of Medicine and Surgery," *Southern Practitioner* (hereinafter cited as *SP*) 33 (July 1911): 366. The Army Medical Museum, founded during the Civil War, was the precurser to the National Museum of Health and Medicine. The author wishes to thank Daniel W. Stowell for comments on this paper, a shorter version of which was presented at the Douglas Southall Freeman and Southern Intellectual History Conferences in Richmond, Va., on Feb. 23, 2002.

2. *Nashville Union and American,* Apr. 8, 1874; *Atlanta Constitution,* May 21–22, 1874. Parts of the latter article are reprinted in [Edwin D. Newton], "Correspondence," *SP* 26 (Oct. 1904): 623–28; and [Margaret J. Stout], "Correspondence," *SP* 32 (Sept. 1910): 461–63. Samuel H. Stout, "An Address: Concerning the History of the Medical Service in the Field and Hospitals of the Army and Department of Tennessee," *SP* 24 (Aug. 1902): 436.

3. *Atlanta Constitution,* May 21, 1874; John M. Johnston to Samuel P. Moore, May 18, 1874, Samuel H. Stout Papers, Special Collections, Robert W. Woodruff Library, Emory University, Atlanta; *Nashville Union and American,* Apr. 8, 1874; Glenna R. Schroeder-Lein, *Confederate Hospitals on the Move: Samuel H. Stout and the Army of Tennessee* (Columbia: University of South Carolina Press, 1994), chap. 7; Irwin Unger, *The Greenback Era: A Social and Political History of American Finance, 1865–1879* (Princeton, N.J.: Princeton University Press, 1964).

4. *Richmond Dispatch,* Oct. 19–21, 1875; "Annual Meeting of the Association of Medical Officers of the Army and Navy of the Confederacy," *SP* 23 (Aug. 1901): 394–95; Samuel P. Moore, "Address of the President of the Association of Medical Officers of Confederate States Army and Navy,"

SP 31 (Oct. 1909): 491–98 (reprinted from *Richmond Dispatch,* Oct. 20, 1875); *Atlanta Constitution,* May 22, 1874.

5. *Richmond Dispatch,* Oct. 21, 1875; Newton, "Evolution of Medicine and Surgery," *SP* 33 (July 1911): 364–65; [Newton], "Correspondence," *SP* 26 (Oct. 1904): 627–28; "Annual Meeting of the Association of Medical Officers of the Army and Navy of the Confederacy," *SP* 23 (Oct. 1901): 488; C. H. Tebault, "History of the Association of Medical Officers of the Army and Navy of the Confederacy," *SP* 32 (Aug. 1909): 399. Joseph Jones led the reorganization attempt at the Chattanooga UCV meeting in 1890. A. A. Lyon, "Annual Meeting of the Association of Medical Officers of the Army and Navy of the Confederacy," *SP* 37 (Aug. 1915): 321–22.

6. Tebault, "History," *SP* 32 (Aug. 1910): 399–402; [Newton], "Correspondence," *SP* 26 (Oct. 1904): 623–24; "Report of the President, Francis L. Parker, M.D., of Charleston, S.C.," *SP* 22 (Aug. 1900): 353; "Obituary [James B. Cowan]," *SP* 31 (Aug. 1909): 389–90.

7. "Qualifications for Membership in the Association of Surgeons of the Confederate States Army and Navy, U.C.V.," *SP* 22 (July 1900): 312. This is about the earliest statement of membership qualifications published in the *Southern Practitioner,* but similar statements (updated as necessary) were published in several issues each year through 1917. [Parker], "Report of the President," *SP* 22 (Aug. 1900): 355.

8. Because of the association's weak dues-collection method (see note 11), it would also have been difficult to pay the UCV's annual assessment on members. A. A. Lyon, "The Association of Medical Officers of the Army and Navy of the Confederacy," *SP* 32 (Mar. 1910): 128. Some early article titles, such as "Qualifications for Membership" and several others published in 1900, confuse the issue by including UCV as part of the title. But later articles indicate that there was no official connection. "Ninth Annual Meeting of the Association of Medical Officers of the Army and Navy of the Confederacy," *SP* 28 (Aug. 1906): 474; "Twelfth Annual Session of the Association of Medical Officers of the Army and Navy of the Confederacy," *SP* 31 (Sept. 1909): 433–34; "Annual Meeting of the Association of Medical Officers of the Army and Navy of the Confederacy," *SP* 32 (July 1910): 343.

9. The meetings were held in Atlanta (1898), Charleston (1899), Louisville (1900), Memphis (1901), Dallas (1902), New Orleans (1903), Nashville (1904), Louisville (1905), New Orleans (1906), Richmond (1907), Birmingham (1908), Memphis (1909), Mobile (1910), Little Rock (1911), Macon (1912), Chattanooga (1913), Jacksonville (1914), Richmond (1915), Birmingham (1916), and Washington, D.C. (1917). Meeting locations can be found in each volume of the *Southern Practitioner* from 1900 to 1917. They are conveniently listed in Appendix 7 at the end of Norman H. Franke and Laura Webb Stone, "A History of the Association of Medical Officers of the Army and Navy of the Confederacy," *Military Medicine* 131 (Apr. 1966): 334. This article presents a straightforward account of the meetings.

10. "Members and Associate Members of the Association of Medical Officers of the Army and Navy of the Confederacy," *SP* 23 (Mar. 1901): 138–48; "List of Members, Associate Members, and Junior Members of the Association of Medical Officers of the Army and Navy of the Confederacy," *SP* 24 (Apr. 1902): 217–20. The largest numbers of medical veterans came from Tennessee (39), Kentucky (37), Georgia (32), Mississippi (28), Virginia (23), and South Carolina (22).

11. Lyon, "Annual Meeting," *SP* 37 (Aug. 1915): 323–24. Because only members attending paid dues of one dollar each year, approximate attendance figures can be deduced from the amount of dues collected by the secretary-treasurer. Dues payments in Dallas were $149 and $159 in New Orleans. "Report of the Proceedings of the Annual Meeting of the Association of Medical Officers of the Army and Navy of the Confederacy," *SP* 25 (July 1903): 408; "Association of Medical Officers of the Army and Navy of the Confederacy," *SP* 27 (Aug. 1905): 442–43; "Sixteenth Annual Meeting of the Association of Medical Officers of the Army and Navy of the Confederacy," *SP* 35 (Aug. 1913): 370; Lyon, "Association," *SP* 32 (Mar. 1910): 128.

12. "Qualifications for Membership," *SP* 22 (July 1900): 312; James M. Keller, "Circular Letter from the President of the Association of Medical Veterans of the Army and Navy of the Confederacy," *SP* 23 (May 1901): 234.

13. "Death of Dr. Preston B. Scott," *SP* 22 (Oct. 1900): 463; Samuel H. Stout, "Some Facts of the History of the Organization of the Medical Service of the Confederate Armies and Hospitals," *SP* 22 (Nov. 1900): 521–23.

14. "Annual Meeting of the Association of Surgeons of the Confederate States, United Confederate Veterans," *SP* 22 (July 1900): 289–312; Tebault, "History," *SP* 32 (Aug. 1910): 404.

15. For accounts of the meetings, all of which follow the same general format regardless of their length, see the appropriate issues of *SP* 22–38 (1900–1916).

16. Stout, "Address," *SP* 24 (Aug. 1902): 434–54; "Annual Meeting of the Association of Medical Officers of the Army and Navy of the Confederacy," *SP* 26 (Aug. 1904): 493–505.

17. J. B. Stimson, "Three Unusual Gun-Shot Wounds," *SP* 22 (Aug. 1900): 363–64; J. A. Hickman, "Remarkable Gun-shot Wound of Brain," *SP* 22 (Sept. 1900): 420–21; Francis Parker, "Explosive Bullets," *SP* 22 (Dec. 1900): 559–62; William Taylor, "Conservatism in Army Surgery—Some Field Reminiscences," *SP* 27 (Nov. 1905): 625–28; Deering J. Roberts, "Remarkable Case of Gun-Shot Wound and Recovery," *SP* 23 (Jan. 1901): 53–54; "Annual Meeting of the Association of Medical Officers of the Army and Navy of the Confederacy," *SP* 24 (June 1902): 338; "Ninth Annual Meeting," *SP* 28 (Aug. 1906): 475–76.

18. "Ninth Annual Meeting," *SP* 28 (Aug. 1906): 471–72; "Association of Medical Officers," *SP* 27 (Aug. 1905): 446, 451–64; "Report of the Proceedings of the Annual Meeting of the Association of Medical Officers of the Army and Navy of the Confederacy," *SP* 25 (Aug. 1903): 449–53.

19. "Report of the Proceedings," *SP* 25 (Aug. 1903): 450–56; John R. Buist, "Some Items of My Medical and Surgical Experience in the Confederate Army," *SP* 25 (Oct. 1903): 579; C. H. Tebault, "Hospitals of the Confederacy," *SP* 24 (Sept. 1902): 508; D. D. Saunders, "President's Annual Address," *SP* 24 (May 1902): 275–76; "Eleventh Annual Meeting of the Association of Medical Officers of the Army and Navy of the Confederacy," *SP* 30 (Aug. 1908): 392; "Sixteenth Annual Meeting," *SP* 35 (Aug. 1913): 372.

20. Samuel E. Lewis, "Samuel Preston Moore, M.D., Surgeon General of the Confederate States," *SP* 23 (Aug. 1901): 384; James M. Keller, "Annual Address at the Meeting of the Association of Medical Officers of the Army and Navy of the Confederacy," *SP* 23 (July 1901): 300, 303; "Annual Meeting," *SP* 23 (Aug. 1901): 388–89; "Annual Meeting of the Association of Medical Officers of the Army and Navy of the Confederacy," *SP* 24 (July 1902): 397–98; "Address of Jno. S.

Cain, M.D., President of the Association of Medical Officers of the Army and Navy of the Confederacy," *SP* 27 (July 1905): 393–94; C. H. Tebault, "Confederate Resources," *SP* 24 (Jan. 1902): 44–50; Carroll Kendrick, "Indigenous Plants Used by Southern People as Medicines during the War," *SP* 31 (Nov. 1909): 534–37. An excellent summary of the standard association view is found in "Circular Letter," *SP* 29 (Apr. 1907): 210–11.

21. "Annual Meeting," *SP* 22 (July 1900): 296; "Annual Meeting of the Association of Medical Officers of the Army and Navy of the Confederacy," *SP* 26 (Sept. 1904): 553–54; "Address of Jno. S. Cain," *SP* 27 (July 1905): 387–88; Lyon, "Association," *SP* 32 (Mar. 1910): 126.

22. "Report of C. H. Tebault, M.D., Surgeon-General," *SP* 22 (Aug. 1900): 358; Lewis, "Samuel Preston Moore," *SP* 23 (Aug. 1901): 384–85; C. H. Tebault, "Treatment of Prisoners during the War between the States—1861–1865," *SP* 27 (June 1905): 321–34; Samuel E. Lewis, "The Treatment of Prisoners of War: The Percentage of Deaths—North and South," *SP* 29 (Oct. 1907): 542–54; V. G. Hitt, "Exchange of Sick Prisoners Discontinued," *SP* 31 (Nov. 1909): 538–40.

23. W. J. W. Kerr, "Annual Address of the President of the Association of Medical Officers of the Army and Navy of the Confederacy," *SP* 25 (June 1903): 335–49; Samuel E. Lewis, "General T. J. Jackson (Stonewall), and His Medical Director, Hunter McGuire, M.D., at Winchester, May 1862," *SP* 24 (Oct. 1902): 553–63.

24. "Annual Meeting," *SP* 22 (July 1900): 296; J. S. Abernathy, "Manual of Military Surgery for the Army of the Confederate States," *SP* 24 (Dec. 1902): 674–79; Buist, "Some Items," *SP* 25 (Oct. 1903): 580–81; "Address of Jno. S. Cain," *SP* 27 (July 1905): 388; "Annual Meeting," *SP* 23 (Oct. 1901): 489; Keller, "Annual Address," *SP* 23 (July 1901): 303; *The Medical and Surgical History of the War of the Rebellion,* 3 vols. in 6 pts. (Washington, D.C.: Government Printing Office, 1870–88); U.S. War Department, *The War of the Rebellion: A Compilation of the Official Records of the Union and Confederate Armies,* 128 vols. (Washington, D.C.: Government Printing Office, 1880–1901).

25. Indications of decline can be found by comparing the contents of the annual meeting reports and other articles in the *Southern Practitioner* from 1900 to 1917. Lyon, "Association," *SP* 32 (Mar. 1910): 127, 130; "Special Notice" [and Circular Letter], *SP* 29 (Apr. 1907): 209.

26. Moore, "Address," *SP* 31 (Oct. 1909): 491–98; Samuel E. Lewis, "Annual Address of the President of the Association of Medical Officers of the Army and Navy of the Confederacy," *SP* 30 (July 1908): 329–38; Newton, "Evolution of Medicine and Surgery," *SP* 33 (July 1911): 360–68. See also other articles by Lewis and Newton. The comments about repetition also apply to the writings of C. H. Tebault.

27. For aspects of the badge/button controversy, see, for example, "Association of Medical Officers of the Army and Navy of the Confederacy," *SP* 27 (Oct. 1905): 565–68; and "Nineteenth Annual Meeting of the Association of the Medical Officers of the Army and Navy of the Confederate States," *SP* 38 (July 1916): 271–72. For attempts to amend the constitution, see, for example, "Nineteenth Annual Meeting," *SP* 38 (July 1916): 269–70; and "Eleventh Annual Meeting," *SP* 30 (Aug. 1908): 392–93. For elections see annual meeting reports for all years except 1914. The tendency to elect presidents from the annual-meeting city is concisely demonstrated in Franke and Stone, "History," 331–33.

28. See annual meeting reports, 1909–16.

29. "Report of the Proceedings," *SP* 25 (July 1903): 408–10. Meeting announcements were printed in many of the spring issues of the *Southern Practitioner.*

30. "Annual Meeting," *SP* 22 (July 1900): 298; "The Great Confederate Reunion," *SP* 25 (June 1903): 364–66. In 1908 Dr. J. C. Abernathy invited the meeting attendees to lunch with him at a nearby restaurant. Luncheons were served through 1906 and again in Little Rock in 1911. "Ninth Annual Meeting of the Association of Medical Officers of the Army and Navy of the Confederacy," *SP* 28 (July 1906): 422; "Eleventh Annual Meeting," *SP* 30 (Aug. 1908): 393; "Proceedings of the Association of Medical Officers of the Army and Navy of the Confederacy—Fourteenth Annual Session," *SP* 33 (Aug. 1911): 411.

31. "Annual Meeting," *SP* 22 (July 1900): 303.

32. Samuel H. Stout, "Some Facts of the History of the Organization of the Medical Service of the Confederate Armies and Hospitals," pts. 1–23, *SP* 22–25 (Nov. 1900–Oct. 1903). There were actually only twenty-two installments, but Roberts seems to have counted Stout's 1902 "Address." "Obituary: Samuel Hollingsworth Stout, A.M., M.D., L.L.D.," *SP* 25 (Oct. 1903): 586–87.

33. See annual meeting reports for each year and contents of the *Southern Practitioner* generally.

34. "Report of the Proceedings," *SP* 25 (Aug. 1903): 458–59; "Annual Meeting," *SP* 26 (Sept. 1904): 567; "Tenth Annual Meeting of the Association of Medical Officers of the Army and Navy of the Confederacy," *SP* 29 (Aug. 1907): 439–40; Lyon, "Association," *SP* 32 (Mar. 1910): 127, 129; A. A. Lyon to Margaret J. Stout, Sept. 12, 1910, Samuel H. Stout Papers, THS 39, Tennessee State Library and Archives, Nashville, Tenn.; "Nineteenth Annual Meeting," *SP* 38 (July 1916): 271.

35. "Announcement," *SP* 39 (Apr. 1917): 141–45; Mrs. James H. Williams, "Reminiscences of a Clerk in the Medical Purveyor's Office and in the Treasury of the Confederate Government, Richmond, Virginia," *SP* 39 (Aug. 1917): 301–5; Mrs. Eliza Clinedinst Crim, "Echoes from the Past," *SP* 39 (Oct. 1917): 394–96; "[Obituary:] Samuel E. Lewis," *Confederate Veteran* 26 (Mar. 1918): 123.

36. Gaines M. Foster, *Ghosts of the Confederacy: Defeat, the Lost Cause, and the Emergence of the New South, 1865 to 1913* (New York: Oxford University Press, 1987), 104–5, 112–13, 119, 137, 139, 163–79. The emphasis here is on the idea that the UCV did not originate because of a desperate need to record their experiences before they died. It is not meant to suggest that the UCV as a whole had no interest in Confederate history because of course they did. David W. Blight, *Race and Reunion: The Civil War in American Memory* (Cambridge, Mass.: Harvard University Press, 2001), places more stress on the importance of memoirs and the attempt to produce a "true" southern history than Foster does. Clearly the Association of Medical Officers fits in that tradition—the members were carrying on the preservation of the Confederate past from the medical perspective. "United Confederate Veterans," *Dictionary of American History,* rev. ed. (New York: Charles Scribner's Sons, 1976), 150. This source suggests the UCV peaked about 1907.

37. "Annual Meeting," *SP* 26 (Aug. 1904): 493–506; Alex G. Lane, "The Winder Hospital, of Richmond, Virginia," *SP* 26 (Jan. 1904): 35–41; Stout, "Some Facts," pts. 1–23, *SP* 22–25 (Nov. 1900–Oct. 1903); Schroeder-Lein, *Confederate Hospitals on the Move,* 173–74. This book uses information from the *Southern Practitioner* quite extensively.

When Charles Francis Adams Met Robert E. Lee: A Southern Gentleman in History and Memory

NINA SILBER

FOR NEARLY FORTY-ONE OF HIS SIXTY-THREE YEARS, ROBERT E. Lee was a military man. Indeed, for a good part of those forty-one years, he was a military man par excellence. He was second in his class at the U.S. Military Academy at West Point, fought brilliantly in the Mexican War, and of course ultimately became best known for his outstanding generalship on behalf of the Confederacy. In the years after his death and down to the present day, Lee has been praised not just for fighting hard and fighting well but also for achieving an unparalleled degree of military genius during his years of command in the Civil War.

But while Lee will forever be entwined with his military endeavors, his life was also shaped by personal and domestic experiences that occurred off the fields of battle, experiences that various biographers, Emory Thomas among them, have helped illuminate.[1] Beneath the polished exterior of the "Marble Man," Thomas explains, was a man with complex human emotions. Lee, we learn, was a man preoccupied with control, order, and propriety, yet one who also tried repeatedly to escape some of the constrictions and confinements of Victorian society. He abided strictly by his husbandly duties and maintained a constant devotion to a wife who was often infirm, yet he also formed close ties with a bevy of young female acquaintances to whom he frequently uttered his most private and revealing thoughts. Similarly Lee tried to project a model of strict paternal authority but was often a nurturing and indulgent parent. No doubt he would have been seen, and would probably have thought of himself, as a foremost example of a "southern gentleman." In fact teaching a sense of gentlemanliness became Lee's central objective when, after the war, he served as president of Washington College. "We have but one rule here," he wrote to a new student, "and that is that every student must be a gentleman."[2] Yet in many respects the label of "southern gentleman" obscures more than it illuminates. Perhaps in no case does it obscure more than in the life of Robert E. Lee.

Certainly Lee conformed to many of the visible markers by which the "southern gentleman" has been judged. He lived a life of outward decorum and exemplary behavior. If he drank, he did so in moderation, careful to avoid any type of excessive indulgences. Like all good gentlemen of the nineteenth century, Lee took a sober and thoughtful approach to his religion, though he was not confirmed in the Episcopal Church until the relatively advanced age of forty-six. Nonetheless he firmly believed in Christian sacrifice and in avoiding the fatal sin of excessive self-absorption. Finally, Lee's notion of race and his thorough acceptance of white superiority also marked him as what nineteenth-century white Americans considered a "gentleman." Indeed, as many saw it, being a "gentleman" denoted superiority, a superiority that was tied to the cultural prescriptions of white society. "The manner in which an individual enjoys certain advantages," Lee once wrote, "is the test of a true gentleman."[3] As a true gentleman, Lee firmly believed in his cultural and racial superiority but tried, as all good gentlemen did, to keep his sense of self-importance in check.

Yet much as Lee became a model of southern gentlemanliness, there are indications—scattered throughout biographical accounts of the Confederate leader—that his behavior was not always consistent with what has often been presented as the typical elements of white southern manhood. In other words, examined from the perspective of both Lee's contemporaries and present-day historians, there were times when he ironically seemed more Yankee than southern. For example, during his West Point years, Lee lived by northern rules: he was a model of discipline and frugality. Other southern cadets—notably Jefferson Davis and Leonidas Polk—lived a more spendthrift and carefree existence that set them apart from the more restrained and parsimonious Yankee boys. Both Davis and Polk, for example, spent liberally on the types of luxuries—clothes, alcohol, groceries—to which they believed "southern gentlemen" were entitled. In contrast Lee received a refund from his educational allowance and, because of his pristine demeanor, completed his time at West Point without receiving a single demerit, a rare occurrence for most students, no doubt even more rare for southern boys.[4]

Lee's sons conformed more to the Davis model of southern high living than they did to the restrained example of their father. Son Rooney Lee, Emory Thomas explains, "inspired classic stereotyping" of southern behavior from his Harvard classmate Henry Adams. Rooney, according to Adams, possessed "the Virginian habit of command and took leadership as his natural habit. . . . For a year, at least, Lee was the most popular and prominent young man in his class, but then seemed slowly to drop into the background. The habit of command was not enough, and the Virginian had little else."[5]

Clearly Adams, who based his analysis of southern manners on observing three Dixie-born boys at Harvard, cannot be the final word on southern character. Yet his description of Rooney Lee, as well as self-portraits by Davis and Polk, share certain similarities with more recent historical representations of white southern manhood—of men who sought, first and foremost, to project a sense of leadership; men who did not totally shun vices, such as drinking and gambling, that many northern men would have condemned; men who could be quick-tempered and even violent. These were men who gave foremost attention to the outward posture they held in their communities rather than to an internal standard of self-improvement. In short, these were men who lived their lives by a distinctly southern notion of honor.[6]

Not that Lee was a dishonorable man. For him, as Thomas explains, honor was crucial in his decision to join the secession movement. Honor bound him to his family, his neighbors, and his local community—though not, as Thomas points out, to abstractions like the Union. Yet in matters of personal behavior, Lee does not seem to have been guided by the proposition that Elizabeth Fox-Genovese views as a hallmark of southern masculinity—that "the value placed on lordship far outweighed that placed on restraint."[7] Robert E. Lee, if nothing else, was a man of supreme restraint.

What, then, made Lee less typical of the classic upper-crust southern white man? Thomas hints at some of the answers, as have other Lee biographers. Certainly Lee's behavior must be at least partially explained by his own personal experiences of hardship and frustration, especially in terms of his formative relationship, or lack thereof, with his father. Although celebrated as a hero of the American Revolution, "Light Horse" Harry Lee left his family with a legacy of worrisome financial instability than of military nobility. This, coupled with the fact that at thirteen Robert Lee became the oldest male in his immediate family, certainly would have made Harry Lee's son more self-reliant than his peers and more determined to avoid the irresponsible behavior that had brought ruin to his father and family. Moreover, since the father-son relationship was such an important factor in transmitting values about leadership and masculinity, Robert would have been deprived of this all-important link.

In addition, Lee's status as a permanent houseguest—a factor in his life to which Thomas gives considerable attention—no doubt affected his ability to assume the part of the domineering southern patriarch. Because he lived much of his life as a resident in other people's quarters, including most of his adult life in his wife's home at Arlington, Lee may have felt less inclined to exert the type of domestic leadership that other southern white men possessed. And because he spent significant time away from home—engaged as he was in a series of military assignments—he had a still more tenuous hold on patriarchal authority. Not until 1857, when his father-in-law died, did Lee have the possibility of pursuing the life of a plantation aristocrat, managing the Arlington estate, and acquiring land, wealth, and slaves. Indeed, if slave ownership helped shape the ideal of southern mastery and command, Lee had little opportunity to immerse himself in that particular experience. In his brief stint as Arlington's patriarch, Lee spent more effort in trying to rid himself of slave labor than in cultivating his relationship with his inherited human property.

Perhaps another factor that influenced Lee's distinctive path of character formation was his immersion in a culture that saw the intermingling of southern traditions with the ideological influences of northern and Victorian society. In fact his formative experience at West Point may have exposed him less to the culture of "southern gentlemen" like Jefferson Davis and more to a northern middle-class culture of self-improvement through educational uplift. Indeed evidence suggests that even within the South the military-school culture departed from traditional southern notions of manhood and spoke more to the career-oriented demands of the region's middle class.[8] Outside of school, southerners like Lee read much of the same prescriptive literature that northerners read and were certainly exposed to many of the same cultural currents that celebrated home, family, and bourgeois respectability. In effect Lee is a prime example of southern society at a crossroads—of a culture in which one's personal code could be influenced as much by Victorian notions of individualism, domestic sentiment, and self-control as by more traditional southern notions of lordly display and honor.[9]

Of course there was another side to Robert E. Lee: the man who committed acts of violence and war for a considerable portion of his life. Lee in fact may have relished his military life because it afforded him an opportunity to exercise more traditionally "southern" traits that he held in check in his civilian life. In the military he certainly could project a preeminent sense of leadership—especially on those occasions when his assignments went beyond the routine and the bureaucratic. Lee may have preferred his military world to his civilian one precisely because it gave him opportunities for leadership, unrestrained living, and even the violence that characterized the lives of southern white male civilians. Indeed embedded in his military record one can find a more definitive portrait of the hard and sometimes vicious side of southern gentlemanliness, especially with respect to race. Throughout the Civil War Lee showed consistent contempt for black slaves and black troops, evincing little concern about atrocities committed by his troops against both. His wartime racism appears starkly, perhaps nowhere as much as in his decision to treat captured ex-slave Union soldiers as little more than cannon fodder in the trenches near Petersburg, Virginia.[10]

Yet even as he accommodated himself to brutality and military atrocities, Lee always maintained a certain self-consciousness about his outward deportment, about how to show the world that he remained a "southern gentleman." Before, during, and after the Civil War, Lee was determined to link himself to a mythic and aristocratic tradition of Virginia gentlemanliness. As Richard McCaslin has explained, Lee lived his life and fashioned many of his personal and military undertakings on the model of his ancestral in-law, George Washington. Michael Fellman concurs, though he sees in Lee's veneration of Washington more of a self-conscious attempt to create a heroic image. In any event, by the time Lee reached maturity, he became attuned to projecting a certain model of manhood and drew on a time-honored ideal of leadership and restrained behavior to do so. In this regard he felt the influence of not only mid-nineteenth-century northern notions of respectability alongside southern notions of honor and leadership but also eighteenth-century notions of control and authority.[11]

Thus, even before his death, the Lee myth was already being spun. Certainly by the time he became president of Washington College, many white southerners viewed Lee as a symbol of the region's civility and nobility, of the South's pure and honorable motives in its quest for independence. Even more, as Fellman explains, because Lee had become such a potent symbol, he helped legitimize the more violent and repugnant qualities of the white South's resurgence during the postwar period, even though Lee himself tried to put a check on some of the worst excesses of racial violence as practiced at his college.[12]

Lee's death prompted an even more self-conscious effort at mythologizing the "Marble Man." Less than two weeks after the Confederate leader had drawn his last breath, a former subordinate, Jubal Early, helped initiate the new project. The celebration of Lee would prove, as Early suggested, that a society that had followed Lee's leadership possessed the same noble and exalted qualities as the leader himself. Such a society, he and others would argue, must be free of the federal government's oversight and must be free to manage race relations as they saw fit. For the next several years, Early and his cohorts raised monuments and tributes to Lee, shaping him to fit their agenda and in the process placing his complicated and complex humanity even further out of focus.[13]

Yet while Early and others sought to remake Lee, northerners, not surprisingly, tended to resist the veneration of the Confederate commander. To most northern minds Lee was still the leader of a treasonous uprising, a man who turned against the nation that had shaped him. He was, even more, the man who commanded tens of thousands of white southerners to kill and maim tens of thousands of northerners, and many Union veterans carried the scars to prove it. Yet toward the end of the nineteenth century, even in the North there were signs that the Lee myth had taken hold. And as he had been in the immediate postwar years, Lee again became a symbol that served a particular political, and personal, agenda for some white northerners. By the turn of the century, he had become a supreme symbol of national reconciliation in part because he seemed to reflect a personal code that was familiar and reassuring to both northern and southern whites. By highlighting certain qualities and downplaying others, writers and publicists, politicians and historians all presented Lee as a model of manhood, one who not only respected leadership and command but also restraint (as opposed to recklessness) and selflessness (as opposed to greed). In his deeds as well as in his character, Lee offered a far better symbol for intersectional celebration than a man like Jefferson Davis.

Lee, though, was not the only southerner to gain northern praise. By the 1890s southern white manhood—portrayed more often as an abstract entity than as specific persons—was increasingly winning laurels from an increasingly reunited nation. Coming with the intensified fanfare that now paid homage to the heroes of the Civil War era, white northerners gave growing respect to Confederate soldiers for their strength and courage, for their firm adherence to principles and willingness to die for them. Indeed more than Union veterans, who had long since drifted into the mundane world of moneymaking, or worse—pension collecting—southern men appeared to be the nation's perpetual soldiers who fought not for personal gain, but for glory. "Southern gentlemen" in particular were singled out for praise, perhaps even more so because they seemed to be a dying breed. Associated as they were with aristocracy, plantation management, and even slave ownership—features of southern life that now receded into the past—many northern white men expressed respect for the "southern gentleman's" ability to command a seemingly unmanageable workforce. As Massachusetts senator George Frisbie Hoar explained, they possessed "an aptness for command which makes the Southern gentleman, wherever he goes, not a peer only, but a prince." Even more, southern manliness revealed a commitment to ideals and principles that stood above crass economic interests. "They have," Hoar explained in an 1889 Senate speech, "that supreme and superb constancy which, without regard to personal ambition and without yielding to the temptation of wealth, without getting tired and without getting diverted, can pursue a great public object, in and out, year after year and generation after generation."[14]

Lee, who combined the fortitude of the Confederate soldier with the restrained leadership of a southern gentleman, presented an ideal model of manhood and was increasingly singled out for praise. Twenty years after his death, he was approaching the status of a national hero, offering the nation, proclaimed one northern observer in 1890, "an education in manliness." A heightened cultural obsession with male physical vigor and military courage, epitomized best by Theodore Roosevelt's celebration of "the strenuous life," no doubt added to the appeal of southern soldiers and commanders. But Lee was hardly the typical representative of strenuousness; he departed, as mentioned earlier, from the more dissipated behavior that so many of his fellow southern white men exhibited. In this regard he instead presented a model for those who felt disturbed at the more blustering and reckless features of fin-de-siècle masculinity; Lee provided a perfect personification of restraint and self-control.[15]

Indeed, to late nineteenth-century northerners, nothing revealed Lee's masculine self-restraint more than his dignified demeanor at the final surrender. "Whatever real anguish Lee may have felt" at Appomattox, explained one turn-of-the-century textbook, "he kept all emotion suppressed while the formal interview lasted; his manner was dignified and impassive." Lee, claimed one Memorial Day orator, deserved respect for the "simple, earnest, manly manner in which he accepted final defeat." If many northerners remained uncomfortable about celebrating his military career, it was no doubt easier to champion

Lee's surrender at Appomattox Court House as an ideal reflection of his restrained character, not to mention an ideal moment of national reconciliation.[16]

But northerners celebrated more than the single act of surrender. They learned to respect, as Lee's foremost northern proponent put it, the "character" of the man who accepted the defeat. Perhaps a more venerable Yankee could not be found than Charles Francis Adams Jr.—proud descendant of the New England Adams clan, Union officer, Harvard overseer, and president of the Massachusetts Historical Society—yet none did more to rehabilitate the stature of Robert E. Lee in northern eyes. Long after his brother Henry had turned his prejudicial judgment on Lee's Harvard-educated son, Charles Francis found his own vision of the world validated in his celebration of the father. Adams, like so many turn-of-the-century white Americans, upheld the notion of Anglo-Saxonism and used his historical inquiries as a way to expose the qualities that supposedly prepared the "Anglo-Saxon" people for a preeminent position of leadership in world affairs. But in his view Anglo-Saxon leadership sprang not simply from empty assertions of power, but from character. To Adams, Lee represented the finest qualities of that character, most especially in his posture of selfless restraint.[17]

Son of Charles Francis Adams Sr., who served as U.S. ambassador to Great Britain during the Civil War, the younger Charles Francis Adams, born in 1835, made his own contribution to the war effort as a Union officer and commander of black soldiers. When the fighting ended, Adams embarked on a career in business, eventually becoming the president of the Union Pacific Railroad. Yet as he aged, he became increasingly disillusioned with the business world and the "low instincts" of its denizens.[18] He criticized too the new departure in foreign relations, especially the aggressive drive for colonial possessions, and eventually aligned himself with the Anti-Imperialist League that emerged during the war in the Philippines. Disdainful of the jingoistic style of late-nineteenth-century politics, Adams condemned the "strenuosity of the day and its empty loquacity." By the early twentieth century, as he put his business career aside to pursue more historical and intellectual introspections, Adams turned to Robert E. Lee as a model of gentlemanly correctness, a man who revealed to the world the American "ideal of manhood."[19]

In Lee, Adams found a man who offered an appealing alternative to the incessant greed of modern American businessmen and an approach to warfare that seemed to differ dramatically from the current trend toward rapacious violence and empty jingoism. Adams first offered praise of Lee in a

1901 presentation before the American Antiquarian Society but saved his most elaborate defense of the general for a 1907 speech delivered at Lee's final place of employment, Washington and Lee University in Lexington, Virginia. In this setting Adams recalled Lee as someone who stood opposed to "the modern university spirit" that favored athletics over textbooks and preached the importance of character in restraining the "wildness of southern youth." Adams also saw Lee as a brilliant representative of selflessness, seen especially in his decision to support Virginia's secession from the Union. Lee, claimed Adams, was not motivated to support slavery but only to protect his much-loved ancestral home.[20]

Like others before him, though, Adams made the strongest case for Lee's selflessness in his interpretation of the general's actions at Appomattox. In his 1901 speech, Adams first called attention to the decision to surrender as a study in contrast with the current course of events in the Boer War. Unwilling to pursue an anarchistic, guerrilla struggle like that urged by Confederate president Jefferson Davis in April 1865, or like the one being pursued by the Boers and British in South Africa, Lee maintained that "as Christian men" it was their duty to lay down their arms. Quoting one Confederate officer, Adams stressed that Lee in particular made his decision in the interest of maintaining a civilized society, fearing that women and children would be "the greatest sufferers in the state of anarchy." Moreover, Adams suggested, he recognized the futility of the Confederate situation and knew that the best hope for the nation's future lay in closing out the struggle. "The service Lee now rendered to the common country," he explained, "the obligation under which he placed us whether North or South, has not, I think, been always appreciated; and to overstate it would be difficult."[21]

Significantly too, Adams had no criticism of either Lee's beliefs or behavior in regard to race or slavery. Calling him a slaveowner "of the patriarchal type," he claimed that Lee found the institution ultimately evil. Even more, Adams regarded slave ownership as merely a "phase, pardonable in passing," in American history, not something morally abhorrent. Expressing tolerance for it, he instead aimed some of his sharpest barbs at abolitionists, especially those who, like Harriet Beecher Stowe, presented a "female and sentimentalist portrayal . . . that the only difference between the Ethiopian and the Caucasian is epidermal." Lee in contrast earned Adams's respect for adhering to the more sensible, and masculine, doctrine of Anglo-Saxon superiority. Lee believed, as his congressional testimony during Reconstruction made clear, that the white people of the South must be the region's natural and total rulers. And while he condemned belligerent racist violence, just as many of Adams's northern cohorts deplored the actions of the lynch mob, Lee—like Adams—saw no room for black southerners in the post–Civil War power structure.[22]

Like all mythmakers, Charles Francis Adams manipulated certain truths about his subject in order to create a picture that served his needs. In particular he drew on the somewhat intangible qualities of Lee's "character"—one that, as noted earlier, had a number of conflicting threads and had already been subject to considerable manipulation by Lee himself—to offer evidence of the general's commendable qualities in action. Thus while Lee did in fact call slavery an "evil," the historical evidence suggests that he was thoroughly willing to accept the institution as a justified means of racial subordination. His inhumane treatment of captured ex-slave Union soldiers and his view that they remained little more than property further demonstrates that compliance.

Moreover Adams portrayed Lee as the civilized warrior, dignified not only in surrender but also in all aspects of battle. "He was humane, self-restrained, and strictly observant of the most advanced rules of civilized warfare," Adams intoned. From his perspective Lee had to be in order to offer a commendable alternative to early-twentieth-century notions of aggressive warfare. And within Lee's own writings, one could find evidence that this was the type of military man the Confederate leader aimed to be. When leading his troops into northern states, Lee took pains to condemn "excesses" or "depredations" committed by the soldiers against the civilian population. But as Emory Thomas and Michael Fellman suggest, Lee's actions, at least as they evolved later in the war, suggest a more complicated picture. Although initially critical of the kind of vicious guerrilla fighting waged by Confederate warriors such as John Mosby, Lee eventually endorsed Mosby's methods and thereby helped initiate a new type of warfare that accepted civilians as legitimate targets of violence.[23]

The point, though, is not whether Adams saw Lee through rose-tinted glasses, but why and how he made Lee into an American icon. Lee probably did possess certain qualities and characteristics that set him apart from other southern white men of his class and his generation, qualities that reflected his own complex notions of "gentlemanliness." His penchant for personal self-restraint—even if not always exercised in warfare—certainly shaped his character and some of the choices he made on and off the battlefields. But Lee himself had lent a hand in creating his own myth; by shaping himself along the lines of George Washington, he reached back to character traits that comforted his own familial anxieties and suggested a model of preeminent greatness. Finally, Lee's personal characteristics also shaped the stories that were told about him in both his wartime and postwar actions, stories that added further luster to the Lee myth, particularly as it was shaped and manipulated by southerners like Jubal Early in the late nineteenth century. By the turn of the century, even for a historian like Charles Francis Adams, stories and history had become so intertwined that it no doubt became difficult to disentangle one from the other. Indeed Adams often relied on the sentimentalized recollections of Lee's cohorts when it came time to piece together his own account. Yet he went further than the previous generation of mythmakers by highlighting those themes that would make Lee a symbol that reasonable and sober northern white men could respect, especially in an age of heightened jingoism and rising imperialism.

In the late nineteenth century, and into the twentieth, Americans would reshape the myth of Robert E. Lee and his "gentlemanly" character to serve a variety of political, ideological, and regional agendas. In the 1870s and 1880s, Early and other Lost Cause devotees made Lee the noble white commander whose unblemished character could serve as a positive reflection of the white South in the postwar years. Twenty years later Charles Francis Adams reclaimed him as the restrained and dignified leader whose Anglo-Saxon character served as a hopeful symbol for a reunited and globally oriented nation.

NOTES

1. The classic biography of Robert E. Lee is Douglas Southall Freeman, *Robert E. Lee: A Biography,* 4 vols. (New York: Charles Scribner's, 1934–35). More-recent treatments include Emory M. Thomas, *Robert E. Lee: A Biography* (New York: Norton, 1995); and Michael Fellman, *The Making of Robert E. Lee* (New York: Random House, 2000). On Lee's image see Thomas L. Connelly, *The Marble Man: Robert E. Lee and His Image in American Society* (Baton Rouge: Louisiana State University Press, 1977); and Alan T. Nolan, *Lee Considered: General Robert E. Lee and Civil War History* (Chapel Hill: University of North Carolina Press, 1991).

2. Lee quoted in Fellman, *Making of Robert E. Lee,* 250.

3. Lee quoted in Thomas, *Robert E. Lee,* 397.

4. Bertram Wyatt-Brown has suggested that Lee, along with a relatively small group of upper-class, evangelical southerners, adopted a notion of honor that was consistent with a broader southern ethos, though they promoted a more restrained, and Christian, view of that principle. See Wyatt-Brown, *Southern Honor: Ethics and Behavior in the Old South* (New York: Oxford University Press, 1982), 145–47.

5. Henry Adams quoted in ibid., 169.

6. Books that consider antebellum southern manhood include Edward Ayers, *Vengeance and Justice: Crime and Punishment in the Nineteenth-Century American South* (New York: Oxford Uni-

versity Press, 1984); Wyatt-Brown, *Southern Honor;* Steven M. Stowe, *Intimacy and Power in the Old South: Ritual in the Lives of the Planters* (Baltimore: Johns Hopkins University Press, 1987).

7. Elizabeth Fox-Genovese, *Within the Plantation Household: Black and White Women of the Old South* (Chapel Hill: University of North Carolina Press, 1988), 200.

8. For more on the culture of antebellum southern military schools, see Jennifer R. Green, "Books and Bayonets: Class and Culture in Antebellum Military Academies" (Ph.D. diss., Boston University, 2002); Rod Andrew Jr., *Long Gray Lines: The Southern Military School Tradition, 1839–1915* (Chapel Hill: University of North Carolina Press, 2001).

9. This notion of shared middle-class values is also discussed in Anne C. Rose, *Victorian America and the Civil War* (Cambridge: Cambridge University Press, 1992).

10. Fellman, *Making of Robert E. Lee,* 207.

11. Richard B. McCaslin, *Lee in the Shadow of Washington* (Baton Rouge: Louisiana State University Press, 2001); Fellman, *Making of Robert E. Lee,* 15–16.

12. Fellman, *Making of Robert E. Lee,* 262–63.

13. Connelly, *Marble Man,* 94; Fellman, *Making of Robert E. Lee,* 301–2.

14. For more on the conciliatory movement and the northern appreciation of Lee, see Nina Silber, *The Romance of Reunion: Northerners and the South, 1865–1900* (Chapel Hill: University of North Carolina Press, 1993), 169–78; and Connelly, *Marble Man.* Senator Hoar quoted in Thomas Nelson Page, *The Negro: The Southerner's Problem* (New York: Charles Scribner's Sons, 1904), 281.

15. Henry M. Field, *Bright Skies and Dark Shadows* (New York: Charles Scribner's Sons, 1890), 301.

16. Ibid.; James Schouler, *History of the United States of America, under the Constitution,* 6 vols. (New York: Dodd, Mead, 1894–99), 6:600; Grand Army of the Republic, *Memorial Ceremonies at Monument Cemetery, Philadelphia, under the Auspices of Post No. 2, Department of Pennsylvania* (Philadelphia, 1890), 24.

17. For more on the Anglo-Saxonist cult, see George Fredrickson, *The Black Image in the White Mind: The Debate on Afro-American Character and Destiny, 1817–1914* (1971; repr., Middletown, Conn.: Wesleyan University Press, 1987), 228–55; and Richard Hofstadter, *Social Darwinism in American Thought* (Boston: Wesleyan University Press, 1955), 172–79.

18. Adams quoted in Vernon Louis Parrington, *Main Currents in American Thought: An Interpretation of American Literature from the Beginnings to 1920,* 3 vols. (New York: Harcourt, Brace, 1927–30), 3:214.

19. Charles Francis Adams Jr., "Shall Cromwell Have a Statue?" *Lee at Appomattox and Other Papers* (Boston: Houghton Mifflin, 1902), 428; Edward Chase Kirkland, *Charles Francis Adams, Jr., 1835–1915: The Patrician at Bay* (Cambridge, Mass.: Harvard University Press, 1965), 182–85.

20. Charles Francis Adams Jr., *Lee's Centennial: An Address by Charles Francis Adams, Delivered at Lexington, Virginia, Saturday, Jan. 19, 1907, on the Invitation of the President and Faculty of Washington and Lee University* (Boston: Houghton Mifflin, 1907), 13–22, 62–63.

21. Adams, *Lee at Appomattox,* 1–3, 26; Adams, *Lee's Centennial,* 49.

22. Adams, "Shall Cromwell Have a Statue?" 410–11, 427; Adams, *Lee's Centennial,* 41–42.

23. Adams, *Lee's Centennial,* 22; Thomas, *Robert E. Lee,* 72, 249–50.

The Last Word

WILLIAM S. McFEELY

NOTHING COULD BE MORE INAPPROPRIATE AS A LAST WORD IN A book about the Confederacy than a frosty note from New England. But I think the man being honored would understand. After all, he and I have traded postcards signed REL to USG, and the reverse, for years. If I was guilty of a biography of a general who did some damage to the Confederacy, Emory Thomas had the last word with his fine study of Robert E. Lee. And symmetry being what it is, I'm not sure how many times he and I ratcheted around the countryside together doing our vaudeville act on the two warriors.

No more congenial companion could be imagined, particularly when, the job done, we could haul up over some of his excellent bourbon. But whiskey played only a supporting role. I do not know another historian who had more fun with history. Serious he could be, as his books amply attest, but he did, after all, teach his Civil War class by playing in a sandbox in which many a gory battle was fought, usually, I suspect, to a draw. His students loved it. And this zest for history is there in everything he wrote.

There is a good deal of his chief subject's grace in Emory Thomas. That overused term "southern gentleman" truly fits him. He put its virtues to the good of the history community in general and the History Department of the University of Georgia in particular. He coaxed good scholarship from students and fellow Civil War historians; he smoothed abrasions in a sometimes abrasive department. He and his good wife, Fran, herself no mean historian, were the very best of hosts to a wonderful parade of gatherings of historians, both local and from far-flung lands. There has even been a New Englander or Manhattanite or two treated to the best of their hospitality.

Nothing could be more fitting than a festschrift—I wish there were a plain old English term for it—honoring Emory M. Thomas. That we have in this fine volume, done in tribute to a fine historian. So, all the best to REL from USG.

Select Bibliography of Emory M. Thomas's Writings

BOOKS

The Confederate State of Richmond: A Biography of the Capital. Austin: University of Texas Press, 1971. Reprinted, Louisiana State University Press, 1998.

The Confederacy as a Revolutionary Experience. Englewood Cliffs, N.J.: Prentice-Hall, 1971. Reprinted, University of South Carolina Press, 1991.

The American War and Peace: 1860–1877. Englewood Cliffs, N.J.: Prentice-Hall, 1973.

The Confederate Nation: 1861–1865. The New American Nation Series. New York: Harper & Row, 1979. Reprinted, Monticello Editions, History Book Club, 1993.

Bold Dragoon: The Life of J. E. B. Stuart. New York: HarperCollins, 1986. Reprinted, University of Oklahoma Press, 1999.

Travels to Hallowed Ground: A Historian's Journey to the American Civil War. Columbia: University of South Carolina Press, 1987.

Robert E. Lee: A Biography. New York: W. W. Norton, 1995.

Robert E. Lee: An Album. New York: W. W. Norton, 2000.

BOOK CHAPTERS, JOURNAL ARTICLES, AND PUBLISHED LECTURES

"Rebel Nationalism: E. H. Cushing and the Confederate Experience." *Southwestern Historical Quarterly* 73 (January 1970): 343–55.

"Honest to Clio: The New History of the Old South." Lamar Lecture Series.

Macon, Ga.: Wesleyan College, 1972.
"To Feed the Citizens: Welfare in Wartime Richmond, 1861–1865." *Virginia Cavalcade* 22 (Summer 1972): 22–29.
"Jefferson Davis and the American Revolutionary Tradition." *Journal of the Illinois State Historical Society* 70 (February 1977): 2–9.
"The Peninsular Campaign." In *The Image of War, 1861–1865,* edited by William C. Davis. Vol. 2, *The Guns of 1862,* 112–23. New York: Doubleday, 1982.
"Reckoning with Rebels." In *The Old South in the Crucible of War,* edited by Harry P. Owens and James J. Cooke. Jackson: University Press of Mississippi, 1983.
"The Paradoxes of Confederate Historiography." In *The Southern Enigma: Essays on Race, Class, and Folk Culture,* edited by Walter J. Fraser and Winfred B. Moore, 217–24. Westport, Conn.: Greenwood, 1983.
"The South and the Sea: Some Thoughts on the Southern Maritime Tradition." *Georgia Historical Quarterly* 67 (Summer 1983): 159–67.
"Richmond, City and Capital at War." In *The Image of War, 1861–1865,* edited by William C. Davis. Vol. 6, *The End of an Era,* 275–98. New York: Doubleday, 1984.
"'The Greatest Service I Rendered the State': J. E. B. Stuart's Account of the Capture of John Brown." *Virginia Magazine of History and Biography* 94 (July 1986): 345–57.
"Everyone's War." In *Touched by Fire: A Photographic Portrait of the Civil War,* edited by William C. Davis, 2:199–205. Boston: Little, Brown, 1990.
"God and General Lee." *Anglican and Episcopal History* 60 (March 1991): 15–24.
"Bibliography and Historiography." In *Encyclopedia of the Confederacy,* 4 vols., edited by Richard Current et al.
"Secession, Succession, and Sumter: The Crisis of 1860–61." In *The David A. Sayre History Symposium: Collected Essays,* edited by F. Kevin Simon. Lexington, Ky.: Sayre School, 1993.
"Rethinking Robert E. Lee." *Douglas Southall Freeman Historical Review* (Spring 1994).
"Eggs, Aldi, Shephedstown, and J. E. B. Stuart." In *The Gettysburg Nobody Knows,* edited by Gabor S. Boritt, 101–21. New York: Oxford University Press, 1997.
"Rebellion and Conventional Warfare: Confederate Strategy and Military Policy." In *Writing the Civil War: The Quest to Understand,* edited by James M.

McPherson and William J. Cooper, 36–59. Columbia: University of South Carolina Press, 1998.

"Ambivalent Visions of Victory: Jefferson Davis, Robert E. Lee, and Confederate Grand Strategy." In *Jefferson Davis's Generals,* edited by Gabor S. Boritt, 27–45. New York: Oxford University Press, 1999.

"The Lees' Marriage." In *Intimate Strategies: Military Marriages of the Civil War,* edited by Carol K. Bleser and Lesley J. Gordon, 32–48. New York: Oxford University Press, 2001.

"Clio at Climax: Apocalypse and the American Civil War." In *Warm Ashes: Issues in Southern History at the Dawn of the Twenty-First Century,* edited by Winfred B. Moore Jr., Kyle S. Sinisi, and David H. White Jr., 12–20. Columbia: University of South Carolina Press, 2003.

Editors and Contributors

EDITORS

LESLEY J. GORDON is associate professor of history at the University of Akron. She earned her Ph.D. under ET's direction in 1995. She is the author of *General George E. Pickett in Life and Legend;* the coauthor, with Daniel J. Sutherland and Michael Fellman, of *This Terrible War: The Civil War and Its Aftermath;* and the coeditor, with Carol K. Bleser, of *Intimate Strategies: Military Commanders and their Wives.*

JOHN C. INSCOE is professor of history at the University of Georgia, where he was a colleague of ET's from 1984. He is the author of *Mountain Masters: Slavery and the Sectional Crisis in Western North Carolina* and coauthor, with Gordon B. McKinney, of *The Heart of Confederate Appalachia: Western North Carolina's Civil War.* He is the editor of several essay collections, including *Enemies of the Country: New Perspectives on Unionists in the Civil War South,* coedited with Robert C. Kenzer.

CONTRIBUTORS

ROD ANDREW JR. is associate professor of history at Clemson University. He earned his Ph.D. at UGA under ET's direction in 1997. He is the author of *Long Gray Lines: The Southern Military School Tradition, 1839–1915,* and is now working on a biography of Wade Hampton.

KEITH S. BOHANNON is assistant professor of history at the State University of West Georgia. He earned his Ph.D. at Penn State University in 2000 and an M.A. at UGA in 1993 under ET's direction. His dissertation is on the Civil War in the mountains of northeastern Georgia. He is coeditor of *Campaigning with "Old Stonewall": Confederate Captain Ujanirtus Allen's Letters to his Wife.*

FRANK J. BYRNE is assistant professor of history at SUNY-Oswego. He earned his Ph.D. at Ohio State University in 2000 and an M.A. at UGA under ET's direction in 1994. His dissertation is a study of merchants in the antebellum and Civil War South.

WILLIAM C. DAVIS is the director of the Virginia Center for Civil War Studies at Virginia Tech University. The author of numerous books about the Civil War and the Confederacy, his work on the latter includes *"A Government of Our Own": The Making of the Confederacy; An Honorable Defeat: The Last Days of the Confederate Government;* and *Look Away! A History of the Confederate States of America.*

PHILIP D. DILLARD is assistant professor of history at James Madison University. He earned an M.A. at UGA under ET's direction in 1994 and a Ph.D. from Rice University in 1999 with a dissertation entitled "Independence or Slavery? The Confederate Debate over Arming the Slaves." He is coeditor of *The Southern Albatross: Race and Ethnicity in the American South.*

RUSSELL DUNCAN is professor of history at the University of Copenhagen. He earned his Ph.D. at UGA in 1989 under ET's direction. He is the author of *Freedom's Shore: Tunis Campbell and the Georgia Freedmen; Entrepreneur for Equality: Governor Rufus Bullock, Commerce, and Race in Post–Civil War Georgia;* and *Where Death and Glory Meet: Col. Robert Gould Shaw and the 54th Massachusetts Infantry.*

THOMAS G. DYER is University Professor of History and Higher Education and director of the Institute of Higher Education at UGA. Both a student and colleague of ET, he is the author or editor of four books, including most recently *Secret Yankees: The Union Circle in Confederate Atlanta.*

JEAN E. FRIEDMAN is a recently retired colleague of ET at UGA. She is the author or editor of several books, including *The Enclosed Garden: Women and Community in the Evangelical South, 1830–1900,* and *Ways of Wisdom: Moral Education in the Early National Period.* She is now at work on a comparative study of northern and southern families and how the Civil War affected their lives and relationships.

JOSEPH T. GLATTHAAR is Alex Stephenson Professor of History at the University of North Carolina, Chapel Hill. His books include *The March to the Sea and Beyond: Sherman's Troops in the Savannah and Carolinas Campaigns; Forged in Battle: The Civil War Alliance of Black Soldiers and White Officers;* and *Partners in Command: The Relationship between Leaders in the Civil War.*

JENNIFER LYNN GROSS is assistant professor of history at Jacksonville State University. She earned her Ph.D. at UGA in 2001 under ET's direction with a dissertation entitled "Good Angels or Dangerous Women: Confederate Widowhood in the Postbellum South."

WILLIAM S. McFEELY is the Abraham Baldwin Professor Emeritus at UGA, where he taught from 1987 to 2000. He is the author of five books, including biographies of Ulysses S. Grant, which won the Pulitzer Prize; Frederick Douglass, which won the Lincoln Prize; and Thomas Eakin, forthcoming. He currently lives in Wellfleet, Massachusetts.

DAVID H. McGEE is associate professor of history at Central Virginia Community College in Lynchburg. He completed a dissertation entitled "'On the Edge of a Crater': The Transformation of Raleigh, North Carolina, during the Civil War Era" under ET's direction in 1999. He is currently at work on a history of the 26th North Carolina Regiment.

JAMES M. McPHERSON is the George Henry Davis '86 Professor of History at Princeton University. Among his many books are *Battle Cry of Freedom: The Civil War Era*, for which he won the Pulitzer Prize; *For Cause and Comrades: Why Men Fought in the Civil War*, which won the Lincoln Prize; and *Antietam: Crossroads of Freedom.*

CLARENCE L. MOHR is professor of history and chair of the Department of History at the University of South Alabama. He received his Ph.D. at UGA in 1975. He is the author of *On the Threshold of Freedom: Masters and Slaves in Civil War Georgia* and coauthor of *Tulane: The Emergence of a Modern University.*

CHRISTOPHER PHILLIPS is associate professor of history at the University of Cincinnati. He earned his Ph.D. at UGA in 1992. He is the author of several books, including *Damned Yankee: The Life of General Nathaniel Lyon;*

Freedom's Port: The African American Community of Baltimore, 1790–1860; and *Missouri's Confederate: Claiborne Fox Jackson and the Creation of Southern Identity in the Border West.*

GLENNA R. SCHROEDER-LEIN, currently with the Abraham Lincoln Library in Springfield, Illinois, has held editorial positions with both the Andrew Johnson Papers Project at the University of Tennessee and the Lincoln Legal Papers Project. She earned her Ph.D. at UGA in 1991 under ET's direction. She is the author of *Confederate Hospitals on the Move: Samuel Stout and the Army of Tennessee* and coeditor of *Andrew Johnson: A Biographical Companion.*

NINA SILBER is professor of history at Boston University. She is the author of *The Romance of Reunion: Northerners and the South, 1865–1900,* and coeditor of *Divided Houses: Gender and the Civil War.* Her essay is an expanded version of a paper she presented as part of a panel on ET's *Robert E. Lee* at the Southern Historical Association meeting in 1995.

JENNIFER LUND SMITH teaches history at North Georgia College and State University. She earned her Ph.D. under ET's direction in 1997 with a dissertation entitled "'T'will Take Some Time to Study When I Get Over': Varieties of African American Education in Reconstruction Georgia."

BRIAN S. WILLS is professor of history at the University of Virginia at Wise. He earned his Ph.D. in 1991 under ET's direction. He is the author of *A Battle from the Start: The Life of Nathan Bedford Forrest* and *The War Hits Home: The Civil War in Southeastern Virginia.*

Index